An Overture to Philosophy
of Communication
The Carrier of Meaning

This book is part of the Peter Lang Media and Communication list.
Every volume is peer reviewed and meets
the highest quality standards for content and production.

PETER LANG
New York • Washington, D.C./Baltimore • Bern
Frankfurt • Berlin • Brussels • Vienna • Oxford

RONALD C. ARNETT & ANNETTE M. HOLBA

An Overture to Philosophy of Communication

THE CARRIER OF MEANING

PETER LANG
New York • Washington, D.C./Baltimore • Bern
Frankfurt • Berlin • Brussels • Vienna • Oxford

Library of Congress Cataloging-in-Publication Data
Arnett, Ronald C.
An overture to philosophy of communication: the carrier of meaning /
Ronald C. Arnett, Annette M. Holba.
p. cm.
Includes bibliographical references and index.
1. Communication—Philosophy. I. Holba, Annette. II. Title.
P90.A8417 302.2'01—dc23 2012034606
ISBN 978-1-4331-1345-1 (hardcover)
ISBN 978-1-4331-1344-4 (paperback)
ISBN 978-1-4539-0910-2 (e-book)

Bibliographic information published by **Die Deutsche Nationalbibliothek**.
Die Deutsche Nationalbibliothek lists this publication in the "Deutsche
Nationalbibliografie"; detailed bibliographic data is available
on the Internet at http://dnb.d-nb.de/.

Cover photo by Millie Arnett

Contents

Acknowledgments

I, Ronald C. Arnett, offer my thanks and gratitude to Duquesne University, the Spiritan community, and my colleagues in the Department of Communication & Rhetorical Studies. I am deeply thankful to Heather Blum, Senior Graduate Research Assistant, for her outstanding work on this project, and I am equally thankful to Susan Carr, my current Senior Graduate Research Assistant, for her thoughtful attentiveness. Additionally, I offer thanks to Mary Savigar, Senior Acquisitions Editor, and am appreciative of the important work of Peter Lang Publishing. Finally, I am grateful to my coauthor, Annette Holba, for the opportunity to work with her on this wonderful project.

I dedicate this work with thanks and appreciation to my family Millie, Adam, Aimee, Rich, Alexa, and Ava.

I, Annette M. Holba, offer my deepest gratitude first to Duquesne University and Plymouth State University. Ronald C. Arnett (Duquesne University) has extended intellectual generosity, patience, and support throughout this project. It has indeed been a pleasure working and learning with him on this endeavor. Heather Blum and Susan Carr (Duquesne University) have been most helpful with every step in the process of this project. It has been delightful working with both of them. I also offer my appreciation to Plymouth State University President, Sara Jayne Steen and Vice-President of Academic Affairs and Provost, Julie Bernier. It is indeed a pleasure to work at an institution that is supportive of intellectual endeavors as I was awarded a sabbatical release to research and write on this project. I also extend my deepest gratitude to Mary Savigar, Peter Lang Publishing, who has endured my many questions and demonstrated patience as we worked through our writing process. Finally, both of us want to thank Deborah Eicher-Catt who read our manuscript and provided valuable feedback that was extremely helpful.

I dedicate this work to my husband Dan for his patience, encouragement, and belief in me.

PART I: OVERTURES TO MEANING

CHAPTER 1

HABITS OF THE HEART

This work, *An Overture to Philosophy of Communication: The Carrier of Meaning*, orchestrates a particular perspective on philosophy of communication, describing philosophy of communication discourse as constituting a dwelling for human meaning. Our position is that philosophy of communication offers a content "why" that sustains, reconstitutes, and builds communicative practices that shape our "habits of the heart."[1] We understand philosophy of communication as an intellectual shaping of habits of the heart, tempering information by moving existential meaning into embodied and contextual understanding. This focus requires one to understand the difference between Aristotle's (trans. 1998) "expert" and "craftsman." Both the expert and craftsman understand the necessary information about a given craft; however, only a craftsman invests in the meaning of the craft. The craftsman is an expert who loves the craft itself. A craftsman adds to the life of an expert, affirming the importance of practices and understanding the particular meaning of those practices. The craftsman understands that there is a meaning-centered story behind practices that announce the "why," the importance of a given craft. Philosophy of communication is akin to a craftsman uniting expertise and meaning, framing a theoretical "why" behind the "how" of practicality. The craftsman gives heart to information and practices, a place within which to dwell; such is our understanding of philosophy of communication.

Introduction

Philosophy of communication takes us to the interplay of ideas, people, and historical situations that shape the dwelling of human meaning. This introductory chapter outlines the significance of this project in four sections: (1) "The Horizon of Philosophy of Communication," (2) "The Interplay of Information and Meaning," (3) "The Texture of Philosophy of Communication," and (4) "Philosophy of Communication and Attentiveness." We contend that philosophy of communication is of pragmatic importance in a diverse world composed of multiple perspectives and meanings; we concur with Richard Bernstein (1983) in his argument that the practical and the philosophical have intersected.

To exemplify this meaning emphasis, we rely upon a literary exemplification of heart and meaning in action through the novel *Zorba the Greek*, which gives

---

1 Alexis de Tocqueville (1835 & 1840/2000) first coined the phrase "habits of the heart" in *Democracy in America* (p. 275).

us a picture of philosophy of communication akin to an existential dance that is ever responsive to human meaning. The characters in *Zorba the Greek* bring to life the importance of passion, heart, and meaning in the meeting of human existence. We contend that philosophy of communication assists meaning construction in a world defined by diversity, difference, fragmentation, and the importance of learning from alterity, otherness.

The Horizon of Philosophy of Communication

A horizon offers a conceptual way to texture a given idea as an impressionistic picture, as suggested by Hans-Georg Gadamer (1960/1986). A horizon indicates possibilities for discerning a general outline of a given identity without eliminating the reality of multiple perspectives. It is possible to have an entity called a philosophy of communication that is composed of multiple conceptions. This ongoing orientation of difference within a horizon is illustrated by Emmanuel Levinas (1997) in his discussion of the interplay of the particular and the universal (p. 136). Levinas states the necessity of beginning with the particular in order to get to the universal.

A philosophy of communication presupposes that there are multiple ideas and stories while rejecting the assumption that one can discern the reality of existence from the vantage point of the one grand and dominate idea or metanarrative. Multiplicity keeps alive the interplay of the particular of a given perspective, forging diverse glimpses of and perspectives on a given horizon. For Levinas, the universal lives in the engagement of the unique, in attending to a particular human face, which points to a fundamental responsibility for another. As we meet a particular human face, we are simultaneously pointed to a universal, an "ethical echo" (Arnett, 2009, p. 200)—"I am my brother's keeper" (Cohen, 1998, p. xii; Levinas, 1998). For instance, there is a universal commitment to being a friend, but if you are to be a friend you must play out that commitment in a unique and particular fashion. There is a particular demand, and a unique caring that is called forth. Anyone who anticipates being a friend knows that each person requires different engagements. The horizon of what one might call a universal is only modestly approachable if one attends to the demands of the particular. Philosophy of communication begins with the particular in hopes of a glimpse of what might be ironically termed a "temporal universal" that works within a horizon of meaning within the human condition that is responsive to the particular and the unique.

This interplay of particular and universal is exemplified in *Philosophies of Communication: Implications for Everyday Experience*, edited by Melissa

Cook and Annette Holba (2008); the authors examine the origins of the terms "philosophy" and "communication." They explore places where the interplay of communication and philosophy rests with particular scholars such as Martin Buber and Hans-Georg Gadamer; the communication insights of Stanley Deetz and others who have examined the world of hermeneutics; and the public structural domains and institutional structures that frame life-world considerations of authors such as Hannah Arendt and Jürgen Habermas. Cook and Holba (2008) offer a definition of philosophy of communication attentive to this structural interpretive interplay: "Communication occurs within tradition, a rationality of existence, a particular social order, between the individual and the community" (p. xvii). For Cook and Holba, philosophy of communication requires life-world attentiveness that is meaning centered and only discernible in the particular.

In another work on philosophy of communication, editor Pat Arneson (2007) cites Calvin O. Schrag (1986), known as a philosopher with a deep kinship with the discipline of communication and rhetoric, with his focus on "communicative praxis." Arneson (2007) also highlights the work of Lenore Langsdorf (2002), who talks about communicative "poiesis," stressing the revelatory elements of communication. The revelatory calls us into reflection and contemplation. The situating of the work of Schrag (1986) and his well-known metaphor of "communicative praxis" and Langsdorf's contribution of communicative poiesis emphasizes the importance of action with a textured attentiveness to meaning. Arneson (2007) discusses philosophy of communication as requiring attentiveness to revelatory significance that emerges in the cracks of everyday life. Philosophy of communication is necessary, pragmatically called forth, when life seems to sever the communicator from sensibility, demanding that a person attend to temporal and existential connectedness. Philosophy of communication functions as an existential dwelling for such temporal meaning awakenings.

In another essay, Arnett (2010) sought to define philosophy of communication with a stress on Arendt's view of public opinion. Philosophy of communication does not presuppose that we have discovered *the* answer, but more modestly offers documented evidence grounded in the form of public opinion, furthering multiplicity of views in the public domain. "Philosophy of communication lives and dies by public opinion, preserved by history of philosophy of communication, ready for resurrection from the reclamation energy of public opinion" (p. 59). Arnett (2010) states that a particular philosophy of communication atrophies in significance when it no longer has pragmatic importance and no longer shapes a sense of meaning in the public domain. What breathes life into the bare bones of ideas are opinions that work with the drama of everyday life. This perspective is consistent with the work of Ricoeur (1984) in his exposition about "emplotment," which includes a sequence of activities and characters that must live through a given story, attentive to historicity that gives rise to a question that calls forth human responsiveness.

Philosophy of communication connected to public opinion is a story in action; it is the testing ground for ideas and their appropriateness in human existence. Philosophy of communication is not method centered, but rather is a form of multi-centered communication. Both Immanuel Kant (1790/1951) and Hannah Arendt (1958) talk about the issue of public as being composed of multiple conversations and diverse possibilities. Philosophy of communication keeps a conversation going (Rorty, 1979, p. 378) about a story, a drama that continues to capture the attention of a given public. Connecting philosophy of communication to public opinion openly acknowledges that each perspective offers biased or "tainted ground" upon which a given philosophy of communication turns and engages the public (Arnett, 2008). It is the responsibility of a communicator to think about a given philosophy of communication, not simply to follow a particular perspective unreflectively.

Arendt (1978) concurs with the insights of Kant, emphasizing that the first dialogue is with oneself, an inner dialogue of self-conversation that seeks to understand origins and implications, recognizing that each path or direction requires deliberation and recognition of limitations. Such an understanding of philosophy of communication applauds difference with a stress on opinion that includes evidence and prior thinking, rejecting the existence of an Archimedean point of reference that guides one's observations, deliberations, and sense of meaning.

Although there are many projects that point to the ongoing academic area of philosophy of communication, there are multiple scholarly books and journals that explicitly use the phrase "philosophy of communication" in the title; these works are listed in the appendix of this project. In addition to these sources, multiple scholars have contributed to the study of philosophy of communication within the discipline. Arguably, the leading philosopher of communication in the discipline is Michael J. Hyde (1982, 2001, 2004, 2006, 2010); he contributes to philosophy of communication, offering communicative insight and application to ongoing human questions. Additionally, Ramsey Eric Ramsey (1998) and Ramsey and David James Miller

(2003), along with Lisbeth Lipari (2004) and Corey Anton (2010), have all made significant contributions in the area of philosophy of communication with one major connecting theme—their work with Calvin O. Schrag (1986) at Purdue University. We have many other scholars in our discipline, from W. Barnett Pearce (1989) to Pat Arneson (2007) to Deborah Eicher-Catt and Issac Catt (2010) to Richard Lanigan (1972, 1988, 1992) to Gary P. Radford (2004) to Pat Gehrke (2009), to name but a small number, whose work bears witness to the ongoing importance of philosophy of communication.

In each case, these scholars provide a way to connect philosophy of communication with the importance of meaning. However, the insights of Cronen and Pearce (1980) and their coordinated management of meaning construct explicitly centered the notion of meaning in a philosophy of communication theory. Although Cronen and Pearce penned their theory more than 30 years ago, it continues to generate scholarly attention today, both inside and outside the discipline of communication.[2] This project continues to connect philosophy of communication to meaning.

Philosophy of communication organizes information and simultaneously offers a sense of meaning without denying the realities of multiplicity and difference. Philosophy of communication meets existence and organizes, coordinates, and offers meaning that can be tested in the public domain. Philosophy of communication is a form of public engagement of thoughtful opinion about presuppositions and evidence that shape our human meaning.

The Interplay of Information and Meaning

This work frames communicative meaning as the differentiating principle between an analytic philosophy and a particular view of philosophy of communication. Observation of a baseball game affords a common example of this difference. If one watches a baseball game and has no knowledge of

2 For example: Bruss, M. B., Morris, J. R., Dannison, L. L., Orbe, M. P., Quitugua, J. A., & Palacios, R. T. (2005). Food, culture, and family: Exploring the coordinated management of meaning regarding childhood obesity. *Health Communication*, 18(2), 155–175; Montgomery, E. (2004). Tortured families: A coordinated management of meaning analysis. *Family Process*, 43(3), 349–371; Rose, R. A. (2006). A proposal for integrating structuration theory with coordinated management of meaning theory. *Communication Studies*, 57(2), 173–196; and Salmon, G., & Faris, J. (2006). Multi-agency collaboration, multiple levels of meaning: Social constructionism and the CMM model as tools to further our understanding. *Journal of Family Therapy*, 28(3), 272–292. Additionally, in June 2011 a conference entitled "IMC and CMM: Finding Common Ground" was held at the University of North Carolina–Wilmington and featured Vernon Cronen as the keynote speaker.

the history and tradition of the game, one only sees human beings engaged in limited exercise, with the participants standing in place waiting for a ball to be "potentially" hit in some direction. For the person who is puzzled by the watching of this game, information alone cannot answer "why" and "how" this slow-paced game continues to inspire loyalty and enthusiasm. But those who have memories of playing with friends all day on a weekend, or perhaps watching the game with fathers, mothers, and siblings, discover later in life the power of that silent communication. For us, the game requires a philosophy of communication in order to meaningfully understand how information about baseball can become a practice and place of human meaning.

Another way of understanding the doing of philosophy of communication is to connect it to the sculpting of information into meaningful engagements. Philosophy of communication is akin to making pottery, in which the clay is information that, through the act of sculpting, gives rise to meaning. Philosophy of communication takes information and turns it into meaningful connections between persons. What unites persons is not simply information, but meaning sculpted between and among them.

In examining books that have captured the hearts of readers, such as Rowling's (1998-2007) Harry Potter series or Tolkien's (1954) *The Lord of the Rings*, one discovers novels that announce the struggle for and about human meaning. In the Harry Potter series, a young boy seeks meaning, in the community of friends, while on a journey charged by a desire to overcome the oppression of, and ultimately destroy, the series' villain, Lord Voldemort. Harry Potter finds the reality of temporal meaning with others in a world of uncertainty. Additionally, in *The Lord of the Rings,* Gollum's eerie words of "my precious" (Tolkien, 1954, p. 267) point us toward the difference between the discovery of meaning and the desire to possess the meaning of existence. Philosophy of communication, as understood in this work, differentiates between meaning and possession. Meaning is temporal and fleeting. Meaning cannot be objectified, reified, or possessed. One must be ever attentive to glimpses of meaning that emerge in given historical circumstances within particular temporal acts, recognizing that meaning can never be taken for granted. Meaning shapes our discourse and is lost when acts of possession, like "my precious," trump. Information can be possessed, but a philosophy of communication is only meaningful when participation, not possession, guides the interaction. Philosophy of communication can only be understood in the doing, just as baseball must be experienced and pottery must be done with one's hands in the clay, sculpting objects that give life for others, functionally and aesthetically. It is in the doing, the praxis of philosophy of communication, that one understands a unique and meaningful communicative texture, turning a two-dimensional understanding of a given event into three-dimensional meaningful understanding that cannot be totally possessed.

The Texture of Philosophy of Communication

Calvin O. Schrag describes the role of communicative texture as a metaphorical sense of topography that gives depth that constitutes meaningful information. Embodied meaning has texture—one can sense and feel the meaningfulness of a given communicative exchange, suggesting that not all communication can be meaningfully understood as a philosophy of communication, nor should all communication be understood as philosophy of communication. We limit philosophy of communication to discourse that houses a sense of meaning and offers interpretive frameworks for understanding. Following Schrag's lead, we offer metaphors that texture our understanding of a philosophy of communication that moves information into a greater sense of meaningfulness, stressing three metaphors: heart, pattern, and fulcrum.

Heart

We argue that the notion of heart is played out in numerous ways in philosophy of communication, stressing the connection between heart and communicative practices. In *Habits of the Heart*, sociologist Robert N. Bellah and colleagues (Bellah, Madsen, Sullivan, Swidler, & Tipton, 1985) outline the problem of individualism in American culture. Bellah et al. counter this perspective with discussion of the importance of practices learned by repetitive practices of the heart that become habits of the heart, in which Bellah and his colleagues record interviews with people in suburban San Jose, California. This work models what George Cheney (2008) and Cheney, Wilhelmsson, and Zorn (2002) term "engaged scholarship." Bellah found that his interviewees articulated one common lament: Why is it that we cannot sustain a sense of community? Bellah and his colleagues (1985) discovered that the answer rested in vocabulary and practices that are highly individualistic, contrary to practices that shape the "habits of the heart" of a community.

The notion of heart, for Bellah, is not a mystical understanding that one person has for another. It is a way of pointing to meaning and the importance of practices. For example, "What is the heart of the matter?" "What is the heart of this issue?" "What or whom is the heart of this organization?" Heart is a metaphor for centering and focusing discourse. The phrase "habits of the heart" announces practices that focus, center, and shape lives in an effort to find direction. We find our habits of the heart through what we practice.

Bellah is conversant with the work of Alasdair MacIntyre, who is known for his stress on the limits of unreflective practices, first described by Alexis de Tocqueville (1835 & 1840/2000) in *Democracy in America*. Tocqueville warned of the dangers of individualism, the impulse to stand above the community and to act as if the restraints, the mores, the traditions, and the impulses of a given group of people, a society, a city, a culture, are largely irrelevant. MacIntyre (1981) follows this lead, discussing a decision-making mechanism that he considers problematic and dangerous for individual people and communities—"emotivism." This form of decision making (emotivism) disregards everything except what I want. Emotive decision making contains no collective foresight or retrospective understanding of history; it has no attentiveness to others. Tocqueville worried that the habits of the heart of individualism would trump attentiveness to others and eclipse the context that must be taken into consideration in a given decision. MacIntyre states that the challenge to individualism and emotivism can only be marshaled with differing practices that shape the habits of the heart in a contrasting direction. Identity emerges from what we practice.

In opposition to emotivism, we turn to Viktor Frankl (1959/1992) and his work with meaning, which he termed "logotherapy." Logotherapy, for Frankl, involves meaning through practices. He talks about three basic ways in which human beings find meaning: (1) through what one *gives* to life—the practices we offer without demand for reward; (2) through what one *gets* in life—the practices that come toward you; and (3) through one's *stand against the inevitable* when it seems as if no matter what you do, no matter what another does, the consequence cannot be changed, giving shape to practice of steadfastness. This final freedom is not necessarily a practice that takes one somewhere; rather, this final freedom demands that one stand upright, directly meeting the event. The practice of taking a stand against the inevitable permits one to engage in an element of dignity at a moment when life seems uncontrollable. At such a moment, one is called to meet existence on its own terms.

Frankl's work reminds us that human beings are in charge of two of the three elements that make life meaningful. We control what we give and our stance against the inevitable. The environment does not simply beat up on us every day; we are in charge of two-thirds of our own lives by practices that give and practices that take a stand against the inevitable. Practices shape our communicative hearts. Our communicative practices form habits of the heart that begin to shape patterns of our interpretative lives.

Pattern

Pattern permits practices to become meaningfully apparent. Philosophy of communication attends to meaning emergent from practices that form a pattern that shapes our "habits of the heart" (Tocqueville, 1835/2000, p. 275; Bellah et al., 1985). This stress on pattern is a central feature in general systems theory, where meaning is tied to the disclosure of pattern (Bertalanffy, 1968). Something becomes meaningful when there is an emergent pattern; practices form communicative patterns.

The connection between meaning and pattern is discerned in the lives of elementary school students as they are invited into a world of music. One must make a selection of an instrument at that time, or be given an instrument to play by the teacher. At that moment, it is unlikely for most students to see playing music as meaningful. It is through hours and hours of practice that playing music takes on a pattern and becomes meaningful. One finds a similar result with athletes and those in love with dance and voice; what binds such people together is the practice and pattern that makes the activity meaningful. The book *Outliers: The Story of Success* by Malcolm Gladwell (2008) makes this point; he articulates that practice separates an amateur from someone who will become a genuine expert at a given activity. The separation is not driven as much by knowledge as it is by the hours that are spent in the engagement of the task. He describes a study of student musicians who began at age five practicing the same number of hours each week, but as they grew, the differences in their practice hours contributed to whether they would be simply good or join an "elite" group of experts—"the elite performers had each totaled ten thousand hours of practice" (Gladwell, 2008, pp. 38–39). Practices offer a pattern that invites us to recognize just how meaningful something is in a given life engaged in the human condition.

Practices that shape a life pattern can transform existence. One of the founders of pragmatism, William James, attempted to discern how to implement free will after he had suffered a nervous breakdown in his late twenties. He stated, "My first act of free will shall be to believe in free will" ("William James," 2010). His decision led to a pattern of health. Pragmatically, *practices* that take the form of *patterns* give shape to *communicative meaning*. Meaning emerges as we witness a pattern of practices. Our heart follows our practices, and meaning follows our practices that emerge as patterns, acting as fulcrums that assist a human being in doing the heavy lifting in existence.

Historical Moment as Fulcrum

For understanding the importance of the notion of fulcrum, we turn to classical antiquity and one of the leading mathematicians of that time, Archimedes of Syracuse (c. 287–212 BCE). Archimedes studied multiple instruments that reduced "...the effort that has to be applied for moving a given load...," including the principle of the lever, a theory that he discussed in *On the Equilibrium of Planes* (Dijksterhuis, 1983, pp. 17–18).

A lever works with a fulcrum point; according to Merriam-Webster (n.d.), a fulcrum is a "prop; specifically, the support about which a lever turns." What Archimedes provided was a further extension of the mathematical law of the lever. Archimedes provided the mathematical and the practical applications that permitted human beings to move massive weight beyond their own body mass. What happened in the 1600s is not that the lever was found anew, but rather that the pivotal point on which the lever rested was named—fulcrum. According to Merriam-Webster (n.d.), the origin of the term "fulcrum" is Latin, from the word bedpost, *fulcire*, meaning to prop; the first use of the term is traced to 1668. "Fulcrum" is an important and pragmatic term for those wanting to move weight beyond the expectation of their own strength.

A philosophy of communication functions as a lever that rests upon a fulcrum that leverages the meaningfulness of philosophy of communication in the ongoing praxis of life. Following the insight of Hans-Georg Gadamer, we contend that the fulcrum for a given philosophy of communication is the historical moment. Without attentiveness to the historical moment, philosophy of communication appears like an abstract, unwieldy instrument of limited utility. When the lever of philosophy of communication joins the fulcrum of the historical moment, its impact far exceeds expectations. The practices and patterns of a philosophy of communication, no matter how theoretically insightful, rise and fall in significance in accordance with attentiveness to the historical moment, the fulcrum that empowers ideas. When one attends to practices and patterns of a given philosophy of communication, that philosophy functions as a lever that is given additional strength by attending to the historical moment.

Philosophy of Communication and Attentiveness

Philosophy of communication engages a story that frames the meaningfulness of human interaction; words permit Hannah Arendt (1958) to describe the transformation of "behavior" to the word "action" through story (p. 45). What separates behavior from action is that the latter has been vetted by and within a story; there is a communicative context behind it. Action requires a background story, which transforms behavior into a meaning context. Communicative significance includes a story that addresses a given historical moment and yields novel and particular insights.

Often what we call miscommunication and misunderstanding comes from our inappropriate pairing of a story (emplotment, main characters, and the historical moment) with a given behavior and a given historical moment. Arendt (1958) stressed the role of a "storyteller" as the one who gives credence or vets a given behavior; the storyteller, for Arendt, has a significant meaning-role in a culture (p. 192). She went to great lengths to articulate the classical understanding of a historian as responsible for recording, not necessarily who was the victor, but great deeds from both sides of the conflict that manifest themselves in battle. The classical "historian" is the recorder of great deeds with a given action becoming great as it addresses the historical moment rightly (Arendt, 1958, p. 194). Additionally, a spectator of great deeds, functioning as a historian, must provide a written story of what has transpired, offering a public account of the significance of a given activity. The notion of "spectator" looms large in the work of Kant (1790/1951), Arendt, and more recently, in the scholarship of Richard Sennett (2006, 2008). Each of these authors attributes an organizing and meaning function to the spectator.

Philosophy of communication assists us in our role as a spectator in order to shape meaning for our role as a participant; we organize material as a story attentive to a given historical moment. In his understanding of story, Paul Ricoeur (1984) stresses three major terms: drama, emplotment, and character. The story gives drama to behavior, and emplotment allows one to see behaviors changing; emplotment keeps the drama going and conveys the ongoing understanding of a given idea as a live tradition. Characters serve as both caretakers and catalysts of a story. For Arendt, the human condition manifests itself in a given historical moment through the stories within which humans find themselves situated.

Martin Buber (1972) held a similar position on the importance of story in his discussion of the "great character." A great character discovers identity within a story. If one asks what creates a great character, the answer from the philosophy of communication perspective of this project, *An Overture to Philosophy of Communication: The Carrier of Meaning*, is that a person situated within a great story that requires practices and commitment to an ongoing drama that has episodes of emplotment in a given historical moment shapes identities of characters within the story.

A story comes alive within the hands of onlookers who invite us into a sense of meaning by uniting the doing and the doers of human activity. There are multiple ways to illustrate philosophy of communication with a meaning focus within the realm of story, from ethnographic inquiry to case studies. This work turns to a story-laden convention of the novel. According to Ian Watt (1957), "...our usage of the term 'novel' was not fully established until the end of the 18th century" (p. 10), and is attributed to the use of the word "original," meaning "novel or fresh in character or style," to describe the genre of novel, which favored plots comprised of individual experiences rather than tales based on classical or renaissance epics, fables, or past history (p. 14). This project follows the lead of Watt, using the novel *Zorba the Greek* as an exemplar of story in action of our view of philosophy of communication as the carrier of meaning.

In the next chapter, we turn directly to *Zorba the Greek*, and then return to this novel at the conclusion of each of the following 13 chapters. We intentionally concentrate on the main character, Zorba, treating Boss as a secondary character in a book that exemplifies the power and significance of human passion and meaning through Zorba. Boss is a significant player in that his life exemplifies the extraordinary manner in which Zorba engages existence. Our focus moves from the dialogue between Boss and Zorba to a description of Zorba's mad rush into and through life, appreciating each moment whether or not it is to his liking. Meaning requires a context, and for that meaning to have persuasive significance, it needs a fulcrum—the historical moment—that moves information into philosophy of communication, giving direction, communicating the "why" that can aid in the bearing of the "how." An enduring and temporally engaged story points to how a given set of ideas shared with others (a philosophy of communication) continues to address a given historical moment that functions as a fulcrum, which brings life, energy, significance, and meaning to the communicative participants.

Telling a Story about Philosophy of Communication

An Overture to Philosophy of Communication: The Carrier of Meaning attends to the existential and emotive characteristics of human engagement, reflecting on how we understand and discern human meaning. Philosophy of communication is story-centered content that engages persons in the meeting of human existence. *An Overture to Philosophy of Communication: The Carrier of Meaning* claims conceptual terrain for philosophy of communication— beyond information accumulation alone. Human passion, meaning, and depth of engagement give life to philosophy of communication. A tourist sees only new buildings, monuments, and cities. Philosophy of communication is not for the tourist but for those who want to build meaningful communicative dwellings between and among persons. The building of such dwellings constitutes the immemorial musical score of philosophy of communication meaningfully orchestrating the human condition.

This book is divided into three parts that engage the process of meaning discernment and formation. Part I, "Overtures to Meaning," comprises chapters one through three. As this first chapter attests, philosophy of communication is akin to habits of the heart that shape our engagement with the world around us. As we meet existence, our understanding necessitates far more than information accumulation. Chapter 2, "Zorba's Dance," turns to an exemplar of this engagement, Zorba the Greek, who dances through life with passion and engagement in and with human existence. Zorba's understanding of existence is propelled by the action metaphor of dance. Habits of the heart and an existential dance do not take place in abstraction, but respond to the realities of the demands of human existence. Chapter 3, "Communicative Dwellings," situates the historical moment of such participation, stressing how and why we understand within communicative dwellings that are only partially of our own making.

Part II, "Situating Meaning," makes up the majority of this work, and begins with Chapter 4, "Knowledge and Meaning through Epistemology," which examines ways in which human beings gather resources for the understanding of human existence. Epistemology seeks to augment human understanding through the continual gathering of knowledge. Chapter 5, "Existential Engagement," offers a counter to epistemology, stressing existential engagement. In Chapter 6, "Philosophical Hermeneutics as Interpretation and Meaning," the work of existentialism offers a foundation for understanding philosophical hermeneutics and our role in interpreting existence. This assumes that an interpretive framework cannot exist without great respect for the object under study; we must meet that which we seek to understand. Chapter 7, "Empathy and the Other: A Phenomenological Perspective," explores a phenomenological perspective that reminds us of the importance of respect for the Other. A phenomenological perspective seeks a rigorous focus upon a given object, other, or phenomenon in order to understand. Understanding unites more closely with control in the analytic tradition of Chapter 8, "Analytic Discernment"; logic and clarity of thought yield understanding centered more on method than on the Other. Understanding yields to consequences and outcomes in Chapter 9, "Pragmatism: An American Practice," which outlines the American attraction to pragmatism. Understanding that is dependent upon differentiation clarifies and shapes insights in Chapter 10, "Dialectical Differentiation." Chapter 11, "Ethics and Diversity," seeks to understand what human beings hold as significant goods and examines the importance of ethics and diversity. These various approaches to human understanding are then framed in communicative action.

The final part of this book, "Meaning in Action," begins with Chapter 12, "Public Domain as the Home of Difference and Opinion," which examines the public domain as the essential home of differing theories and opinions that question one another and at times collide. Chapter 13, "Individualism as Misstep," takes a pejorative view of what the authors consider a problematic path in application of understanding. We then turn to Chapter 14, "*Sensus Communis*: The Community Matters," as a counter to individualism, stressing the significance of human community. Finally, we return in Chapter 15 to "Story-Centered Meaning: Beyond Information," reengaging the theme that propelled the introduction of this work—philosophy of communication is a form of story-centered meaning that contours understanding, framing the public domain and propelling us into human communities of communicative engagement.

CHAPTER 2
ZORBA'S DANCE

This chapter is the heart of the book, exemplifying communicative meaning in action in philosophy of communication. In the novel *Zorba the Greek*, we find two contrasting characters, Boss and Zorba; together they shape the story through their communicative relationship, illustrating meaning as the fulcrum of philosophy of communication. Each character embodies a particular philosophy of communication; the principal character, Zorba, lives life with passion and attentiveness to the sensations of life. Boss attempts to discover meaning in life through ideas and classical texts. Zorba seeks temporal/particular answers to the "why" of existence as he meets life on its own terms. Additionally, we witness Nikos Kazantzakis, the author of *Zorba the Greek*, writing with deep affection for Zorba's world, educating us with a testimony about the importance of meeting the historical moment of existence.

Introduction

The selection of *Zorba the Greek* emerged from three basic assumptions: (1) familiarity with the character of Zorba through the novel, cinema, and theater;[1] (2) the significance of the philosophical background of the author, Nikos Kazantzakis; and (3) the existential passion that the character of Zorba exhibits for the pursuit of meaning. Zorba is an exemplar of philosophy of communication as a carrier of meaning.

We begin with a discussion of the author, Nikos Kazantzakis, and background related to the book *Zorba the Greek*. The majority of this chapter describes events of the novel in relation to the two main characters in the work, Zorba and Boss. The aim of this chapter is to set the context for the novel, outline action within the novel, and provide material that is referenced in later chapters in this project, as an exemplification of philosophy of communication in action.

Zorba, in raw form, offers insight into Eugen Rosenstock-Huessy's book, *I Am an Impure Thinker* (1970/2001). One can hear a background conversation related to Rosenstock-Huessy's project, with Boss as an analytic thinker and Zorba as an existential thinker. Zorba is indeed the "impure thinker" who engages a raw form of philosophy of communication that seeks meaning as he attends to the historical moment.

---

1 The novel *Zorba the Greek* was originally published in 1946. The film version starring Anthony Quinn as Zorba appeared in 1964, and the theatrical production opened on Broadway in 1968.

> This is the world of the "pure" thinker; it is also the academic world. It teaches us to analyse but it knows nothing about life and death and does not help when we are concerned with "the survival of a truly human society."...Under the impact of life we are "impure thinkers"; we have to change, to give in, to balance, and to respond to the unforeseeable. (Rosenstock-Huessy, 1970/2001, p. v)

This project, *An Overture to Philosophy of Communication: The Carrier of Meaning*, celebrates impure thinking that lives in the tension of a conflicted heart that passionately seeks to live and understand. Philosophy of communication is the communicative task of making sense of and discerning meaning in the demands of everyday life, not with the aim of perfection, but with the aspiration of living in the world while resisting the temptation for blind pursuit of the perfect, the pristine, and the pure.

Philosophy of Communication in Story Form

Zorba the Greek was published in 1946 by Nikos Kazantzakis (1883–1957), who, at the time of its publication, had already experienced considerable success. Kazantzakis published numerous other works, including fiction, travel guides, and poetry.[2] Kazantzakis's dramatic hero of choice was Odysseus (Kazantzakis, 1960, p. 36), the major figure in the writings of Homer's *Odyssey*, reflected in Kazantzakis's epic poem *The Odyssey: A Modern Sequel* (1938). Kazantzakis was born in a region now known as Crete. He completed a Doctor of Laws in 1906 at the University of Athens, where he wrote his dissertation on Friedrich Nietzsche (1844–1900). Shortly after his university experience, Kazantzakis went to Paris and studied philosophy with Henri Bergson (1859–1941) (Lea, 1979, pp. 14–15). Bergson's work was central to Kazantzakis's literary challenge of a mechanistic view of life. Bergson received the Nobel Prize for Literature in 1927. Thirty years later, in 1957, his student, Kazantzakis, lost out to Albert Camus by a single vote for the same prize; however, Kazantzakis was awarded the Lenin Peace Prize in 1956. Additionally, it is interesting to note that Kazantzakis worked with Giorgos Zorbas, the inspiration for his novel, while operating a lignite mine in the Peloponnese in 1917 (O'Neil, 2004, p. 714).

---

2 Kazantzakis's published English works include: *The Odyssey: A Modern Sequel* (1938), *Zorba the Greek* (1946), *The Greek Passion* (1953), *Freedom or Death* (1956), *The Last Temptation of Christ* (1960), *The Saviors of God: Spiritual Exercises* (1960), *Saint Francis* (1962), *Japan-China* (1963), *Spain* (1963), *The Rock Garden* (1963), *The Fratricides* (1964), *Toda Raba* (1964), *England: A Travel Journal* (1965), *Report to Greco* (1965), *Journey to the Morea* (1965), *Journeying: Travels in Italy, Egypt, Sinai, Jerusalem and Cyprus* (1975), *Buddha* (1982), and *Alexander the Great* (1982).

Kazantzakis also lived in Berlin and Vienna, where he studied Buddhism, from 1922 to 1924, exemplifying real-life connections to the character Boss in *Zorba the Greek* (O'Neil, 2004, p. 706).

Kazantzakis was not only an active writer; he also spent a number of years in public service and later worked for UNESCO (1947–1948). In 1919, he was appointed director general for the Greek Ministry of Public Welfare, having responsibility for the repatriation of more than 150,000 persons of Greek ancestry who were caught by the civil war (1918–1920) in the Caucasus region of Russia (O'Neil, 2004, pp. 705–706). Kazantzakis's own philosophy contained elements from the philosophies of Bergson, Nietzsche, and Karl Marx (1818–1883), as well as aspects of Christianity and Buddhism (Lea, 1979, ix). According to biographer Peter Bien (1972), Kazantzakis's *The Saviors of God: Spiritual Exercises*, which he wrote in Berlin between 1922 and 1923 (Kazantzakis, 1960, p. 13), was "the book in which he eventually expounded his Bergsonian ideas with Nietzschean passion" (Bien, 1972, p. 13). This Bergsonian view emerges in the prologue's oft-quoted opening words: "We come from a dark abyss, we end in a dark abyss, and we call the luminous interval life" (Kazantzakis, 1960, p. 43). Kazantzakis centered his writing on the importance of assuming responsibility for light announced by the courage to act while surrounded by darkness.

Kazantzakis wrote *Zorba the Greek* while on the island of Aegina from 1941 to 1943 (O'Neil, 2004, pp. 706–708). The 1964 movie starring Anthony Quinn, the 1968 Broadway musical of *Zorba the Greek*, and the 1983 musical revival also starring Anthony Quinn brought this work into the consciousness of many. Those who watched the film and attended the stage performance experienced the image of Anthony Quinn inspirationally dancing to Greek music. It is the passionate love of life that personifies this novel, even in the midst of suffering and death. One finds, within the novel's characters, philosophy of communication in the everyday trenches of human life that meets existence on its own terms with clarity of response and the ongoing recognition of the importance of loving life.

The novel addresses the passion and existential wisdom of the working class and brings forth Bergson's (1911) commitments that countered a mechanistic view of human life. Boss, Kazantzakis's intellectual character, attempts to answer one question after another posed by the more existentially minded Zorba, who takes the reader into a messy meeting of the demands of existence. There is no walking away from raw realities of life; the novel takes the reader directly to the realities of death, murder, and relational endings that cast a shadow upon existence, providing the background that makes genuine light visible. Yet, in the meeting of these events, the novel reminds us that there is a tenacious sense of joy that permeates life, even in the final goodbye to a friend. We witness ongoing efforts to engage a philosophy of communication in life's traumas and sufferings, in the banalities of the everyday, and through the joys and achievements discovered in existence.

Boss and Zorba—Their Meeting

The roots and origins of each man, Boss and Zorba, are left as "enthymemes" for the reader to fill in the blanks and discern the meaning of their entrance into the story (Aristotle, trans. 2007, pp. 33–34); we have just enough knowledge to form an impressionistic view of their formations. We quickly discover that Boss wants to escape something. Interestingly, Boss is both writing a book on Buddha and beginning his foray into the role of a capitalist as he works in a mine in a small town where he employs Zorba and a number of local men. It is the dramatic interplay between Zorba and Boss that captures our imagination. Each event ignites a conversation between the two men in moments of triumph, quandary, deep suffering, and joy. Zorba centers his life on passion, good food, good wine, and agreeable women. He is an unlikely equal for an intellectual who unexpectedly becomes his friend and his student.

The relationship between Zorba and Boss shapes this novel. Zorba is in his 60s, a man without formal education and a veteran of various odd jobs who plays the *santuri*, a musical instrument from Turkey. Boss is a younger man who is book learned as well as spiritual, attending to the insights of both Dante (1265–1321) and Buddha. Zorba lives within the demands of existence, and Boss lives more comfortably within the confines of the pages in his books. It is hard to imagine two more contrasting characters. Yet they unite in their questions about the meaning of life that originate from very different places.

The novel begins with Boss as the narrator; we discover in the last few pages that shortly after Boss learned of Zorba's death, he quickly wrote an account of his life with Alexis Zorba. An opening description of the character Zorba and the phenomenon of *Zorba the Greek* comes from a *Time* magazine quotation that answers the question "Who is Zorba?" with the following:

> He [Zorba] is Everyman with a Greek accent. He is Sinbad crossed with Sancho Panza. He is the Shavian Life Force poured into a long, lean, fierce-mustached Greek whose 65 years have neither dimmed his hawk eyes nor dulled his pagan laughter. Author Kazantzakis tried to kill him off in a letter. But he reckons without his own talent. He has created Zorba, but he cannot kill him. (Kazantzakis, 1946/1952, p. 1)

In the study of philosophy of communication and human meaning, the phenomenon of Zorba exemplifies passion for life, and the character of Boss reveals both the importance of and the limits of books—Zorba and Boss open and limit our worlds with the conviction of their perspectives. Their messages are reminiscent of Martin Buber, the great Jewish philosopher, who stated that he loved books, but if he ever had to choose between books and a human being, the choice would be the latter (Friedman, 1981, p. 56). To never read again would be a great tragedy; to never meet another would be a greater wrong, an existential sin.

Zorba engages people, and Boss, the bookworm, consistently makes choices that move him away from the recognition of the fundamental importance of others. The existential journey of Boss is more akin to that of most human beings; he is engrossed with successes, mistakes, and regrets that give rise to the question of why one should continue. Boss lacks the existential courage of Zorba. The book begins with Boss parting ways with a friend who calls him a "bookworm" at their departure (Kazantzakis, 1946/1952, p. 12). When Boss reflects on that moment, he states: "If only I could live again the moment of that anger which surged up in me when my friend called me a bookworm! I recalled then that all my disgust at the life I had been leading was personified in those words" (Kazantzakis, 1946/1952, p. 12). The book will later end with a similar lament with Boss missing his friend Zorba. Boss wants so desperately to "…live with simple men, workmen and peasants, far from the race of bookworms!" (Kazantzakis, 1946/1952, p. 13). Boss later contemplates the choices he made in life before meeting Zorba.

> I was envious of the man. He had lived with his flesh and blood—fighting, killing, kissing—all that I had tried to learn through pen and ink alone. All the problems I was trying to solve...this man had solved up in the pure air of the mountains with his sword. (Kazantzakis, 1946/1952, p. 255)

Boss then understood the difference between meeting life on its own terms and living with ideas in abstraction.

The novel is an account of Boss's search for meaning in the existential meeting of others, rather than solely looking for universal answers in books. Boss does, however, find meaning in books and language, exemplified in his description of compassion:

> But at times I was seized with compassion. A Buddhist compassion, as cold as the conclusion of a metaphysical syllogism. A compassion not only for men but for all

life which struggles, cries, weeps, hopes and does not perceive that everything is a phantasmagoria of nothingness. Compassion for the Greeks, and for the lignite mine, and for my unfinished manuscript of Buddha, for all those vain compositions of light and shade which suddenly disturb and contaminate the pure air. (Kazantzakis, 1946/1952, pp. 21–22)

However, as Zorba becomes the teacher, the novel reveals that both books and people can open and close the world. This project on philosophy of communication assumes that we need interaction of the two—books and human relationships.

Boss rents a "disused lignite mine" on the coast of Crete facing Libya (Kazantzakis, 1946/1952, p. 13). His life changes as he takes a boat to his destination and meets Zorba, who immediately asks to accompany Boss. Boss, who does not know Zorba, asks why, as any of us might. Zorba then counters with a statement that few intellectuals would want to hear. "'Why! Why!' he exclaimed with disdain. 'Can't a man do anything without a why?'" (Kazantzakis, 1946/1952, pp. 14–15). Boss, with his Dante in hand, is met with the energy of one of those "simple men" who would challenge him more than any other (Kazantzakis, 1946/1952, p. 13).

Boss discovers that Zorba has the skills of a miner, and Boss has just rented a mine. Zorba ends up talking about his santuri and his singing of "... old Klephtic tunes from Macedonia" before he introduces himself as Alexis Zorba (Kazantzakis, 1946/1952, p. 16). Zorba explains what the santuri means to him, stating, "[s]ince I learnt to play the santuri, I've been a different man. When I'm feeling down, or when I'm broke, I play the santuri and it cheers me up. When I'm playing, you can talk to me, I hear nothing, and even if I hear, I can't speak" (Kazantzakis, 1946/1952, p. 17). Boss makes his first discovery; it is in the doing, the engagement of life, that Zorba lives. In the doing one finds a particular identity. Perhaps the reluctance for doing is the reason we are left with a narrator known only as "Boss," a man without a particular name. The meeting of Zorba and Boss ends with them leaving together and with Boss saying, "'May God be with us,...'Let's go!'" and with Zorba following with his typical contrariness, "[May] God and the devil [be with us]!" (Kazantzakis, 1946/1952, p. 20). Zorba and Boss, as contrasting human caricatures, leave for Crete together to work in the mine, beginning a friendship of remarkable depth.

Crete—A Welcome and Imagining the Real

Zorba was not a novice on Crete soil. He had been there before, during the revolution in Crete with the Turks where he found himself in combat; Zorba felt ashamed of the "madness" of that war (Kazantzakis, 1946/1952, p. 27).[3] The conversation about the war dominated their time until the two reached the village where the mine was located, with Boss as the manager and Zorba as the daily supervisor. They lodged that first night at Madame Hortense's boarding house. This older French woman becomes an illustrative relational character in the novel, a walking witness to the disappointments and moments of joy that shape a life. Zorba immediately pays close attention to her, making her feel special and young once again. Kazantzakis (1946/1952) describes Madame Hortense as "A dumpy, plump little woman, with bleached flax-colored hair...waddling along on her bandy legs" (p. 35). From the moment of "welcome" from Madame Hortense, Zorba ignites her sense of hope. As Zorba begins a relationship based upon actions that are, at best, only partially deceitful, Madame Hortense begins to fall in love with him. In the meeting of this woman, however, Zorba recognizes what others do not; he sees the outline of a life as it once was, now cloaked by age and pain, far from public clarity and notice—yet Zorba notices.

The next few chapters are largely devoted to Zorba's relationship with Madame Hortense. The reader is encouraged to take notice of the appearance of Madame Hortense; she is tired and beaten by life. Yet with Zorba, she finds a new sense of life and energy. She owns a hotel establishment that "...consisted of a row of old bathing-huts joined together" (Kazantzakis, 1946/1952, p. 38). Additionally, Zorba and Boss begin work in the mine with hopes of paying expenses within three months. After work, Madame Hortense feeds Zorba and Boss well with meat, bread, and wine, while Zorba makes his normal sensual comments about her. She wrestles with his comments, reflecting on how she

---

3 Zorba is referring to the first Greco-Turkish war of 1897, which is also called the Thirty Days' War. The Greeks were concerned about the deteriorating relations between Christian civilians and Muslim leaders on the Turkish-led island of Crete. In 1896, a rebellion on the island gave Greece the opportunity to annex Crete. In February 1897, Greek troops landed on Crete, with Greek union being proclaimed. Soon after, the European powers erected a blockade in order to stop the spread of disruption to the Balkans, which prevented Greece from sending assistance to the island. Greek forces, led by Prince Constantine, were sent to attack the Turks in Thessaly. However, the Greeks were inadequately prepared and were overwhelmed by the German-organized Turkish army. On May 27, 1897, yielding to pressure from European powers, Greece withdrew their troops from Crete and accepted an armistice on the mainland ("Greco-Turkish Wars," 2011).

and other women somehow continue to care for and assist men who seem to be forever unappreciative. Madame Hortense is angry at the ingratitude of men. In Madame Hortense, we find a person who has endured a demanding life in a world centered on men, creatures who consistently seem to demand more than they give, offering little thanks. In spite of all this suffering, Zorba somehow permits Madame Hortense to imagine and hope once again; this anticipation conjures up an increasing rush of sadness as Madame thinks of death and of men fighting against one another, too often senselessly. She reflects and begins to weep.

Zorba gives insight into imagining a reality that is not empirically present. He recognizes Madame Hortense phenomenologically, as a woman with a beautiful heart, giving reality to the sexual language that no longer coincides with her current physique. Zorba's use of common and raw language with insight into the heart of another is anything but common. He is able is see a "sacred and mysterious face" (Kazantzakis, 1946/1952, p. 50) unseen by others, a humanness not additive of individual characteristics.

As Zorba returns from spending a long evening with Madame Hortense, he recounts a story to Boss about his grandmother, who cursed him and young people for not seeing what was phenomenologically present in an empirically old face. It is not the empirical fact that shapes a human life; it is the phenomenological meaning that we discover with others that shapes human lives. On Sundays, Zorba and Boss dress up and go to dinner at Madame Hortense's hotel; she provides a fowl for them to eat each week, offering meals with hospitality and kindness. Zorba witnesses the truth of Martin Buber's statement about the power of "imagining the real" (Anderson & Cissna, 1997, p. 23). Zorba sees what is not empirically present; he is able to imagine a reality more authentic than the visual proclaims.

Earthly Brutes and Reading Buddha

Later, Zorba defines "man," for Boss, as a "brute" (Kazantzakis, 1946/1952, p. 64). He warns Boss to keep his distance and never to let the other get the upper hand. Zorba has earthy wisdom.

> That man has not been to school, I thought, and his brains have not been perverted. He has had all manner of experiences; his mind is open and his heart has grown bigger, without his losing one ounce of his primitive boldness. All the problems which we find so complicated or insoluble he cuts through as if with a sword, like Alexander the Great cutting the Gordian knot. It is difficult for him to miss his aim, because his two feet are held firmly planted on the ground by the weight of his whole body. (Kazantzakis, 1946/1952, p. 74)

Boss is the counter to this vision of having one's feet "planted on the ground," even as he sees something special in Zorba. Boss wakes in the morning with a pen in his hand, having fallen asleep writing.

The beginning of a new day quickly takes the conversation back to Zorba's discussion of the importance of woman, eating, and dancing; Zorba dances with such vigor that Boss grows scared and repeatedly screams, "That's enough!" (Kazantzakis, 1946/1952, p. 83). He wants Zorba to quit before his heart stops beating. Never has Boss seen a dance of life that simultaneously invites the thought of death. Zorba states that there is a devil in him and wonders why Boss cannot laugh at the sight of a dance that lets out the devil. Zorba also admits that his joy was choking him and that he needed to find an outlet because he admitted that words were insufficient to describe how he felt. "What could I do, boss? My joy was choking me. I had to find some outlet. And what sort of outlet? Words? Pff!" (Kazantzakis, 1946/1952, p. 84). Zorba "dances" at his misfortunes (Kazantzakis, 1946/1952, p. 86). Boss then ponders how much he both envies and feels sorry for Zorba.

> In other, more primitive and creative ages, Zorba would have been the chief of a tribe. He would have gone before, opening up the path with a hatchet. Or else he would have been a renowned troubador [sic] visiting castles, and everybody would have hung on his words—lords and ladies and servants.... In our ungrateful age, Zorba wanders hungrily round the enclosures like a wolf, or else sinks into becoming some pen-pusher's buffoon. (Kazantzakis, 1946/1952, pp. 87–88)

As Boss continued to think, Zorba states out loud that as he grew older he simply became more wild, more a part of the earth and existence.

Zorba has been married before, more than once; he is a survivor of many relationships. He understands that he is often simply a "passerby" in many of his relationships (Kazantzakis, 1946/1952, p. 97). His language about women is macho and places him in control. Yet each discussion with Boss has a hint of deep care that is more profound than his speech. It is as if Zorba speaks a language that overrides his speech. This language is deeper than the speech that unites Zorba and Boss, as Boss holds out his hand to the rain and feels the sorrow of the earth. Zorba then states, "A man's heart suffers when it rains" (Kazantzakis, 1946/1952, p. 107). The discussion then goes to "crude realism" about birth that sounds more like Shakespeare to Boss than the ranting of an uneducated laborer (Kazantzakis, 1946/1952, p. 114). The discussion between Zorba and Boss then moves to comments about the widow woman in the town, which begins with a focus on her beauty that invites uncontrolled jealously in the village that will eventually lead to violent deaths. She, like Madame Hortense, becomes a relational character of consequence in the novel and again we are given little information about her background. The focus is on Zorba, who takes them back to a discussion of women, stating that once a woman called him to her and he did not answer. Zorba contends that his deafness to that woman's call would send him to Hell. His earthly commitment to the Other was not a pretense, but more of a sacred pledge to existence out of an obligation to enjoy life while assisting others in finding joy in existence as well.

Zorba states that God must be like him, only that he, Zorba, is crazier and his brain is not the correct weight. He then pauses and wonders why Boss continues to put up with him. Zorba's moments of reflection remind him that he does not belong in this changing world; his focus of attention is passionately intense and outside of normative convention.

> He [Zorba] was busy, he did not wish to speak. "Don't speak to me when I'm working," he said one evening. "I might snap!" "Snap, Zorba? Why?" "There you go again with your 'whys' and 'wherefores'! Like a kid! How can I explain? I'm completely taken up by my work, stretched taut from head to foot, and riveted to the stone or the coal or the *santuri*. If you suddenly touched me or spoke to me and I tried to turn round, I might snap. Now, d'you see?" (Kazantzakis, 1946/1952, p. 126)

The defining characteristic of Zorba is his intensity, his passion for life.

Zorba is both intense in what he does and in his not knowing. His passion makes it possible for him to appreciate mystery. Zorba and Boss both seek knowledge or belief about God, but neither character is able to make a commitment regarding the existence of God.

> "Boss, d'you believe that? That God became man and was born in a stable? Do you believe it, or are you just pulling our legs?"

> "It's difficult to say, Zorba." I replied. "I can't say I believe it, nor that I don't. What about you?"

> "I can't say I do either. I can't for the life of me. You see, when I was a kid and my grandma told me tales, I didn't believe a word of them. And yet I trembled with emotion, I laughed and I cried, just as if I did believe them. When I grew a beard on my chin, I just dropped them, and I even used to laugh at them; but now, in my old age—I suppose I'm getting soft, eh, boss?—in a kind of way I believe in them again.... Man's a mystery!'" (Kazantakis, 1946/1952, p. 133)

Zorba and Boss share similar questions about religious teachings. They also share skepticism about their beliefs, stemming from their individual experiences. What separates them is the intensity that Zorba brought to his questioning of life.

The force of Zorba's engagement with life is central to all his relationships. Zorba finds meaning in life through passionate immersion in life's experiences and relationships with others; Boss, of course, continues to seek meaning through ideas and books. Zorba acknowledges this difference in a discussion about living life.

> Yes, you understand with your brain. You say: "This is right, and that's wrong...." But where does that lead us? While you are talking I watch your arms and chest.... They're silent. They don't say a word. As though they hadn't a drop of blood.... Well, what do you think you understand with? With your head? Bah!" (Kazantzakis, 1946/1952, p. 250)

Zorba points to the meeting with others within contexts as being the experiential location for determining meaning in one's life.

One morning before sunrise, Zorba is worried. He feels a premonition. Later that day, the premonition comes true—the gallery roof of the mine shuddered. Zorba yells telling the mineworkers to escape. All the men follow the demand of Zorba's voice; they run, leaving Zorba alone. Zorba stands alone in the mine; he props up the wall and then runs, saving his life only after all others are safe. The mine collapses and the men are alive due to Zorba's actions. When Zorba finally begins to speak, he takes that moment to yell at the men for what they left behind—their tools.

> Zorba had just made firm the great prop and was running, slithering in the mire, towards the exit. Rushing headlong in the darkness, he ran into me and we accidentally fell into each other's arms. "We must get out!" he yelled. "Get out!" We ran and reached the light. The terror-stricken workmen had gathered at the entrance and were peering inside.... "You left your picks down there!" Zorba shouted angrily. The men said nothing. "Why didn't you take them with you?" he shouted again, furious. (Kazantzakis, 1946/1952, pp. 127–128)

Zorba stands before the men as a practical moral reminder of the importance of work and the practical sacredness of tools that permit one to do their work. The work matters and taking care of the tools is a pragmatic acknowledgment of the importance and the gift of work. Zorba is a brute of a man, who not only knows how to work but also understands the sacredness of the doing of the work and the value of the tools that permit one to labor.

Relational Demands

Kazantzakis increasingly connects us to the ongoing relationship between Zorba and Madame Hortense, and the emerging relationship between the widow and Boss. As Boss thought obsessively about the widow, Zorba reminds Boss that all is simple in life; we just have a habit of making life's decisions unnecessarily complicated. Zorba wants Boss to attend to the essentials of life, such as food, work, friendship, and love. Zorba wants Boss to meet life on its own terms, but Boss understands that there is a unique sense of timing that life demands—a timing that, when violated, brings hurt to people and existence itself.

> My breath had forced the butterfly to appear, all crumpled, before its time. It struggled desperately and, a few seconds later, died in the palm of my hand. That little body is, I do believe, the greatest weight I have on my conscience. For I realize today that it is a mortal sin to violate the great laws of nature. We should not hurry, we should not be impatient, but we should confidently obey the eternal rhythm. (Kazantzakis, 1946/1952, p. 139)

The reality of hurt continues, as Boss wonders who will be the first person he will meet in the new year, and it is, of course, the widow. Zorba naturally begins the new year with much food, wine, and time with Madame Hortense. There appears to be a harmony between Zorba and the universe, even as much did not proceed as he wanted. The harmony results from Zorba meeting life on its own terms.

Boss then returns to his books, thinking once again about Buddha and referring to him as the "last man" (Kazantzakis, 1946/1952, p. 154). At the same time, existence enters into his life with the realization that he and Zorba are running out of money. The conversation directed by the narrator turns to Zorba and his view of the universe. "He lived the earth, water, the animals and God, without the distorting intervention of reason" (Kazantzakis, 1946/1952, p. 156). Boss then reflects on letters from his friend whom he had left earlier on the boat, before meeting Zorba. The postscript of the letter is of importance. "P.S. I haven't forgotten the agreement we made on the boat the day I left. If I have to 'leave' this earth, I shall warn you, remember, wherever you are; don't let it scare you" (Kazantzakis, 1946/1952, p. 163). The reading of the letter happens when Zorba is gone, supposedly for a few days to fetch supplies for their work in the forest, which turned into 12 days.

During this time, Zorba writes to Boss, "But don't you worry yourself, boss, I'm looking after your little affairs, too. Now and then I go and look round the shops. I'll buy the cable and all we need, don't you worry" (Kazantzakis, 1946/1952, p. 170). Zorba's letter also includes numerous comments on the "disgrace" of old age, death, and his "relationship" with a young woman while he is away (Kazantzakis, 1946/1952, p. 165). As Boss slowly reads Zorba's letter, he reflects on how he admires "this primitive man" who understands that all is "miraculous" in existence (Kazantzakis, 1946/1952, pp. 171–172). Boss then sends a telegram to Zorba, urging him to "[c]ome back immediately" (Kazantzakis, 1946/1952, p. 175). Boss reflects to himself, "…I was for a while in two minds—no, three. I did not know whether to be angry, or laugh, or just admire this primitive man who simply cracked life's shell—logic, morality, honesty—and went straight to its very substance" (Kazantzakis, 1946/1952, p. 171). Boss misses his primitive and unconventionally inspiring friend.

As Boss waits for Zorba, so does Madame Hortense, who impatiently anticipates Zorba's return. When Madame Hortense approaches Boss and asks him about Zorba's return, Boss reads Zorba's letter to her. Out of pity for her, Boss does not read the part where Zorba has taken up with another woman. Much worse, Boss adds a lie at the end of the letter, stating that Zorba wants to marry her. She says, "I accept" (Kazantzakis, 1946/1952, p. 180). Boss's attempt at polite optimism offers her great joy and places Zorba in a demanding position when he returns. Boss's false conversation about marriage provides a concrete example of fantasy that masquerades as imagination (Kant, 1800/2006, p. 75). Madame Hortense becomes scared and sick. The reason for her sickness is the fear of loss—for the first time in years, she is afraid, afraid of death. Boss's lie about Zorba in relation to Madame Hortense has the unintended consequence of making her increasingly fearful about the loss of love and joy.

Boss is then interrupted by more sad news. He overhears someone stating that Pavli, Mavrandoni's son, drowned himself because of his unrequited love for the widow woman. The responses to this news in the village are frightening, with one woman suggesting that some man of courage must step up and cut the widow's throat. Manolakas, Pavli's cousin, lifts up the corpse of his cousin and begins to walk the still body to the village. Boss hears the commotion and remembers Zorba telling him repeatedly, if the widow comes by your path, you need to "Get married, have children, don't hesitate! Troubles were made for young men!" (Kazantzakis, 1946/1952, p. 186). At that moment, and quite unexpectedly, a gift of oranges comes to Boss from the widow who is thankful that he has been kind to her. With the gift, Boss's "…heart was ready to burst for joy" (Kazantzakis, 1946/1952, p. 187). Thought and reflection move Boss,

from the changing of seasons of loneliness of existence to his connection
with the widow. Additionally, he thinks that after his Buddha manuscript is
complete he will be "delivered," made fully complete with his manuscript and
relationship guiding him. He then meets a gift-bearing Zorba, who has just
returned (Kazantzakis, 1946/1952, p. 198).

Zorba has brought presents, but his gift giving is interrupted by Boss's
confession about the "marriage lie" that he told to Madame Hortense. Zorba says
that such things are not for joking, making Boss feel ashamed. Zorba tells Boss:

> You shouldn't do things like that, boss, if you don't mind my saying so. That sort of joke,
> you know is…women are weak, delicate creatures—how many times have I got to tell
> you that? Like porcelain vases, they are, and you have to handle them very carefully, boss.
> (Kazantzakis, 1946/1952, p. 200)

During dinner, the confrontation between Madame Hortense and Zorba
seems inevitable, as the marriage lie told by Boss becomes known. We do not,
however, have a resolution; Kazantzakis leaves this encounter abruptly, only
to return later, turning instead to another side character, a monk.

Zorba and Boss are on a trek to the monastery to say their prayers and to
buy land. During their journey, they meet a monk who encourages them to
turn around and go back. The monk warns Zorba and Boss that the monastery
has only one trinity, "Money, pride, and young boys!" (Kazantzakis, 1946/1952,
p. 213). The monk is running away; he can no longer endure the monastery
environment, but Zorba asks him to go back to the monastery with them.
The monk states that he has a devil in him by the name of Joseph, who takes
a drink and a cigarette from Zorba. This new character in the story confesses
that he became a monk to escape poverty. Zorba wants the angry monk to
assist as he and Boss try to buy the nearby forest for half its going price; they
need wood in order to shore up the mine and restart their work after the
collapse of the mine. At the monastery they hear a gunshot, and both Zorba
and the monk assume that another monk has been killed. They buy the forest
and then quickly leave behind the oddities of the monastery.

Zorba then returns home to "marry" Madame Hortense with Boss as his best
man. Zorba is also the one who performs the ceremony, during which Madame
Hortense almost collapses, saying that Zorba will be her husband forever.
Zorba knows he has appointed himself the director of the marriage bureau and
answers the unspoken criticism with "I've got a heart" (Kazantzakis, 1946/1952,
p. 246). Indeed, he does have a heart for life, as he lives out this fictional and
simultaneously real drama of marriage to Madame Hortense. Boss understands

that when this man's soul is touched, one finds fire, a great passion for life, and a passion for others. Zorba lives outside the routine expectations of a normal life. "Rescued from my country, from priests, and from money. I began sifting things, sifting more and more things out. I lighten my burden that way. I—how shall I put it?—I find my own deliverance, I become a man" (Kazantzakis, 1946/1952, p. 253). Zorba refuses to fight for abstract principles that seem to corrupt people. Zorba did not engage in combat for a country, but for people that mattered to him. Zorba then went to work and "…was completely absorbed in the job" (Kazantzakis, 1952, p. 258). Zorba fights for existence, for others, and for a love of life, escaping the demands of abstract principles. In this fictional yet real drama, we witness the struggle of Zorba in action.

Meeting the Inevitable

The novel then shifts to the reality of a number of difficult endings: the meeting of death, implications for those left behind, and Zorba's acknowledgment that they too will someday be simply "worm meat" (Kazantzakis, 1946/1952, p. 254). This part of the work gives insight into death in numerous forms, each final and each painful. We first find Madame Hortense ill. On Easter day, she is very sick and Zorba is concerned; he tells Boss to look for a woman to love while he can—life is short. Zorba checks on Madame Hortense when she does not show for Easter dinner. Upon Zorba's return, he tells Boss that Madame Hortense caught a cold but he gave her some rum and a massage. Zorba makes a toast to her health and her quick recovery, adding that he hopes the devil does not take her too soon.

The story abruptly shifts to another ending—that of Boss's completion of the Buddha manuscript and then to Madame Hortense calling for Zorba with only Boss able to see her. Boss relays to her that Zorba is not feeling well. Walking home, Boss finds the widow woman cornered in the midst of much yelling with knives drawn. The crowd calls her a "Wretch! Slut! Murderess!" (Kazantzakis, 1946/1952, p. 273). Old Mavrandoni, father of the drowned Pavli and Manolakas's uncle, takes out his knife and wants to kill the widow. Zorba enters the room in which the widow is cornered and fights on her behalf, calling them all cowards. He eventually fights with Manolakas, only to lose and watch Mavrandoni cut the widow's throat, taking off her head. That night Zorba cannot eat. Existence has been violated—men have behaved as beasts. Boss tries to console him, only to have Zorba shout, "Shut up!" (Kazantzakis, 1946/1952, p. 279). The next time Zorba and Manolakas meet, Manolakas seeks to kill Zorba as revenge for Zorba's attempting to stop him from killing the widow. Boss intervenes, explaining why he should not kill Zorba.

> "And don't forget, Zorba is a foreigner, a Macedonian, and it's the greatest disgrace we Cretans can bring on ourselves to raise a hand against a guest in our country…. Come now, give him your hand, that's real gallantry—and come to the hut, Manolakas. We'll drink together and roast a yard of sausage to seal our friendship!" I took Manolakas by the waist and led him a little apart. "The poor fellow's old, remember," I whispered. "A strong, young fellow like you shouldn't attack a man of his age." (Kazantzakis, 1946/1952, p. 282)

With these comments, the fight ceases. Manolakas says he will not raise a hand against Zorba ever again.

The next day Zorba visits Madame Hortense, who is dying. Zorba holds her hand as she says she does not want to die. Meanwhile there are people outside the room hoping she will expire quickly so they can claim her things. Zorba yells at them, calling them "old magpies" (Kazantzakis, 1946/1952, p. 291). Zorba holds Madame Hortense. "'Forgive me, dear lady,' he said to her, 'forgive me, and may God forgive you. If sometimes I spoke a harsh word, we're only men…. Forgive me'" (Kazantzakis, 1946/1952, p. 289). Madame Hortense dies, and Zorba wants to weep but refuses to do so in front of the scavengers. He spits and states, "A bit of earth" (Kazantzakis, 1946/1952, p. 295). Later, with Boss, Zorba is very quiet and says, "Well, all those damned books you read—what good are they? Why do you read them?" (Kazantzakis, 1946/1952, p. 300). Zorba grieves over the loss of life and his friend, Madame Hortense.

Zorba again sees the monk who describes how he has killed Joseph, the other personality within the monk, the devil inside him. The monk appears to be mad. Zorba's response is that without the devil in him, he is without a sense of purpose, "…completely empty, finished!" (Kazantzakis, 1946/1952, p. 309). At this juncture, Boss offers his most profound description of human beings:

> I think, Zorba—but I may be wrong—that there are three kinds of men: those who make it their aim, as they say, to live their lives, eat, drink, make love, grow rich, and famous; then come those who make it their aim not to live their own lives but to concern themselves with the lives of all men—they feel that all men are one and they try to enlighten them, to love them as much as they can and do good to them; finally there are those who aim at living the life of the entire universe—everything, men, animals, trees, stars, we are all one, we are all one substance involved in the same terrible struggle. What struggle?… Turning matter into spirit. (Kazantzakis, 1946/1952, pp. 309–310)

Zorba is confused as he hears these comments. He goes outside and when he returns, he tells Boss that he found the monk with his heart no longer ticking, laying face down on his stomach. Zorba shaves the dead monk's face and then explains to all the other monks that God has done this task—a miracle has happened. Zorba wants the monastery to become a "miracle factory" (Kazantzakis, 1946/1952, p. 313); he pulls off this strange act of shaving the monk and trying to turn it into a miracle.

> *"Kyrie eleison! Kyrie eleison!"* murmured the villagers in terror. "That's not all," added the monk, swallowing his spittle. "When we bent down to lift up the accursed Zaharia we stood aghast: for the Virgin had shaved off his hair, moustache and beard—like a Catholic priest!" Controlling my laughter with the greatest difficulty, I turned to Zorba. "Scoundrel!" I said in a low voice. (Kazantzakis, 1946/1952, p. 316)

Zorba wants to infuse a sense of awe in the life of the monks once again. He senses the need to re-instill the sacred that begins with a sense of awe. His action honors the life and the death of his newly encountered friend—the monk.

Learning to Dance

Boss then asks Zorba to teach him to dance. Zorba begins to dance with such energy and defiance that Boss can only register a deep sense of awe. "Watching Zorba dance, I understood for the first time the fantastic efforts of man to overcome his weight. I admired Zorba's endurance, his agility and proud bearing. His clever and impetuous steps were writing on the sand the demoniac history of mankind" (Kazantzakis, 1946/1952, pp. 323-324). Zorba wants to know if Boss could live and sense the "showers of sparks" (Kazantzakis, 1946/1952, p. 324); they both begin to laugh. Boss then reads a letter from his friend whom he left on the boat and realizes his friend is in great danger. He abruptly tells Zorba that he is leaving and has many more papers to write. The two men have wine together but Zorba does not play the santuri because it requires a "happy heart" (Kazantzakis, 1946/1952, p. 333). Zorba wants this ritual of goodbye to end quickly. Their "separation was as clean as a sword cut" (Kazantzakis, 1946/1952, p. 337); the two men never see one another again. Later, Boss receives a telegram stating that his old friend from the boat, who was mentioned at the start of the novel, has died of pneumonia—his premonition was correct.

Zorba continues to send letters to Boss after their departure, asking him to come and stay with him. Boss declines, at which time Zorba writes back for the last time: "My God, sometimes when I had no work, I asked myself the question: Is there or isn't there any hell? But yesterday, when your letter came, I said: There surely must be a hell for a few pen-pushers like the boss!"

(Kazantzakis, 1946/1952, p. 340). Boss never hears from or about Zorba until one day he senses Zorba speaking to him in a dream, which left him with a taste of death. Zorba marries and has a child. A schoolmaster in the town writes to Boss, confirming the death of Zorba. The note recounts Zorba's last minutes on earth.

> "Listen, just another minute. If some priest or other comes to take my confession and give me the sacrament, tell him to clear out, quick, and leave me his curse instead! I've done heaps and heaps of things in my life, but I still did not do enough. Men like me ought to live a thousand years. Good night!" These were his last words. He then sat up in his bed, threw back the sheets and tried to get up. We ran to prevent him—Lyuba, his wife, and I, along with several sturdy neighbors. But he brushed us all roughly aside, jumped out of bed and went to the window. There, he gripped the frame, looked out far into the mountains, opened wide his eyes and began to laugh, then to whinny like a horse. It was thus, standing, with his nails dug into the window frame, that death came to him. His wife Lyuba asked me to write to you and send her respects. The deceased often talked about you, she says, and left instructions that a santuri of his should be given to you after his death to help you to remember him. (Kazantzakis, 1946/1952, p. 346)

The man who so deeply loved life reminds us of the importance of passion, love for music, and the memory of a friend. Zorba, the man who danced, offers a life that was a philosophical picture of the joy of meeting existence on its own terms.

As the carrier of meaning, philosophy of communication engages existence—the joys of friendship, the toils of labor, the intensity of love, the pain of relational loss, the reality of regret and bad decisions, and the anticipation of death. In each case, the meaning we derive is shaped within a communicative dance. Zorba the Greek suggests the pragmatic importance of such meaning, as we meet life on its own terms.

Chapter 3

Communicative Dwellings

In the context of communication, we paint a philosophical picture of what we perceive. We do not dwell in pristine truth; we dwell in fuzzy horizons of meaning that shape communicative understanding. We contend that philosophical pictures, which this chapter describes, are historical dwellings that give rise to meaning and profile our communicative lives. We will begin by offering an example of this perspective with what is commonly called historical periods. We will then examine multiple philosophical approaches that contribute to philosophy of communication through the lens of philosophical pictures as communicative dwellings.

We comprehend a specific historical period, or historical moment, as a communicative dwelling that illuminates and shelters a given "philosophical picture," enabling a particular textured communicative comprehension (Piercey, 2009, p. 5). We use the controversial discussion of historical periods to illustrate philosophical pictures at work. They are not pristine presentations of truth; rather, they point to communicative dwellings that shape the character and texture of communicative meaning. Our understanding of philosophical communication lives in a world of fallible human meaning, forgoing the demand for absolute and undeniable truth. We engage and respond to philosophical pictures that guide, giving perspective to a fuzzy horizon that calls forth our active participation.

Introduction

This chapter illuminates philosophical pictures that contain particular insights and questions that guide discourse, suggesting implications for communicative meaning. We are aware of the danger of solidification of moments in time, limited by a Western perspective (Kuklick, 1984). We acknowledge those limits while emphasizing the importance of doing philosophy of communication as a task of connecting us to unique historical moments. We follow Piercey's (2009) assertion that there are "aspects of human nature" that invite us to acknowledge historical moments that assist the emergence of philosophical pictures (p. 70). These communicative dwellings provide insight into how human beings engage communicative meaning together. Additionally, Charles Taylor (1984) reminds us of the link between history and philosophy. Taylor (1984) argues that in order to understand ourselves today, "we are pushed into the past" (p. 26). Taylor, like the authors of this project, does not reify historical moments; however, he engages historical periods as dwellings that embody questions relevant to a unique moment in time.

This chapter connects philosophy of communication attentive to meaning with communicative dwellings of philosophical pictures in action. This chapter consists of four major sections: (1) an examination of Robert Piercey's painting of philosophical pictures; (2) an overview of philosophical pictures that contain aspects of narratival neighborhoods and conversational horizons as discussed by Calvin Schrag; (3) a review of historical moments, from the Classical period through postmodernity, as explicated through the work of Charles Taylor; and (4) implications of historical moments as philosophical paintings for the study of philosophy of communication exemplified through the novel *Zorba the Greek*, the central story used throughout this project. Understanding philosophy of communication as the carrier of meaning through historical and philosophical pictures enables us to witness the embodiment of communicative dwellings that inform our making sense of the world.

Acknowledging that historical moments guide us is central to what Piercey (2009) terms "doing philosophy historically" (pp. 41–42). This interpretive task necessitates historical engagement and responsive creativity that function as starting places for situating philosophy of communication within historical moments that give insight into the temporal discernment of meaning.

Piercey's Philosophical Pictures

Robert Piercey earned his Ph.D. in philosophy from the University of Notre Dame in 2001. Currently, Piercey is an associate professor of philosophy at Campion College at the University of Regina in Canada. His research interests and publications are located at the intersection of history and philosophy with special emphasis on Georg Wilhelm Friedrich Hegel and Paul Ricoeur. Piercey is also interested in the intersection of philosophy and literature, and his interest in philosophical hermeneutics runs through his scholarship. Piercey's (2009) *The Uses of the Past from Heidegger to Rorty: Doing Philosophy Historically* highlights four philosophical perspectives that offer different philosophical pictures of the human condition; this work takes front stage in this chapter, setting up an understanding of philosophy of communication that is exemplified throughout the remainder of this project. Philosophical perspectives rest within a given historical moment and begin a conversation that shapes a given view of existence.

History and Philosophy: Four Perspectives

The human conversation belongs to all of us; as Lucius Annaeus Seneca (1969) stated, "[a]nything said well by anyone also belongs to me" (p. 65). Calvin Schrag (2010) suggests that historical moments remind us that "to converse is to reminisce, to remember, and in remembering to ruminate and reflect" (p. 8). We are placed within particular conversations that permit us to experience and recall stories that are no longer proximate to us. In these explorations of past historical moments, we do not illuminate facts in a chronological or spatially organized series of events; rather, we illuminate human experience intimately connected with historical moments. Philosophical pictures frame conversations and exchanges between people in a manner that informs our comprehension of human experience.

Doing philosophy of communication historically requires awareness of shifting historical content and context. Lorenz Krüger (1984) accounts for changing historical content and context through intellectual responsiveness to emerging questions across and between historical periods (p. 80). Piercey (2009) states that doing philosophy historically is different from studying the history of philosophy. In doing philosophy historically, one meets earlier thinkers in a given context and time, seeking to understand the questions they sought to answer.

Doing philosophy historically emphasizes revelatory insights that emerge through philosophical pictures within a historical lens. These perspectives are dynamic, ever changing, and dependent upon our responsiveness. Doing philosophy historically occurs when philosophers articulate and refine pictures of reality in response to existence (Piercey, 2009). Piercey (2009) states that doing philosophy historically is a practice of "tracing the development of philosophical pictures," which illuminates the strengths and weaknesses of a particular reality and the broader potentiality of a given historical moment (p. 23).

Piercey (2009) asserts that *philosophical pictures do not remain static*; they are dynamic, complex, and embedded within a conversational situatedness that is unique and responsive to communicative action, interaction, and transactions between and among communicants. Philosophical pictures shift and augment meaning as new phenomena emerge and then coexist in communicative exchange (Piercey, 2009), opening communicative participants to novel and renewed understandings that shape communicative life between and among persons.

In *The Uses of the Past from Heidegger to Rorty: Doing Philosophy Historically*, Piercey (2009) identifies four approaches (philosophical pictures) to understanding philosophy historically, including narrative (Richard Rorty, 1931–2007), critical (Alasdair MacIntyre, b. 1929), diagnostic (Martin Heidegger, 1889–1976), and synthetic (Paul Ricoeur, 1913–2005). These approaches have rich scholarly traditions, which he unpacks in the context of his key metaphor, "philosophical pictures."

Rorty and narrative. A narrative is a story composed of practices agreed upon by a group of people; it is this collective sense of agreement that separates a story from a narrative. According to Piercey (2009), Richard Rorty used narrative and historical moments to do philosophy historically. Piercey (2009) traces the development of a philosophical picture of narrative beginning with "seeing as," which he contends Rorty privileged (p. 31); once we realize that we see something *as* something, we understand that we have made an interpretive judgment about the situatedness of the object. "Seeing as" is dynamic and driven by a framework that permits a shift in perception from singular recognition to genuine perception. "Seeing as" invites multiple interpretive possibilities, contrary to a totalizing "seeing is" that restricts interpretive meaning. Rorty (1979) suggests that doing philosophy historically accounts for the notion of "as" or "aspect" of a historical moment that is assumed or taken for granted by identifying emerging questions within a given historical narrative (p. 105). For example, one of the authors sees black bears in her backyard on a daily basis in the spring and summer. If we perceive the bears as a "seeing is" event, our understanding of the bears remains fixed and flat, limited to a wild animal. However, if we see the bear as something, interpretive judgments create multiple possibilities about the story of bears in a backyard.

Rorty (1984) asked readers to rethink and perhaps abandon positions and presuppositions whenever limits are discerned. He stated that the world constantly changes, moving, not in a straight line, but in a curve; we cannot always see what stands before us until we engage in reflection (Rorty, 1979). Rorty embraced a world that is dynamic, unpredictable, and uncertain. He found ambiguity inherent in language that is largely responsible for uncertainties of perception. Rorty attended to metaphors, not declarative statements that determine our convictions. The metaphors are understood within a narrative web that invites a philosophical picture of our lives, understood as story-laden action. Narratives are philosophical pictures that assist our negotiation in and with the world. Piercey (2009) then identifies the critical approach of Alasdair MacIntyre, attending to MacIntyre's critique of the Enlightenment.

MacIntyre and the critical. Alasdair MacIntyre's critical approach is described as being "concerned with the philosophical significance of history" (Piercey, 2009, p. 82). Piercey identifies MacIntyre's work as a critical historical study that provides an alternative to the Enlightenment project. Piercey suggests that we cannot fully understand MacIntyre's work if we have not critically explored key arguments that MacIntyre states are inherent within given historical moments. MacIntyre critiques what governs our thinking through attention to emergent questions within particular historical moments. Piercey (2009) concurs with MacIntyre's commitment to learn from history, as ideas change over time in response to the demands of shifting historical moments.

MacIntyre's critical approach is important to philosophy of communication, providing the necessary distance for interpretive possibilities that are constitutive of meaning. Critical distance permits one to comprehend emergent questions within a given horizon. Historical distance sanctions a critical perspective that offers attentiveness to questions and potential responses that can historically decenter an interpreter, giving birth to new insights. MacIntyre offers a critical philosophical picture, understanding that the existence of multiple philosophical positions is a critical key. Our critical insights come from assuming the vantage point of different and contrasting perspectives, and then coming to a judgment in terms of the good offered by a given perspective. Piercey then moves to another critical perspective, stating that Martin Heidegger provided a diagnostic approach that examined the forgotten and the forsaken in Being itself.

Heidegger and the diagnostic. According to Piercey (2009), Martin Heidegger brought a diagnostic approach of discovery to doing philosophy historically. Through the practice of diagnosis, regardless of whether there is intentional or unintentional deception or bias in the philosophical picture, Heidegger diagnosed the disclosure of particular understandings. Pictures are deceptive when we do not reflect upon them. The act of diagnosis accompanies the reflection process that examines the modes of Being. In a diagnostic approach, one attempts "to uncover the true nature of ways of thinking that are widely accepted but deceptive" (Piercey, 2009, p. 128). Heidegger's (1962) approach assisted in unmasking and identifying questions that ordinarily go unknown and unasked.

Heidegger moved us toward diagnosing matters that we normally do not think to question, such as the possibilities of Being and the obtrusion by a failed Western project. He demanded that we diagnose the limits of status quo Western conceptions of life. Heidegger outlined a path to ontological discovery that pushes us toward a greater range of interpretive possibilities. Heidegger framed a philosophical picture of the failed Western project of agency; he diagnosed the problem, revisited early Greek thought, and outlined an alternative path. The task of the human is to disclose the possibilities of Being that open up opportunities for the human being, a task that continues until death. Piercey concludes with his summary of the creative work of Paul Ricoeur, who framed a philosophical picture that synthesizes and reconciles ideas and events in the human condition.

Ricoeur and the synthetic. Ricoeur's philosophy reconciled perspectives, finding significance in contrasting and invaluable positions (Piercey, 2009). A synthetic approach gathers different and potentially competing philosophical pictures and then reconciles the contrasting perspectives in order to discover an alternative and multidimensional picture. Piercey pieces together Ricoeur's synthetic approach through exploration of multiple works completed by Ricoeur. Piercey concludes that Ricoeur's doing of philosophy involves uniting multiple projects with an underlying interconnectivity, a synthetic approach that reconciles different philosophical pictures that are in tension with one another.

Ricoeur brings together diverse texts that, in conversation with one another, offer new insight. His goal of synthesis was "to explore *possibilities* [emphasis added] for thinking: to articulate a new way of approaching philosophical questions" that avoid the limitations of past predicaments (Piercey, 2009, p. 203). Ricoeur's (1970) approach teaches us to reject the reification of philosophical pictures; such pictures are never fixed or finished. The synthetic approach used by Ricoeur opens new questions and creative insight.

Piercey suggests that the above four approaches ground the importance of doing philosophy through attentiveness to human connectedness that creates a context from which we can interpret relationships and experiences. The narrative approach provides stories that illuminate relationships in a given historical moment. The critical approach identifies the significance of taking a critical distance and understanding philosophical differences in competing narratives. The diagnostic approach uncovers historical truths about the possibilities of Being that influence what the human perceives and conceptualizes in existence. Finally, the synthetic approach offers an integrated picture of human relationships through co-creating that results in the synthesizing of meaning in everyday life.

Texturing Philosophical Pictures

The above approaches offer multiple philosophical pictures. We will use the notion of philosophical pictures throughout this project, emphasizing the diversity of approaches to philosophy of communication. Additionally, we texture Piercey's perspective with insights from Calvin Schrag. He provides the metaphors of "narratival neighborhoods" and "conversational horizons," giving us insight into the communicative practices of a given philosophical picture about philosophy of communication.

Philosophical Pictures and Narratival Neighborhoods

Philosophical pictures are further illuminated by Calvin Schrag's (2010) connection of communication and philosophy with historical and temporal dwellings that he identified as "narratival neighborhoods" (p. 55). These dwellings are illuminated within "conversational horizons" that shape historical moments and inform our understanding (Schrag, 2010, p. 63). Philosophical pictures are formed within narratival neighborhoods; they clarify how meaning is co-created, revealing the emergence of a lived historical memory.

Narratival neighborhoods demand recognition of a basic reality—there are others who came before us, as well as all those around us; we live in a socially framed world. Schrag (2010) argues that the "other" is "inextricably tied to the unfolding of that which is 'my own'" (p. 55). Human history is given birth in a narratival living space shaped through the communicative lives of both the seen and the unseen. This communicative dwelling is a space of association that is a result of communicative reminiscing and reflecting within a life-world, keeping communicative meaning clear, yet dynamic and open. Such neighborhoods resonate with Piercey's (2009) four approaches (narrative, critical, diagnostic, and synthetic); Piercey's approaches can be understood as situated within a particular narratival neighborhood where perspectives, behaviors, and communicative conditions exist and compete for interpretive attention. Within a narratival neighborhood, we discover a conversational horizon of meaning that assists change, adaption, and response to historical moments.

Conversational Horizons of Meaning

Philosophical pictures are shaped by communicative actions occurring within narratival neighborhoods, situated within a backdrop of "conversational world horizons" (Schrag, 2010, p. 63). Schrag describes a conversational horizon as a place where different spheres of interest and knowledge are accommodated in response to changes and shifts in and to a given historical moment. Schrag admits that within these horizons we experience multiplicity and differences related to vocational, generational, ethnic, and cultural demarcations, which give rise to different temporal insights and revelations—a hallmark of shifting philosophical pictures.

Horizons of meaning bind the temporal textuality of narratival neighborhoods to conversations, reminiscences, and reflections (Schrag, 2010); these punctuations guide the excavation of narratival neighborhoods, announcing that there is no *one* communicative meaning in a historical event. An illumination of the hermeneutic of everyday life enables sense making to undergird human understanding and comprehension through philosophical pictures framed in narratival neighborhoods that are responsive to conversational horizons. Approaching philosophy of communication via historical moments attends to the interplay of narratival neighborhoods and conversational horizons that carry meaning within what Piercey termed philosophical pictures. The following section illustrates philosophical pictures in action, as we examine the work of Charles Taylor and his reliance upon historical periods. We often use the term "historical moments" instead of historical periods due to the legitimate controversy about these historical conceptions. We are not interested in the accuracy of these dates or gatherings of historical data; rather, our communicative point is both more modest and, perhaps, more essential in that we stress that humans live in different historical moments. Our ideas, theories, and actions are foreground responses to the background of a given time. In short, whatever we call these gatherings of lived human experience, they constitute historical moments that were unique and important in their own right. The historical moment of another lends insight on its biased terms; just as we seek to understand that moment out of our own situated prejudices (Gadamer, 1960/1986). We cannot state what another's life was "really" like, but we can, at least, begin with pragmatic respect that recognizes differences from our own formation.

Historical Moments

The discovery of meaning carried from one historical moment to the next permits novel interpretations and reinterpretations of previous events that live in current perceptual memory. Such interpretive engagement is done within contexts and relationships, permitting us to learn from the actions of others via attention given to issues in a particular historical moment. Piercey offers us narrative, critical, diagnostic, and synthetic approaches to examine philosophy tied to historical moments. Another perspective akin to Piercey's insights comes from the work of Charles Taylor (b. 1931), whose scholarship manifests a historically embedded thinking perspective. Taylor was a prize fellow at All Souls College at the University of Oxford from 1956 to 1961, professor of political science at McGill University from 1961 to 1998, and Chichele professor of social and political theory at All Souls College at the University of Oxford from 1976 to 1981. He was awarded the Templeton Prize for research in 2007 and the Kyoto Prize in arts and philosophy in 2008.

Taylor (1989) summarizes his historical approach to philosophy by examining successive historical understandings. Taylor uses this approach of historical narratives in *A Secular Age* (2007); he sketches qualitative distinctions of varying historical moments, providing a successive understanding of how society has become increasingly secular. The corpus of his scholarship assumes the importance of history. Taylor attends to historical moments as keys for interpretive understanding. For our stress on meaning in philosophy of communication, we now turn to Taylor's (1989) *Sources of the Self: The Making of Modern Identity.*

Taylor's (1984) thesis situates the relevance of doing philosophy historically; he recognizes and explores the nature of narratives, taking a critical distance in his interpretive positions, asking diagnostic questions of why and how, and synthesizing what he gathers, permitting all of his interpretations to inform judgments and future communicative actions. Taylor (1984) argues that histories and actions of people situated within a historical horizon provide meaning, offering the context of a philosophical picture. These pictures are comprised of narratives that weave together a tapestry of re-described human experiences. Taylor (1989) explores background pictures of human experiences within historical narratives that are demarcated by particular moments in history. Taylor (2007) suggests it is the search for meaning that enables human beings to make sense out of questions situated within a given historical moment.

In *Sources of the Self: The Making of Modern Identity,* Taylor (1989) traces the making of the self through historical frameworks. He argues that we cannot understand ourselves without comprehension of changing moments in history that affect human identity. Taylor (1989) contends "frameworks are problematic" in that they set limits that can obscure meaning and understanding; people also do not necessarily share the same frameworks (p. 17). He argues that frameworks are "inescapable"; we need them to aid our understanding (Taylor, 1989, p. 17). Taylor (1989) begins his examination of historical frameworks with the Classical era and Plato, who "helped set the form of the dominant family of moral theories in our civilization" (p. 116). As the source of our moral selves, Plato established thought as pivotal, distinguishing it from the Enlightenment stress on reason.

The Classical moment generally denotes a period ranging from the middle of the second millennium BCE (before the common era or before Jesus Christ) to the 6th century AD (after the death of Jesus Christ), although the typical consensus focuses on the time range between 800 BCE and 300 AD (Hornblower & Spawforth, 2000). This historical moment includes Homer's writings through the fall of the Roman Empire (Griffin, 1986). Many consider this historical moment the philosophical and cultural foundation of the Western world. Taylor's (1989) historical perspective of the Classical world narrative situates the self as being dependent upon and subservient to Truth tied to the polis; identity was shaped by one's role within the polis.

Scholars refer to the end of the Classical world as the period of late antiquity, beginning with the fall of the Roman world (Kristeller, 1979). The Middle Ages (medieval), connotes an epoch within European history that ranges between the 5th and the 15th centuries. Scholars typically denote this period to range from 600 AD to 1350 AD (Kristeller, 1979). Taylor (1989) states that during this time, Christian theology incorporated Platonic thought through the tenet that self-definition comes from external means (God) rather than from within one's self; the center of meaning shifted from the polis to the Church. There was a break from Platonic thought that accepted a higher level of thinking, placing thought within the soul. Understanding the discontinuity from the Classical period creates a philosophical picture that shifts from one's role in the polis to one's allegiance to a Christian metanarrative in the Middle Ages.

During this time in the West, classical learning flourished mainly in Ireland and England; there is little evidence of scholarly advancements in the schools of Western Europe. Monastic education was the primary form of education and philosophy (Kristeller, 1979). The Middle Ages included sociocultural transitions that revealed the tensions between pagan and Christian traditions and the ultimate downfall of pagan philosophy (Pieper, 1960/2001). The influence of religious values was imbued within the cultural horizons of medieval Europe. Toward the end of the Middle Ages, individuals began to rebel against the dominance of religious association, giving rise to a renaissance of learning.

Charles Taylor (2007) described the Renaissance as interested in nature and science, which would ultimately lead society toward secularism. The Renaissance is typically demarcated between 1350 and 1600. Contrary to the Church's power over rhetorical education in the medieval period, the Renaissance demonstrated an expansion of rhetorical education and practices. This rhetorical revolution generated a rebirth of thought and philosophy, provoking the beginning of the Enlightenment, a significant era of invention and progress. A renaissance of thought lifted the constraints on human reason and shifted power from the influence of the Church to the autonomy of the human being in a secular environment.

Taylor (1989) states that the Renaissance led to a completion of God's creation of man by human beings themselves, emphasizing human action in "bringing the cosmos to it fullest nature" (p. 200). At this time, human beings knowingly worked at creating their own identities. This moment did not, however, mark the fall of a religious paradigm, but it did give birth to the Protestant Reformation in the 16th century and increasing emphasis on the individual. The philosophical picture of human meaning moves from concrete institutions (the polis of the Classical period and the Church of the medieval period) to individual creativity in the Renaissance, and then to individual reason in the Enlightenment.

Taylor (1989) identified a "dialectic of the Enlightenment" in which reason was a liberating force that, ironically, gave rise to domination (p. 116). The Enlightenment is generally considered to be the focus of the Western world in the 18th century, although some scholars and historians include the 17th-century Renaissance period as well. The Enlightenment is complex in nature; a recent critique of this period juxtaposes two actual Enlightenments, the moderate and the radical, suggesting that the moderate Enlightenment was unable to create and maintain the liberation that the radical Enlightenment sought. Unfortunately, the radical Enlightenment was pushed underground, stifling its influence on human thought. The conceptual victor was the moderate Enlightenment, which disembodied the person from tradition. The radical Enlightenment situated the person with traditions and acknowledged diversity in cultures and ideas (Arnett, Fritz, & Holba, 2007). It is the disembodied conception of the moderate Enlightenment that propels what we conventionally call the Enlightenment. The philosophical picture of humans during this time shows increased distance from sociality and fewer ties to traditions and others.

Taylor (1989) identified the notion of individual "freedom" as predominantly modern (p. 117). He stated that the "autonomous individual [is] at the centre" of the system of law (Taylor, 1989, p. 195). Modern views of identity are "strongly human-centered" (Taylor, 1989, p. 506). Modern identity of the self relies upon "human poietic powers" that cultivate a sense of control over one's environment (Taylor, 1989, p. 200). Taylor's (2007) critique of this new ethic of freedom is carried forth in A Secular Age, as he argues that the modern world is captured in "malaises" (p. 299). Society turns toward the individual and places the "buffered self" at the epicenter of a culture driven by an individual ethic of freedom, displacing the Greek notion of the polis (Taylor, 2007, p. 300). The modern philosophical picture consists of the individual fractured from a sense of community, having little feeling of individual responsibility toward the other.

This modern era is marked by a privileging of progress, science, and fractured human communities. The modern era was responsible for advancements in science and technology while at the same time losing a commitment to an "enlarged mentality" (Arendt, 1958) that was concerned about others with a constant stress on "individual independence" (Taylor, 1989, p. 192). The dark side of the modern period brought political unrest through colonialism, imperialism, and totalitarianism. The troublesome side of modernity led to a fractured spirit, giving rise to postmodernity.

The postmodern period is a condition rather than a specific period. Postmodernity is an intertextual cacophony of historical voices coexisting with multiple narratival neighborhoods. We situate an awareness of postmodernity somewhere in the latter part of the 20th century. This moment has been described as a time in which the idea of a grand narrative or metanarrative was replaced by the idea of petite narratives (Lyotard, 1984). Stuart Sim (1999) identifies postmodernity as an announcement of the loss of a grand narrative with the emergence of smaller narratives and the breakdown of singular hegemonic discourse and politics. Postmodernity denotes uncertainties in economic markets, political and religious contentions, and the restructuring of the human fabric of existence. In other words, postmodernity announces change without the assurance of progress, recognition of competing narratives, and, ironically, a rediscovery of multiple traditions, which modernity lambasted. Historical moments understood as narratival neighborhoods function as conversational horizons guided by an unlimited number of philosophical pictures that shape the background of philosophy of communication.

Philosophical pictures illuminate questions that emerge in particular historical moments. These different moments give rise to different and ever contrasting philosophical pictures of human meaning. Understanding historical differences broadens our understanding, opening a hermeneutic door for increasing interpretative possibilities. Philosophy of communication presupposes a historical context from which a given philosophical picture of human meaning emerges.

Philosophy of Communication: *Zorba the Greek* and Philosophical Pictures

How we interpret and understand our communicative lives relies upon our understanding of the past and meaning that history imparts upon our current experiences. Presence is a foreground that is situated and interpreted within a dwelling of the past that is simultaneously made present in the act of interpretation. Taylor (2007) argues, "history cannot be separated from the situation it has brought about" (p. 776). History and the past function as backdrops for our understanding of the significance of philosophical pictures. Philosophical pictures "trace the changes...that produce our present predicament" (Taylor, 2007, p. 773). This chapter stresses a narrative approach, in which narratival neighborhoods and conversational horizons illuminate the historical moment, providing multiple stories that shift our perceptual insight as information is added, edited, and removed. The critical engagement with the historical moment identifies questions that shape our understanding. The diagnostic approach to the historical moment considers why there are particular demarcated shifts in thought and cultural practices. Finally, the synthetic approach to the historical moment provides for a variety of perspectives in order to gain comprehension of any given circumstance. Philosophy of communication connected to history, narratival neighborhoods, and conversational horizons offer a background, a philosophical picture, for understanding and meaning. Philosophy of communication as the carrier of meaning, understood from the vantage point of historical background, assumes the necessity of an interpretive backdrop. The drama and action within the novel *Zorba the Greek* offers an interpretive backdrop for understanding a philosophy of communication that is existentially engaged.

Zorba recognizes the power of history; he attends to questions of particularity in a historical understanding that enables a comprehensive understanding of something or someone. Boss knows that Zorba had a deep understanding of the meaning of life; Zorba lives a life embedded within a historical moment that offered a philosophical picture in action. Zorba acknowledges multiple meetings and experiences with others that cultivated meaning. Boss reflects upon the presence of Zorba and connected him to a traditional culture or historical moment quite different from the 1930s setting of the novel. Boss conceptualizes Zorba as "the chief of a tribe…a renowned troubador [sic]… and everybody would have hung on his words" (Kazantzakis, 1946/1952, p. 87). Zorba also has a particular philosophical picture of Boss. Zorba states:

> Yes, you understand with your brain. You say: "This is right, and that's wrong...." But where does that lead us? While you are talking I watch your arms and chest.... They're silent. They don't say a word. As though they hadn't a drop of blood.... Well, what do you think you understand with? With your head? Bah!" (Kazantzakis, 1946/1952, p. 250)

Boss understands Zorba as an anachronism, out of place and out of time, while Zorba understands Boss as a man unable to meet life. Boss understands Zorba through the unique pictures he paints from the canvas of a life attentive to narratival neighborhoods and conversational horizons. Zorba experiences history and responds to emerging questions of a given historical moment. Zorba understands that the historical moment and his experiences shaped his understanding of life. Zorba meets the historical moment; he makes decisions based upon his reflections of narratival neighborhoods and conversational horizons that shape the historical frames from which he found meaning. Doing philosophy of communication historically guides our understanding, our philosophical picture of existence, offering meaning as we experience the world before us.

This chapter has outlined the significance of communicative dwellings for understanding, engaging, and doing philosophy of communication in action. We conclude this chapter by revisiting four central points:

1. History assists in discerning meaning in philosophy of communication. Nikos Kazantzakis situates *Zorba the Greek* in a time that is responsive to the aftermath of war. The town that is at the center of the novel lives with the wounds of war. Zorba's responses to past events announce throughout the novel his ability to find meaning in historical realities.

2. Our understanding of history is shaped by different and often contrasting approaches that sketch and frame multiple philosophical pictures. Zorba, Boss, and those who fought on opposing sides of the war bring different philosophical pictures that shape the understanding of that experience and its implications. It is not simply the event in a given historical moment that marks us; it is our response that ultimately shapes human identity.

3. Philosophical pictures presuppose a context situated within narratival neighborhoods and conversational horizons. A philosophical picture is not a snapshot; it can only be understood within a context grouped with other pictures, conversations, and the sharing of perspectives. Throughout the novel, both morning and evening are peppered with conversation between Boss and Zorba, providing a horizon that permits them and the reader to make sense of their time together.

4. Philosophical pictures are carriers of meaning, aiding our temporal understanding and responsiveness. Philosophical pictures carry meaning. They are guides along the way, illuminating existence. Boss has a picture of Zorba that is out of place and out of time. He understands Zorba as part of an era in which a tribal leader would gather the significance and power of a people. In offering this philosophical picture of Zorba, Boss provides insight into the present moment in which Zorba and Boss are situated, which still require this anachronism from the past.

In the spirit of this chapter, *Zorba the Greek* provides insight into the power of philosophical pictures in everyday life, revealing how they inform and shape understanding and meaning in a historical moment within a communicative dwelling that did not always conform to their expectations, hopes, desires, or wishes.

PART II: SITUATING MEANING

CHAPTER 4

KNOWLEDGE AND MEANING THROUGH EPISTEMOLOGY

Knowledge shapes meaning, enabling human beings to make sense out of their surroundings. There are multiple epistemological perspectives that explain how we gain and maintain the knowledge that shapes our worldview. Epistemology assumes that meaning rests with what and how we know. This chapter examines epistemology as an explication of a particular philosophical picture of what we term a philosophy of communication. Epistemology assumes that knowledge informs and shapes our communicative lives.

Introduction

Epistemology is derived from the Greek word *episteme*. There are two general interpretations of this Greek term; the first is knowledge and the second is logos. Epistemology, as the study of knowledge, considers four different ways of apprehension: (1) empirical knowledge based on evidence we observe; (2) non-empirical knowledge that is a priori, things already known without empirical evidence; (3) knowledge by acquaintance or inference based on what others tell us about events, ideas, or actions; and (4) technical knowledge that informs us how to do something (Audi, 1995/2001). Epistemology is the study of the modes through which we gather what we know.

This chapter consists of three sections: (1) a general overview of epistemology offered by Vincent Hendricks; (2) a biographical portrait to the life and philosophy of Immanuel Kant, focusing on his critique of epistemology; and (3) implications of epistemology for the study of philosophy of communication understood as a philosophical painting exemplified through *Zorba the Greek*. Epistemology, understood as a philosophical painting, provides a textured understanding of how we learn and how we come to know prior to making decisions. The study of epistemology outlines what composes epistemic judgments as we encounter the world before us.

This chapter relies on the philosophical painting of epistemology offered by Vincent F. Hendricks's *Mainstream and Formal Epistemology* (2007). Hendricks provides a textured landscape in philosophical studies, offering a cogent perspective on contemporary epistemologies. We then turn to Immanuel Kant's *Critique of Pure Reason* (1781/1965), which is considered the cornerstone text on epistemology in modernity. Kant attempted to reconcile reason and knowledge with the objective of moving beyond what he understood as the failures of traditional epistemological philosophy. Kant countered with a transcendental epistemology; his work is an Enlightenment exemplar of the connection between epistemology and individual responsibility.

A General Overview of Epistemology

Vincent Hendricks (2007) frames epistemology as a systematic accumulation of knowledge that informs deliberation, decisions, and action. Hendricks is a professor of philosophy at the University of Copenhagen and Columbia University. HHe held several prestigious editor-in-chief positions with top philosophy publications, including *Synthese: An International Journal for Epistemology, Logic, and Philosophy of Science*; *Texts in Philosophy Book Series*; *Palgrave Innovations in Philosophy Book Series*; and *Stanford Encyclopedia of Philosophy*. In order to give the reader an appreciation of the importance of the contribution of epistemology to philosophy, Hendricks (2007) begins with the primary historical counter to epistemology—skepticism. Hendricks contends that skepticism challenges epistemology, questioning knowledge in the sphere of perpetual debate.

Skepticism

Skepticism recognizes the primacy of uncertainty that naturally leads to errors in understanding. According to Hendricks (2007), "[e]rror is the starting point of skepticism" (p. 1). Skepticism presupposes the possibility of continual errors regarding the how and why of knowledge gathering. Skepticism is a philosophical view grounded in doubt that is cautious of how we form belief structures. The Greeks introduced two schools of skepticism: academic skepticism, which bluntly and absolutely stated that no knowledge is possible; and Pyrrhonian skepticism, which originated from the attributes of Pyrrho of Elis (360–275 BCE) and stated that there is insufficient and inadequate evidence to determine if knowledge is possible, leaving us in a state of perennial doubt (Hendricks, 2007). These two categories of skepticism give us a range of perspectives, from absolute denial of knowledge to unending doubt.

An academic skeptic, or global skeptic, holds that knowledge of any kind is not possible. This view was supported by Socrates, who stated in *The Apology*, "well, although I do not suppose that either of us knows anything really beautiful and good, I am better off than he is—for he knows nothing, and thinks that he knows. I neither know nor think that I know" (Plato, trans. 2010, pp. 7–8). Socrates is associated with skeptic wisdom: "all I know is that I know nothing" (Popkin, 2003, p. xvii). For the global skeptic, we cannot know because all presuppositions we make with our senses are unreliable, resulting in faulty reasoning. From this perspective, we lack a standard from which to determine how to judge.

Pyrrhonian skepticism suggests that human beings cannot have sure knowledge about anything. This perspective suggests that in propositions related to things we cannot see, we have a belief that we can understand; we cannot have absolute knowledge. The Pyrrhonian skeptic suspends judgment and is no longer concerned with finding absolute truth. Pyrrhonian skepticism accepts appearances of a truth based on faith or beliefs. Hendricks (2007) offers four different conceptions of epistemology that counter skepticism: empiricism, rationalism, traditionalism, and contemporary epistemologies. These perspectives fundamentally contend with skepticism, in that each assumes the importance of gathering knowledge for decision making and the pursuit of a good life.

Empiricism

As an alternative to skepticism, empiricism is grounded in knowledge based upon observation and experience. The Greek notion of experience, *empieria*, is a theory of knowledge that privileges experience in human knowledge. The notion of empiricism has many different threads (Hendricks, 2007); however, there are generally two main categories of empiricism, concept empiricisms and belief empiricisms. Both shape the horizon of this conception of knowledge acquisition. Concept empiricisms identify the concept that is connected to an experience. For example, the concept of motion sickness is directly tied to the experience of motion sickness. This orientation assumes that all concepts are related to or derived from an experience. In contrast to skepticism, empiricism holds that we can know what we see through observation and evidence.

Belief empiricists approach experience with the assumption that belief resides inherently in the individual rather than in the interaction with the experience. For example, belief empiricists connect a belief with an observation. The experience is not interactive, but is understood and sensed internally. Belief empiricists also accept testimony about an observation from another person as acceptable knowledge. Hendricks (2007) states that a "claim to knowledge requires the connection between the belief condition and the truth condition… [though] beliefs may be the result of blind luck, clairvoyance, [or] random guessing" (p. 14). Belief does not amount to undisputed knowledge because the risk of error in the belief lacks connection to evidence of truth. However, belief attends to the testimony of another's experience.

Challenges to empiricism revolve around the question of what constitutes evidence, concepts, or beliefs. The idea of inferential beliefs counting as evidence has provoked much debate regarding empirical qualities inherent in justification of evidence. An inferential belief involves assumptions about our observations, but the possibility of an epistemic error is high because the inference comes from a belief. Hendricks (2007) considers inferential beliefs a form of contextual epistemology, because everything possible in a contextual setting provides an account of what one knows. Hendricks argues that contextual experiences engage inferential knowledge and provide opportunities for broader access to knowledge even though the possibility of error remains.

Hendricks admits to the decline of the traditional category of empiricism in light of contemporary epistemologies designed to account for and reconcile limits in empiricism, including the debate surrounding belief and knowledge. Another traditional epistemology that emerged as a response to skepticism was rationalism, which seeks to connect logic and evidence and often weaves together empiricism and skepticism.

Rationalism

The epistemology of rationalism uses reason in constructing what and how we know. Rationalism seeks to use reason to explain what is not immediately measurable or observable. The term "rationality" comes from the Latin word *ratio*. The rationalist perspective asserts that perceptions and observations are generally fallible and untrustworthy (Joachim, 1997). Rationalism is divided differently than skepticism and empiricism, with skepticism having two main schools of thought (academic and Phyrrhonian) and empiricism also having two main schools of thought (belief empiricists and concept empiricist). In contrast, rationalism does not unfold into discrete categories. In general, rationalism uses reason, logical argument, and epistemic proof when direct observation is unavailable. As a result, the appeal to good reasoning is the crux or foundation of rationalism. This perspective functions without a focus on observation or inference.

In rationalism, beliefs are justified through reasoning and logic—not through our senses. According to Hendricks (2007), with rational inquiry, the "reasons for believing [something] are truth-conducive" (p. 6). What we know comes from logical reasoning. Basic syllogistic reasoning undergirds this perspective and is contrary to proof by our senses or the skeptical contention that we cannot know anything. To the rationalist, math and logic are primary modes of proof, telling us what we know and justifying how we know. The idea of pure reason can be exemplified by considering the number seven. We understand the number seven to be an odd number because it cannot be divided evenly. We define what "odd" means and then argue that seven holds the qualities of that definition. We do not rely solely on perception, though it might be part of the evidence. The focus is on logical reasoning and rationality. Some propositions are self-evident and require little or no argument to provide evidence, such as knowing that seven is larger than six. This evidence is considered a rational expression in nature.

Hendricks (2007) focuses on contemporary epistemologies that offer counter measures to the stark, delineated categories of skepticism, empiricism, and rationalism. He also does not include traditionalism in his discussion of formal and mainstream epistemologies, though the concepts that constitute traditionalism are integrated in aspects of two of the countermeasures, epistemic reliabilism and contextual epistemology, which we will consider in the next section on contemporary epistemologies. In epistemic reliabilism, knowledge has limits in cognitive reliability, similar to traditionalism, which accepts imperfections in cognitive reliability as tradition relies on the past to enliven the present. In contextual epistemology, knowledge comes from conversational contexts that happen between people. Conversation is embedded within a context that is part of other conversations and other contexts—conversational contexts establish traditional conventions informed by the past. Traditionalism points to the context in which people come to know and generate meaning in their lives together. Traditionalism assumes an interplay of cognitive reliability and contextual aspects that help to generate knowledge. To explore traditionalism further, we look to René Guénon.

Traditionalism

During the 20th century, traditionalism received less attention than skepticism, empiricism, and rationalism (Sedgwick, 2009). According to Mark Sedgwick (2009), René Guénon (1886–1951), a French philosopher of metaphysics, is the intellectual voice that drove the traditionalism movement in the 20th century. Traditionalism emerged as a response to the intellectuals of the 19th century who were distressed that insight from religious and traditional thought was intentionally ignored. Traditionalism was a movement suspicious of modernism, the loss of faith, and the absence of ground from which one could find truth. Traditionalists rejected epistemologies that relied on premises governed by modernity—empiricism and rationalism. Referring to the historical moment after World War I, René Guénon emerged as the voice of the movement as he identified modernity as a form of dark ages; his project critiqued epistemological certainty, rebelling against the scientific revolution of the 20th century (Sedgwick, 2009).

Traditionalism is a foundational epistemology that includes continuity of past practices that are renewed and textured in their ongoing use; meaning emerges in the practices. Sedgwick (2009) argues that the experience of World War I gave birth to the traditionalist movement as the world sought stability and peace. By the 1930s, the traditionalist intellectual movement was active but remained on the periphery of the intellectual community. The intellectuals who advanced traditionalism were contestants battling against modern power structures and their reliance on science and progress. Traditionalism occurred in response to the uncertainties of the early 20th century; similarly, Hendricks (2007) describes contemporary scholars seeking alternatives to empirical, rational, and traditional epistemologies that speak to this contemporary historical moment.

Contemporary Alternatives

According to Hendricks (2007), "contemporary epistemologies have developed a family of countermeasures for standing up to the skeptical challenge" of error (p. 2). These countermeasures are an "epistemological forcing" that shows there are always possibilities of error, and "they fail to be *relevant* possibilities of error" (Hendricks, 2007, p. 2). Hendricks suggests that the possibility of error is not relevant enough to be meaningful to the acceptance or rejection of knowledge. He states that the possibilities of error are "simply not genuine—they are too remote, too speculative, or too much" (Hendricks, 2007, p. 2). The possibility of error "forces out" the possibility of possibility (Hendricks, 2007, p. 2). The reality of error makes possible novel insight that emerges in response. Hendricks offers a contemporary approach to ongoing problems in epistemology through these possibilities.

Hendricks (2007) identifies four main contemporary epistemologies as examples of the notion of "forcing out" from an error that was not ultimately an error, but a turn to novel insights: epistemic reliabilism, counterfactual epistemology, contextual epistemology, and computational epistemology. Epistemic reliabilism acknowledges limits in cognitive ability, forcing out the possibility of error. Counterfactual epistemology shows that the possibility of error is so remote that semantics governing conditions are assured, forcing out the possibility of the possibility of error. Contextual epistemology assumes knowledge is in a conversational context and that knowledge begins from conversation, forcing out the possibility of beginning with error. Finally, computational epistemology suggests that one focuses on the "intrinsic solvability" of epistemic problems, determining the set of possibilities that force out the constraints that limit the possibilities within a problem (Hendricks, 2007, p. 4). These contemporary epistemological theories confront the starting place of skepticism.

Empiricism, rationalism, and traditionalism emerged out of skepticism as a way to reconcile the inadequacies of incomplete knowledge. Epistemic considerations involve both knowledge and belief as we perceive and experience the world through a finite lens. As a result, we conceptualize some things clearly, while others are obscured. Epistemologically, theories of knowledge privilege different kinds of knowledge and manners of gathering knowledge. Traditionalism, rationalism, empiricism, and Hendricks's contemporary epistemologies are alternatives to skepticism. The language used to talk about epistemology, in the domain of philosophy, has begun to shift toward a new language of forcing out error as an alternative skepticism.

Although Hendricks provides us with a historical overview of epistemology, the central figure in the movement was Immanuel Kant (1724–1804). One cannot understand the Enlightenment without attending to the thought of Kant. His project addressed the limits of empiricism and rationalism. Kant's view on epistemology offers an Enlightenment view of epistemology, giving us what he termed transcendental knowledge.

Kant on Epistemology

Immanuel Kant was a central Enlightenment figure; one must study Kant to understand the evolving story of Western philosophy and culture. Kant was a German philosopher who published in a wide array of disciplines, including history, law, ethics, aesthetics, philosophy, and religion. A pivotal philosopher of the 18th century, Kant's work was a resounding response to and expansion of the ideas that shaped the historical moment in which he lived. Kant's influence to philosophical discourse is unmatched in breadth.

Kant's lasting influence on the West emerged from his ideas. His travel experiences were minimal. He was one of the major intellectual architects and a product of the Age of Reason. Kant was born in Königsberg in 1724, which at the time was the capital of East Prussia, a province in Germany that is now Russia. Kant grew up in poverty with five sisters and one brother. His mother was a great influence upon his moral character; she was an uneducated, pious woman who shaped his desire to frame a way in which individuals could discern the right action (Kuehn, 2001).

Kant attended eight years of Pietist schooling, becoming impatient with a strict religious system that limited opportunities for understanding and acquiring knowledge. Kant demonstrated significant intelligence and a deep desire to learn. He attended the University of Königsberg as a theological student from 1742 to 1746, but quickly became disenchanted and bored with religious studies. Kant's interest was in math and physics; Isaac Newton's (1642–1727) work greatly influenced him during this period. However, Kant's father died when Kant was 22 years old, leaving him penniless. Thus, he did not complete his degree until he was 31 years old (Kuehn, 2001). Kant published on Isaac Newton, Gottfried Wilhelm Leibniz (1646–1716), and David Hume (1711–1776), who ignited Kant's great work, Critique of Pure Reason (1781/1965), which was completed 11 years after he became professor of logic and philosophy at the University of Königsberg. After Kant's continuing interest in metaphysics and speculative philosophy, he published Critique of Practical Reason (1788) and Critique of Judgment (1790). Kant lived to the age of 80, dying after a stroke from which he never fully recovered (Kuehn, 2001).

Kant's philosophical perspectives covered a vast number of ideas and subjects with a major focus on metaphysics, which he framed in Critique of Pure Reason (1781/1965). Kant resurrected and reestablished metaphysics as a legitimate form of inquiry. He understood metaphysics as a science that privileged theoretical principles over physical or natural principles. Kant sought to recapture the relevance of metaphysics as a form of investigation in an era when logical positivism and the reliance on scientific and rational reasoning were the dominant forms of inquiry (Kuehn, 2001).

In general, Kant's analysis of traditional epistemologies involved what he referred to as synthetic a priori judgments as opposed to traditional analytic judgments supported by logical and scientific means. A priori judgments are true before experience; Kant's basic questioning of synthetic a priori judgments required asking how judgments are even possible. Kant illuminated a new metaphysics that considered space and time as categories of understanding in making synthetic judgments that are not simply empirical calculations. Kant did not consider space and time to have qualities that are scientific or analytic. He understood space and time as non-empirical broad categories, dismissing physics and other hard sciences that were based upon theoretical principles (Kuehn, 2001).

In Critique of Pure Reason, Kant (1781/1965) stressed the importance of experience. He stated that "experience is, beyond all doubt, the first product to which our understanding gives rise...[e]xperience is therefore our first instruction...[but] it is by no means the sole field to which our understanding is confined" (Kant, 1781/1965, p. 41). Kant argued that there is no true universality that can accurately interpret the wide variation of individual experiences. Because of Kant's critique of empiricism, he sought to reconcile empiricism and rationalism. In doing so, Kant detailed a transcendental epistemology that accounted for his understanding of the imperfections of empiricism and pure rationality. In *Critique of Pure Reason*, Kant (1781/1965) attempted to forge a rational argument to prove the existence of God as an exemplar of a universal divine aspect. He demonstrated the use of reason and observation in framing the case for the existence of God but determined that his discovery was insufficient as proof for the existence of God. As Kant attempted to blend empiricism and rationality, he concluded that there are phenomena that are simply not empirically observable. Kant argued that rationality cannot be limited to empirical observation, thus leading to his transcendental emphasis.

Kant's transcendental argument accounted for the weaknesses of both empiricism and rationality. He wanted a foundation for both observation and experience (empiricism) and logical arguments (rationality). His work gave rise to transcendental epistemology. Kant (1781/1965) admitted "the transcendental object lying at the basis of appearances...is and remains for us inscrutable....[f]or it is of the very essence of reason that we should be able to give an account of all of our concepts, opinions, and assertions, either upon objective or, in the case of mere illusion, upon subjective grounds" (p. 514). Kant indicated that there is another way to knowledge; his alternative embraced the transcendental as a corrective to empiricism and rationality. Transcendental arguments account for what is not observable or empirically experienced; he argued that we must base evidence on transcendental deductions (Kant, 1781/1965).

Kant believed we are able to know by observation and experience. He reminds us of the importance of a transcendental mode of inquiry that requires synthetic judgments about information not implied in the original experience or observation. The gathering point of insight is what Kant (1781/1965) understood as the transcendental. For Kant, the transcendental mode permits one to engage synthetic arguments; this perspective is not to be confused with analytical arguments. The enactment of the transcendental through synthetic arguments relies upon what Kant termed an inherent subjectivity that permits one to make arguments relative to the autonomous judgment of the person called to render a decision. Kant offered the metaphysical category of the transcendental as a way of conceptualizing this form of judgment and argument that accounts for how we understand, beyond the immediacy of experience and observation. His work provides insight into the gathering of perspectives that permits one to go beyond senses alone and understand a given situation. His insights give us a philosophical picture of practical reason in action.

Kant resurrected metaphysics, giving birth to a new metaphysics. Kant (1781/1965) argued that knowledge from "pure intuition," a priori, is "infallible," unlike empirically and rationally based knowledge (p. 657). As an alternative, Kant framed a new metaphysics that involves both speculative and practical pure reason. He argued that knowledge necessitates transcendental philosophy. Kant (1781/1965) contended that transcendental philosophy's, and therefore transcendental epistemology's, "sole preoccupation is wisdom; and it seeks it by the path of science, which…permits no wandering…[but can be] discharge[d] only…aided by a knowledge through reason from pure concepts…which is nothing but metaphysics" (p. 665). Kant's perspective was an alternative to empiricism and rationalism. How we understand knowledge is important to how we understand the world and others; for Kant, transcendental knowledge provides us a basis from which we communicate with those around us. In each epistemological perspective, the goal is to ground knowledge, providing us with a textured understanding of evidence that drives decisions and shapes what we know. Epistemology informs our philosophy of communication and our experiences through the manner and perception of knowing.

Philosophy of Communication: *Zorba the Greek* and Epistemology

Epistemology grounds knowledge as we construct meaning in our lives. Epistemology is tied to experiences and beliefs that inform varying levels of proof and skepticism. Epistemology frames an understanding of how knowledge is gained and perceived. We are guided to insight and meaning by carefully engaging with and understanding knowledge. Epistemology offers a way to understand the gathering of information, moving beyond sensory impressions to the assimilation of information guided by a transcendental bringing together of observation, experience, and practical reason. We are susceptible to making errors in judgment because of how we understand knowledge; when we understand that knowledge weaves between the universal and the contextual, we create an opportunity to conceptualize imperfections in the gathering of knowledge as we prepare to make a judgment. Kant gives us practical reason as a mode of rationality that rests between the universal and the contextual. His work brings the transcendental to the play of reason as a gathering point, not as a universal assurance of truth. Philosophy of communication situates knowledge as central, stressing accumulation and precision. Zorba offers an exemplar of the necessity of knowledge accumulation in the meeting of existence. Zorba accumulates knowledge in his hands and in the practices of his labor.

In this chapter, we discussed various theories of knowledge and how we come to know how something impacts our knowledge of human meaning. Throughout the story of *Zorba the Greek*, we witness numerous examples of how people come to know their environments and how this knowledge influences interaction with others. When we enter the story of *Zorba the Greek*, we encounter the meeting of two people; these people directly shape the knowledge that will situate epistemic judgments about events in the novel. We gain meaning about a place within a communicative environment that is understood. Situated understanding and knowledge of a particular meeting between persons, according to Kant, requires transcendental insight that helps us make sense of empirical experience, rationality of observation and consideration, and the practices of tradition.

In Zorba's conversations with Boss, we witness skepticism about God. Zorba asks Boss:

"Boss, d'you believe that? That God became man and was born in a stable? Do you believe it, or are you just pulling our legs?" "It's difficult to say, Zorba." I replied. "I can't say I believe it, nor that I don't. What about you?"

"I can't say I do either. I can't for the life of me. You see, when I was a kid and my grandma told me tales, I didn't believe a word of them. And yet I trembled with emotion, I laughed and I cried, just as if I did believe them. When I grew a beard on my chin, I just dropped them, and I even used to laugh at them; but now, in my old age—I suppose I'm getting soft, eh, boss?—in a kind of way I believe in them again.... Man's a mystery!"" (Kazantakis, 1946/1952, p. 133)

Zorba counters his own skepticism with empirical and rational approaches to his question about God. He takes time to reflect upon his question, engaging Boss in his quest. Zorba also comments about how, as a young man in war times, he made decisions about killing that he would not choose again. His knowledge and understanding of the manner of gathering knowledge independently no longer makes the same decisions possible. Zorba's knowledge and reflections about his past meetings with others reconfigures all he knows with new transcendental insights; his epistemic judgments change with new knowledge. Zorba comprehends the world differently as he gains experiences of more meetings with others without falling into the trap of undue assurance. Zorba questions how he actually knows, recognizing that he does not know everything. For Zorba, knowledge changes him without making him into a fool with undue self-assurance.

Philosophy of communication as the carrier of meaning, understood from the vantage point of epistemology, reminds us of our desire for knowledge and its limits. We conclude this chapter by revisiting five central points:

1. All communication originates from some form of knowledge gathering. Zorba does not gather knowledge from encyclopedias or great books, but he is a knowledge gatherer. He is propelled by questions; he understands the practical necessity of knowledge in his hands for the doing of labor and the protecting of those around him.

2. Knowledge provides grounding that allows us to make judgments. Zorba is not shy about his judgments, but they are grounded in knowledge he has gathered throughout his demanding life. His knowledge emerges from past experiences that shape his judgments.

3. In order to understand knowledge, we also need to understand *how* we came to understand and *what* we then claim as knowledge. If Zorba were to hear the "how" and "what" of knowledge, he would shake his head, wondering why such terms were necessary. For Zorba, the how and the what emerge as by-products of simply living life. Epistemological rigor moves the stress on the how and what of knowledge to the forefront; they are no longer simply emerging by-products.

4. What we know about knowledge has limits, prohibiting us from assuming that the extremes of knowing all or nothing should guide us. The notion of limits is a central theme throughout *Zorba the Greek*; Zorba's questions to Boss repeatedly announce awareness of his own knowledge limits. Zorba does not simply tell or accumulate questions about what he does not understand; he engages in existential confession with his questions.

5. Limits to knowledge can be negotiated through transcendental approaches to knowledge that acknowledge limits and create space for creative possibilities. Limits to knowledge are broken through in transcendental moments in which insight is transformed. For Zorba,

such insights did not emerge from a book, but from experiencing life. For Boss, ultimately, the experience of life is the place of hope for new transcendental insights that would move him beyond the limits of his own book knowledge.

Philosophy of communication relies upon knowledge, giving us a base from which to make judgments about people, places, and things. Knowledge undergirds a worldview and an evolving philosophy of communication.

CHAPTER 5

EXISTENTIAL ENGAGEMENT

Existentialism is a practical and responsive philosophical movement that emerged out of the Western crisis of World War II; the existentialist task was to make sense of a life-world in turmoil. Europe[1] was in a historical moment of narrative and virtue collapse, unsure of its direction. For those fighting the Nazi machine and for families throughout Europe, normative daily existence was under siege, turned upside down. For instance, the intense bombing of London ("The Blitz") lasted from September 1940 to May 1941, France was occupied by Germany from 1940 to 1944, and Japan and the U.S. were at war from 1941 to 1945. These events were followed by the communist revolution in China and the Chinese Civil War (1945–1949). The Western world was torn asunder. Existentialism addressed lost trust in narrative foundations and structures; the hope was to enact individual choice when trust in institutions was lost for many.

Introduction

This chapter relies on a philosophical picture of existentialism painted by William Barrett's (1958) *Irrational Man: A Study in Existential Philosophy*; his work is a classic portrayal of existentialism that offers insight into its nature and origins. Additionally, this chapter turns to a compilation by Walter Kaufmann (1956), *Existentialism from Dostoevsky to Sartre*, which offers a thoughtful introductory essay on existentialism and provides the reader with a number of excerpts from original works penned by well-known existentialist writers.

This chapter consists of two major sections: (1) Barrett and Kaufmann's renditions of existentialism; and (2) implications for the study of philosophy of communication understood as one philosophical picture exemplified through *Zorba the Greek*, the central story used throughout this project. Existentialism is a philosophy that offers a modern answer, a calling forth of individual choice, to an emerging problem later identified, using a postmodern description, as the collapse of narrative consensus. There was no consensus regarding the viability of progress, which had been the master narrative of modernity.

Existentialism, understood as a philosophical picture, counters the collapse of historic institutions with what seems to be the only answer left in an era of narrative collapse—reliance upon the self. For existentialism, hope lives in

---

1 World War I lasted from 1914 to 1919, ending with the Treaty of Versailles. World War II began in Europe in 1939 and ended in May 1945.

meeting existence on its own terms, finding the last stand of hope resting in individual choice. Existentialism underscores a philosophy of communication that meets existence with a stress on the communicative agent as a choice maker capable of addressing a world in perceived narrative collapse.

Barrett and Kaufmann on Existentialism

Barrett and Kaufmann offer insight into a story about navigating the loss of narrative and institutional and structural guidance, calling us to meet existence on its own terms and demanding that we take responsibility for our own individual choices. William Barrett (1913–1992) was a professor of philosophy at New York University from 1950 to 1979. He served as both editor of the *Partisan Review* and as a literary critic for *The Atlantic*. He is widely credited for introducing European existentialism to the United States. *Irrational Man: A Study in Existential Philosophy* is regarded as a definitive study of existential philosophy for the general reader (Honan, 1992). Walter A. Kaufmann (1921–1980) was a member of the philosophy department at Princeton University from 1947 to 1980. Promoted to full professor in 1962, he was appointed to the Stuart Chair in 1979. He also held visiting appointments at numerous national and international universities throughout his career, including Fulbright Professorships at Heidelberg and Jerusalem ("Walter A. Kaufmann," 2011). Kaufmann (1956) paints an impressionistic portrait of what existentialism is and is not, as he considered existentialism "not a philosophy" (p. 11), but a rebellion against abstract philosophical systems. Existentialism moves one out of an unreflective meeting of life that finds support from undue specialization, resulting in "professional deformations" (Barrett, 1958, p. 4). Existentialism is an effort to resurrect passion for the challenge ahead, which required countering the loss of traditions and institutions while rejecting mindless specialization that resembled an intellectual version of the assembly line.

A General Overview of Existentialism

After World War II, the principal home for existentialism was France, led by Jean-Paul Sartre (1905–1980), Simone de Beauvoir (1908–1986), and Albert Camus (1913–1960).[2] Existentialism has rich European roots as it offered an

---

2 Albert Camus did not like the term "existentialism"; he later parted ways with the near-Marxist insight of Sartre, as he shifted from the notion of the absurd to the idea of moral "rebellion" ("Albert Camus," 2010).

alternative voice to Anglo-American philosophy and American optimism, which viewed existentialism as driven too extensively by despair and nihilism. "Anxiety, death, the conflict between the bogus and the genuine self, the faceless man of the masses, the experience of the death of God are scarcely the themes of analytic philosophy. Yet they are themes of [existential] life…" (Barrett, 1958, p. 9). Existentialism embraced the reality of human moods and their vitality in the meeting of existence; they shape our participation in the human condition.

It was not Camus, but Sartre, however, who brought recognition of existentialism to the United States. Sartre's primary sources were Karl Jaspers (1883–1969), Martin Heidegger (1889–1976), and Edmund Husserl (1859–1938). Sartre's intellectual task began with those interested in "philosophical anthropology" (Barrett, 1958, p. 11), such as in the work of Max Scheler (1874–1928), who claimed that modernity had made the human a problem unto himself.

In addition to Sartre, early versions of existentialism found champions in the work of Gabriel Marcel (1889–1973), a Catholic who often was at odds with Sartre, along with the American idealist Josiah Royce (1855–1916), and the French intuitionist Henri Bergson (1859–1941). Throughout Europe there were numerous scholars actively discussing existentialism in Russia, Spain, and Germany. The work of Martin Buber (1878–1965) provided "a necessary corrective to more ambitious systematizers like Heidegger and Sartre" (Barrett, 1958, p. 17). Additionally, the work of William James (1842–1910) is often understood as being more vibrantly existential than pragmatic; existentialism contrasted with Anglo-American philosophy of "analytic philosophy, Logical positivism, or sometimes merely 'scientific philosophy'" (Barrett, 1958, p. 21). Barrett painted a caricature of positivist[3] man as a curious creature who dwells on a tiny island of light composed of what he finds scientifically "meaningful"; yet the majority of ordinary persons live from day to day in a darkness constituted by a sense of "meaninglessness" (Barrett, 1958, p. 21). To people in such crises of meaning, existentialism frames a hopeful response to existence, providing an alternative to the 19th-century Enlightenment stress on scientific progress, played out in positivism and in Marxism.

Existentialism emerged in response to an era of narrative collapse in the West, promoting a form of "self-consciousness" of the self in action (Barrett,

---

3 Defined by the work of Auguste Comte (1789–1857), within philosophy, positivism refers to any system that excludes a priori or metaphysical opinions in favor of only data discovered through experience ("Positivism," 2011).

1958, p. 23). "The loss of the Church was the loss of a whole system of symbols, images, dogmas, and rites which had the psychological validity of immediate experience, and within which hitherto the whole psychic life of Western man had been safely contained" (Barrett, 1958, p. 25). The lack of context for the meaning of historically grounded ideas is the reason Barrett stated that one could no longer write Dante's *Divine Comedy* today; that Aquinas could no longer connect rationality with God as Aquinas did in the 13th century; and Kant's 18th-century critique of "unbounded rationalism" required the social tremors of his time (Barrett, 1958, p. 26). Without a given particular historical context, great works are not possible; the ideas respond to real moments and real problems in a particular human context.

The focus on the individual continued with Barrett (1958) emphasizing the Protestantism of Martin Luther (1483–1546), which called into question reason. At the same time, religion lost an increasing number of traditions, with science offering hope of "progress" in the Enlightenment (Barrett, 1958, p. 27). For Barrett, the rapid march away from tradition opened the door to an encounter with "nothingness" (p. 29). The move from feudalism to capitalism shifted the focus from the concrete life of a community to an abstract conception of living, leaving us with only a "fragment of man" (Barrett, 1958, p. 30). Such an era placed hope in technique and as an external, removing hope from the concrete center of existential life. The person entered what Karl Jaspers called in 1930 (three years before the rise of Hitler) "depersonalizing forces" of modernity (Barrett, 1958, p. 32). The onset of World War I (1914) to 1930 was deemed a time of raw "materialism," which gave rise to a "feeling of homelessness, of alienation…intensified in the midst of a bureaucratized, impersonal mass society" (Barrett, 1958, p. 34). Homelessness is the consequence of the emergence of a bureaucratic and faceless society, a milieu within which a genuine sense of place is no more.

Immanuel Kant's (1724–1804) 18th-century focus on the limits of reason found support in 20th-century science by Werner Heisenberg's (1901–1976) "Principle of Indeterminacy" (1927), which stated that our ability to accurately know the position and momentum of a physical particle is limited; Aage Niels Bohr's (1922–2009) "Principle of Complementarity" (1913), which stated that an electron can be both a wave and a particle, dependent on its context; and Kurt Gödel's (1906–1978) findings that mathematics could never be a formalized system due to its insoluble problems (Barrett, 1958, pp. 38–39). Such discoveries pointed to "the collapse of human *hubris*" (Barrett, 1958, p. 40). Modernity sought a "labor of denudation" that moved existence into the banal (Barrett, 1958, p. 41). Edmund Husserl (1973) offered an alternative to a banal engagement of existence with his return to origins, "the things themselves," calling us to take life before us seriously and concretely.

In addition to science, the arts called our attention to this era of disruption, offering testimony against the assurance of modernity. One finds questions and warnings in works from the impressionist painter Claude Monet (1840–1926), to the Fauvist movement leader Henri Matisse (1869–1954), who led a short-lived expression of wild colors and non-natural movements. These efforts began with the generation after World War I (1914–1918). They made a statement about crumbling traditions; their work was termed nihilistic as it deconstructed the canon of Western traditions. They challenged the West for no longer being able to "nourish its most creative members" (Barrett, 1958, p. 47). Barrett then argued that from Cubism, detachment from the object of art was discovered. The world was then critiqued as two-dimensional with a flattening of "planes" (with the presentation of past and present together), "climaxes" (leaving the classical understanding of beginning, middle, and end), and "values" (questioning the hierarchy of Western values), igniting increasing interest in the East (Barrett, 1958, pp. 50–58). In such a portrait, the human became a "faceless hero" with the charge of meeting "Nothingness" (Barrett, 1958, p. 62). As Max Scheler (1874–1928) stated, the human became a problem unto himself and existentialism sought to offer an answer, with Barrett (1958) continuing his review of the ancient roots of existentialism (p. 64).

Historical Roots

Barrett (1958) traced the origins of existentialism to the Hebraic tradition and the 19th-century work by Matthew Arnold (1822–1888), who defined the Hebraic world by "practice" and the Greek world by "knowledge" (p. 70). The Hebraic model of Job calls God into account and is contrary to a Protestant world. The Hebrew engagement is a passionate, not detached, meeting of the concrete existential moment. The Greeks, on the other hand, had Plato (428/427–348/347 BCE), who differentiated the psyche from the body, and Aristotle (384–322 BCE), who continued the rational ideal with a metaphysical position of Being as "First Cause" (Barrett, 1958, p. 89). These ideas were in contrast to the early Greek thought of Parmenides (c. 515 BCE), the visionary poet who held that many changing forms and motions of things are only the appearance of the eternal reality of Being, as Heraclitus (540–480 BCE), the describer of all things being in "flux," stated (Barrett, 1958, p. 83; "Parmenides, 2010"). The task of bringing light out of the darkness began with Plato, but this perspective was not the totality of the Greek world. Just as existentialism challenged the prevailing assumptions after World Wars I and II, there were competing orientations during the reign of Plato. In contemporary terms, however, "Kierkegaard and Nietzsche in the nineteenth century were the first to reverse this Platonic scale of values and to establish the individual, the single one, precisely in the way in which he is an exception to the universal norm, as taking precedence over the universal" (Barrett, 1958, p. 85). Friedrich Nietzsche (1844–1900) was the first to return to the insight of Heraclitus's flux, contrary to the Western reliance upon a hierarchy of values.

The argument between East and West, Hebrew and Greek, is played out, according to Barrett, by early Church fathers. For instance, there is the work of St. Paul (c. 4 BCE–64 AD) and later that of Father Tertullian (c. 150–225 AD), who stated that faith finds affirmation in the "absurd" and the "impossible"; faith is simply beyond reason (Barrett, 1958, p. 95). The insights of St. Augustine (354–430 AD) are existential; he meets existence and asks, "Who am I?" (Barrett, 1958, p. 95). It is the project of theodicy,[4] of connecting good to the cosmos, that Gottfried Wilhelm Leibniz (1646–1716) extrapolated from Augustine, which was later lampooned as undue optimism in Voltaire's (1694–1778) caricature of Dr. Pangloss in *Candide* (1759/1993). Barrett stressed the disagreements between theologians focused on faith and dialecticians centered on logic. St. Thomas Aquinas (1224–1274) attempted to bring the forces of faith and logic together in his *Summa Theologica*. He placed the intellect before the will, while Duns Scotus (1266–1308) reversed the order, stressing "voluntarism" over the intellect (Barrett, 1958, p. 101). Another Church father, Miguel de Unamuno (1864–1936), argued that Aquinas missed existence and placed support of the institution of the Church as his primary objective. However, Étienne Gilson (1884–1978) and Kierkegaard (1813–1855) re-acknowledge the existential nature of Aquinas, stating that the argument between these two members of the Church centers on the difference between existence (Aquinas) and essence (Scotus). "The essence of a thing is *what* the thing is; existence refers rather to the sheer fact *that* the thing is" (Barrett, 1958, p. 102; emphasis in original). Existentialism

---

4 According to Barrett (1958) "Theodicy is an attempt to deal with God as a metaphysical object, to reason demonstratively about Him and His cosmos, to the end that the perfection of both emerges as a rational certainty. Behind this lies the human need to seek security in a world where man feels homeless. But reason cannot give that security; if it could, faith would be neither necessary nor so difficult...[witness] the modern revolt against theodicy..." (p. 97).

assumes that existence is a priori to essence. Individual choice emerges with its connection to essence in the meeting of existence.

One can understand Pascal (1623–1662), an outstanding mathematician, as an existentialist. In Dante's (1265–1321) *Divine Comedy* (1555), Virgil (70–19 BCE) functions as the leader of reason, only to be replaced by Beatrice (1266–1290) as a "symbol of Divine Revelation" (Barrett, 1958, p. 111). This happy cosmos is contrary to Blaise Pascal's negative assessment of the human condition. Pascal's negativity about "habit" and "diversion" conceals the human from "nothingness," reviving pessimism that later shaped the insights of Sartre, who took this position the farthest (Barrett, 1958, p. 112).

Pascal understood that human life could not be grasped through the eyes of geometry alone, stressing the importance of the "intuitive mind" that later gave rise to the work of Henri Bergson (Barrett, 1958, p. 114). Bergson stressed the importance of intuition that permits one to navigate ambivalences and contradictions and understand significance that goes beyond reason. Pascal stressed a radical contingency of existence that acknowledges the finitude of human life, an emphasis that moved us far afield from the world of Tertullian (c. 150–225 AD) and Augustine to a new consequence derived from this reality of "homelessness" (Barrett, 1958, p. 118), or what was deemed much later as "existential homelessness" (Arnett, 1994). Pascal died in 1662; his death was followed by a century of blinding light in the form of the Enlightenment, which was propelled by the hope of progress and the expectation that reason would be the savior of Truth. However, an unrestrained hope in reason resulted in optimism, not in realism, in the meeting of existence.

Optimism disconnects one from the world, which led Barrett to emphasize Jonathan Swift's (1667–1745) *Gulliver's Travels* (1726) and the voyage to Laputa, an island that floats in the air whose people are Platonists and cerebral, committed to geometry and "harebrained schemes of research" (Barrett, 1958, p. 122). Interestingly, many assume that this work was Swift's revenge against Trinity College, which had failed him for his lack of comprehension of logic. Whether or not this assumption is correct, Swift did predict intellectual movements that emerged after him, such as the Romantics who protested against industrialization and reason through the works of William Blake (1757–1827), William Wordsworth (1770–1850), and Samuel Taylor Coleridge (1772–1834).

Wordsworth led Romanticism's return to the past as the period's most philosophical poet. He liked the German poet Friedrich Hölderlin (1770–1843), who opposed the industrial impulse of dissection, consistent with

Alfred North Whitehead's (1861–1947) stress on process theory and the "togetherness-of-things" (Barrett, 1958, p. 126). It was Coleridge who took us closest to existentialism with his personal description of his failing as a poet as he began to lose a love of nature in *Dejection: An Ode*. Coleridge's melancholy is akin to Goethe's (1749–1832) version of *Faust*. "Faust to a reckless attempt to master all of human learning, which Goethe dismisses in the final statement of intellectual disenchantment: '*Gray is all theory, green is life's glowing tree*'" (Barrett, 1958, p. 128). Faust, like Nietzsche's Superman, attempts to transcend humanity. The original Faust was a medieval scholar who dabbled in the black arts and was brought to public consciousness by Christopher Marlowe (1564–1593) in *The Tragical History of Doctor Faustus* (1604/1905). This emphasis on magic is framed within Chinese ideograms where the notion of "men of virtue" is translated as "men of magic"; such was the power of alchemy at that time (Barrett, 1958, p. 129). "It is in later French Romanticism, as it passes over into Symbolism, that this spiritual craving of poets for magic and alchemy becomes more noticeable" (Barrett, 1958, p. 130). For instance, Charles Baudelaire's (1821–1867) "correspondences" take poetry to arcane and obscure images, an "aesthetic perversion" that is put into extreme practice by Arthur Rimbaud (1854–1891) with a focus on violence, calling the moment an "era of assassins" and breaking with Western civilization (Barrett, 1958, pp. 130–131).

Rimbaud was one of the first to stress "primitivism," followed by Paul Gauguin (1848–1903) and D. H. Lawrence (1885–1930), who understood modernity, in the hands of academics and artists, as generally a form of "decadence" (Barrett, 1958, p. 132). Barrett (1958) concludes by stating that Rimbaud eventually succumbed to the call to action, the "demon" of the West (p. 132).

During this same period, we find the power of Russian authors. Leo Tolstoy (1828–1910) denounced Baudelaire in *What Is Art?* as Tolstoy continued to counter modern writers. In 19th-century Russia, there is a desire to join the West with change occurring at break-neck speed. The reaction to this unreflective love of the West leads to the negative use of the term "intelligentsia," which begins in Russia at the same time as communism (1917). Also, the insights of Franz Kafka (1883–1924) emphasized the problem of self-delusion and the effort to hide behind words such as duty and patience, missing one's own call of responsibility. The intellectuals are the embodiment of reason and are cut off from concrete life in Russia. It is Heidegger (1889–1976) who later turns to the work of Tolstoy and Dostoevsky (1821–1881) as he seeks an alternative to modernity. Dostoevsky's (1862/1965) return from imprisonment in Siberia shapes his first major work, *Memoirs from the House of the Dead*, which understands the human as "demoniacal" rather than rational (Barrett, 1958, p. 136). In *The Possessed* we find an ongoing critique of "progress," "reason," and "socialism" (Barrett, 1958, p. 139). In *Notes from the Underground*, we discover the clearest rejection of modernity's commitment to "morbid mediocrity" (Barrett, 1958, p. 141), persons who become "monsters of frustration and resentment" (Barrett, 1958, p. 139). Modernity finds a literate foe in Dostoevsky's strident critique of the metaphysical construct of progress.

Walter Kaufmann's introduction to *Existentialism from Dostoevsky to Sartre* (1956) begins with a description of Dostoevsky's contribution to the existential expression. Kaufmann states that Dostoevsky's *Notes from Underground* (1864/1956) is far from the Romanticism of Keats (1795–1821) and Wordsworth, in that Dostoevsky does not seek any form of deliverance from existence. Dostoevsky's work is an "uncompromising concentration on the dark side of man's inner life" (Kaufmann, 1956, p. 13). Unlike Jean-Jacques Rousseau (1712–1778), Dostoevsky did not believe that a good society could ever rid itself of the natural depravity that follows human beings.

Kaufmann begins with the work of Dostoevsky, even though Kierkegaard, whom many consider the father of existentialism, was dead nine years before the publication of *Notes from Underground*. Dostoevsky gave us a "world" understood through the gaze of Kierkegaard's "individual" (Kaufmann, 1956, p. 14). Dostoevsky wrote as a man formerly exiled in Siberia, whose insights inspired Nietzsche. "Our choice is usually mistaken from a false view of our advantage. We sometimes choose absolute nonsense because in our foolishness we see in that nonsense the easiest means for attaining a supposed advantage" (Dostoevsky, 1864/1956, p. 72). Dostoevsky assumed that human history could not be understood as rational; it is a "vulgar folly" (Dostoevsky, 1864/1956, p. 75). The themes of the *Underground* revolve around the rejection of reason as the link to progress, the difficulty of respect, and the power of vanity and lying. Dostoevsky offers a story-laden version of Kierkegaard's insights.

Additionally, Tolstoy wanted the human to stand face to face with the drama of life, from its joys to its deepest sorrows, providing a critique of modernity as a mistaken path. Struggles of life do not find security in "intellectual" truth, but in the temporal meeting of "existential truth" (Barrett, 1958, p. 143). Tolstoy would have rejected Spinoza's (1632–1677) assertion that the free person only thinks of life and not of death; to do so misses the existential demands of the everyday. Such a perspective is in stark contrast to the writing of Kant. The work of Kierkegaard, Nietzsche, and Kafka, who was born in Prague and worked as a German writer, shaped what Karl Jaspers (1883–1969) called *Existenzphilosohie*.

Jaspers did not begin with philosophical content; he was interested in the embedded nature of our making sense of the world. Instead of philosophy, he generally used the term "communication," connecting all knowledge to "interpretation" (Kaufmann, 1956, p. 34). Jaspers (1956) understood the importance of Kant's four questions connected to this historical moment: (1) "What can I know?" (2) "What shall I do?" (3) "What may I hope?" and (4) "What is man?" (p. 139). In applying these questions to existence in the historical moment, Jaspers (1956) reworked Kant's questions, offering five of his own that he considered appropriate to his historical existence: (1) "What is science?" (2) "How is communication possible?" (3) "What is truth?" (4) "What is man?" and (5) "What is Transcendence?" (pp. 142–152). Jaspers rejected abstract systems, making personal engagement with ideas and existence. He understood both Kierkegaard and Nietzsche as critics functioning as philosophical prophets, calling for the reconnection of deeds and statements. Jaspers's (1956) commitment to "transcendence" was an effort to honor existence and to refuse to reify the meaning of that which is before one (p. 142).

Jaspers is important to 20th-century existentialism, but it is the 19th-century insights of Søren Kierkegaard (1813–1855) and Friedrich Nietzsche (1844–1900) that made this perspective philosophically visible. Kierkegaard, as a Dane living in Copenhagen, created difficulties for others as he challenged faith that was unduly abstract. Kierkegaard brought us the irony of despair, the reality of a public with a heightened self-consciousness regarding their own reactions and judgments. He gave us insight into the "absurd" and the suggestive nature of his own epitaph: "That individual" (Kaufmann, 1956, p. 16). Kierkegaard rebelled against the wisdom of the Greeks and stressed the temptation of Abraham as "a decision," a "choice…made in fear and trembling" (Kaufmann, 1956, p. 17), offering an existential critique of reason and an existential description of rebellion. Kierkegaard placed passion far ahead of reason—meeting existence requires energy fueled by something beyond rationality.

Kierkegaard challenged abstract intelligence inattentive to existence and to the necessity of individual choice. Kierkegaard followed German forerunners Johann Georg Hamann (1730–1788) and Friedrich Wilhelm Joseph von Schelling (1775–1854), who were outspoken critics of the manic imposition of rationalism on our understanding of and participation in the human condition. Kierkegaard rejected the "cosmic rationalism" of Hegel (1770–1831), a position that has ancient roots dating back to Parmenides,[5] who understood "Absolute Reality" as pure and good and able to swallow up each finite evil (Barrett, 1958, p. 155). This commitment to idealism lifted existence out of Hegel's system. The Hegelian dialectic worked without reliance upon existence. Such idealism was opposed to Kierkegaard's melancholy and more akin to that of Hamlet; fortunately, Kierkegaard's melancholy was tempered by irony and humor. He functioned like a 19th-century Socrates, who called himself "the gadfly of Athens," recognizing the fact that existence cannot be created or conceived by reason (Barrett, 1958, p. 157).

Countering Certitude

Kierkegaard's insights were in direct contrast to Kant, who some contend gave birth to "positivism" (Barrett, 1958, p. 162). For Kierkegaard, existence cannot be understood as a concept; we are enveloped in existence. Kierkegaard's existentialism has three major dimensions: aesthetic, ethical, and religious (Barrett, 1958, p. 163). For Kierkegaard, the aesthetic is driven into flight from "boredom" (Barrett, 1958, p. 164), making oneself a spectator and turning life into a theater. The aesthetic stays on the periphery of life, unlike the "ethical" that requires us to choose (Barrett, 1958, p. 165). Kierkegaard did not propose a formal theory of ethics but stressed the importance of choice in existence. It is in the life of the "religious" that one walks into the realm of the "absurd" and the "exception," transcending rules and moving into the "suspension of the ethical," and rejecting the abstractness of modern society with acknowledgment of the importance of moods (Barrett, 1958, p. 167). The moods of despair and anxiety actually turn against us as we become increasingly more "willful" against existence (Barrett, 1958, p. 170). Kierkegaard reconnected with Augustine, rejecting the 13th-century Thomistic stress on truth and its relation to the intellect while rejecting institutionalized religion. Like Dostoevsky, Kierkegaard stressed choice and the ethical, connecting choice with "the agony of [genuine] selfhood" (Barrett, 1958, p. 174).

    As suggested above, Kierkegaard's (1956) work protested the perversion

---

5 The Greek philosopher Parmenides founded Eleaticism, a prominent pre-Socratic school of Greek thought. Parmenides is also considered a founder of metaphysics due to his method of basing claims about appearances on the concept of Being ("Parmenides," 2010).

of Christianity that was lessening the power of choice and responsibility that must rest in the "individual" (p. 92), calling forth attentiveness to the "crowd" (p. 93). "Ethico-religious" thinking and action rested with the individual, not the crowd (Kierkegaard, 1956, p. 97). Kierkegaard's (1956) understanding of humanity is that the whole or the species must pass through the individual, not the "crowd"—the person and place of responsible action (p. 96). This emphasis on abandoning the crowd is also central to Nietzsche's project.

Nietzsche continued this existential focus with a deconstructive religious turn (Barrett, 1958, p. 177). Nietzsche was a professor of classical philology at the University of Bassel and focused on interpretation of classical and Biblical texts. He brought great gifts in classical languages and in music. He resigned after ten years due to ill health. Nietzsche turned to the Greek God Dionysus, framing the importance of a God of ecstasy and tragic festivals as an alternative to the modern movement of "fatigue and decline" (Barrett, 1958, p. 178). Nietzsche's emphasis on Dionysus gives us insight into a man who was torn apart and, at the end of life, "homeless" (Barrett, 1958, p. 180).

Nietzsche's autobiographical work *Ecce Homo* (1888) is translated as "Behold the Man!" with Nietzsche self-identifying with Dionysus (Barrett, 1958, p. 182). Nietzsche worked at tearing himself from his Western roots. Both Goethe's Faust and Nietzsche's Superman portray individual efforts that transcend past views of humanity. From Nietzsche's disgust of mediocrity, he insisted there must be an "Eternal Return" where the "Superman" has the courage to repetitively bear the test of existence with an ongoing commitment to say "yes" to existence (Barrett, 1958, p. 195).

Unlike Kierkegaard who attempted to bring passion to Christianity, Nietzsche deconstructed Christianity and reason. Nietzsche attacked the hypocrisy that was masquerading as Christian morality. His work, when little understood, was connected with the Nazis, who were fond of citing him. However, such a comparison was "...like linking St. Francis with the Inquisition in which the order he had founded played a major role" (Kaufmann, 1956, p. 100). Like Kierkegaard, Nietzsche called for an individual who rejected the demands of the crowd. Nietzsche understood Kant as a follower of fashion and critiqued Arthur Schopenhauer (1788–1860) as a "lonely philosopher" who tried to make a difference in a time of emerging narrative collapse (Nietzsche, 1956, p. 102). Such a person, functioning as a creative individual, is the "Superman," a person who rejects social convention and the temptation to live life as a "mouse" (Nietzsche, 1956, pp. 111–112). Nietzsche (1956) called "nihilism" the natural consequence of values and morality that no longer guide; they simply mask (p. 110). Nietzsche worked like the "Dionysian poet" Rainer Maria Rilke (1875–1926), who was "…considered the greatest German poet since the death of Goethe" (Kaufmann, 1956, p. 113); Rilke's *The Notes of Malte Laurids Brigge* (1910/1956) gives insight into the "inauthentic" life of the wretched, persons who do not complain and simply fade into the woodwork (Kaufmann, 1956, p. 113). Both understood the necessity of finding new ways to meet existence.

Many suggest that Nietzsche was an unsystematic thinker; this position is contrary to Heidegger's position, who called Nietzsche "the last metaphysician in the metaphysical tradition of the West, the thinker who at once completes and destroys that tradition" (Barrett, 1958, p. 197). Nietzsche understood that the classical world was not just a humanistic tradition, but composed of "virtue, *arête*, the clanging tone of Ares, god of battle" (Barrett, 1958, pp. 198–199). He framed a theory of the "will to power" that, when lived out in its extreme, leads to "nihilism" (Barrett, 1958, p. 203). He viewed power as the last value in modern life. It is out of this dark conception of the human condition that Heidegger responded.

Martin Heidegger underscored the importance of "thinking," differentiating it from "reason" (Barrett, 1958, p. 206), which moves the human into estrangement from Being. Heidegger worked within a 25,000-year history of Western philosophy of Being as he sought to dismantle the assumptions of modernity. He did not view Being as a concept, but as a fundamental response to existence with the task of the human bringing Being to light. Truth rests in thinking, not in rationality, rejecting Descartes's view of rationality in "…*Cogito, ergo sum*, 'I think therefore I am'" (Barrett, 1958, p. 216). Heidegger contended that one cannot think above the world; one thinks in the world, revealed through an expanding sense of Being—"Being-in-the-world" (Barrett, 1958, p. 217). The field in which Being reveals itself is *Dasein*, or what another might more conventionally call the practices of the human being where the task is to illuminate additional possibilities of Being. The human exists in a "fallen-ness" in which one is an "impersonal One," not yet an "I" (Barrett, 1958, pp. 219–220). What separates the "One" from the "I" is an existential choice of "inauthenticity" ("chatter" and the crowd) or "authenticity" ("speech" and a responsiveness to existence) (Barrett, 1958, pp. 220–223).

This unexpressed context of understanding consists of presuppositions rooted in existence. Heidegger's Field Theory of Being is contextual. Being is the context within which beings become known. Because the human stands in the context of Being, this open space of Being permits one to communicate with others. Humans exist "within language" (Barrett, 1958, p. 223). Prior to uttering sounds, humans exist within a mutual context of understanding, which in the end is nothing but Being, itself.

Heidegger's work assumes the existential reality of "death," "anxiety," and "finitude" (Barrett, 1958, p. 225). The human's acceptance of death is a meeting of finitude and anxiety that is the realization of "Nothingness" (Barrett, 1958, p. 226). Such a trinity of existential reality moves the human to live in the "distance," to be ahead of oneself (Barrett, 1958, p. 227). The human does not live in the present, but always in the "to be" (Barrett, 1958, p. 228). Heidegger objected to the Greeks detaching "beings from the vast environing ground of Being" (Barrett, 1958, p. 230). The separation of figure and ground in Gestalt terms is the divide between East and West, with Truth pursued with rationality connected to light in the West and every light coming with a "shadow" in the East (Barrett, 1958, p. 231).

Heidegger moved us closer to the Orient, taking our conception of Being out of representation and into the embeddedness/contextual understanding of being human. Heidegger rejected "representational thinking" that relied upon metaphysics and stressed thinking that "recalls" (Kaufmann, 1956, p. 39). He sought to recall missed roots of the West, taking us back to the Greeks and the "unconcealedness" of Being (Heidegger, 1949/1956, p. 208). The existential task is "overcoming of metaphysics" (Heidegger, 1949/1956, p. 209) by attending to the reality of being in existence, standing in and caring for Being; such acts open up new possibilities. Heidegger's work de-centered the role of the human, placing the human in the shadow of Being.

Martin Buber critiqued Heidegger, stating that Heidegger stressed the individual at the expense of the community, consistent with Heidegger's attraction to Hölderlin, considered to be the German poet of "loneliness" (Barrett, 1958, pp. 236–237). Heidegger, as an existential thinker, turned us from ethical and religious passion situated within the individual choice of Kierkegaard to the disclosure of Being. The French existential connection rests largely with Sartre, who did not follow the thought of Heidegger rigorously; instead, Sartre stressed the passion of individual choice characterized by Kierkegaard.

Sartre wrote as he watched Léon Blum's (1872–1950) Popular Front government[6] drift, unable to confront "the crisis of the times" (Barrett, 1958, p. 241). Sartre took evil seriously along with the notion of *Nausea* (his first novel), offering a response to atmospheres of decay (Barrett, 1958, p. 241). To fight both, Sartre offered the defining element of human freedom in negative terms—the act of "No" (Barrett, 1958, p. 241). Sartre had a strong Descartian bent of "Systematic Doubt" (Barrett, 1958, p. 242), functioning as a "Cartesian rationalist" (Barrett, 1958, p. 249). Sartre was different from Descartes in that he connected human consciousness with "transcendence" (Barrett, 1958, p. 248); however, Barrett suggested that Sartre's project was a combination of Descartes and the French Resistance of World War II.

Sartre's work was based on a dualism of "Being-for-itself" (a consciousness of Being that is consistently beyond itself) and "Being-in-itself" (the thingness of a given object) (Barrett, 1958, p. 245). Security resists thingness, and in order to avoid objectifying Being, one is left with "radical insecurity," "fragility," and the negativity of "No" that permits one to resist Evil in the midst of Nothingness—the Sartrian understanding of the absurd (Barrett, 1958, p. 246). "Man's existence is absurd...the only meaning he can give himself is through the free project that he launches out of his own nothingness" (Barrett, 1958, p. 247). Sartre understood absurdity as giving rise to Nothingness, an "abyss" into which we can fall at any time (Barrett, 1958, p. 116). Additionally, Sartre emphasized the "will to action" (Barrett, 1958, p. 249) contrasted with Nietzsche's "will to power" (Barrett, 1958, p. 197); Sartre used literature to exemplify the "will to action" with No Exit as a rhetorical exemplar about social change. His focus was on a "rootless" state of an active choice maker committed to a Radical "No" (Barrett, 1958, p. 250). "Sartre's freedom is demoniacal. It is rootless freedom" (Barrett, 1958, p. 261). Barrett ended with the suggestion that as society becomes increasingly totalitarian, the freedom of a Sartrian "No" makes increasing sense. Existentialism requires meeting existence on its own terms, choosing a response and the responsibility for yes or no.

Philosophy of Communication: Zorba the Greek and Existentialism

Existentialism privileges the importance of meeting existence on its own terms without the aid of a tidy theory. One meets existence and responds without ideological certainty, giving insight into the importance of existential

---

6 From 1936 to 1937, Blum, the first Socialist premier of France, presided over the Popular
   Front coalition government, which introduced social reforms such as a 40-hour work week,
   paid vacations, and collective bargaining for workers, as well as nationalized the Bank of
   France and war industries. However, his plans for state control over private industry and
   finance aroused hostility among French business leaders, forcing Blum to resign his post in
   1937 ("Léon Blum," 2011).

responsiveness. Existentialism views existence as an essence that is timeless and existence is existentially understood as relational and embedded, as the predicate of the human condition, allowing the human to figure out a choice and direction within existence. Zorba the Greek is the poster child for this chapter; his raw instincts meet existence, not on his terms, but on the terms of existence itself. His meeting with existence is not passive; rather, he is like a fighter, a boxer, or a wrestler struggling with and against existence to his final breath. Additionally, Zorba deeply respects that which he wrestles. He does not demean life; he struggles with it and, in doing so, enlarges all those around him.

Existentialism reminds us that we are responsible; like it or not, our choices matter. The major characters, Boss and Zorba, offer stark differences. Zorba is the existential character and Boss is the caretaker of books. Kazantzakis (1946/1952) exemplifies this point when Boss reflects upon the last moment he spent with a friend, who called him a "bookworm" before he departed (p. 12). When Boss, as the narrator, reflects on that moment, he states:

> "If only I could live again the moment of that anger which surged up in me when my friend called me a bookworm! I recalled then that all my disgust at the life I had been leading was personified in those words." (Kazantzakis, 1946/1952, p. 12).

Boss wants desperately to "live with simple men, workmen and peasants, far from the race of bookworms!" (Kazantzakis, 1946/1952, p. 13). He is absorbed in books, but Zorba becomes the teacher. Zorba lives in existence; he is an existential exemplar that meets existence on its terms and then wrestles with life until the last breath.

Philosophy of communication as the carrier of meaning, understood from the vantage point of existentialism, requires the meeting of existence on its own terms; meaning emerges in our response. We conclude this chapter by revisiting four central points:

1. There is no theory that will ultimately protect or guide—the demand of humanity is choice. If we asked Zorba what theory guided him, the response would be a wicked laugh. Zorba is guided by no theory, no a priori, just simply a responsive engagement to that which is before him.

2. We cannot stand above existence—we live within an already created and ongoing world that we must meet and address. Zorba's irritation with Boss is not his focus on books, but rather Boss's inclination to want to stand above existence and avoid the mud of everyday life. The events of the novel take Boss into the center of such mud, pain, and

difficulty. To embrace life is to embrace not only that which brings us joy, but to meet that which we would not ever request.

3. We are situated and embedded within existence—our sense of choice is blurred. Zorba's questions reveal his being unsure at times, that the choice is often blurred, unclear; we do not always know what is right. Zorba tells Boss of a conversation he had with a 90-year-old grandfather: "And he, bent as he was, turned round and said: 'My son, I carry on as if I should never die.' I replied: 'And I carry on as if I was going to die any minute.' Which of us was right, boss?" (Kazantzakis, 1946/1952, p. 42). There is no right answer, for the choice and the response are blurred, ever dependent upon the context and the moment.

4. Life finds identity within limits and in the acknowledgment of finitude—we cannot know all and existence will rebuff our demands for control. The novel reminds us that existence is composed of limits: the beginning of friendships and the end, the beginning of relationships and the end, the beginning of a life and its conclusion. Our identity and our meaning fit between the bookends of an often unnoticed beginning and an abrupt end, sometimes with, sometimes without, even a moment of goodbye.

Barrett (1958) stated that the Radical "No" takes us to "The Place of the Furies," where we find abstractness from undue rationality and technological/bureaucratic life. "Existentialism is the counter-Enlightenment..." (p. 274). The Furies remind us of a darker side that cannot be ignored, regardless of how hard we try. Existentialism assumes that negativity is needed to battle naïve idealism.

CHAPTER 6

PHILOSOPHICAL HERMENEUTICS AS INTERPRETATION AND MEANING

Philosophical hermeneutics unites three coordinates—the interpreter, the text, and the historical moment—in dialogue. In this chapter, we turn to two works that lend insight into this perspective: Georgia Warnke's (1987) *Gadamer: Hermeneutics, Tradition, and Reason*, which focuses on Hans-Georg Gadamer's theory; and Charles E. Reagan's (1996) *Paul Ricoeur: His Life and His Work*, which engages Paul Ricoeur's contribution with a stress on biography tied to the historical moment. Together, these two works unite theory and life-world exemplification of philosophical hermeneutics, giving insight into philosophy of communication's contribution to meaning in communicative engagement.

Introduction

This chapter relies on a philosophical picture painted by Gadamer and Ricoeur, the German and French representatives of philosophical hermeneutics, each engaging a given interpretive project of philosophical hermeneutics. This perspective joins the prejudice or bias that one takes to a text with respectful interpretative engagement. Philosophical hermeneutics attends to the horizon (the identity) of a given text, offering an interpretative alternative to both objective and subjective proclamation. The importance of Gadamer's and Ricoeur's insights for this project hinge on a "unity of contraries" (Buber, 1965/1966, p. 111)—they give us information that reclaims the natural and inevitable nature of bias while honoring the communicative text under examination.

This chapter examines philosophical hermeneutics in three major sections: (1) an examination of Gadamer's insights with particular attention paid to his reclamation project about the importance of tradition; (2) Ricoeur's stress on story and emplotment as exemplified through his own life; and (3) the contributing issues of philosophical hermeneutics to the study and practice of philosophy of communication exemplified through Kazantzakis's (1946/1952) *Zorba the Greek*.

Philosophical hermeneutics offers a philosophical picture of knowledge advanced through respect. First, the interpreter must respect the ideas and positions that shape his or her interpretive identity; positions and standpoints give rise to a particular perspective on what is discovered or understood. Second, respect must guide engagement with the text under consideration, which has a life of its own; we cannot make something say what we demand.

Philosophical hermeneutics is the home of dialogue that unites respect with our interpretive limits.

Hans-Georg Gadamer's Reclamation Project

Hans-Georg Gadamer was born in Marburg, Germany, in 1900 and died in Heidelberg in 2002 at the age of 102. He grew up in Breslau, Poland (Germany until 1945), where his father was a professor of pharmacy at the university (Malpas, 2009). Gadamer's father had little engagement with the humanities and focused on teaching his son science to no avail—Gadamer was more interested in the humanities. In 1922, at age 22, Gadamer earned his first doctorate at Marburg (Malpas, 2009). He then took summer classes at the University of Freiburg in 1923 where he encountered the teachings of Martin Heidegger (1889–1976) (Clearly, 2005, p. 500). In 1923, Gadamer worked as Heidegger's assistant at Marburg; he earned a second doctorate in 1928 (Mueller-Vollmer, 1985/2006, p. 256).

Gadamer's teaching career commenced at Marburg in 1929 as an instructor of philosophy, becoming a "professor extraordinary" in 1937 (Mueller-Vollmer, 1985/2006, p. 256). He then taught at the University of Leipzig from 1938 to 1947 where he became a full professor in 1939, dean of faculty in 1945, and rector in 1946 (Malpas, 2009). In 1949, Gadamer was asked to succeed Karl Jaspers as chair at the University of Heidelberg, where he would retire in 1968 as a professor emeritus (Mueller-Vollmer, 1985/2006, p. 256). After his retirement, Gadamer traveled and taught throughout North America; he held visiting professor positions at numerous universities for nearly two decades, forming a close association with Boston College (Malpas, 2009).

Re-engaging Prejudice

Georgia Warnke's[1] (1987) *Gadamer: Hermeneutics, Tradition, and Reason* quickly references and stresses the importance of Gadamer's (1960/1986) *Truth and Method* as his "magnum opus" (p. 1). Gadamer was 60 years old when he published *Truth and Method* in 1960; this work continues to generate considerable interest in hermeneutic study and practice. In *Truth and Method*, Gadamer reclaims the importance of "prejudice," providing a counter to the Enlightenment proposal that attempted to "eradicate prejudice" (Warnke,

---

1 Georgia Warnke is a professor of philosophy at the University of California, Riverside. She has published five scholarly books, 25 articles, and has contributed to the *Cambridge Companion to Gadamer* (2002).

1987, p. 4). Gadamer's work returns us to an understanding of "embedded history," in that we cannot escape the prejudice of our own situatedness (Warnke, 1987, p. 4). The human condition is not something we can stand above; we are embedded within a given place, a given historical moment.

Warnke states that the context for Gadamer's philosophical hermeneutics has numerous points of origin beginning with Matthias Flacius (1520–1575), who argued for interpretation of the Bible, moving us to acknowledge differences within a common text. The emphasis on interpretive differences was a predecessor to Wilhelm Dilthey's (1833–1911) notion of the "hermeneutic circle," in which interpretation comes from the interplay of insight into the interpretive interplay of part and whole with each lending insight into the meaning of the Other (Warnke, 1987, p. 5).

Dilthey's work was an alternative and response to Friedrich Schleiermacher's work (1768–1834), which focused hermeneutics on grammar and psychology with the intention of delineating the intentions of the author and the "individuality" of the author at work (Warnke, 1987, p. 14). Dilthey sought to liberate hermeneutics from the "dogmatic" (Warnke, 1987, p. 6), insisting on essence or correct meaning that shaped Biblical hermeneutics as he opened the conversation to the importance of consistency of "method" (Warnke, 1987, p. 14). Gadamer rejected Dilthey's move to method as too closely tied to the Cartesian view of certainty, "I think therefore I am" (*Cogito ergo sum*); this cognitive certainty led, ironically, to the desire to doubt all of existence, framing a mind/body dichotomy with the mind as the ruling agent (Descartes, 1637/2008). Gadamer concurred, however, with Dilthey's differentiation of the human sciences from the natural sciences, which reflects the reality of different "modes of experience"; this insight influenced Gadamer in his rejection of unreflective reliance on method and a psychological reading of human history (Warnke, 1987, p. 26).

Gadamer's position was more akin to Arthur C. Danto's (1997) stress on our situatedness within a given historical moment, shifting the focus from individual motives to a given embedded historical actor. "Historical situatedness" (Warnke, 1987, p. 21), or "historicity of historical understanding" (Warnke, 1987, p. 27), suggests that bias is present in the historical question before us. "There can therefore be no 'objective' self-understanding free from the 'life-relations' (*Lebensbezüge*) in which one finds oneself. One cannot leap out of one's situation to gain impartial access to one's past" (Warnke, 1987, p. 29). Gadamer's view of the historical situatedness of interpretation rejects Dilthey's "life-philosophy" as both too methodological and too subjectivist

(Warnke, 1987, p. 31). Gadamer contended that Dilthey refused to publicly proclaim bias.

Gadamer's alternative ground for existential understanding of interpretation begins with what is before us, not pristine abstract truth. This perspective came first from the "life-world" conception of Husserl's (1970) later work, *The Crisis of European Sciences and Transcendental Phenomenology*, and the insights of Heidegger, with the "…insistence on historicity, on a situatedness or 'thrownness'…" (Warnke, 1987, pp. 36–37). Gadamer was concerned about "meaning," not certainty of truth based on the myth that one can stand above the messiness of the human condition (Warnke, 1987, p. 38). Gadamer's truth claims are historically situated in tradition, prejudice, and bias.

The dialogue of prejudice and tradition is controversial and fundamental to Gadamer's project. Jürgen Habermas disagreed with Gadamer, stating that we are vulnerable to "ideologically distorted claims" (Warnke, 1987, p. 117). Gadamer, in contrast, states that we cannot escape prejudice. Habermas (1977, 1980) published two major essays in response to Gadamer's work, arguing the dangers of distorted communication propelled by tradition. Habermas sought an "ideal speech situation," which Gadamer rejected as idealism (Warnke, 1987, p. 129). Gadamer embraced a pragmatic recognition of bias that one publicly brings to a given text. His view of interpretation was within a tradition without desiring universal validity, inviting understanding without guaranteeing an undisputable grasp of truth.

Gadamer eschewed "authorial intention" (asking what did the author really mean) and rejected certainty of interpretive truth (Warnke, 1987, p. 42). Gadamer stressed the importance of "shared meaning" between the text and the interpreter (Warnke, 1987, p. 47). He supported his position with discussion of Aristotle's notion of "mimesis" (Warnke, 1987, p. 48). Mimesis is a form of imitation that does not seek to duplicate the "real." Mimesis reveals a truth not present in reality alone. The doing of mimesis is akin to a game that one knows is not real, but must be taken seriously while attending to all the rules. This analysis requires Gadamer to differentiate between "distortion" and "situated interpretation," with the latter being inevitable; we are all situated in a given historical moment (Warnke, 1987, p. 72). Gadamer emphasized historicity, situatedness, and embeddedness of perception that naturally result in prejudice or bias in the act of interpretation. Gadamer "rehabilitates" prejudice and tradition, rejecting the efforts of the Enlightenment's call for neutrality and objectivity (Warnke, 1987, p. 75). Reason emanates from the perspective of prejudice of a tradition that shapes how a person thinks, what a person values, and how that person reasons.

Respect for the Text

Gadamer began with an assumption of "good will toward the text," contrary to deconstructive critics such as Jacques Derrida (1930–2004), who asserted that we must attend to an interpretive "rupture" (Warnke, 1987, p. 88). Otherwise, according to Derrida, tradition can lead us to support Hitler's *Mein Kampf*. Derrida wanted critique and questioning of a given interpretive tradition. Gadamer contended that a given interpretative tradition is challenged by the existence and interpretive use of another tradition. Multiple traditions permit one to transcend the prejudice of a given tradition, as one learns from and about different ones. For Gadamer, wisdom emerges from understanding multiple and competing traditions. This awareness of multiplicity of traditions permits the discernment of bias and prejudice, "interests" in Habermasian terms (Habermas, 1987). Gadamer conceptualized the act of understanding as a dialogue between the universal and the particular, which invites the discernment of truth.

Gadamer insisted that one must meet the object under study with serious respect in order to "avoid opportunism" of subjective imposition of meaning upon a text (Warnke 1987, p. 99). His work represents a pragmatic honoring of the traditions from which both the interpreter and text under study reside. The interplay of interpreter, prejudice of a given tradition, and the questioning of the text announces a form of interpretive "dialogue" (Warnke, 1987, p. 100), a "fusion of horizons" that brings together multiple traditions in conversation (Warnke, 1987, p. 103). What makes dialogue or the fusion of horizons possible is not neutrality, but the prejudice of a given tradition that situates an interpreter and the meeting of a given text. The interplay of prejudices permits new insights to emerge. Gadamer's task is one of interpretive enrichment. Understanding tradition requires the importance of "temporal distance," which gives one increased interpretive insight, uniting writing, interpretation, and editing with the necessity of temporal distance (Warnke, 1987, p. 115). One gains distance from one tradition as one learns from other traditions.

Karl-Otto Apel (b. 1922) agrees with Gadamer while questioning the limits of Gadamer's theory. In response, Apel calls for "unconstrained communication" (Warnke, 1987, p. 129). Gadamer, to the contrary, accepted natural restraint as the heart of his project—we must restrain our subjective impulses or we eclipse that which we want to interpret and learn about. Gadamer's acknowledgment of restraint lessens the result of solipsism that confuses one's own view with universal truth. Gadamer stressed the dialectic of illumination and darkness; he rejected the assumption that the task of human life is to lessen darkness with ever increasing amounts of illumination. He countered the Enlightenment hope of obtaining universal access to rationality that makes prejudice and tradition passé, replaced by the continual expectation of progress. Gadamer's rejection of progress and universal rationality of the Enlightenment gives new life to traditions and to the importance of respect when learning about what we do not yet know. His project called for a literate and humble interpreter, someone willing to admit limits and learn from difference.

Warnke (1987) ends her book with a connection between Gadamer and the "new pragmatism" of authors such as Richard Rorty and Richard Bernstein (p. 137). Rorty stressed the importance of hermeneutics in outlining the tradition/prejudices of all forms of knowledge. Rorty used Gadamer's work as a counter to the emphasis on epistemology (Warnke, 1987, p. 150). Rorty understood philosophical hermeneutics as closer to poetry than to rationality, taking power from the philosopher who desires to be the final valuator of meaning. Rorty recognized in Gadamer's work the importance of giving an account of a given interpretation. Gadamer stressed "practical reasoning" (Warnke, 1987, p. 51) as an idea of "giving an account," which gives one cultural interpretation coping skills (Warnke, 1987, p. 162). The act of accounting offers a public map of the interpretive process after the meeting of horizons of interpreter and text.

Gadamer offered a dialogical account of interpretation that recognizes the pragmatic reality of the fusion of horizons of interpreter and text, stressing an understanding of rationality that is situated, always open to challenge, and resistive of pleas for universal assurance. The next section exemplifies philosophical hermeneutics through the interplay of Paul Ricoeur's personal interpretive responsiveness to the events before him in the midst of his own life struggles.

Paul Ricoeur—Interpretation in Demands of Existence

Charles E. Reagan's[2] (1996) *Paul Ricoeur: His Life and His Work* offers insight into the doing of philosophical hermeneutics in the life-world of "the mud of

---

2 Charles E. Reagan is a professor of philosophy at Kansas State University and the author of six books.

everyday life" (Arnett, Fritz, & Bell, 2009, p. 36). Reagan's biographical essay illuminates the work of Ricoeur through an examination of the demanding engagements in Ricoeur's life. Ricoeur was a prisoner of war for five years. This event was one of many that situated his life within a dialectical tension; he participated in the war and had a commitment to pacifism (Reagan, 1996, p. 2). Ricoeur was orphaned during World War I, imprisoned during World War II, and led the opposition to France's role in the Algerian civil war (1954–1962) (Reagan, 1996, p. 2). Ricoeur's personal and scholarly life continually addressed the problems of evil and war; his life was defined by war.

The Meeting of Evil

Ricoeur was born February 27, 1913, in a small town about 42 kilometers south of Lyon, France. His mother died when Ricoeur was seven months old and his father was killed in World War I. His paternal grandparents were "devout Protestants"; they raised him and his sister (Reagan, 1996, p. 4). Throughout Ricoeur's education, he received support from the state that was offered to orphans of those killed in the Great War. After his grandmother died in 1928, his aunt cared for him and his sister. At the age of eight, Ricoeur met his sister's friend Simone, who became his wife in 1935. Ricoeur lost both his grandfather and sister before he began his studies at the Sorbonne, where he met Gabriel Marcel (1889–1973), who became a lifelong friend. From 1935 to 1940, much of Ricoeur's writing was on Christian Pacifism. When France declared war on Germany (September 3, 1939) after Germany had invaded Poland, Ricoeur went to war, only to be captured in 1940, becoming a prisoner of war for five years.

The prison years were unique in that Ricoeur and a number of prisoners who were scholars and novelists formed university courses and taught one another (Reagan, 1996, p. 10). Ricoeur's (1950/1966) first book, *Freedom and Nature*, emerged from that experience. After the war, "he received the Croix de Guerre with three palm leaves, but never wore it and never spoke about it" (Reagan, 1996, p. 8). Ricoeur's views toward war were contemptuous; he disconnected himself from honors he received from the conflict.

The reality of war and death made questions of the human condition ever so salient to Ricoeur. His friend Emmanuel Mounier, a Catholic intellectual, pacifist, and founder of the journal *Esprit*, died in 1932; they had been friends since college. Ricoeur paid his respects to his friend and mentor in "Emmanuel Mounier: A Personalist Philosopher," an essay first published in the December 1950 issue of *Esprit*. This article is a long intellectual biography that reviews

Mounier's philosophy and a whole generation of French intellectuals (Reagan, 1996, p. 20). Ricoeur's connection with war and evil gave rise to multiple interpretive projects; he sought to understand the text before him.

Shortly after the war, Ricoeur and Simone met André Philip (1902–1970), a French socialist who served as an interior minister for the Free French during the war and as a finance minister from 1946 to 1947. Philip told them about a small town in southern France, Le Chambon-sur-Lignon, where Pastor André Trocmé and his wife had given sanctuary to 2,500 Jews during the war and education was provided by Collège Cévenol. Ricoeur taught there from 1945 to 1948 and co-authored a major work on Karl Jaspers, who was known for his work on existentialism and his "…'situation-limit,' such as death, suffering, war, and evil" (Reagan, 1996, p. 16). Ricoeur also wrote a book that brought the work of Marcel and Jaspers together, examining the connections between "Marcel's 'incarnation'" and Jasper's stress on "situation-limite" and the understanding of "freedom, communication, and Transcendence" (Reagan, 1996, p. 16). During that time, he met Albert Camus, who was in the audience as Ricoeur discussed Camus's (1947/1948) *The Plague*. This period in Ricoeur's life was intellectually rich and served as an important transition from the war.

In Ricoeur's three-volume set of *Phenomenology of the Will*, he framed an account of Husserl's "eidetic method," which sought to disclose the essential ingredients of a phenomenon (Reagan, 1996, p. 18). For Ricoeur, the coordinates that constitute "will" include both the voluntary and the involuntary; he wanted to avoid a Descartian separation of mind and body. He worked with the notion of dialectic as a practical way to lessen a Descartian interpretive split of mind and body. Ricoeur rejected the assumption that the mind was the supreme agent of control. Ricoeur situated his project of examining the dialectic of the voluntary and involuntary under the genre of "philosophical anthropology," which attempts to understand the human condition (Reagan, 1996, p. 19).

Finding Direction

From 1956 to 1957, the Ricoeurs stayed in a building at *Les Mur Blancs* that had been bought by Mounier, which later housed Mounier's friends and widow. At this time, Ricoeur went beyond the "eidetic method" and into the "…'disproportion' within us between our possibilities and our limitations [that] renders us 'fragile'" (Reagan, 1996, p. 23). Ricoeur examined evil, both symbolically and metaphorically. Working with such issues took his phenomenology into a hermeneutic turn, represented by *Finitude and*

Culpability, which he published in two parts as *Fallible Man* and *The Symbolism of Evil* in 1960.

Ricoeur's interest in engaging evil was reflected in his scholarship and his politics. He rejected French policy related to the civil war in Algeria that began in 1956. He supported Algerian independence and was arrested on suspicion of harboring guns for the cause; he was later released, becoming "one of the most famous and well-known professors in France" (Reagan, 1996, p. 25). During that era, Ricoeur developed great interest in Freud, stressing hermeneutics of "suspicion," "culpability," "guilt," "semiotics of desire," and a dialectical interplay of "demasking" and "revelation of the sacred" (Reagan, 1996, p. 27). Ricoeur worked within a hermeneutic phenomenological dialectic of the "archeology of the subject" tied to a "teleology," which he understood as design or purpose (Reagan, 1996, p. 29). This study took Ricoeur to the examination of "symbols" that announce a sense of direction in "regressive" and "progressive," momentary paralysis in "guilt" and "consolation" (Reagan, 1996, p. 29). These terms assisted in his teleological interpretation of "forgiveness" and "hope," which returns a sense of direction to a human life (Reagan, 1996, p. 29). Ricoeur's "architectonic," an organized design that takes on a meaningful sense of structure, included Freud's notion of "illusion" with a dialectic of "revelation of the sacred" (Reagan, 1996, p. 31)— Ricoeur's task was to follow and detail the coordinates of human direction.

Ricoeur wrote a number of critical essays on the condition of the university in France that reshaped his own direction. Due to his critiques, Ricoeur took the opportunity to go to the University of Nanterre, a new university, which would later become the heart of the largest general strike in French history in 1968. Ricoeur left the Sorbonne in 1967 and became the doyen of the Faculty of Letters of the University of Nanterre one year later. As a pacifist and critical thinker, he did not expect the intensity of disruptions from leftist students and the constant battles between Maoists and Communists. On March 16, 1970, Ricoeur resigned as doyen due to ill health. One moment personified the ironical demands of the situation, when students abused guards at the university to the point of threatening them with lynching:

> The real irony of the situation became apparent when one of the guards said to a student, "I am a working man from a poor family, and you are the rich son of a wealthy family who is not working; so why are you attacking me in the name of the working class and calling me bourgeois? You are a spoiled bourgeois brat." (Reagan, 1996, p. 35)

At the juncture of his resignation, Ricoeur was deeply discouraged and turned his attention to his work on *The Symbolism of Evil*, within which he differentiated from the structuralism of Claude Levi-Strauss (1908–2009) with a stress on "…'accusation,' 'consolation, 'testimony,' 'guilt'…" (Reagan, 1996, p. 41). Ricoeur continued to examine the dialectic between existence and interpretive choice, which makes direction possible.

Looking for a necessary change in direction, Ricoeur joined the faculty at the University of Chicago, succeeding Paul Tillich (1886–1965) in the Divinity School where he completed *The Rule of Metaphor* (1975). Ricoeur discussed metaphor as requiring a referent that breaks with convention and opens the world of a text anew. Ricoeur then completed his groundbreaking work, *Time and Narrative* (1984). Ricoeur stated, "human action is a referent" for interpretive understanding (Reagan, 1996, p. 46). The focus on narrative yielded understanding of depth and clarity situated within emplotted events that capture the imagination, commitment, and actions of people, giving us insight into referents for interpretive understanding.

From Imitation to Genuine Testimony

In addition to emphasizing multiplicity of referents, Ricoeur stressed "mimesis," which gives rise to insights otherwise than imitation (Reagan, 1996, p. 47). With the notion of mimesis, Ricoeur stressed creative disclosure of a given text within time and narrative, neither of which remains stagnant and each reconfigures the other in the interpretive process (Reagan, 1996, p. 47). One finds the different, not the same, in interpretation. This work was met with acclaim and brought Ricoeur back to France, where many were rediscovering his scholarly insights. Ricoeur had outlived structuralist critics and was once again in intellectual demand, only to meet tragedy again with the death of his son, Olivier, by suicide. Life is not an imitation of some other event, but real drama that demands our participation. After the death of his son, Ricoeur increasingly used the terms "suffering" and "human action" (Reagan, 1996, p. 64). In the midst of great pain, Ricoeur completed a collection entitled *From Text to Action* (1986), as well as *Oneself as Another* (1990), framing identity over time as an act of "promise-making" (Reagan, 1996, p. 50). Ricoeur took seriously emotions that connected human beings with the demands of existential engagement; emotions remind us of the uniqueness of a given life. The combination of emotions awakens us, encouraging interpretive resiliency in the meeting of existence that shapes identity.

Ricoeur's work began to unite identity and ethics, stemming from the events at the University of Nanterre, the actions of the Lacanians,[3] and the sad loss of his son. Ricoeur worked with the dialectic of *idem* (self) and *ipse* (self and other) (Reagan, 1996, p. 75). Indeed, his earlier experience as a prisoner of war was of little consequence in comparison to the loss of his son. His work contrasted with the foundational claims of *cogito*; he stressed the weaker and more vulnerable understanding of information, *doxa*, or opinion, which is similar to testimony that there is both true and false (Reagan, 1996, p. 76). Ricoeur's interpretive work rests between skepticism and undue certainty, and in the meeting of human existence gives rise to human testimony.

Ricoeur's understanding of identity emerges through the communicative act of testimony and includes both "agent" and "action," with agent being the "referent" for action that gives rise to an identified referent that moves an event into action. He stated the importance of "who," "what," and "why" as a form of "ascription," which names the agent without moving to the level of "attribution" of motives (Reagan, 1996, pp. 79–82). Ricoeur pointed to "narrative identity" as the mediator between the character of sameness and promises of change of selfhood (Reagan, 1996, p. 85). Narrative identity resides between description and prescription, between sameness of character that can be counted on and a selfhood able to change in acts of responsibility. This stress on identity emerges from the responsibility of witnessing and led to Ricoeur's discussion of ethics and morals.

Ricoeur tied ethics to a teleological conception (a given direction) of the good life and tied morals to deontology shaped by norms and rules. Ethics lends itself to a life of "self-esteem," which includes a commitment to practices that move one toward "standards of excellence" and morals to a life of "self-respect" (Reagan, 1996, pp. 86–87). Ricoeur places ethics over morals in terms of significance, giving primacy to the former (Reagan, 1996, p. 86). The "good life," for Ricoeur, includes self-esteem and "solicitude," concern for others (Reagan, 1996, p. 87). Friendship is a form of solicitude inherent in interpersonal relationships and the institutional view of solicitude is justice; an ethics of friendship is reciprocal and the moral injunction of justice is "asymmetrical" (Reagan, 1996, p. 88). Friendship mediates self and other, inviting recognition of "irreplaceablity" and "nonsubstitutability" (Reagan, 1996, p. 88). Ricoeur conceptualized the justice dimension at the ethics/

---

3 The Lacanians were followers of Jacques Lacan (1901–1981), a French psychoanalyst who gained international fame as the interpreter of Sigmund Freud's work.

teleological level of interpersonal relations and the moral/deontological at the level of institutions. "Distributive justice" is the intermediary between ethics/teleology and morals/deontology[4] (Reagan, 1996, p. 90). The notion of a "social contract" is central to Rousseau (1762/2008), Kant (1959), and Rawls (1971); Ricoeur, however, counters with the fact that the social contract is a fiction and that we must strive to live with Others and within institutions, finding hope not in a contract, but in "practical wisdom" with one another (Reagan, 1996, p. 92).

Practical wisdom is an alternative to moral formalism played out in the notion of the universal and in institutions, and when the human limits of institutions meet bad decisions, they invite human "tragedy" (Reagan, 1996, p. 92). Ricoeur rejected both Habermas's assertion that all institutions and traditions yield a "crisis of legitimacy" and "Kant's categorical imperative: the universality of humanity and the individuality of each person as an 'end-in-himself'" (Reagan, 1996, p. 93). Practical wisdom requires us to meet existence with our actions offering a testimony that provides one side of justice, while the rules and norms of institutions hold up the other side. Testimony and institutional norms call for the importance of promise keeping that keeps selfhood connected to Others, finding a middle way of "critical solicitude" that walks between the universal and the communal/contextual (Reagan, 1996, p. 94).

Ricoeur stressed the importance of practical wisdom connected with testimony that works hand in hand with suspicion; for there is both good and bad testimony. Suspicion "haunts attestation" (Reagan, 1996, p. 97), but Nietzsche's suspicion cannot carry the day or we will fall into another form of "dogmatism" (Reagan, 1996, p. 98). Ricoeur's sense of testimony rejected "foundationalism" without succumbing to the extremes of selfhood on the one hand, and morality of institutions on the other (Reagan, 1996, p. 99). Ricoeur's practical wisdom works within limits and recognizes tragedy that necessarily haunts institutions and individual lives.

Ricoeur rejected "intuitionist" projects, from the tradition of Plato (427–347 BCE) to certain aspects of phenomenology, leaning closer to the work of

---

4 Teleology, from the Greek words *telos* (end), is described as "final causality." Aristotelian teleology states that a full explanation of anything must consider the final cause, the purpose for which something exists or was produced, in addition to the material, the formal and the efficient causes ("Teleology," 2011). Deontology, from the Greek word *deon* (duty), is, in contemporary moral philosophy, a normative theory regarding which choices are morally required, forbidden, or permitted. As a moral theory, deontology guides and assesses one's choices of what one ought to do ("Deontological Ethics," 2011).

Ernst Cassirer (1874–1945) and the "system of symbols," with hermeneutics engaged in the task of "explication of all the symbolic systems" (Reagan, 1996, pp. 100–101). Ricoeur's work rests between Gadamer's stress on "tradition" and Habermas's suspicion of "authority" (Reagan, 1996, p. 102). Ricoeur discarded Habermas's use of "communicative rationality" over "instrumental rationality" as inattentive enough to narrative reality (Reagan, 1996, p. 114). Additionally, the insights of Heidegger and the notion of suspicion shaped Ricoeur's emphasis on "conflict of interpretations" and "conflict of convictions" (Reagan, 1996, pp. 95–96). Conflict of interpretations and conflict of convictions require determination of the criteria or referent; it can be understood as the clashing of testimonies.

Ricoeur detailed a discourse of action that moves from descriptions to narration to prescription (Reagan, 1996, p. 118). Any reading of a text is not "innocent" (Reagan, 1996, p. 108), but "tainted" (Arnett, 2008) by a narrative referent. Narrative invites a telling, a testimony that has temporal limits and understands identity as embedded within narrative. Narrative carries debate of opposing views. Ultimately, for Ricoeur, the narrative of the human condition requires us to act and respond to existence even when the human condition demands suffering. How we act in response to suffering shapes the identity of our human responsibility in a particular moment and time.

Philosophy of Communication: *Zorba the Greek* and Philosophical Hermeneutics

Philosophical hermeneutics gives us insight into limits between and among competing traditions while stressing the importance of respect for that which we seek to understand. Through the interplay of difference and respect, responsibility becomes the signature for interpretation. Additionally, a confessional orientation shapes philosophical hermeneutics; one makes public the biased perspective that guides one's entrance into a given interpretive task. What we proclaim as an interpretive insight is a display of human testimony that then invites others into the conversation, beginning another cycle of difference, respect, and responsibility as interpretive keys. Uniting difference, respect, and responsibility is a demanding task but is the heart of Zorba's existential engagement with others.

In *Zorba the Greek*, Boss and Zorba bring contrasting bias or prejudice to their daily engagement with existence and with one another. Each narrates life quite differently, resulting in contrasting views on life. Boss asks Zorba to define what a human being actually is, and Zorba responds by saying the human being is a "brute" (Kazantzakis, 1946/1952, p. 64). Zorba gives advice to Boss: keep your distance, stay away from human beings. The narrative contrast between the two men is clear.

> That man [Zorba] has not been to school, I [Boss] thought, and his brains have not been perverted. He has had all manner of experiences; his mind is open and his heart has grown bigger, without his losing one ounce of his primitive boldness. All the problems which we find so complicated or insoluble he cuts through as if with a sword, like Alexander the Great cutting the Gordian knot. It is difficult for him to miss his aim, because his two feet are held firmly planted on the ground by the weight of his whole body. (Kazantzakis, 1946/1952, p. 74)

Zorba's feet are on the ground. Boss has his head in books and is writing a book on Buddha. Boss even becomes sick as he watches Zorba dance with such passion. He demands that Zorba stop before the dance claims him through death. Zorba's life is a dance that testifies to the power of life against an inevitable foe. For Zorba, dance is the bodily form of philosophical hermeneutics. He reminds us of the importance of the doing, engaging in interpretation, and, in this case, offering a testimony through the necessity of dance.

Zorba is an exemplar of Gadamer's and Ricoeur's use of contradictory terms that frame a unique contribution to philosophy of communication, relying on terms such as "bias" and "respect" in the interpretive process.

1. Bias or prejudice is inevitable. Zorba brings a clear bias to life that gives him insight and a sense of character. It is not our neutrality that shapes identity, but the uniqueness of the perspective that we bring to a given event. Creativity comes from what we bring to a typical event, moving the normative to the unexpected.

2. We bring positions to the table of conversation, giving us different insights and opinions about information. Zorba understands that much of life rests with our views about information, not just information alone. We bring opinions that texture and shape discourse and our perception about human events. Information is the text that begins the conversation; it is opinion that moves one into communicative action.

3. Whenever we interpret, we need to have respect for a given text, curtailing the impulse to overwhelm a text with our own subjective demands. Zorba displays bias in his particular view of life throughout

the novel. He also reveals the ability to offer respect to others in his own inevitable fashion. Zorba extends respect to others throughout the novel; he is able to affirm persons who bring difference to the table of conversation. Additionally, he is able to struggle and fight for opinions that require active communicative support.

4. The movement from behavior to action requires situating events within a narrative that provides a meaningful context for understanding. Zorba's behavior is often odd—at first glance and without knowing the "why" of his actions. In the novel we read the context, the "why" for his behavior, that often rests outside the pale of normative conventions. The story about the place, Zorba's life, and the relationship with Boss and all the other characters shift the stress from behavior alone to action that is story laden.

Zorba reminds us that the task of interpretation in philosophical hermeneutics begins with novel understandings of tradition, respect, and the pragmatics of dialogic learning and understanding. Philosophical hermeneutics offers testimony for what one understands, taking interpretive insight into the public arena, a dwelling composed of different interpretative conceptions— often on the same event and topic.

CHAPTER 7

EMPATHY AND THE OTHER: A PHENOMENOLOGICAL PERSPECTIVE

The notion of empathy has deep roots in philosophical scholarly understanding; it is rooted in the German word *Einfühlung*. The term, coined by German philosopher Robert Vischer (1847–1933) in 1873, was first tied to aesthetics, then connected to psychology in the work of Theodor Lipps (1851–1914) (Wispé, 1987, p. 18), and, perhaps most importantly, found in the insights of Sigmund Freud (1856–1939) (Wispé, 187, p. 25). In scholarly communication journals, there have been more than 55 articles published with the word "empathy" in the title between 1946 and 2010. The term has been an active metaphor for discussion of a human sense that attends to the subjective meaning experienced by another. From a philosophical perspective, one of the most important scholarly figures associated with the notion of empathy was Edith Stein. The task of this chapter is to exemplify the notion of empathy through one of the term's most energetic advocates, centering on the life and scholarship of Edith Stein. This particular scholar connects empathy with the development of personhood and with her scholarly interest in phenomenology.

Introduction

Stein was an exemplar of the significance of empathy in the shaping of personhood in the human condition. Stein's existence was a rich combination of philosophical insight and religious commitment that brought her to the study and application of empathy. Stein's life is a tragic witness to what happens when empathy is eclipsed in our engaging of another. The Nazis killed Edith Stein on August 9, 1942, because she was born Jewish, ignoring her conversion to Christianity in 1921 and her becoming a Catholic nun in 1934. Her life and scholarship offer a phenomenological conception of empathy.

This chapter explores the vitality of empathy in the human condition through three major sections: (1) a biographical portrait of Edith Stein's life and philosophy, offering some insight into the drama that shaped her half-century on this earth; (2) an examination of Stein's understanding of empathy and its foundational importance for the development of personhood; and (3) the implications of empathy for philosophy of communication illustrated through the novel *Zorba the Greek.*

Communicative life, understood and engaged without an underpinning of empathy for and toward others, opens the door to the shadow side of our living with one another, a flawed and raw form of what Herbert Spencer (1820–1903) detailed as the "survival of the fittest" (1866, p. 444). The work of Francis Charles Montague (1885) considered this notion deeply problematic in that the "survival of the fittest" is void of attentiveness to the struggles of others. However, Stein's description of empathy is closer to the insights of Montague than to the modern connection of empathy with psychology. Stein's life and death revealed some of the horrors that emerge when the refusal to extend empathy becomes normative.

Stein: Consciousness of Light, Engulfed in Darkness

Stein (1891–1942) was a German Jewish–Christian intellectual. She was born a Prussian citizen in Breslau and was intellectually engrossed from the beginning of her life, "taking [in 1915] a supplementary examination in Greek at Johannes Gymnasium in Breslau" (Stein, 1989, p. 119). She became a nun at the age of 42 and then lost her life at the hands of the Nazis at Auschwitz at the age of 50. Alasdair MacIntyre (2006), in his major work on Stein, begins his philosophical analysis with two basic assumptions: (1) Edith Stein is worthy of much study, an outstanding scholar who became a Catholic nun who has been canonized (October 11, 1998) with the full name of St. Teresa Benedicta a Cruce; and (2) Stein's integration of philosophy and practice renders insight into the creative potential of the life-giving character of the study and the doing of philosophy.

Phenomenological Beginnings

Stein's work in phenomenology is recognized because of her independent thinking, innovative scholarship, and long-term work and collaboration with Edmund Husserl (1859–1938), the founder of phenomenology. In Herbert Spiegelberg's two-volume work on *The Phenomenological Movement*, there are seven references to her phenomenological scholarship (Baseheart, 1997, p. ix). The contention of Mary Catharine Baseheart (1997) is that "Stein is a philosopher of consciousness" (p. x). Consciousness in phenomenology assumes a referent—consciousness of/about something and of/about a given object. Empathy is a particular expression of a phenomenological consciousness that occupied much of Stein's life. Stein understood the human being as more than a thinking subject who assumes that one should embrace relentless certitude as an achievable reality in a world of human finitude. She contended that a phenomenological consciousness is more fundamental than thinking, and empathy is an expression of a phenomenological consciousness that bridges chasms between persons.

Stein understood phenomenology and Husserl's commitment to the "things themselves" while being ever aware of the impact of culture, history, and particularity of perspective in the development of ideas. She sought a re-discovery of what is termed "perennial philosophy" (Baseheart, 1997, p. 123). "She defines *perennial philosophy* [as] 'the never-resting search of the human spirit for true being'" (Baseheart, 1997, p. 123). Stein's philosophy of the person and her connection of phenomenology with faith add a unique flavor to her work. She was a scholar who sought to understand the person without forgetting a basic assumption—we are temporal creatures with limited insights living within a world that connects to the eternal, to a God who walks with us in our lived experience.

Stein's faith commitment is akin to a well-known story about a person looking back on one's life after death and seeing footprints in the sand, sometimes one set and sometimes two. The person asks why at times there is only one set of footprints. The answer is that at such times God carried the person. This manner of faith and thought was more than a popular poster for Edith Stein; she lived the faith. When the Nazis took her, one can imagine Stein taking time to thank God for carrying her one last time before she was about to be killed. Stein's philosophy and faith shape what it means to be a person, connected to the eternal and responsive to the temporal demands of the everyday.

Edith Stein's life stresses the notion of "chiaroscuro," the study of the interplay of light and darkness (Baseheart, 1997, p. 1). Leonardo da Vinci used this method in painting with shades of darkness and light; he was the technique's most famous leader (Upgren, 1998, p. 139). Additionally, in Jewish theology, confidence in "holy sparks" comes from and out of dwellings of darkness (Buber, 1958, p. 187). This interplay of dark and light lends clarity to the manner in which Stein, as a scholar and as a person of faith, met and understood existence. Stein was able to discern darkness in the midst of human life; her faith gave her courage to attend to what was, forgoing what she demanded of life.

Interestingly, her second publication, entitled *An Investigation Concerning the State*, examined the relationship between the person and the community and emerged out of her hospital service during World War I. Unlike Husserl, Stein was attracted to metaphysical questions. From the years 1922 to 1931, as Stein taught at St. Magdalena's Girls Academy and at a training institute for teachers in Speyer, she continued to work with various dimensions of Thomas Aquinas's scholarship. She maintained her mutual friendship with Edmund

Husserl until his death in 1938. In between the years of 1928 and 1932, Stein engaged in an active series of lecture tours in Germany and Austria; her theme was women in education. In 1931, she left her teaching post to devote more time to researching and writing these lectures. Then, in the spring of 1932, "she was named to the chair of scientific pedagogy at the German Institute for Educational Theory at Münster in Westphalia, where her first series of lectures was on the structure of the human person" (Baseheart, 1997, p. 25). Edith Stein recognized the Nazi threat early on, as well as the danger of Hitler's appeals to pride that were locally and internationally grounded and cemented by hatred of a people—the Jews. In the early 1930s, she requested a private papal visit and was given the opportunity to meet in a small group; Stein refused (Baseheart, 1997, pp. 25–26). Stein was denied the opportunity to be of any service in Nazi Germany; she resigned from teaching at Münster in 1933 and entered the Carmelite convent on October 12, 1933.

In the Company of Others

Stein was the youngest of 11 children, growing up in Germany in an area that is now Poland. Of her ten siblings, four of them died in infancy. She wrote an unfinished autobiography, *Life in a Jewish Family*, which was published in 1986 and outlined her life in a Jewish family from the years 1891 to 1916. In school, her classmates often resented her; she brought to learning a combination of ambition and intelligence. Fortunately, she was able to make friends easily and displayed a deep sense of social responsibility. She had an in-depth knowledge of and interest in beginnings/origins, preparing her for later work in phenomenology.

Stein transferred to the University of Göttengen in the spring of 1913, close to the time in which Edmund Husserl was doing his early writing on phenomenology. Husserl had published his book *Logical Investigations* (1900–1901) a decade earlier. Stein was impressed with Husserl's work and with the insights of another professor, Max Scheler (1874–1928), whose approach to phenomenology was different than that of Husserl; he founded what is now known as "philosophical anthropology" (Gálvez, 2010, p. 7). Additionally, Stein was impressed with Adolf Reinach (1883–1917), one of Husserl's finest students. Reinach was known for his ability to make Husserl's ideas accessible to students; he even offered clarity to Husserl about his own writing. Stein met Reinach when she was 29; Reinach increasingly introduced Stein and others to an understandable version of Husserl. Reinach, like Husserl, moved in a direction contrary to the "psychologism" of Gottlob Frege (1848–1925) and Theodor Lipps (MacIntyre, 2006, p. 17), announcing the power and the uniqueness of the notion, "to the things themselves."

Husserl extended an intellectual tradition initiated by Franz Brentano (1838–1917) and Kazimierz Twardowski (1866–1938). These two men stressed the notion of "intentionality" in understanding a given phenomenon (MacIntyre, 2006, p. 23). According to Husserl (1931/1991), "Conscious processes are also called *intentional*; but then the word intentionality signifies nothing else than this universal fundamental property of consciousness: to be consciousness *of* something; as a *cogito*, to bear within itself its *cogitatum*" (p. 33). Reinach understood Husserl's conception of intentionality, which contended with Immanuel Kant's (1724–1804) understanding of "necessity"; Reinach sided with Hume's view of "the immediate grounding of necessity through experience" (MacIntyre, 2006, p. 51). David Hume (1711–1776) had stated what Reinach, and later Stein, understood as a view of social acts that could unify "I," "me," and "my" in the making of "promises" (MacIntyre, 2006, pp. 59–60).

Husserl connected with the intentionality of Franz Brentano, was cognizant of differences between Hume and Kant, and affirmed Hume's stress on "sensations" (MacIntyre, 2006, p. 29), which led Husserl to emphasize the "nonphilosophical" or "prephilosophical" understanding of perception that begins with "sense impressions" (MacIntyre, 2006, p. 29). Husserl read Hume with openness to his perspective, viewing his insights as phenomenological. Husserl's insights were also contrary to Kant's infatuation with "Newtonian" laws and more akin to "quantum mechanics"; intentionality assumes that understanding sensations and experience involve the interplay of subject and object (MacIntyre, 2006, p. 48). Stein agreed with intentionality, which united a life of faith. Stein, however, rejected Husserl's assertion that each standpoint will render a different perception (MacIntyre, 2006, pp. 59–60). Stein contributed to her own view of intentionality, which contained the possibility of perceptual consistency.

One of many empathic turning points for Stein was when she turned in her thesis in November of 1915 and immediately reported to Mährisch-Weisskirchen, a Red Cross hospital in Moravia, Austria, that served those with contagious diseases. The patients were largely connected to the military academy; Stein was so selfless in her service that she was awarded a medal of valor for her volunteer work. During her time at the hospital, she had but two books to read—Husserl's *Ideen* (1913) and Homer's epic poems. During the First World War, Stein had no doubt "that the values at stake in the conflict were those of *Kultur*, values threatened by French cynicism, British commercial self-seeking and Russian barbarism" (MacIntyre, 2006, p. 69).

Stein lived in Germany because she had a desire for excellence without forgetting the importance of the local. Stein endorsed this aspirational principle in an effort to assist teaching and scholarship, which she did by studying half into the night. Eventually, Stein's teaching impacted her health; she resigned in 1916 from her old school, Realgymnasium of the Viktoriaschule (secondary school of the Victorian school), in order to find time to finish her manuscript on empathy.

Stein's *On the Problem of Empathy* was her doctoral dissertation; upon completing the manuscript, Stein went to Freiburg where she met Martin Heidegger (1889–1976). At dinner with Heidegger and others, she was surprised that his conversation was consistent with his inaugural lecture, "What Is Metaphysics?" His words undercut and critiqued phenomenology and Husserl without much subtlety. Stein's keen interest in phenomenology was tempered by her commitment to metaphysical philosophy and classical and Catholic perspectives. She was a prolific writer; *On the Problem of Empathy*, one of her most important works, was completed under Husserl at the University of Freiburg. Stein commented on Husserl's *Logical Investigations*, stating, "they seemed to find his work a turning away from idealism toward a new form of realism" (Baseheart, 1997, p. 21). She understood the "I" as consciousness in an ongoing flux or stream of what we call lived experience; she did not assume, contrary to Husserl, that one could engage in a phenomenological reduction that suspended all judgment. Even in her dissertation, Stein's intellectual independence was present. Her first experience at university, specifically the University of Breslau, had her specializing in psychology. The University of Göttingen then offered the opportunity for Stein to connect to the insights of Edmund Husserl and philosophy, and with two major characteristics that would remain consistent throughout her life: love of learning and love of God.

After Husserl read Stein's (1989) thesis, originally entitled "The Empathy Problem as It Developed Historically and Considered Phenomenologically," Husserl was impressed (p. xiii). However, during her association with Husserl, Stein continued her interest in Catholicism and religion; she was significantly influenced by Max Scheler (1874–1928). Scheler inspired many of his pupils, helping them find their way back to religion that connected phenomenology to faith. The interplay of phenomenology and Catholicism led Edith Stein, at the age of 42, to enter Carmel convent in 1933 as a postulant in the contemplative life of the Carmelites. Six months later, Edith Stein became

Sister Teresa Benedicta of the Cross and donned the brown and white habit that was characteristic of the nuns of the Carmelite order.

Sister Teresa

When Edith Stein began to read the autobiography of Sister Teresa Benedicta of the Cross, she sensed a call to enter the Catholic Church. According to MacIntyre (2006), Stein associated four major issues with Sister Teresa's life: (1) history connected to God and a life of prayer; (2) the importance of shedding obstacles that get in the way of God's presence; (3) a flat rejection of false spirituality that fails in understanding God as embodied within human nature and human interaction; and (4) the danger of being deceived, which requires one to distinguish between "natural and worldly prejudices" (MacIntyre, 2006, p. 168). Stein took this commitment with the name into cloistered life in 1933. Immediately upon her entrance, Stein began to work on an important project entitled *Finite and Eternal Being*; her writing did not cease.

As Teresa Benedicta of the Cross, Stein was assigned the task of research and writing. Her first assignment was to index the translation of Aquinas's *De Veritate*; this manuscript was composed of more than 1,300 pages. Additionally, she completed her treatise *Finite and Eternal Being*. This work brought together phenomenological and Thomistic elements, displaying her analysis of the metaphysical structure of being. Her understanding of being began with the first Being (God) and one's connection to the first Being. She also spent a great deal of time reading the work of Jacques Maritain (1882–1973). Her last work, *The Science of the Cross*, remained uncompleted when the Gestapo arrested her before losing her life at the hands of the Nazis in August 1942. The thread that runs through her work is the importance of empathy, the connecting link between the person and the community.

On Christmas Eve 1936, her sister Rosa visited and was a baptized into the Catholic Church. In 1938, at the time of voting, Sister Benedicta had to declare her non-Aryan status. This made her presence at the Carmel convent dangerous for her and the other nuns. Stein left for the Carmel at Echt in Holland, which offered to house her, in April 1938.

In 1940, Stein welcomed her sister Rosa into the convent at Echt; the two were planning to escape German-occupied territory, but were unable to do so due to complications of trying to find a place for Rosa. This delay made it difficult for them to quickly escape. Although the Catholic bishops issued a pastoral letter in 1942 protesting the persecution of Catholic Jews, Nazi reprisal against the letter ordered all Catholic Jews to be deported within a few days. On August 2, two S.S. officers ordered Teresa and Rosa to leave the convent, after which they were promptly taken to a prison camp at Amersfoort in the Netherlands. On August 7, the sisters were transported from Westerbork to Auschwitz. Judicial testimony later reported that no one on the transport survived. "In 1950, the official Dutch Gazette published the names of all Jews who had been deported from Holland on August 7, 1942. Among them was the name of Edith Stein, and the date of death was listed as August 9, 1942" (Baseheart, 1997, p. 20). The Nazis killed Edith Stein at the age of 50; she left behind a legacy of empathic building between cultures, offering reconciliation between persons in her faithful walk in the midst of hatred and human darkness, announcing the importance of an empathy that sheds light and hope.

Empathy: A Phenomenological Bridge

Stein's conception of the human person and the necessity of sociality gave her natural rationale for the study and the importance of empathy between persons. The background of empathy begins with the importance of a "givenness," which consists "of primordial experience to phenomenological analyses of person and community" (Baseheart, 1997, p. 30). Stein claimed that Husserl's notion of empathy followed the early work of Theodore Lipps's notion of empathy, beginning with an acknowledged lack, a grasping at a "foreign consciousness" (Baseheart, 1997, p. 32). Alternatively, empathy, for Stein, was both primordial in its present experience and simultaneously non-primordial in terms of its content; "empathy is a kind of act of perceiving" (Baseheart, 1997, p. 33). Stein disagreed, however, with Lipps's understanding of the goal of empathy as a coming together, the complete oneness of two subjects. For a similar reason, Stein rejected Scheler's "theory of imitation," the transfer of feeling from one to another (Baseheart, 1997, p. 34). Stein rejected the notion of "inner perception" and talked about the importance of an "inner intuition" (Baseheart, 1997, p. 35). She was even harsher on Hugo Münsterberg's (1863–1916) theory that attempted to understand "foreign acts of will" that were imposed from the outside (Baseheart, 1997, p. 35).

For Stein, empathy involved the unity of the "I," which grasps the other "both cognitively and affectively" (Baseheart, 1997, p. 37). She situated the "I" within a living body, terming this a form of "sensual empathy" (Baseheart, 1997, p. 38). Empathy rests in the interplay of an intersubjective world between persons. The spiritual person begins with concentration on feeling; Stein understood human sentiment as fundamental in shaping what we call rationality (Baseheart, 1997, p. 40). Stein acknowledged that there is a controversy over what the notion of empathy is, with her understanding of empathy as beginning with "sensory appearance" that makes known data comprehended from the encountering of "foreign experience" (Stein, 1989, p. 6). Empathy is not an outer perception, but rather an inner one; it is not primordial. "It [empathy] is neither the primordial experience nor the 'assumed' one" (Stein, 1989, p. 14). Empathy becomes a form of "reflexive sympathy" Stein (1989) cited Scheler, who understood empathy as perceiving "foreign" consciousness with an "inward 'I'" (p. 27). She differentiated between primordial and non-primordial experience; this distinction permits one to understand the complexity of difference between sympathy and empathy (Stein, 1989, p. 34). Sympathy is primordial; sympathy is the manner in which we are wired as human beings to one another. Sympathy assists us in the sensual engagement of a given environment. Empathy requires the same sympathetic attentiveness, and in addition, includes the reflective act upon the senses that affects the body and/or comes from an internal response to an external sensation; in both cases, reflection from the inner workings of the person make empathy possible.

The "pure 'I'" finds constitution from the continuing creation of a sense of "selfness" that only emerges when one meets foreignness or otherness; selfness generates "individuality" as one learns to make "qualitative variations" between selfness and otherness (Stein, 1989, pp. 38–39). This pure sense of "I" lives in what Stein understood as the living soul of the human being. The "I" lives and grows from "sensations" of feelings, situated within a "living body" that senses (Stein, 1989, p. 43). Phenomenologically, this statement finds validity in what is called the "phantom limb" phenomenon (Murray, 2010). The sensations of feelings give rise to "general feelings" that are "non-somatic" or what we commonly call "moods" (Stein, 1989, p. 49); they are secondary to primary senses that shape a body and give rise to a particular understanding of character in a given day. Stein does not, however, connect sensations and feelings to causality alone; she acknowledges the power of the human will in which "what is truly creative about volition is not a causal effect" (Stein, 1989, p. 56). The reality of will makes it possible to emit coldness, as well as empathy, to another in an otherwise pleasant conversation. Unlike sympathy, empathy has a connection to human will, permitting one to assist another when all sensations demand otherwise.

Stein engaged a phenomenological rendering of empathy as the natural act beyond sympathy. Her work traced back to Wilhelm Dilthey (1833–1911), whom she called "the Newton of the Human Studies" (Baseheart, 1997, p. 42). She was interested in the human sciences, which offered a corrective to Hume by connecting sensations to the "life-force" of humanness (Baseheart, 1997, p. 42). Stein understood empathy as including the psychic and spiritual dimensions of being human. She defined the notion of person as the gestalt that connects a "three-fold oneness" of "body-soul-spirit" (Baseheart, 1997, p. 56). She moved the human person from causal and rational engagement alone to a "realm of grace" without losing the individuality of the "I" (Baseheart, 1997, p. 56). This unique conception of the human person meets the notion of community. Human community calls forth the spirit of the "I." Human community, the spirit, and the "I" require a bridge that connects one person to another. The human function of empathy is that it functions as a phenomenological bridge between persons.

Community

Human community is constituted by a sociality that can lead one constructively and also in problematic directions. One can be deceived by empathy and find that the "unity of meaning" has generated a "false" comprehension (Stein, 1989, pp. 84–85). What permits correction to take place is yet another emphatic response of the senses that has one reflect upon the unity of the meaning of a given activity. For Stein (1989), empathy has both a "nature" and a "spirit" functioning together, with the latter offering a theoretical framework from which to situate or structure a given empathic understanding and corrective to an initial emphatic gesture (p. 112).

Stein moved from discussion of sympathy as primordial to a non-primordial form of reflection tied to empathy. The individual becomes a person through empathy that attends to foreignness, reflects on difference, and attends to sensations that emanate from otherness, which give rise to the uniqueness of personhood in the ongoing reflective understanding of selfness—we are shaped by that which we meet that is not our "I." Empathy assists in the recognition of the differences between and among us. For Stein, empathy is the communicative link that connects a person to community, education and existence, human essence in existence, and the finite and the eternal, with each connection enlarging a sense of the person.

Stein concerned herself with the surrounding world, *Umwelt*. She understood that one of the ways in which an individual becomes a person is through three different forms of collective association: "mass," "society," and "community" (Baseheart, 1997, p. 62). Mass association assumes that people are grouped together in a given place; they are part of a temporary herd, an "ensemble of individuals" (Baseheart, 1997, p. 62). Society, or Gesellschaft, has both a personal and spiritual sense of bond with a commitment to a "common goal" (Baseheart, 1997, p. 62). A society has a number of "functions" that assist in the obtaining of common goals—the nature of these goals and functions shape identity in a given society, announcing its "character" (Baseheart, 1997, p. 63). There is interplay between the character of a society and those who live within a given society.

Stein's view of community was largely connected to the work of German sociologist Ferdinand Tönnies (1855-1936).[1] "Ferdinand Tönnies…considers community as a natural, organic grouping of individuals, in contrast to society, which he described as an artificial union resting solely on the rational deliberation regarding means to the end or goal" (Baseheart, 1997, p. 63). The essence of community is a common life of a subject meeting a subject, which is in contrast to a subject meeting an object. Communities require an "authentic" rather than an "inauthentic" existence, which supports common practices (Baseheart, 1997, p. 65).

Stein did not confuse a community with a society; she rejected the Nazi connection of Das Folk, which required a blood connection, to society. Society is a place of many communities and should not be constructed with one privileged sense of gathering that excludes all others. Stein stated that when faith and society clash, the former must trump; however, no healthy society can require total religious agreement—both the faithful and not-so-faithful must have a place within a society. Stein considered the State a natural act, ignoring the assertions of Rousseau (1712–1778) and Locke (1632–1704). The State protects sovereignty of a place, which makes individual freedom possible as long as multiple communities have a place within the society. In each case, "mass," "society," and "community" are central to human association and fundamental to the framing of the person. For Stein, the task of society is not simply to enhance individual freedom, but to augment empathy that has a moral obligation to attend to all, not just those like me. Additionally, education has the same social function as society, opening the way to new social insights, reminding persons of meaning and

---

1 A German sociologist, Tönnies's theories reconciled the organic and social-contract conceptions of society. A teacher at the University of Kiel, Tönnies was known throughout Great Britain for his English-language editions of Thomas Hobbes's writings ("Ferdinand Tönnies," 2011).

labor for something larger than oneself.

Education and Existence

Stein was an advocate for woman in education. She understood the human being as composed of "double species" of man and woman (Baseheart, 1997, p. 81). The human condition requires differing perspectives of man and woman. Stein worked from the 1919 Constitution of the Reich, which gave women full equality and citizenship. These rights, however, were not played out in higher education. As stated above, Stein was denied positions, first due to her gender at the Universities of Göttingen, Freiburg, and Breslau, and then because of anti-Semitism. After Stein completed her Ph.D. at the University of Freiburg, she became Husserl's assistant but left shortly after, largely because Husserl refused to treat her as a colleague; he would not read her material or comment on her insights. Gender limitations propelled her commitment to an educational system open to widening the horizons of women.

Stein wanted to bring forth the perspective of women, stressing their "special characteristics" and contrasting perspectives that must be taken into account if one is to study and understand the sociality of the human being (Baseheart, 1997, p. 80). Schooling is essential for intellect, will, and feeling to work together creatively. Stein did not demand that women be eligible to become priests in the Catholic Church, but she repeatedly stated that nothing "dogmatic" in Church teaching precluded such a possibility (Baseheart, 1997, p. 87).

Stein was interested in "essential structures" of the person in various dimensions of life (Baseheart, 1997, p. 88). She worked with the metaphysics of essence and existence and was more inclined to "realism" than Husserl (Baseheart, 1997, p. 88). She asserted that each being has one essence with an "individual essence" tied to a "universal essence" (Baseheart, 1997, p. 90). Her insights differed from Husserl in the formal manner in which she understood essence, stressing terms that Husserl did not use: (1) "being-in-the-mind," which is a second way of describing "at hand"; (2) "being-in the-divine intellect," which points to the "timeless realm of essential meaning" posited by God; and (3) *Existenz*, which includes the notions of real and ideal objects in being (Baseheart, 1997, pp. 92–93). Stein's major difference with Husserl was the focus upon essences. Human life consists of two basic formations: "material-formed life" and "spiritual-personal interior life" (Baseheart, 1997, p. 99). Stein's work centered on the movement from individual to person; she sought to make present structures and essences that abide in this transformation. Increasing individuation leads to a deeper and richer understanding of the essence of personhood.

Stein connected her work to Husserl's with her view of "intuition," understood outside the trappings of "mysticism" and "irrationalism" (Baseheart, 1997, p. 102). Following Husserl's lead, she understood intuition as propelled by the "bodily eye" (sensation) and the intellect supported by the "mental eye" (Baseheart, 1997, p. 103). "This is Husserl's so-called *categorical intuition*, which is a complex act, founded on sensory intentions, in which the sphere of sensibility (*Sinnlichkeit*) is left, and the sphere of intellect is entered" (Baseheart, 1997, p. 104). It is through experience that "individual essence" is brought to "givenness" and cannot be phenomenologically understood without "eidetic reduction," which seeks to bracket all things that cloud the possibility of getting to the thing itself phenomenologically (Baseheart, 1997, p. 104). Stein sought to understand the thing itself, never assuming that human beings could have perfect knowledge. All knowing is temporal and partial. Stein wanted to know an essence without perfect knowledge; she understood life as bigger than individual perception. Stein's commitment to phenomenology, limits, and engagement with the eternity of the faith took her naturally to the examination of the ongoing dialectic of the finite and the infinite in the ongoing development of sociality.

Finite and the Eternal

Stein's incorporation of the "consciousness-conscious philosophy" and "God-conscious philosophy" took her work to the interplay of the "finite" and the "infinite" (Baseheart, 1997, pp. 110–111). This move separated her insights from those of Martin Heidegger, who understood anxiety unto death, with Stein having a confidence in God that is a "pre-apprehension," placing life on the firm ground of eternal assurance (Baseheart, 1997, p. 113). Stein did philosophy and phenomenology within a faith commitment in an effort to understand the "flux" or stream of consciousness against a background of an eternal promise (Baseheart, 1997, p. 119). She united temporality and finitude with infinity and eternity through discussion of "potency and act," with eternity as an act without an end (Baseheart, 1997, p. 117). Unlike the apodictic impulse for pure and certain knowledge, Stein embraced the mystery of not knowing as central to being human, even as one seeks greater and greater insight into given phenomena and experience. The interplay of the finite and the eternal is central to Stein's attraction to both Husserl and Aquinas.

Stein considered Husserl's insights as vital and necessary preparation for her later work with Aquinas. On Husserl's 70th birthday, Stein published an essay in honor of Husserl that examined what she considered the close connections between Aquinas and Husserl, entitled "Husserl's Phenomenology and the Philosophy of St. Thomas Aquinas: Attempts at a Comparison." As stated above, one of the major influences on Husserl was Franz Brentano;[2] it is through Brentano that the connection to Aquinas became clearer. Brentano was educated within a strict Catholic setting and had constant interaction with those citing Aquinas and the importance of the "logos" or "ratio," with both Aquinas and Husserl committed to the power of reason (Baseheart, 1997, p. 130). Husserl only emphasized "natural reason" and Aquinas stressed both "natural reason" and "supernatural reason" that was connected to the faith (Baseheart, 1997, p. 131).

Husserl was interested in getting to the things themselves. Aquinas revealed a truth in whatever was possible that emerged from the ground of faith and offered a "philosophy of life" (Baseheart, 1997, p. 135). Husserl worked with a "transcendental phenomenology" that moved increasingly away from a medieval task of framing philosophy for living within the material conditions of a given place and time (Baseheart, 1997, p. 136). Husserl separated the terms "ontology" and "metaphysics," which is common in phenomenological work. Aquinas wrote from a metaphysical position without ignoring the world around him.

Interestingly, the study of phenomenology was used by some to encourage a revival of scholasticism in a common commitment to "essence-analysis" (Baseheart, 1997, p. 138). Both phenomenology and scholasticism begin with the senses, involving the intellect in understanding, then parting ways on the question of active or passive intellect, with scholasticism being the former and phenomenology the latter. Ultimately, the common feature between Aquinas and Husserl, for Stein, was the pursuit of truth, with Husserl beginning with consciousness and Aquinas commencing with faith. Both were methodical in their work and attempted to gather insight through meticulous inquiry, with Aquinas, like Stein, understanding that the ultimate rests in faith, not in the penultimate certainty of worldly knowledge. Stein's life and scholarship united phenomenology and faith, Husserl and Aquinas, and metaphysical and existential concerns, leading her to an explication of the human person formed

---

2 Franz Brentano (1838–1917) was a German philosopher generally regarded as the founder of intentionalism or act psychology, which is more concerned with the mind's acts rather than its contents ("Franz Brentano," 2011).

in community and connected to others in and with a phenomenological understanding of empathy connected to the faith.

Philosophy of Communication: *Zorba the Greek* and Empathy

Edith Stein offers a meaning conception of philosophy of communication through her scholarship and life. It is so common to find separation between theory and practice or words and action that when we do discover such a union, we must acknowledge that we are in the presence of something quite special. Edith Stein was, indeed, a special person, giving us hope when hope for many seemed ever so silent. In Stein's life and faith, we find a congruence that offers confidence of response from another. If one is looking for a friend or someone to whom one can offer advice, the hope is that such a person will unite word and deed, giving us a chance to witness ideas in actions. One can make the case that if one cannot unite word and deed, at least on some occasions, doing philosophy of communication is not possible. Stein goes even further than the typical expectation for such congruence—her life and work united word and deed in an exemplary fashion with the Catholic Church bestowing upon her the title of saint. Zorba, on the other hand, will never be confused with a saint. However, he gives us insight into the possibility of congruence of word and deed in the life of an ordinary man with an extraordinary capacity for friendship.

When Zorba is on a trip, he pens a letter to Boss, who then reads the letter to Madame Hortense. Boss does not, however, simply read Zorba's words. He adds material to the letter that Zorba did not write, stating that Zorba wants to marry Madame Hortense. Zorba returns and discovers the lie told by Boss. Zorba is furious, but with a deep sense of empathy, he finds a way to "marry" Madame Hortense. Boss is Zorba's best man, and Madame Hortense almost collapses with joy as Zorba becomes her "husband." Note, however, that Zorba has appointed himself the director of the marriage bureau, allowing him to officiate his own "marriage" (Kazantzakis, 1946/1952, p. 246). Zorba's empathy for Madame Hortense functions as a phenomenological bridge to another human being; Zorba finds a way to orchestrate a fictional, but phenomenologically real, marriage. Zorba manifests a passion for life and others.

Zorba's empathy is for the non-trodden; he is not propelled by abstract principles. Zorba has learned empathy for the other before him. He states that he was "rescued from my country, from priests, and from money. I began sifting things, sifting more and more things out. I lighten my burden that way. I—

how shall I put it?—I find my own deliverance, I become a man" (Kazantzakis, 1946/1952, p. 253). Zorba does not have empathy for abstractions. Zorba is "completely absorbed in the job" (Kazantzakis, 1952, p. 258)—an emphatic job that calls him to attend to real people and their needs.

Zorba lives a philosophy of communication that unknowingly embraces empathy as a phenomenological bridge that connects his life to others. Zorba loves life, stating, "Men like me ought to live a thousand years" (Kazantzakis, 1946/1952, p. 346). Perhaps Zorba is correct; more people with an empathic bridge to others are seemingly needed in each historical moment. However, we must end this chapter stating that human beings like Edith Stein should live a thousand years in our hearts, calling us to empathically attend to the lives of others.

Zorba points to philosophy of communication as the carrier of meaning that embraces the importance of the interplay of sensations, ideas, and human action, the ingredients for doing and understanding empathy.

1. Existence matters; all of life that surrounds us affects us with sensations. Zorba lives a life of "to the things themselves." He does honor to all that he meets by taking the person or event seriously on its own terms. Zorba does not ignore the power of sensations in him that are elicited from existence. What is before us matters.

2. A metaphysical story matters, shaping lives of those who made this moment possible. Zorba is puzzled by Boss, who is drawn to metaphysical stories about life. Zorba is irritated with Boss's preoccupation with books, but his questions to Boss reflect a desire for something more than raw existential meeting. Zorba, in primitive fashion, announces why Edith Stein was not satisfied with phenomenology alone. The story within which we are situated gives meaning to the events that we meet.

3. Unity of word and deed gives witness to the power of ideas. Stein exemplified the union of word and deed, as did Zorba. Each worked within a given horizon of a story that guided action. Zorba is crude and, at the same time, predictably honorable in his behavior. He does not abide by rules; he attends to a story about the nature of existence and how his actions need to conform to such a perspective.

4. Empathy is a human phenomenological bridge connecting persons in a community. The final part of the story for Stein centers on human empathy that requires the integration of sensations, experiences, and

learning. Empathy requires us to reach out to others from the baseline of all we know. Community emerges from many bringing unique contributions that care for the other differently. Indeed, Zorba's manner of caring would be difficult to teach; however, in his life with others, empathy for another propels his communicative encounters.

Stein's insight into the power of empathy suggests its pragmatic importance as a primal counter against human evil. Stein gives us a view of empathy that acts as a phenomenological bridge between persons of difference, assisting in understanding a particular moment in the life of another. In the unlikely character of Zorba, we find such empathy in action.

Chapter 8
Analytic Discernment

Philosophy of communication is a phrase that is not typically associated with analytic philosophy. Eli Dresner (2006) acknowledges this omission, stating that philosophy of communication is an important "body of work" and requires closer attention in analytic philosophy (p. 155). One of the major branches in analytic philosophy is the philosophy of language. Within the field of philosophy of language, the central question of linguistic meaning revolves around logical analysis; likewise, in philosophy of communication, questions regarding the use of language and how it functions logically are pursued. From an analytic tradition, when human communicants construct meaning they are conducting, knowingly or otherwise, philosophical analysis of language related to linguistic concepts and propositions. The analytic task requires a systematic logical analysis of linguistic choices that identify and test assumptions. Analytic philosophy examines the structure of language and explores the relationship of language to the world through a logical linguistic process.

Introduction

This chapter relies on a philosophical picture of analytic philosophy painted by Aaron Preston's historical rendering, *Analytic Philosophy: The History of an Illusion* (2007); this work is a comprehensive macro-history of the analytic philosophical tradition. We texture his portrait though the innovative work of Ludwig Wittgenstein[1] (1889–1951). Wittgenstein's (1953) philosophy is explicated in his major work, *Philosophical Investigations*, while his radical revisioning of his own perspective about language is explicated in *Tractatus Logico-Philosophicus* (1922). His insights propelled the analytic philosophy tradition into the realm of everyday language. Wittgenstein's philosophy identified daily language issues between people and the world that convey meaning in everyday existence. Analytic philosophy explores aspects of language in terms of clarity, ambiguity, semantics, and meaning. An analysis of the language choices people make, the way they choose to structure sentences, and the evidence from which they draw upon shapes analytic philosophy. The objective is to understand the function of linguistic choices and explore more ideal ways of communicating meaning. Analytic philosophy presupposes that

---

1 Ludwig Wittgenstein (1889–1951) was an Austrian philosopher who studied logic, math, philosophy of the mind, and philosophy of language. He was a professor in philosophy at the University of Cambridge and wrote two main philosophical books, *Tractatus Logico-Philosophicus* (1922) and *Philosophical Investigations* (1953), as well as multiple philosophical essays related to language, the mind, and human communication.

there are inherent logical and semantic dysfunctions in language use, which can cause misunderstanding and misinterpretation.

This chapter examines analytic philosophy in three basic sections: (1) the philosophical picture Preston illuminates of the history of the analytic tradition in philosophy; (2) Wittgenstein's contributions to the analytic philosophy tradition; and (3) implications for the study of philosophy of communication understood as one philosophical painting exemplified through *Zorba the Greek*, the central story used throughout this project.

Analytic philosophy, understood as a philosophical picture, provides thoughtful reflection on how human beings use language to make meaning clearer through logical analysis of propositions. This position is academic and considered abstract by the later work of Wittgenstein. He shifts analytic philosophy into the examination of the interplay of language and everyday life. The objective of analytic philosophy is to examine language and logical analysis of language, seeking a way to use language that effectively generates linguistic insight.

Preston and Analytic Philosophy

Aaron Preston is an associate professor and chair of philosophy at Valparaiso University in Valparaiso, Indiana. His scholarship focuses on analytic philosophy and he has been published in the *Bertrand Russell Society Quarterly*, *Metaphilosophy*, *The Monist*, and *Axiomathes*. Preston's significant contribution to philosophy is *Analytic Philosophy: The History of an Illusion* (2007). Preston has spent the majority of his career providing clarity about the application of analytic philosophy, acknowledging that his primary research forges a critical account of the history of this tradition. Preston's astute interest in the analytic tradition informs our general examination of analytic philosophy.

No One Common Perspective

Preston (2007) argues that the histories that identify various phases in analytic philosophy are contradictory and incomplete. He provides an example of the complexity of these competing histories by comparing different historians of the analytic tradition. For example, Morris Weitz (1966) identifies four phases in analytic philosophy: realism, logical analysis, logical positivism, and conceptual analysis. Alternatively, Barry Gross (1970) identifies five stages: realism, logical atomism (a logical system that is ultimate and cannot be reduced or parsed down), logical positivism, Wittgenstein's ordinary language, and Ryle's ordinary language. This brief illustration confirms Preston's (2007) contention that "there is no clear answer to the question, what is AP [analytic philosophy]" (p. 42). Preston suggests that there is no one definition of analytic philosophy that permits one to appreciate the rich nuances that resonate from differing perspectives within the analytic-philosophical tradition.

There are numerous versions of analytic philosophy. The task of forging a unifying perspective is beyond the scope of Preston's project, and unlikely to produce as much insight as the current varied tradition now offers. Preston eagerly rejects any effort to confine the analytic tradition; he abhors a comprehensive or universal definition of analytic philosophy and its tradition. His position pragmatically recognizes that "Historians of analytic philosophy have not been able to identify *any* set of features common to all and only canonical analysts" (Preston, 2007, p. 42; emphasis in original). Preston provides an overview of analytic philosophy and does, however, offer clarity between and among the differing schools or threads of the analytic tradition. Analytic philosophy is better understood as a tapestry composed of the differing elements that comprise this category of philosophical inquiry.

This lack of unifying features that frame a single view of analytic philosophy is interesting in that this perspective has at its root the desire for logical precision. Perhaps it is this demand for precision that makes precise agreement impossible, making agreement on what analytic philosophy "really is," a natural outcome of this philosophical picture. Despite this lack of a single driving definition, Preston provides a helpful description of the tradition, illuminating the differences among major analytic philosophers that we associate with the tradition: George Edward Moore (1873–1958), Bertrand Russell (1872–1970), Gilbert Ryle (1900–1976), and Ludwig Wittgenstein (1889–1951).

A Textured Story

In order to begin our discussion of the insights offered by Wittgenstein, we situate the story of analytic philosophy within Preston's scholarship. Preston (2007) states that the term "analytic philosophy" originates from the 1930s and became the "norm" when referring to the philosophy of language (p. x); he suggests that this label demarcated a radically new approach in philosophy that centered upon "the analysis of language," which focused on the logical analysis and precision of linguistic structures (p. 2). Preston (2007) identifies the mid-1960s as a moment when "AP [analytic philosophy] lost its linguistic character…this was also the period when AP achieved dominance in the

British and American universities" (p. xi). At this moment, analytic philosophy became "an ideationally unified school," a philosophical school that primarily focused upon logical analysis of language related to reality that recognized the limits of logical analysis in the search for an ideal language (Preston, 2007, p. x). The notion that an ideal language exists is untenable, according to the latter part of this story framed by Ludwig Wittgenstein. Analytic philosophy was primarily comprised of English-speaking philosophers who responded to one another and became isolated and ignored by the larger philosophical community, resulting in a closed system of inquiry that focused only on the ideology of logical analysis.

Both the analytical and continental philosophical traditions "originated around the turn of the twentieth century, and though they are opposed in many respects, both involve significant departures from the norms of traditional philosophy" (Preston, 2007, p. 1; emphasis in original). One distinction that Preston points out is that analytical philosophy is primarily connected to Great Britain and the United Kingdom, and the continental perspective emerged primarily from France and Germany. Continental philosophy differs substantially from analytic philosophy in that analytic philosophy examines language, ambiguity, and verification, while continental philosophy explores Being and being in the world with others, intentionality, perception, temporality, existentialism, historicity, ethics, and otherness. Preston (2007) states that analytic philosophers are concerned with logical analysis of language; they pursue a "linguistic thesis," which Preston refers to as a "metaphilosophical view" of language, suggesting that "philosophy is wholly or largely a matter of linguistic analysis" (p. 31). Preston suggests, however, that analytic philosophy is no longer characterized in this manner. The definitive statements about the past practices of analytic philosophy no longer carry the same agreement, as the diversity of positions within this tradition suggests.

Preston (2007) argues that the first analytic philosophers, such as G. E. Moore, Bertrand Russell, and Gilbert Ryle, failed to actually identify a successful system of analysis, causing a "slow retreat" from the linguistic thesis (p. 2). Recognizing that Richard Rorty is one of the most current critics of analytic philosophy, Preston states that Rorty redefines the analytic tradition as the name for "a set of problems being discussed by philosophy professors in certain parts of the world" (quoted in Preston, 2007, p. 7). Rorty rejects the narrow focus of logical analysis and the narrow community of thinkers who were involved in the analytic tradition. As stated above, Wittgenstein's work pushed beyond these narrow conventions, and is actually known within both the continental and analytic traditions.

Preston (2007) identifies the normative function of analytic philosophy as the practice of doing "good philosophy," which seeks linguistic understanding (p. 9). Preston (2007) suggests that in the early development of the analytic tradition, the process of analysis was central to the philosophical method. One general notion held by most early analytic philosophers was that the surface form of language (what we "see") often obscures meaning, concealing logical structures and misleading the user. Analysis developed by analytic philosophers was based upon logic and mathematical structures, which meant that the process followed strict rules that seemed unchangeable and unresponsive to variations in our changing environment.

Understanding Differences in the Tradition

Preston offers four general phases of analysis that highlight the evolution of the analytic tradition: realism, logical analysis, logical positivism, and conceptual analysis. Each phase addresses logical problems in linguistic concepts and propositions that generate misunderstanding and misinterpretation. Additionally, each phase reaches limits, which moves the analytical structure to the next phase. It is the fourth phase, conceptual analysis, where we witness a traditional understanding of analytic philosophy that ends with Wittgenstein influencing both the analytic and continental philosophical traditions.

Realism. Realism concerns how concepts and propositions connect with what is real. Preston (2007) states that the history and evolution of analytic philosophy started with the realism of "Moore and Russell to logical atomism, to linguistic philosophy ideal and ordinary, and finally to post-linguistic eclecticism" (p. 158). Moore exemplified realism in his 1903 work, "The Refutation of Idealism"; in this essay, Moore argued against idealism and referred to it as spiritualism. Moore's main critique against idealism was that the world is not what it seems to be; we impose upon the world properties that the world does not really possess. Therefore, we have to control how we perceive; we must cease adding properties that are not present in the world. Moore indicated that all objects and subjects are experienced internally and externally, both in our minds and in our experience. Moore made a distinction between philosophical analysis and linguistic analysis. For Moore, linguistic analysis, or analysis of verbal expression, is concerned with "dissecting the symbols out of which it was composed and noting their manner and combination," whereas philosophical analysis was concerned with broader philosophical categories (Preston, 2007, p. 104). The key is to control the manner of linguistic perception by attending to the real.

Realism was, however, a broader category that did not satisfy Moore or Russell. Realism, as a form of analytic philosophy, involves: (1) the ideas of mind and matter and the universal and particular as ultimate aspects in language, (2) the theory of external relations, and (3) an explication of the nature of truth. Analytic philosophy adheres to the correspondence theory of truth, which states that truth is related to a fact that is a relational property connected to factual reality. Realism assumes that external property is necessary to prove the existence of any given factual reality (Russell, 1912/2011). Preston (2007) states that while the dogma of realism was clear, the refinements and modifications attempted through analytic discourse were not obvious, resulting in numerous misunderstandings. The failure to provide an understandable case for realism in analytic philosophy led both Moore and Russell to turn toward logical analysis of language.

2. **Logical analysis.** The turn toward logical analysis by Moore and Russell marked a new phase in the analytic philosophical tradition. Preston (2007) indicates that "*logical, or ideal language analysis*" included three main schools of thought (p. 32; emphasis in original): Bertrand Russell's theory of descriptions, Gilbert Ryles's systematic misleading expressions, and Ludwig Wittgenstein's initial call for the discovery of an ideal language (Preston, 2007). Russell's theory of descriptions works to resolve propositions that contain symbols of unreal and self-contradictory objects. For example, if we say "the author of *Zorba the Greek* is Greek," we invite ambiguity in that we assume there is only one author; however, we do not know this to actually be the case. Russell's theory of descriptions calls us to rephrase this assertion as, "one and only one person wrote *Zorba the Greek* and whoever wrote *Zorba the Greek* was Greek," making the case clearer that the author of *Zorba the Greek* was actually Greek.

Russell's theory of descriptions provided a way of clarifying and working with symbols that enhanced communicative clarity, repositioning symbols into a comprehensible reality. Gilbert Ryle's concern for misleading expressions involved the idea that if an expression is misleading, then it can generate misunderstanding or function as an intentional subterfuge, as in the case of red herrings in arguments. Misleading expressions often dominate the political landscape, especially during negative political campaigning when candidates attack the character of opponents and misrepresent actions of opponents in hopes of diverting attention from their own inadequacies. The use of misleading comments can derail their opponents' potential success.

Ryle's perspective on logical analysis focused on the intentional or mistaken ways people select and use language. Attempts at logical analysis can pave the way for a more precise system of language analysis. This perspective united with scientific consideration leads to the next phase of analytic philosophy, "logical positivism."

3. **Logical positivism.** This approach to analytic philosophy emerged in philosophical circles around 1922 and lasted until the beginning of World War II (Preston, 2007, p. 62). Logical positivism is known as a doctrine that includes verifiability, the rejection of metaphysics and theology, the unity of science, and the idea of language as logical and mathematical (Preston, 2007). Preston identifies Rudolf Carnap (1891–1970) as a leading advocate of logical positivism. Carnap (1934) suggested that the principle task of logical positivism is to determine the reality of verifiability. In direct verifiability, a proposition is true only if we can attest to the reality of a given proposition. For example, stating "the line is red" suggests that the line is only true as we refer to it having a quality of redness, which permits us to comprehend the quality of red. The statement is verified when observations confirm the existence of particular qualities.

Verifiability is determined through perception, which can be problematic. Even if we do not see the red line, we indirectly verify the truth of the proposition by verifying an assertion through: (1) a proposition that is already considered logically present or true that is intimately related to the original proposition; (2) another person who saw the line; (3) someone who took a picture of the line; and (4) corroboration by another person independently. Verifiability functions through direct observation and can be corroborated by an independent source that offers linguistic proof; this action extends the possibility of verification outside the realm of individual observations.

According to Preston (2007), Carnap claimed that analytic philosophy was concerned with linguistic form and arrangements of symbols that compose propositions without providing a reference point to reality. According to Preston (2007), Carnap indicated that without a referent, the rules for analysis cannot be applied to symbols. Carnap stated that systematic and verifiable analysis based upon mathematical and scientific modes of proof are meaningless without a referent. Preston (2007) asserts that the failure of analytic philosophers to agree upon and identify a unified system of logical analysis fueled a move toward "conceptual analysis" that unites premise and linguistical thesis (p. 126). This move failed, however, pushing analytic philosophers away from the ideal and toward ordinary language. Preston

(2007) does not employ the term "conceptual elucidation" as many traditional histories of analytic philosophy offer. Instead, Preston uses "conceptual analysis" as the final step in analytic philosophy (Gross, 1970; Weitz, 1966), referring to this orientation as the conceptual move of analytic philosophy into the realm of ordinary language.

According to Weitz (1966), "conceptual analysis" focuses on the analysis of concepts while "conceptual elucidation" focuses on the roles of concepts (p. 1). He admits that the analytic tradition typically refers to this fourth part as conceptual analysis, but he provides a corrective, changing the metaphor to "conceptual elucidation" because the "method" actually explores the roles of concepts and is not limited to analysis. Preston, on the other hand, argues that Weitz's contention is too limiting. Instead, Preston (2007) augments his definition, suggesting "conceptual analysis" as an appropriate term because it is not only a general linguistic analysis but is also an attempt to understand language by carefully studying its "elements and their interrelations" (p. 37), including, but not limited to, roles.

Conceptual analysis. Preston considers this late-emerging understanding of analytic philosophy to be distinct from earlier analytic positions. According to Preston (2007), conceptual analysis rejected: (1) a purely scientific or mathematical method, (2) the importance of a systematic analysis, and (3) the assumption that there is only one specific descriptive systematic method in the analysis of language. Conceptual analysis marked the search for ordinary language that opens language and celebrates possibilities. Conceptual analysis dismisses the idea of an ideal language and liberates philosophers to discover new ways to question language and find understanding. For example, in the traditional analytic tradition of analysis of language, one might ask, "What is the nature of X?" In conceptual analysis, the questioning shifts from "what is" to "What does X do to a language?" or "How does X do something to language?" Conceptual analysis recognizes that questions of meaning shift over time, revealing that the notion of an ideal language is an illusion. Conceptual analysis assumes the existence of conceptual complexity in all linguist environments.

This amalgamation of analytic philosophy approaches reveals problems in language related to: (1) the articulation of the reality of language and experience, (2) the manner in which we do logical analysis of language and meaning, and (3) the enactment of doctrines of verifiability and inferential meaning. Ludwig Wittgenstein then stepped forward, bringing us a philosophy of ordinary language. His work opens conversation; he tried to reconcile problems he conceptualized in analytic philosophy. His work began with understanding language as an infinite system of communication; his work was in contrast with the assumption that it is possible to discover a correct, finite system of analysis. Wittgenstein's project moved analytic thought into engagement with everyday language.

Wittgenstein and Analytic Philosophy

Ludwig Wittgenstein is arguably one of the most significant philosophers to come out of the analytic tradition (Warnock, 1958); his work disrupted the paradigmatic unity among analytic philosophers. He was born in Vienna in 1889 and was home schooled until he was 14 years old, at which time he entered formal education outside the home. In 1908, at the age of 19, Wittgenstein became an engineering student at the University of Manchester, where he was exposed to Bertram Russell's *Principles of Mathematics*. In 1911, Wittgenstein transferred to Trinity College at Cambridge to study philosophy with Russell. At Cambridge, Wittgenstein initiated research that would later ground *Tractatus Logico-Philosophicus* (1922). He left England in 1913 and moved to Norway before entering the army in World War I. After the war, Wittgenstein first taught in a small school in Austria, returning to Cambridge in 1929 where he subsequently became Russell's successor as chair of philosophy in 1939. Wittgenstein taught at Cambridge until 1947; after his retirement, Wittgenstein continued to write and philosophize about language and meaning (Weitz, 1966).

Wittgenstein's two most significant works are *Tractatus Logico-Philosophicus* (1922) and *Philosophical Investigations* (1953), which was published posthumously. Both of these scholarly contributions influenced 20th-century philosophy. Wittgenstein's philosophical perspectives on language and meaning developed, evolved, and changed—represented in his two major works. Wittgenstein made substantial contributions to the study of language and meaning, contributing to both the analytic and continental philosophical traditions (Weitz, 1966). The major themes that run through Wittgenstein's philosophy of language assume that philosophical difficulties emerge from logical and linguistic tensions and contradictions. Early Wittgenstein approached these philosophical difficulties in an effort to discern/discover an ideal language. He believed that language must show a relationship to the reality that language represents in order for propositions to signify something in reality with hopes of discerning ideal forms of language. Later, Wittgenstein moved from the ideal-language project to connecting language with everyday life.

Due to the difference in early and later Wittgenstein, his contributions to philosophy are often divided into two periods of thought: (1) his early thought, represented by *Tractatus Logico-Philosophicus* (1921); and (2) later Wittgenstein, represented by *Philosophical Investigations* (1953). Wittgenstein's (1921) *Tractatus* engages everyday language. At this early juncture of his thought, Wittgenstein supported the linguistic thesis of the early analytic movement, while endorsing a "logical picture" of the facts that construct the world (Preston, 2007, p. 115). Wittgenstein's first perspective was that the structure of the proposition is identical to that which is real. From this orientation, meaning is a matter of a structurally equal relationship between the proposition and the reality to which it refers. Preston (2007) indicates that Wittgenstein admitted that these logical forms are not stated; they are made manifest through logical pictures. Early Wittgenstein emphasized meaning through "picturing" and "logical form" (Preston, 2007, p. 116). Wittgenstein's *Tractatus* was initially misread by philosophers, who disagreed with the notion of logical pictures and interpreted them as purely linguistic. They failed to understand the additional importance of logical forms, which transcend the limits of logical propositions (Preston, 2007). This insight led to the later Wittgenstein, whose focus on ordinary language helped us to move beyond the ideal and logical that was placing limits on analytic philosophy.

Preston (2007) offers an interesting perspective, arguing that the differences in Wittgenstein's early and later philosophical thought on language were exaggerated. Preston (2007) suggests that there are two main discontinuities between *Tractatus* and *Philosophical Investigations*. First, in *Tractatus*, Wittgenstein writes in crafted propositions, but in Investigations, he criticizes generalities of any kind. Second, in *Tractatus*, Wittgenstein writes in a careful and logical manner, but in *Investigations*, his writing rambles and is less organized. However, in both works, Wittgenstein is concerned with connecting language and objects; he shifts from an early perspective, which seeks out an ideal language, toward his later perspective, which seeks understanding of ordinary language.

Philosophical Investigations, his later work, presents a revised understanding of the relationship between language and reality. By the time Wittgenstein finished *Philosophical Investigations*, he had abandoned his pursuit of an ideal language and began to identify the action and role of language in everyday life. Wittgenstein's (1953) *Philosophical Investigations* demonstrated a development in philosophical thought from the *Tractatus* with a shift from ideal language to the implications of ordinary language. Wittgenstein stated that the relation between language and reality is intersubjective; linguistic meaning comes from communicative interaction between persons in everyday use of language.

Wittgenstein (1953) did not apologize for his shifting perspective on language; he believed that language caused a "bewitchment of our intelligence" (p. 109). Because of the multiplicity in words and sentences, language offers multiple renderings of a given focus of attention, whether idea, object, or person. We use the effects of linguistic multiplicity to naturally give rise to differing interpretations. For example, the manner in which one asks a question elicits a particular language that can assist and at the same time mislead and misdirect attention, which can confound meaning and generate multiple interpretive possibilities. Wittgenstein (1953) contended that philosophical problems are a consequence of using language, rather than a problem within language; this realization shifted his work to the task of understanding ordinary language.

In *Philosophical Investigations*, Wittgenstein (1953) suggested that language has more than one meaning. There is no ideal language; there is no way that one can avoid the messy give and take of language use in daily intersubjective exchange between persons. Wittgenstein (1953) argued that "the more narrowly we examine actual language, the sharper becomes the conflict between [language and its referent]" (p. 107). This conflict is due to the variety of possible usages of words and the incredible number of existing languages. Wittgenstein's (1953) shift of perspective on the structure of language asserted that "[t]o imagine a language means to imagine a form of life" (p. 19); the structure of language is as diverse as all the different forms of life. Our use of language shapes our worldviews and our interaction with all of existence.

From pristine conceptions of language in analytic philosophy to the confusing array of ordinary language, Wittgenstein offered insight. He, like others in this diverse analytic tradition, was attracted to questions related to language, ambiguity, misleading expressions, misuse of words, vagueness in word choice, and the lack of a universal language—all played out in everyday ordinary use of language. Analytic philosophy focuses on how we use language as we attempt to confer meaning. In *Zorba the Greek*, the main characters must meet language that is difficult and, at times, impossible to control; meeting language in everyday life is both joyous and ever so demanding, to the point of life and death.

Philosophy of Communication: *Zorba the Greek* and Analytic Philosophy

Analytic philosophy explores the imperfect system of language that seeks the best way to use and understand language. This perspective assumes that if we want to communicate more effectively and thoroughly, we must consider what makes language inherently challenging as we communicate our thoughts to others. The manner in which we approach language impacts human meaning. Wittgenstein's work is a testimony to the importance of a shift from the demand to control language to a willingness to learn from the diversity of language. Wittgenstein asserts that there is no ideal language; we are taught by ordinary language that connects us to objects and realities. We fall short of the ideal of controlling language, but we are given the opportunity to learn from language, discovering insights not yet understood or imagined. It is difficult to imagine a character more tied to the ordinary language of a place than Zorba; he is exceptional and simultaneously a routine player in that place.

The characters in the story of *Zorba the Greek* exemplify many of the concerns addressed in analytic philosophy related to seeking an ideal or ordinary language. Even when Boss discusses compassion, there is an analytic dimension that constitutes his understanding and use of language.

> But at times I was seized with compassion. A Buddhist compassion, as cold as the conclusion of a metaphysical syllogism. A compassion not only for men but for all life which struggles, cries, weeps, hopes and does not perceive that everything is a phantasmagoria of nothingness. Compassion for the Greeks, and for the lignite mine, and for my unfinished manuscript of Buddha, for all those vain compositions of light and shade which suddenly disturb and contaminate the pure air. (Kazantzakis, 1946/1952, pp. 21–22)

For Boss, analytic engagement with language offers a necessary distance between him and the rawness of human experience.

Boss is the image of early work in analytic philosophy, and Zorba captures the position carved out by Wittgenstein; together they provide a backdrop for a particular view of philosophy of communication, emphasizing problems in language that impede how people communicate with each other. Analytic philosophy provides us with insight from the various systems of analyzing structures in language and how people attempt to create meaning with language. There are no answers that open a path to perfect communication. As human beings, we commence with the assumption that there is no perfect or ideal language. Our very lives verify the importance of Wittgenstein's later work. Philosophy of communication continues within a Wittgensteinian spirit, acknowledging and pursuing ordinary language in the give and take of daily life.

Boss and Zorba offer unique insight into the shifts in analytic philosophy and its impact on philosophy of communication.

1. All attempts to communicate our thoughts are mediated in some form through linguistic signs. Boss interprets signs with book-laden precision. He is often unable to meet the abrupt events and changes that accompany ordinary existence. Zorba, on the other hand, is an example of how the extraordinary emerges as one meets everyday life on its own terms.

2. Communication involves adjustment in word choice, sentence structure, or other linguistic decisions. Zorba is able to make changes in his discourse more rapidly than Boss. The simple reason for his flexibility is that life called forth language. Boss, on the other hand, is too eager to impose language on existence in hopes that he might change or control that which is before him.

3. Systematic analyzing of how we use language provides insight into assumptions about language and its usage. Boss understands systems and the necessity of analyzing the assumptions that give rise to particular forms of discourse. He is able to save Zorba's life near the end of the novel. Boss finds assumptions that another would take seriously, offering a face-saving path that permitted an alternative for not destroying Zorba.

4. Language has inherent limits; identifying those limits is key in meaning creation. The language we use has obvious limits when the world before us does not conform to our expectations. Zorba naturally understands the reality; we are part of life, not the dominators of existence. In contrast, Boss has to learn this.

5. Wittgenstein's emphasis on ordinary language enables communication to connect with objects of reality that are understood in the messy life between persons trying to understand meaning in everyday life. Wittgenstein's work makes the life of Zorba more textured. We encounter a character that encounters ordinary life with ordinary language, transforming the communicative environment in the process. Zorba exemplifies the extraordinary found within the ordinary.

Boss embraces an analytic philosophy that is narrowly focused; he deals with issues related to the logical analysis of linguistic structures used in communication. The logical analysis advanced by analytic philosophers restricts logical analysis to concepts and propositions often outside of a particular context, understood within a closed analytical system. Wittgenstein opened this conversation to language in everyday engagement, the terrain in which Zorba dwells and excels.

CHAPTER 9
PRAGMATISM: AN AMERICAN PRACTICE

Pragmatism emerged as an influential philosophical movement in the United States in the early 20th century as a rival to traditional philosophical traditions. Pragmatism considers meaning in relation to context and experience, with language being part of the consideration when assisting pragmatic discernment. Pragmatism seeks to understand meaning between people in shared experiences and contexts. A pragmatic perspective is attentive to everyday experience and the pursuit of meaning in our lives. This chapter explicitly paints a philosophical picture of how pragmatism informs philosophy of communication and assists in discerning meaning in everyday experience.

Introduction

This chapter relies on a philosophical picture of pragmatism painted by H. S. Thayer's (1968) historical perspective that identifies the difficulties and challenges of pragmatism framed in his significant contribution to the legacy of pragmatism, *Meaning and Action: A Critical History of Pragmatism*. Thayer's critical history of pragmatism offers a textured picture of pragmatic thought that stresses the role of individual philosophers in the development of pragmatism. Additionally, this chapter turns to Richard Rorty (1979), who explores the nature and meaning of truth, knowledge, and language in *Philosophy and the Mirror of Nature*, which offers insight into Rorty's perspective on how we engage meaning with others. Rorty is significant to any contemporary discussion of pragmatism; he is the most recent original contributor to the philosophy of pragmatism, and his work influenced the renewal of conversation about this perspective.

Through the historical background about pragmatism offered by Thayer and the pragmatic philosophy of Rorty, we explore the relationship between pragmatism and philosophy of communication in three main sections: (1) a general overview of pragmatism offered by H. S. Thayer; (2) a biographical portrait of Richard Rorty and his unique contribution to pragmatism; and (3) implications of pragmatism for the study of philosophy of communication understood as one philosophical painting illustrated through the characters in *Zorba the Greek*, the central story used throughout this project. Pragmatism, understood as a philosophical painting, provides an alternative to the philosophical limits of the analytical and continental traditions in philosophy. Pragmatism focuses on contextual meaning between people that enables us to make sense of the world in which we live; it is through pragmatism that we find meaningfulness in the pursuit of meaning.

Pragmatism is considered the unique American contribution to the study of philosophy. Pragmatism privileges consequences and outcomes, shaping what many would contend as the American spirit of innovation. Pragmatism is more interested in what gets accomplished than in the exact elements that guide the "why" of actions. Pragmatism lives within the realm of impact and consequence with attentiveness to everyday outcomes. There is controversy over the American claim of pragmatism; however, there is little question that this philosophical perspective has had and continues to have a massive influence on decision making in the United States.

Thayer: An Overview

H. S. Thayer (1923–2008) provides a historical look at the development of pragmatism. Thayer was a professor of philosophy at the City College of New York (CCNY) and wrote numerous works on pragmatism. Some of his most significant books include: *The Logic of Pragmatism: An Examination of John Dewey's Logic* (1952); *Newton's Philosophy of Nature: Selections from his Writings* (1953); *Meaning and Action: A Critical History of Pragmatism* (1968); and *Pragmatism: The Classical Writings* (1982). His book *Meaning and Action: A Critical History of Pragmatism* is considered the definitive study of pragmatism for the general reader. In *Meaning and Action*, Thayer (1968) notes that the word "critical" in the subtitle does not denote criticism in a normative sense, but is used to situate his study as an examination of "the cardinal ideas of pragmatism" (p. vii). Thayer pays attention to the nuances and differences in the evolution of pragmatic thought. Thayer's commitment to the study and understanding of pragmatism comes from a passionate assumption that pragmatism is a vital and important philosophical force for decision making and accomplishing work.

Thayer (1968) offers a critical history of pragmatism that sheds light on the concerns of pragmatic thought and its evolution through early pragmatic philosophers. Thayer's history of philosophy, seen through the lens of pragmatism, provides critical connections between this philosophical perspective and the pragmatic and historical developments within the West. Thayer (1968) provides a historical and contextual overview of pragmatism, identifying pragmatism as philosophical thought connected to the discernment of meaning and human direction (p. 420). Thayer (1968) views pragmatism as part of a larger "paradigm of moral activity" (p. 421). Thayer's (1968) story of pragmatism includes a descriptive account of philosophical problems associated with the "relation between the nature of scientific knowledge and the status of moral values" (p. 4). The chief contributors to pragmatism include Charles Peirce (1839–1914), William James (1842–1910), and John Dewey (1859–1952); from their work, Thayer renders a critical survey of pragmatism that explores how American pragmatism has influenced, and continues to influence, the larger world community.

Pragmatism is concerned with practical implications. Originating in the United States, it is recognized as the American contribution to philosophical thought (Smith, 1978). Before Thayer (1968) makes his case for the American experience of pragmatism, he rightly reminds the reader that an isomorphic linking of pragmatism and the American experience is a "mistake" (p. 6). Pragmatism took root on American soil, but to limit this philosophical perspective to one geographical location makes pragmatism "an essential irrelevance" (p. 6). Thayer's comment indicates that while it is interesting to understand pragmatism as uniquely connected to American life, the beginnings and the implications of this philosophical and practical perspective extend beyond a provincial American vision. The roots of pragmatism span from the Classical world of Greek and Roman philosophy to insights from Native American thought (Wilshire, 2000); there is diversity in the history of pragmatism that goes well beyond the connections to displaced Europeans starting a new life in a new country. However, the major contributors to pragmatism are unquestionably scholars connected to the American fascination with results. The early pragmatists, including Peirce, James, and Dewey, engaged questions related to knowledge, truth, and experience. The rich history of pragmatism represents influences from beyond the United States, although pragmatism became an American focus in philosophical thought by the late 19th and early 20th centuries.

Pragmatism Grounds Decision Making

Peirce considered pragmatism to be essential, as one had to make judgments and decisions that had enduring consequences. He understood pragmatism as a "method of philosophizing…for deciding and ruling upon the meaning of beliefs, ideas, and uses of language" (Thayer, 1968, p. 79). Peirce described the method of pragmatism as "characteristic of the experimentalist's procedure in the laboratory" (Thayer, 1968, p. 79). Peirce's pragmatism mediates between theory and action, informing how people communicate with one another. Peirce called for an epistemology based upon cognitions or intuitions, either empirical or rational. Peirce advocated for gathering multiple sets of evidence from which one could make pragmatic judgments. His approach to decision making and action taking was inductive in nature, which limited the potential of his perspective for subjectivity and self-interest. Peirce aligned pragmatism with action; his theoretical entrance into understanding that action was based upon the interpretation of communicative signs (Thayer, 1968). Central to Peirce's philosophy is the clarity with which human beings make sense of ideas and frame their conception of objects.

Peirce maintained objectivity between language and action by insisting upon evidence that is both empirical and rational, involving good reasoning. Peirce demonstrated the relationship between one's language and action through measurable evidence in decision making. He wanted to justify decisions based upon objective truth that supported the decision. Peirce's insistence on objective realities marked the difference between his *pragmaticism* and James's subjective *pragmatism*.

Thayer (1968) indicated that Peirce conceptualized pragmatism as a "maxim of logic" (p. 421). Little attention was given to Peirce's pragmatism until James revived this perspective. Peirce accused James of misunderstanding and misappropriating his method. Thayer (1968) stated that as James introduced Peirce's work to the academy, he concluded that Peirce's pragmatism was both a "method for analyzing philosophic problems and a theory of truth" (p. 135). Peirce sought to correct James, clarifying that "pragmatism was a method of explicating meaning, not a *theory of truth*" (Thayer, 1968, p. 135). James applied subjective tendencies in his interpretation of pragmatism, which opposed the objective approach taken by Peirce. With that distortion, Peirce shifted his language from pragmatism to *pragmaticism* to distinguish his objective perspective from James's subjective one (Apel, 1981). To understand this distinction clearly, Thayer begins with Peirce's pragmatism that mediates between theory and action, informing how people communicate with one another. Peirce called for an epistemology based upon cognitions or intuitions, either empirical or rational. James employed a subjectivity that accepted less measurable evidence and deductive inferences in his view of pragmatism; James's system was designed to be open to possibilities of truth without being limited to measurable outcomes.

James's pragmatism diverged from Peirce's objective attempts at understanding truth, perception, and experience, and leaned toward a more subjective perspective that highlights relational aspects between knowledge, truth, and experience. The major connection between James and Peirce occurred when James became interested in pragmatism after learning that Peirce had asserted that pragmatism actually solves no problems. James was interested in a philosophy that opened one's mind to receiving various forms of evidence that can assist in decision making (Thayer, 1968). Unlike Peirce, James considered multiple types of evidence; he was open to serendipitous discoveries and transcendent realities if they connected relationships and meaning in our lives. Opening the mind moved James to question the existence of God, truth, the meaning of life, and the purpose of being human. James's focus on these subjective sensibilities from within the individual mind, as a method of analysis and a theory of truth, led Thayer (1968) to describe James's pragmatism as having a "bifocal vision" that Peirce "renounced as unpragmatic" (p. 135).

Thayer contended that James's position on pragmatism came from observations that were influenced by his experience and interest in a functional psychology. Thayer (1968) stated that James's theory of truth was left unfinished in rough-draft form, but the insights of James's work did spark Dewey's interest and desire to reformulate James's ideas in hopes of finishing his theory of truth. According to Thayer (1968), Dewey thought there were two unfinished aspects of James's theory of truth involving misuse of the concept "relative" and the assumption that truth and falsehood can be attributed to the use or operation of ideas, beliefs, or statements (p. 162). Dewey worked out the definition of relativity, its application, and its usefulness to ideas, beliefs, and statements, explicating a theory of instrumentalism out of his extension of James's project.

Instrumentalism

John Dewey is considered a reformer of American education, a philosopher of education interested in a wide range of subjects, including democracy, truth, knowledge, experience, aesthetics, and ethics. Dewey referred to his conception of pragmatism as instrumentalism for institutions as an "activity of knowing as a social institution" (Thayer, 1968, p. 53). Dewey's philosophy related to education, knowledge, art/aesthetics, and ethics had a practical appeal that centered upon the relationship between human beings. Dewey acknowledged that the dialectical relationship between people is key to how people live and work together. His perspective on pragmatism privileged the dialectical relationship between persons as the most practical aspect of understanding, decision making, and judgment, void of the extremes of pure subjectivity or objectivity (Thayer, 1968).

Dewey coalesced the critical and objective motives of Peirce with the subjective and moral ideals of James. Thayer (1968) stated that Dewey spent his lifetime "devoted to exploration and analysis" of consequences of Peirce's and James's pragmatism related to multiple philosophical contexts (p. 165). During Dewey's lifespan, he witnessed the emergence of Darwin's (1859) *Origin of Species*, the theory of Einstein's (1905) relativity in physics, and the realization of the atomic age in the middle of the 20th century—these scientific advancements gave Dewey a unique perspective in pragmatic philosophy, "instrumentalism" (Thayer, 1968).

Thayer (1968) described Dewey's instrumentalism as an embodied theory of inquiry comprised of two objectives: (1) to determine how thought functions by "working out a descriptive interpretation of thinking," identifying how thinking emerges as a "natural growth of knowledge," and determining how knowledge is relevant to logical forms of thinking (p. 170); and (2) to explicate "the assumptions and implications" of how thought functions by making explicit the assumptions and implications involved in understanding the functions of thinking (p. 170). Dewey's objective was to frame a specific understanding of how people make decisions and the underlying pragmatic assumptions and implications of their decisions and actions. Dewey offered a more "theoretical" and a more "explanatory" view of pragmatism in thinking and decision making (Thayer, 1968, p. 170). The "meditative function" of thinking plays an "instrumental role in establishing consequences" and assists in explaining conditions for pragmatic understanding of outcomes (Thayer, 1968, p. 170). Thayer's elaboration suggested that we know what matters most due to gradual consideration of situations through theory and consequential experience. Dewey emphasized the importance of considering what undergirds actions and the necessity for pragmatic reflection upon the consequences.

Dewey's understanding of truth emerges somewhere between the beginning and end of a given inquiry. Dewey shifted James's theory of truth that relied upon verification to a theory of correspondence between subjects and objects, attending to a real instrumental consequence. The question of truth is inescapably connected to the structure of knowledge, which emphasizes Dewey's understanding of instrumentalism (Thayer, 1968). The foundation of Dewey's instrumentalism is a "primary importance of knowledge…as a guide for action" (Thayer, 1968, p. 423). Deliberate action is guided by some level of reflection that stresses "the result of valuation"; people make value judgments upon specific actions that they consider and/or engage (Thayer, 1968, p. 423). All actions have consequences, and when actions are deliberate, there is a moral consequence. Behavior that is deliberate is committed with choice, interest, and valuation, operating within the realm of pragmatism. We decide what to do and in that decision, we assign value to our choices. It is the aforethought that measures pragmatic action; we then assign value for the future, predicting that a given action will be "satisfactory to someone" (Thayer, 1968, p. 424). Dewey stated that moral reflection is a natural instrumental part of every pragmatic action.

Dewey's perspective on knowledge aligned with his pragmatic and instrumental philosophy; he viewed the term "epistemology" as a flat experience, something outside of experience. Dewey's theory of inquiry implies a relationship and a co-creation of experience (knowledge) that occurs between people within a given context. Dewey's perspective exemplifies an instrumental dialectical engagement between people, places, and things; it situates participatory action and interaction as a requirement for experiencing a given environment. Thayer (1968) distinguished Dewey's theory of inquiry from other earlier perspectives because of the focus on dialectical instrumental pragmatism.

Two distinct threads representing pragmatism emerged in Thayer's (1968) history of pragmatism: (1) the early formulation of pragmatism by Peirce as a mode of logic, and James's revival of Peirce, which announced tensions between objective (Peirce) and subjective (James) perspectives; and (2) a fuller comprehensive development of pragmatism initiated by Dewey that carved out specific areas including knowledge, a theory of inquiry (truth), and valuation of experience that shaped an instrumental perspective on pragmatism (p. 421).

Thayer provides a rich historical overview of pragmatism in philosophical thought, which includes American and European developments in pragmatic thought. He concluded with definitions of pragmatism that synthesize the complexity of his historical survey. Thayer indicated that pragmatism concerns the practical nature of thought and reality that explicates meaning, suggesting that thoughts are an adaptation that assist us in controlling experience and reality. Such action aligns perception with the task of satisfying interests and needs. Thinking includes pragmatic considerations of future experiences and consequences of action. Pragmatism is a philosophical attitude that meets and understands the necessity of pragmatic decision making. We now move to the perspective of Richard Rorty, the most significant pragmatic voice since John Dewey.

Keeping the Pragmatic Conversation Going

Richard Rorty's (1931–2007) position on pragmatism is thoughtfully framed by Alan Malachowski's[1] (2002) book, *Richard Rorty*, which illuminates Rorty's contribution to pragmatism. Malachowski's insights guide much of our conversation on Rorty, along with Rorty's (1979) *Philosophy and the Mirror of Nature*, a key representation of his philosophical pragmatism.

Richard Rorty was born on October 4, 1931 in New York. He was an only child and his parents quickly knew their son was intellectually gifted. At age 15, Rorty entered Hutchins College at the University of Chicago, a unique educational program designed by Robert Hutchins (1899–1977) that accepted high school students into a great books program in the Western tradition and culminated in students earning a B.A. from Hutchins College, University of Chicago (Voparil, 2010). Many of Rorty's philosophical positions were shaped by the time of his entrance into Hutchins College, which emphasized religion and philosophy. Rorty did not tend to religious studies as rigorously as he did to philosophical studies; he fell in love with philosophy (Voparil, 2010).

Rorty earned a Ph.D. in philosophy from Yale University in 1956. He taught at Wellesley College from 1958 to 1961 and Princeton University from 1961 to 1981. In 1982, Rorty became Kenan Professor of the Humanities at the University of Virginia, and in 1997, he was honored with the position of Professor Emeritus of Comparative Literature at Stanford University. Christopher Voparil (2010) reflects upon Rorty's work as generating "intellectual height" (p. 1), describing the significance of Rorty's work with the fact that his scholarship was translated into more than 20 languages, influenced multiple disciplines, and pushed against mainstream analytic philosophy while reigniting mainstream interest in pragmatism. Whether in agreement with his work or not, Rorty has been referred to as the most significant philosopher of the 20th century (Voparil, 2010).

The Pragmatic Alternative

Richard Rorty offers a pragmatic alternative to the manner in which we discern meaning through experience. Rorty's philosophy was based upon the pragmatic

---

1 At the time Alan Malachowski (2002) wrote *Richard Rorty*, he was an honorary lecturer at the University of East Anglia, Norwhich, U.K. His philosophical interests focus on pragmatism, the philosophy of Richard Rorty, and business ethics. He has published several volumes on pragmatism, the pragmatism of Richard Rorty, and articles related to ethical practices in business. Malachowski is also a fellow of the Centre for Applied Ethics at Stellenbosch University in South Africa.

principle that action must be meaningfully connected to experience. He wanted the philosophical to meet the demands of the lived world. Rorty questioned both analytic and continental traditions in philosophy; his project explored feminist studies related to epistemology, gender-biased assumptions, and the influence of these assumptions on literary theory (Malachowski, 2002).

Richard Rorty was dissatisfied with analytic philosophy. He believed that much of the analytic tradition missed the importance of the direct consequences that emerge from human experiences (Malachowski, 2002). Rorty tried to rectify this position in *Philosophy and the Mirror of Nature* (1979) and a subsequent collection of articles published under the title *Consequences of Pragmatism* (1982). These two works marked his split from analytic philosophy and clarified his continuing ideas on pragmatism. Rorty identified the futility of realism(s) and idealism(s), two categories that earlier philosophical traditions privileged. Rorty (1982) suggested that in both realism(s) and idealism(s) there is an accepted conception of truth that does not align with human experience. Truth became a central pragmatic matter in Rorty's pragmatism—he suggested that truth emerges from social practices that enable human beings to cope with beneficial aspects of their lives. Malachowski (2002) describes Rorty's pragmatism as "answerable to those practices and their reality-oriented demands rather than some practice-independent, 'unspecified and unspecifiable,' and therefore, 'well lost' world" (p. 73). Rorty's pragmatism reminds us that philosophizing involves experiences that are contextually situated within social practices. He rejected philosophizing about anything independent and separate from lived experience.

Rorty's (1979) description of his work in *Philosophy and the Mirror of Nature* is akin to our discussion in Chapter 3 on the importance of philosophical pictures. Rorty (1979) summarized his work as a collection of "pictures rather than propositions, metaphors rather than statements, which determine most of our philosophical convictions" (p. 12). Rorty (1979) argued that traditional philosophy sees the mind as a "great mirror" that contains accurate and inaccurate representations of reality that are studied through non-empirical methods (p. 12). Malachowski (2002) suggests that the mirror, for Rorty, exemplifies a single vision of reality that is misguided; there is always more than what is immediately represented. The idea of a single vision led to Rorty's opposition to an "anti-authoritarian streak" in his early writings (Malachowski, 2002, p. 98). Rorty then decided to write *Philosophy and the Mirror of Nature* (1979) as a way of describing how something "could look on the other side" of the idea or situation (Malachowski, 2002, p. 98). Rorty's attempt at dismantling the single vision led to a "post-epistemological philosophy" that focused on pragmatic aspects of truth, meaning, and experience (Malachowski, 2002, p. 98). In this liberation from authoritarian single visions, Rorty (1979) suggested we make assumptions in our interpretations. He suggested that making assumptions about the accuracy of impressions and reflections is risky. Assumptions about representation can be inaccurate, requiring one to constantly inspect, repair, and polish the mirror through which we conceptualize reality.

Rorty explored the mind related to experience, truth, and knowledge (Malachowski, 2002). One of the main threads of his philosophical inquiry involved exploring foundations of knowledge through the mirror in our minds related to the exterior world. In the second part of *Philosophy and the Mirror of Nature*, Rorty (1979) critiqued philosophical positions based upon epistemology; he contended that knowledge can be theorized as privileged representations while discounting the assumption that knowledge serves as pure reason, separate from culture and communication (Malachowski, 2002). In Rorty's (1979) critique of representational knowledge and a foundational view of knowledge, he countered with the assertion that "we understand knowledge when we understand the social justification of belief, and thus have no need to view it as accuracy of representation" (p. 170). Rorty situates knowledge as *conversational*, not foundational. Rorty rejected privileged representation (Malachowski, 2002). He argued that "we will not know what would count as a 'rational reconstruction' of our knowledge" and we will also not know "what epistemology's goal or method could be" (Rorty, 1979, p. 169). Rorty's commitment to his critique of privileged representations remained strong throughout his writing on pragmatism, contending that unrestrained and unchallenged bias obscures reality.

Rorty's Legacy

Rorty's understanding of experience is pragmatically situated within conversation. The conversation, for Rorty, takes place in the environment in which we learn, understand, and experience others in relation to ourselves. If knowledge is clearly representational knowledge, it cannot be connected to experience and therefore it is a contradiction (Malachowski, 2002). Rorty (1979) understood "culture as conversation" instead of culture as erected upon a set foundation, separate and nonresponsive to the conversation (p. 319). Rorty's understanding of experience was action oriented among people and within particularities of culture.

Malachowski (2002) states that Rorty's task in the engagement of pragmatic truth was to "make for 'better human lives'" (p. 172). Rorty believed that philosophy ought to be an open-ended conversation. Malachowski (2002) argues that Rorty shifted the pragmatic conversation in philosophy toward a "redescriptive" philosophical justification of language and action (p. 181). Rorty described redescription as inquiry that liberates one from the authoritarian single vision. Rorty argued for a pragmatism that forgoes this privileged vision that attempts to stand outside experience. He stressed "the webs of belief" that constitute us as human beings (Voparil, 2010, p. 34). In redescriptive philosophy, we continually reconceptualize and redescribe our own experience. Malachowski (2002) understands description of "conversational norms" as meaningful to "internal communities of inquiry" that ask themselves redescriptive questions (p. 181).

Malachowski (2002) asserts that because Rorty broke through the limits of traditional epistemologies through his call for ongoing conversations in the engagement of knowledge, he "democratized" philosophy (p. 183). Interestingly, Rorty was at the center of issues in business ethics because of his argument for the enlargement of the cultural conversation at a time when business discussions were evolving globally (Malachowski, 2002). Rorty's philosophy still faces criticism, but Malachowski (2002) asserts that the real value of Rorty's work has yet to be realized. Malachowski (2002) suggests that Rorty's early works are not explored in enough detail, his connection to the continental tradition has not been fully developed, his views related to natural science require careful attention, his ruminations on the history of history call for exploration, and his rationale for rejecting essentialism contribute to the scholarly community.

Malachowski (2002) suggests that Rorty advocated avoiding "conflicts of ethnocentric interests" by engaging "practical palliatives" such as tolerance and the moral imagination (p. 184). Rorty's redescription of truth and epistemology opened connections with feminist theory, literary theory, and ethics (Malachowski, 2002). The corpus of Rorty's works provides significant opportunity for consideration of his philosophical insights and exploration of their implications for the academy. Malachowski ends with a clear message— Rorty's scholarship has much to offer as we seek a meaningful understanding of knowledge and justification in experience, ever examining and considering the pragmatic consequences of those encounters.

Philosophy of Communication: *Zorba the Greek* and Pragmatism

Pragmatism privileges experience, acknowledging the importance of pursuing truth and knowledge based upon experience that gives shape to meaning in our lives. Pragmatism frames the significance of human experience, displaying a unique perspective in the pursuit of truth and knowledge as we respond to our experiences in existence. Pragmatism begins with experience that is continually tempered and shaped by recognition of and response to human consequences in and beyond our immediate context. For Zorba, music has a pragmatic role in assisting him through the rough and tumble of a life of labor and rugged demands.

An example of pragmatism in the story of *Zorba the Greek* involves Zorba's love for the santuri, a beautiful instrument that Zorba carries with him on his travels. Before Boss and Zorba formally meet, Zorba talks about his santuri and his singing of "old Klephtic tunes from Macedonia" (Kazantzakis, 1946/1952, p. 16). As Boss begins to know Zorba, he finds it intriguing that a man of Zorba's life experience has such passion for music. As Boss and Zorba begin their journey together, Boss and Zorba talk about the pragmatic role of music in Zorba's life. Zorba states "[s]ince I learnt to play the *santuri*, I've been a different man. When I'm feeling down, or when I'm broke, I play the *santuri* and it cheers me up. When I'm playing, you can talk to me, I hear nothing, and even if I hear, I can't speak" (Kazantzakis, 1946/1952, p. 17). Near the end of the story with Zorba's impending departure, Boss asks Zorba to play his santuri and Zorba replies that he cannot; he needs a "happy heart" to play (Kazantzakis, 1946/1952, p. 333). Zorba is saddened by their impending separation. He does not feel the passion to play for Boss. Pragmatically, Zorba's playing will lighten his heart, which at that time he does not want. Zorba is sad; he allows his world to be shaped by the pain of the departure.

At the end of the story, Zorba leaves the santuri to Boss. The santuri played a pragmatic role in Zorba's life—it helped Zorba negotiate tension, pain, and joy. With this final gesture, the santuri plays one final pragmatic role in Zorba's life. The giving of the instrument is a pragmatic gesture, a pragmatic reminder that friendship matters. Zorba's communicative actions are informed by a pragmatic philosophy of communication that permits him to understand and engage his communicative environment throughout his life, pragmatically meeting experience and living with the consequences.

Philosophy of communication as the carrier of meaning, understood from the vantage point of pragmatism, assumes that consequences matter and that one must find pragmatic outlets for expression—Boss turns to books, and Zorba turns to labor and music that permits him to hear more deeply.

1. There is no one theory of pragmatism that informs how we understand the world around us. One can envision Zorba overhearing this statement, walking away, thinking "one must do what one must do." Our comment is yes—pragmatism has such a vein of responsibility tied to attentiveness to human consequences.

2. The coordinates of experience and consequences are present in each pragmatic theory. Pragmatism offers answers that rest between the coordinates of experiences and consequences. Zorba is better equipped for engaging these two perspectives than Boss. Zorba looks to the problems before him, and Boss relies on ideas he imposes. Pragmatism demands that one's eyes be open to the world.

3. Pragmatism requires acknowledgment of particularities in experience, requiring one to comprehend each experience uniquely and respond to a given set of circumstances. Pragmatism has one set system—it is responsive. For this reason, Zorba is able to pragmatically respond to the unexpected, and Boss finds this skill set one that he had seldom practiced and understood even less.

4. We are situated and embedded within experiences that pragmatically influence our perspectives and future actions. Zorba is so embedded that he is part of the soil, the earth, the very place where he lives. Boss attempts to walk above the world whenever he meets the unexpected. We witness this difference between the two men during the final moments of the novel.

5. We learn from experiences; this learning cannot remain static. We do find in Boss an ability to learn from experience. He actually helps Zorba. Then, it is as if Boss concludes that the learning is too painful; he abruptly states that he will go home. The old cliché of the "school of hard knocks" is the classroom that Boss requires and ultimately, the classroom he cannot endure.

6. Pragmatic communicative literacy requires an openness and flexibility as we make sense of the world and are attentive to the consequences that follow. Zorba's openness to existence permits him to learn, not like Boss, but in a manner that makes creative responses to unwanted circumstances possible.

We found in Thayer's historical overview of pragmatism and Rorty's redescriptive approach to pragmatism a consistent reminder about the importance of experience, pragmatic decision making, and the reality of consequences. We concur with communication philosophers who argue that pragmatism assumes and proposes a philosophy of communication (Langsdorf & Smith, 1995). Russill (2003) verifies this position in his literature review, which announced the significant extent to which pragmatism has influenced philosophy of communication. Russill (2007) suggests that "unreflective reliance on a positivist philosophy of science and utilitarian social theory" is inadequate for questions concerning communication; he advocates the significance of "pragmatic perspectives" as more helpful in negotiating issues related to human communication and human relationships (p. 126). Zorba's theory surfaces daily and is tested on the spot, emerging from the coordinates of experience and consequences.

CHAPTER 10

DIALECTICAL DIFFERENTIATION

The notion of dialectic is practically responsive to shifts, changes, and conflicts related to perspectives and movements of innovation. Plato's dialogues portray Socrates as offering dialectical insight in an effort to arrive at higher-order thinking and truth. After Plato's use of dialectic, multiple schools of dialectic emerged, spanning from antiquity to the present. The philosophical picture that dialectic offers philosophy of communication is a cultivation of intellectual literacy that informs both speaker and audience by shaping information, guiding communicative exchange, and using one position or idea to sharpen another. Dialectic is a mode of philosophical inquiry that provokes consideration of assumptions and evidence that advance multiple perspectives within varied communicative environments. Dialectic reveals positions and assumptions that are often overlooked, providing alternatives for complex situations.

Introduction

Dialectic is a broad philosophical category that spans cultures, peoples, and environments. Dialectic informs philosophy of communication as it constitutes philosophical inquiry, relying upon tension and difference in order to understand people, environments, and ideas. The historical development of dialectic in human thought and action provides insight into how we move from the known to the not yet conceptualized.

This chapter outlines the contributions of two of the most well-known creators and users of the dialectic, Plato and Hegel. This chapter consists of four major sections: (1) a general biographical portrait of Nikulin and the philosophical picture he paints of dialectic; (2) a review of Plato's individual explication of dialectic in the Classical era; (3) an explication of Hegel's method of dialectic in the modern era; and (4) implications of dialectic for the study of philosophy of communication understood as one philosophical painting exemplified through *Zorba the Greek*, the central story used throughout this project.

This chapter relies on a philosophical picture of dialectic painted by Dmitri Nikulin's (2010) historical and philosophical illumination of this mode of inquiry, which sets the background for our understanding of the nature and importance of dialectic. Dialectic involves reasoning that is based upon acceptable and honorary opinions. It also implies a communicative structure that, understood as a philosophical painting, provides a way for communicators to engage philosophical inquiry in a practical and constructive manner.

A General Overview of Dialectic

We begin discussion of dialectic with reliance on the philosophical picture of this idea/method offered by Dmitri Nikulin (2010). Nikulin is professor of philosophy and director of undergraduate studies at the New School for Social Research in New York City, a renowned institution that attracts various scholars from around the world and invites creative exploration of philosophical perspectives. Nikulin earned his Ph.D. in philosophy from the Institute for Philosophy of the Academy of Sciences in Moscow in 1990. He has held professorial positions at Essen, Heidelberg (Germany), Oslo (Norway), Universidad de Los Andes (Chile), istitutio de italiano per gli studi filosophici (Italy), and ecole pratique des hautes etudes (Paris), and has published volumes on dialogue, dialectic, ontology, metaphysics, and ethics.

Nikulin identifies two broad schools of dialectic: (1) dialectic in antiquity (dialectic via *antiqua*), based upon the Platonic dialectic; and (2) dialectic in modern times (dialectic via *moderna*), based upon Hegelian dialectic. Plato's example of dialectic is a classical procedure in discerning truth in political environments. Plato's (trans. 1951) *The Republic*, which is representative of classical dialectical thought, is central to Nikulin's broad dialectic category, dialectic via *antiqua*. Hegel's dialectic philosophy reengaged dialectic as philosophical inquiry. Today, dialectic is taught both as a form of argumentation and as a form of philosophical inquiry. Georg Wilhelm Hegel's *The Science of Logic* (1811–1816/1969) and the *The Encyclopaedia of Logic* (1816/1991) exemplify Nikulin's second broad dialectic category, dialectic via *moderna*. Nikulin (2010) generally defines dialectic as a sophisticated way of accessing something by a process of reasoning that makes visible the taken-for-granted side of an issue, action, or idea.

Nikulin (2010) describes dialectic as having many forms and faces, leaving its description open and flexible; this understanding of dialectic permits the notion to evolve and adapt to particular circumstances. Nikulin (2010) contends that dialectic is a process that "builds itself up as a logical enterprise, as the art and method of constructing correct philosophical arguments in accordance with certain rules, and of choosing the right presuppositions as starting points" (p. xi). Nikulin (2010), employing three presuppositions, constitutes dialectic as (1) questioning the kind of thing something is; (2) asking simple and clear close-ended questions that have yes or no answers; and (3) asking questions in a certain order that marches the inquiry toward an answer, a particular truth, in an established order.

Plato's dialogues feature Socrates as questioner, who begins with short clear questions and then asks more sophisticated questions, revealing the dialectic process of questioning in action. Nikulin (2010) argues, "dialectic is a science...by means of question and answer" (p. 46). Reducing dialectic to a mode of logical disputation shifted dialectic from philosophical inquiry in antiquity (800 BCE–300 AD) to a mode of argumentation during the medieval scholastic tradition (600 AD–1350 AD). Dialectic separated from its philosophical ground when Plotinus (204/5–270 AD) asserted, "dialectic itself is not a philosophy but it permits us to talk about philosophy" and engage in philosophical inquiry (Nikulin, 2010, p. 46).

Nikulin (2010) asserts that dialectic adheres to classical "skill in reasoning" (p. 48). A recent employment of the classical view of dialectic is represented by Hans-Georg Gadamer (see philosophical hermeneutics outlined in Chapter 6). Gadamer strengthens the potential for "bring[ing a classical sense of] dialogue back into philosophizing" (Nikulin, 2010, p. 69). According to Nikulin (2010), the modern dialectic is a dwelling place for Hegelian and Marxist dialectic. Nikulin does not break these traditions into separate schools; instead, he explores how dialectical perspectives overlap with and inform other perspectives. Nikulin states his purpose is to reconcile dialectic with dialogue, as both have a fundamental relationship to human communication. Dialogue "requires conversational and communicative skills," and it constitutes the "very *conditio humana*" (Nikulin, 2010, p. x). Dialectic comes about through "oral dialogic exchange" and seeks "to channel dialogical conversation on to a course that would produce a proof or argument through joint deliberation" (Nikulin, 2010, p. xi). The connection of dialectic allied with dialogue begins with Plato. Nikulin explores Plato's dialectic as an example of *antiqua* (antiquity) and then turns to Hegel's dialectic as an example of *moderna* (modernity). Nikulin recognizes their dialectic work as exemplary and generative of continuing scholarship associated with dialectic.

The Classic Dialectic

Plato (427–347 BCE) was a classical Greek philosopher and a student of Socrates. Plato was a teacher; he founded a school that taught young men to be responsible citizens in the polis through dialectic discernment of truth. Plato is considered one of the founding fathers of Western philosophy and the academic tradition propelled by dialectic insight.

A Response to Social Turmoil

Plato was likely born in 427 BCE into a wealthy family in either Athens or Aegina, Greece. It was a moment of division, a consequence of the Peloponnesian War that lasted from 431 to 404 BCE (Johnstone, 2009). Plato's early life witnessed:

> the rupture of public morality in Athens, the rise of demagogues in civic life, acts of great brutality at the hands of the demos, the city's military defeat by the Spartans and their allies, the rule of a ruthless tyranny, a bloody civil war, the execution of Socrates by a restored democracy, and the reemergence of Athens as an aspiring imperial power. (Johnstone, 2009, p. 147)

Even though this period was politically contentious, marked by wars and shifts in political power, Plato seldom mentioned these events in his dialogues (Johnstone, 2009). The execution of Socrates for "impiety" and refusal "to take part in the wicked arrest of one of their friends" was a personal change of direction for Plato (Johnstone, 2009, p. 163). He criticized the treatment of Socrates—this marked the beginning of a period in his life defined by a contemplative retreat from politics. Plato then left Athens for 12 years, travelling to Megara, Northern Africa, and Italy, until returning to Athens to open his school that would come to be known as the "Academy" (Johnstone, 2009, p. 163).

Plato witnessed the consequences of ambition in politics and public service; consequently, he turned away from a public career and devoted his life to philosophy. After his return to Athens and during this era of social turmoil, Plato founded the Academy in Athens; he devoted his life to teaching young men while writing significant works in philosophy that are considered foundational in understanding Western philosophy and the Western world. Plato has been considered the most famous and significant student of Socrates, with Plato's most famous student being Aristotle (Johnstone, 2009).

From Dialectic Reflection to Truth

During Plato's time away from Athens, he devoted himself to philosophical thought that would come to undergird his school and his later philosophical musings (Johnstone, 2009). The time Plato spent away from Athens enabled him to reflect upon Socrates, the corrupt Athenian political system, and the laws and customs in the Athenian polis. In seeking wisdom, Plato had withdrawn from "the realm of the practical, political action and a rejection of the uncertainty and transience of sensory experience, in favor of a realm of pure thought and rationality" (Johnstone, 2009, p. 165). Plato sought universal truth by envisioning "a path to knowledge that rejects the evidence of the senses for the insights of a disembodied Reason" (Johnstone, 2009, p. 165). Out of his disgust for the polis that executed Socrates, Plato believed a philosopher king should rule the polis, subordinating those with weaker intellects (Johnstone, 2009). The execution of his former teacher contributed to Plato's critique of political leadership.

Plato expanded upon the nature of the soul of a human being in questioning what he observed and experienced. Plato's threefold division of the soul consisted of a myth of the charioteer: (1) the appetitive (black horse), (2) the spirited/emotional (white horse), and (3) the rational (the charioteer). In *Phaedrus*, Plato described a charioteer and two horses that represent each part of the soul. A noble white horse represents love of truth, modesty, and temperance; an ignoble dark horse represents love of the flesh and fails to listen to the charioteer. The charioteer represents the one driving the soul to heaven. The allegory begins with the idea that the soul wants to go to heaven, but most souls lose their wings and fail to reach heaven because of their nature. The story foretells a moral that "when it [the soul] is joined with flesh at birth, [it] is pulled down from the heavenly realm by certain unruly passions and becomes burdened...thereby lose[ing] sight" and wisdom (Johnstone, 2009, p. 169). The moral of the story suggests that to attain wisdom, one must descend into the essence of one's soul and move away from worldly matters of the flesh in order to remember "the unchanging truths of the cosmos" (Johnstone, 2009, p. 169). The relationship between the charioteer and the horses is a dialectical one that tests the charioteer's ability to negotiate between the earthly and the heavenly, or a priori good, in pursuit of wisdom. Johnstone (2009) states that people need knowledge that emerges from one's soul, which is a dwelling of recollection of knowledge. The soul composed of wisdom, along with reasoning responsive to the correct order in the polis, makes a leader possible.

Plato described the soul's path as a dialectical exercise. He advanced that "the soul's path to...moments of epiphany involves a laborious course of dialectical and discursive reasoning, beginning with the particulars of sensory experience and then concentrating one's inquiries on ever more abstract conceptions until one is finally to the realm of pure intellection" (Johnstone, 2009, p. 171). To gather wisdom, Plato turned to dialectic. His dialogues exemplify dialectical inquiry in a variety of contexts and cover a variety of philosophical topics including truth, justice, and social order.

Plato's insights are often presented in the form of dialogues. He uses Socrates as the main protagonist, who models dialectical reasoning. Plato's dialectical engagements are a collection of concrete instances of a "thing, action, or event" followed by "rigorous analysis of logical implications" aiming at "constructing a conception that is free from self-contradiction or internal inconsistency" (Johnstone, 2009, p. 171). The Platonic dialectical process involves a pattern of statements and refutations that lead to the revelation of "genuine wisdom" (Johnstone, 2009, p. 173). For Plato, dialectic inquiry leads to wisdom necessary for the recovery of the proper form of governance in the Athenian polis.

Systematic Use of the Dialectic

The proper form of governance assumed by Plato was the backbone of his view of philosophical education, which emerged with an objective of establishing the correct form of political order; he framed his education about the proper political order with a stress on dialectic (Gadamer, 1960/1980). "Plato was the first writer to use dialectic systematically and to reflect on [...its] usage and... limits" (Nikulin, 2010, p. 46). He gave us a dialectical method that engages direct conversation, guiding the interlocutor through a set of propositions in order to arrive at a particular truth that is determined through the conversation. In Plato's *Republic* (trans. 1951), dialectic is described as a kind of inquiry that "systematically attempts to grasp with respect to each thing itself what the being of it is, for all of the other crafts are concerned with human opinions and desires" (531d–534a). The telos connected to dialectic tends to the heart of a given matter, outside the realm of *doxa* (opinion) or persuasion.

Plato's dialectic is a means to philosophical first principles, enabling one to discover truth; dialectic illuminates what is hidden, bringing truth into visibility (531d–534a). Plato elevated dialectic over the scientific process, justifying the supremacy of philosophy over science and at the same time situating dialectic as a method of philosophical inquiry that functions as a foundation for knowledge (Janssens & Johnstone, 1968).

According to Nikulin (2010), Plato's dialectic reveals two aspects: division and analysis. One puts forth a proposition and then parses out or divides the proposition, which permits one to learn to come to a new understanding. Nikulin (2010) distinguishes Plato's dialectic from Aristotle's dialectic. Plato focused on philosophizing through asking questions instead of using logical analysis to analyze propositions. Nikulin (2010) argues that Plato's dialectic abandons the focus on logical analysis in favor of the process of question and answer that leads to something else. In Plato's (trans. 2005) *Phaedrus*, dialectic was connected to natural intelligence. Socrates suggested that dialecticians were people able to engage in "divisions and collections" of evidence of something through a natural capacity (266b). Plato held a broader position on the use of dialectic, indicating that anyone could learn the process of dialectical philosophizing through division and analysis of ideas.

In most of Plato's dialogues where dialectic is exemplified, Socrates illuminates contradictions through question and answer, the process of division and analysis. Plato's interlocutor is usually unprepared to deal with contradiction once it emerges. When the contradiction is identified, the opponent makes concessions in the dialectical encounter. Plato uses contradictions to push dialectical tension toward illumination of a truth, whether known or unknown by participants in the discussion. Plato's dialogues that move into dialectical encounters are not usually antagonistic; however, the opponents of Socrates become defensive because their original position is in danger of losing logical ground.

Dialectic prepares one to think and to speak. In this sense, dialectic owes its origin partially to dialogue because it emphasizes an interactive exchange of ideas between people (Brownstein, 1965). For Plato, dialectic is a process that informs his worldview and shapes his experiences with others. Hegel further develops the method of dialectic, demonstrating the connection between dialectic and a modern view of history.

The Modern Dialectic

Georg Wilhelm Friedrich Hegel (1770–1831) was a German philosopher who, after completing his dissertation, accepted a position at the University of Heidelberg. Hegel attended the seminary of the Evangelical-Lutheran Church in Württemberg, Germany from 1788 to 1793, although he felt confined by the narrow religious perspectives. In an attempt to broaden his learning and experience, Hegel sympathized with the revolutionists in the French Revolution (1789). He would later write in *The Philosophy of History* (1825–1826/1956) that his interest in the French Revolution came from the early Enlightenment philosophy that undergirded the revolution. After receiving his theological certificate in 1793, he accepted a position as house tutor for a family in Bern until 1796; in 1797, he accepted a position in Frankfurt as a tutor, staying until 1801. During this time, he maintained friendships with

Friedrich Wilhelm Schelling (1775–1854) and Friedrich Hölderlin (1770–1843),[1] both of whom influenced the development of his later philosophy (Pinkard, 2001).

In 1801, Hegel held the position of unsalaried lecturer at the University of Jena. Hegel lectured on logic and physics and participated in collaborative lectures with Schelling, who also influenced Hegel's philosophy, especially related to philosophy of art and natural philosophy. Hegel was promoted in 1805 to the position of extraordinary professor at the University of Jena, which was still an unsalaried position. In order to earn a salary, he published *Phenomenology of the Spirit* (1807) and accepted the position of editor of a newspaper in Bamburg. In 1808, Hegel was appointed headmaster of a gymnasium where he produced multiple publications. In 1818, Hegel was appointed chair of philosophy at the University of Berlin, later becoming the rector in 1830. In August of 1831, a cholera epidemic broke out and Hegel, along with many others, fled from Berlin to Kreuzberg out of fear; he returned to Berlin in November for the semester to begin, but the epidemic had not subsided and Hegel died from cholera on November 14, 1831 (Pinkard, 2001).

Hegel's *Phenomenology of Spirit* (1807), *The Science of Logic* (1811–1816; revised in 1831/1969), *Encyclopaedia of Logic* (1816/1991), and *Elements of the Philosophy of Right* (1820) exemplify his philosophical thought and system of historical dialectic. The cornerstones of Hegel's philosophy include consciousness, freedom, mind/spirit, and difference/dialectic. Hegel's project influenced numerous scholars, such as Edmund Husserl (1859–1938) (related to phenomenology and phenomenological method) and Judith Butler (b. 1956) (related to feminism and the dialectic) (Pinkard, 2001).

Hegel's method of dialectic, according to Gadamer (1960/1980), is exemplified by identifying contradictions through thinking about events and objects. Hegel (1816/1991) considered philosophy to be a "thinking consideration of objects" that puts concepts into "forms of thought" (p. 24). Pinkard's (1988) suggestion is that the Hegelian dialectic is an attempt at explanation, which demonstrates a difference from Plato's dialectic that centers on making truth visible. According to Nikulin (2010), Plato demonstrates

---

1 Friedrich Wilhelm Schelling (1775–1854) was a German philosopher who became friends with Hegel and Hölderlin when they roomed together at seminary. Schelling was a professor at the University of Jena when Hegel taught there. Friedrich Hölderlin (1770–1843) was a German intellectual and poet who became friends with Hegel and Schelling when they roomed together at seminary. They remained friends and colleagues throughout their lives.

dialectic through an active engagement of question and answer. Hegel, on the other hand, privileged systematic explanation in order to distinguish between concept and conception—Hegel employed a systematic explanation, expressed through propositions. This view of dialectic was quite different from the conversational emphasis on question and answer offered by Plato.

Hegel's distinction between conception and concept is fundamental to his understanding of dialectic. Conception includes specific or inductive aspects of thought. A concept is abstract, a general understanding about something (Dworkin, 1986), such as the concept of justice. We might share the same conceptual understanding about justice, but our conceptions or specific accounts of justice might differ dramatically. For example, we could share the idea or *concept* that it would be unjust to let someone get away with murder. However, our *conceptions* of what justice is could be quite different. In your conception of justice, you might advocate that the death penalty is an appropriate punishment for murder. On the other hand, I might advocate that life in prison is an appropriate enactment or conception of justice. Our conceptions are shaped by our embeddedness and experiences, which are individualized. Thus, conceptions are so diverse that explanation is a necessary act of discovery for Hegel's dialectical method.

Hegel identified a process of dialectic that permits explanation, which involves thesis, antithesis, and synthesis (James, 2007). The thesis in Hegel's dialectic is understood as a position that involves a particular, finite, or single idea; the antithesis is a conflict of the original idea or a contradiction of that concept that may or may not be originally clear or certain in the first place; and the synthesis is the original thesis transformed into a new one that is nearer to the truth of reality (Downs, 2010). This transformation occurs through the interplay of the thesis and the antithesis that reveals a contradiction (Nikulin, 2010). Dialectical engagement, for Hegel, requires one to deconstruct and then construct what then begins a new synthesis, the consequence of moving through the dialectical explanation.

Dialectic and Contradiction

The basic point of agreement between Plato and Hegel rests with their uniting of dialectic with *contradiction* (Nikulin, 2010). "Dialectic is based on spelling out the contradictions that arise in dialogical investigations of our common opinions about things" (Nikulin, 2010, p. xi). Dialectical engagement illuminates contradictions—Plato through reasoning and Hegel through rich explanation of historical developments.

Contradictions "entangle" our thinking and create internal inconsistencies in our logic, adding to disparity of understanding (Hegel, 1816/1991, p. 35). When information does not make logical sense, dialectic permits specific questions that announce the contradictions, opening up limitations from a previous position. Contradiction is necessary for dialectic to transform meaning, to reveal what is limited or wrong, providing openings for improvement and new directions. Contradiction allows for other voices and positions to play a role in shaping communicative understanding. Dialectical positions inform one another; they permit the contrasting of ideas to disclose a truth. Some contradictions are easy to identify; others are more obscure. For example, political candidates engage in dialectical exchanges by identifying contradictions in the messages of their opponents. During a political debate, candidate A might point out that candidate B has voted for every tax increase over the course of the last ten years; yet the statement made by candidate B suggests she has been the catalyst for tax reform. This position functions as a contradiction of the initial statement about candidate B. Once this contradiction is illuminated, further discussion, whether by logical reasoning or by explanation, is generated with the potential for moving the argument to a new understanding of both candidates. The key is to understand the differences between the candidates.

Dialectic and Difference

Contradiction has also been explored as central to *differentiation* in the philosophy of Hannah Arendt, who was significantly influenced by Hegelian dialectic. Acknowledging that Arendt never explicitly wrote on communication nor used the metaphor of dialectical communicative labor, Arnett (2007) argues that dialectical communicative labor is an apt descriptor of Arendt's social and political philosophy of differentiation; her work provides us with a "dialectically texturing communicative understanding" of her social and political positions (p. 69). Arnett (2007) describes "dialectical communicative labor" as "conceptual shorthand for the unity of philosophical, reflective, and differentiated understanding of ideas and practices that undergird and shape communicative interaction in the public and private domains of communicative life" (p. 79). The work of dialectical communicative labor is a synthesis shaped by multiple perspectives.

Differentiation makes "possible public and private communicative life contentious with demands for conformity in the social sphere. The realm of 'the social' sacrifices the critical questioning mode for an unreflective sense of belonging" (Arnett, 2007, p. 80). Arendt pointed to the Hegelian antithesis, or conflicting tensions, inherent in public and private environments. Arendt's social and political critique of the public realm is consistent with Plato's more general dialectical form in that she explores and analyzes the public domain through a process of division and differentiation.

When we fail to engage in dialectical questioning, as Arendt's critique demonstrates, we move into the realm of the social, unable to differentiate, enacting what George Ritzer (1996) referred to as "the McDonaldization of society," where we live in "extreme commonness" with little to differentiate (pp. 80–81). Dialectical communicative labor denotes a philosophy of communication that embraces both Platonic and Hegelian attributes of dialectic that reach beyond argumentation, pointing to the dialectical ground of the human condition.

The work of Arendt and the insights of Plato and Hegel situate dialectic as a mode of argumentation and a form of philosophical inquiry. Plato and Hegel provide perspectives on dialectic that help us understand how communicators dialectically discern meaning together. Dialectic shapes how people get to the heart of matters that are hidden or obscured. Nikulin (2010) argues that modern dialectic is "suspicious of dialogue" in that dialogue is less structured and less formalized than dialectic; however, it is important to remember that dialectic also "originates in dialogue" (p. xi). Dialectic is a logical enterprise in the pursuit of philosophical arguments and discoveries that contribute to multiplicity and texture in human understanding, enlarging the possibilities for human dialogue.

Philosophy of Communication: *Zorba the Greek* and Dialectic

Dialectic seeks to learn from contradiction in the discernment of truth. The philosophical use of dialectic acknowledges difference in a constructive manner, cultivating a habit of inquiry for learning that extends and sophisticates knowledge beyond what we currently know. Meaning emerges out of dialectical tension. Plato and Hegel offer dialectical frameworks that are central to the cultivation of a philosophical mind. We communicate with others who have differing and opposing perspectives. Dialectic assists in clarity of learning as we differentiate perspectives. We witness dialectic in action as Boss and Zorba encounter the world and one another from dramatically contrasting perspectives.

Zorba the Greek demonstrates dialectic as both a mode of argumentation and a form of philosophical inquiry, displayed in the communicative experiences between Zorba and Boss. After Zorba and Boss establish their plans for their work in the forest, which involves constructing a pulley system to bring cut lumber down from the mountain, Zorba prepares a list of supplies to purchase in the city that they need in order to finish their task. Boss gives Zorba the money to purchase what they need. Zorba's trip should have taken just a few days; however, many days pass—Zorba is gone for over a week. Boss receives a letter from Zorba, who writes, "But don't you worry yourself, boss, I'm looking after your little affairs, too. Now and then I go and look round the shops. I'll buy the cable and all we need, don't you worry" (Kazantzakis, 1946/1952, p. 170). Zorba shares what he has been doing, which involves social and romantic experiences instead of the actual business he was sent there to do—to buy supplies. As Boss reads the letter, he becomes very angry, but at the same time Boss misses Zorba and their conversations. Boss reflects to himself, "I was for a while in two minds—no, three. I did not know whether to be angry, or laugh, or just admire this primitive man who simply cracked life's shell—logic, morality, honesty—and went straight to its very substance" (Kazantzakis, 1946/1952, p. 171). Boss struggles with dialectical tensions that enable him to reflect deeply on the contradictions within Zorba.

In this dialectical experience, we witness Hegel's threefold action of dialectic: thesis, antithesis, and synthesis. The thesis comes in the form of the agreement between Zorba and Boss for the trip to purchase building supplies. It is a propositional statement that Zorba would go to the city to purchase particular equipment. Both Boss and Zorba agree upon this thesis. The antithesis comes in the letter written by Zorba to Boss after Zorba fails to return as they originally agreed. Finally, the synthesis occurs when Boss is able to synthesize this experience and call Zorba back home, to which Zorba attentively responds. When Zorba returns home, he has fulfilled his responsibility, and Boss has come to a new understanding about Zorba's serendipitous engagement with life.

The contradiction in this dialectical encounter emerges when Zorba does not return as originally agreed upon. This contradiction brings Boss to a new understanding about living within a world of contingencies. In the end, dialectic enables Boss to forgive Zorba and allows both men to move forward with their business.

Throughout the novel we observe the dialectic of conflicting tensions and the revelation of new possibilities and truths about given moments within human experience. Contradictions nudge the tension and help shape new meaning in ideas and actions. It is the dialectic in our lives that keeps moving us toward cultivating relationships and learning about others and ourselves. Both ancient and modern perspectives of dialectic inform how we discover possibilities and cultivate relationships. Philosophy of communication engages dialectic as both a philosophical form of inquiry and as a mode of argument determined for discovery. Dialectic enriches the nature of philosophy of communication and breathes new insight into our understanding of the human condition.

Philosophy of communication as the carrier of meaning, understood from the vantage point of dialectic, learns from difference and comparison.

1. Contradiction and illuminating differences are central to dialectical philosophical inquiry. The interplay between Zorba and Boss lends insight into the dialectic in human action. The two men approach life in a contrasting fashion; yet at the end, they unite in a kinship, a bond that goes beyond description. We observe the importance of what Charles Taylor (1989) termed the "inarticulate" (p. 343) that emerges from their dialectical encounter.

2. We cannot assume one mode of inquiry is sufficient for exploring all questions. Dialectic calls into question given positions, assuming that we only learn from contrast and difference. Zorba takes this learning in stride, attending to the power of everyday life that instructs us with novelty we often do not want or expect. Boss finds dialectical learning in everyday life more demanding; such experiences almost do him in—he leaves before his education is concluded.

3. By the nature of our embeddedness within changing environments, contradictions are necessary to provoke philosophical interrogations. Zorba learns from Boss, who is not from turf that is familiar to Zorba. Boss also learns from Zorba and his environment. This reality of dialectical learning emerges each time a person goes abroad and discovers new insights, as one seeks to make sense of a place that is not one's home.

4. Meaning ultimately comes from contradictions and the manner in which we engage and respond to such discoveries. Meaning emerges in the interplay of differences. Without dialectical learning, we are left with routine, which does not require the same attentiveness. Meaning emerges in the meeting of difference, offering assurance about the importance of what we have and lending an education from alterity that we meet. Zorba and Boss find meaning in their engagement of difference.

Zorba and Boss announce the dialectic in action; we observe pushing and pulling actions created by the tensions of the contraries existing within a given issue. Dialectical friction emerges from the interplay between contraries, which creates dialectical texture. The experience of dialectical friction is central to human knowing; we learn from the act of comparison and contrast, moving from the known, to the newly discovered, and then to new insights that renew this cycle of learning once again.

Chapter 11

Ethics and Diversity

Ethics is closely tied to philosophy of communication from the perspective and practice of privileging the meaningfulness and importance of a sense of "why" for human action. From the perspective of philosophy of communication as the carrier of meaning, the study of ethics emphasizes the importance of "why" in terms of a person's ideas, convictions, and actions. To illustrate this standpoint of ethics, this chapter examines two major works on ethics: Alasdair MacIntyre's *A Short History of Ethics* (1966) and Henry Sidgwick's 19th-century classic, *The Methods of Ethics* (1874/1981).

Introduction

The focus on Alasdair MacIntyre (b. 1929) and Henry Sidgwick (1838–1900) provides both a modern and a historical perspective on the study of ethics. According to Thomas D. D'Andrea (2006), "It is no exaggeration to say that, since...[MacIntyre's] *After Virtue* was published in 1981, it has changed the way ethics is written and studied in many parts of the English-speaking world and beyond" (p. xiv). Additionally, Margaret Urban Walker (2007) considers Sidgwick's *The Methods of Ethics* "not just a classic of moral philosophy and of utilitarian philosophy, but a pivot in the course of the emergence of the dominant twentieth-century notion of a certain type of moral theory as 'what to do' in moral philosophy" (p. 36). These two scholars are key figures in the development of ethics as a philosophical area of study.

This chapter examines ethics through the work of MacIntyre and Sidgwick in three major sections: (1) a reading of MacIntyre's *A Short History of Ethics*; (2) an examination of Sidgwick's *The Methods of Ethics*; and (3) the implications of ethics for philosophy of communication as the carrier of meaning exemplified through the characters in *Zorba the Greek*.

This chapter exemplifies the importance of ethics, stressing two major scholarly summaries that outline the development of ethics and the assumption that some things simply "matter" more than others (Cooren, 2010, p. 64). We privilege things that "matter," placing them within the category of ethics. We open this chapter on philosophy of communication and ethics with admission that some things matter more than others; when ideas and actions matter, we seek to protect and promote such perspectives, giving birth to particular ethical perspectives and differences.

MacIntyre: A Story of Ethics

Alasdair MacIntyre was born in Glasgow, Scotland, in 1929. He taught at several institutions in the United Kingdom before moving to the United States in 1970. He is currently the Senior Research Fellow at the Centre for Contemporary Aristotelian Studies in Ethics and Politics (CASEP) at London Metropolitan University and the Rev. John A. O'Brien Senior Research Professor of Philosophy at the University of Notre Dame. MacIntyre invites the reader of his *A Short History of Ethics* (1966) to embrace one basic assumption—there is an intimate connection between ethics and our ability to think philosophically. MacIntyre does not understand philosophy in the abstract; he contends that all philosophical conversations rest within problems and questions of a given historical moment.

> ...the Athenians who condemned Socrates to death, the English Parliament which condemned Hobbes' *Leviathan* in 1666, and the Nazis who burned philosophical books were correct at least in their apprehension that philosophy can be subversive of established ways of behaving. Understanding the world of morality and changing it are far from incompatible tasks. (MacIntyre, 1966, p. 3)

Philosophy permits the human being to understand the social, political, religious, and historical questions of a given historical moment. MacIntyre enacts a reading of given ethical positions that emerged over time in response to genuine issues, questions, and problems that shaped a particular era.

Ethics and Philosophy

MacIntyre unites ethics with philosophy, beginning with discussion of the pre-philosophical era in early Greece. "In Homeric society the dominant hierarchy of functional roles determines which are the dominant qualities; skill, cunning, and courage of various sorts" (MacIntyre, 1966, p. 9). When the viability of the roles collapsed, philosophy emerged as a way to make sense of positions that had previously been assumed. Philosophy was needed when an agreed-upon perspective was no longer shared. There was never just one set of philosophical assumptions about ethics; the assumptions were tied to locality and different city-states, learned and professed by the sophists.[1]

---

1 The term "sophists" applies to any Greek lecturer, writer, or teacher in the 4th and 5th centuries who traveled throughout Greece and provided instruction in a wide range of subjects in exchange for a fee ("Sophist," 2011). According to MacIntyre (1966), "They begin from a situation in which the prerequisite of a successful social career is success in the public forums of the city, the assembly, and the law courts. To succeed in that milieu it was necessary to convince and to please" (p. 14).

MacIntyre (1966) stressed the sophistic insistence upon the reality of "cultural relativism" attached to differing localities—such was the contribution of the wondering scholars called sophists (p. 14). Unlike the sophists, Plato (427–347 BCE) turned to the importance of a priori structured ideas that exist before the fact, which support the unreflective respect of the "common life" of persons in a given locality (MacIntyre, 1966, p. 32). Plato's task in writing The Republic was to outline a political structure expressive of a priori common life, gathering people into cooperative association and productivity in his Republic.

The Republic framed the common life with Plato, removing the "arbitrariness" between virtue and happiness in his rendition of life within the Republic (MacIntyre, 1966, p. 35). Plato organized the Republic into a "tripartite soul" of artisans and laborers, soldiers, and scholar/rulers (MacIntyre, 1966, p. 36). For Plato, form, structure, and order mattered, as he tried to counter the decline of the aristocracy of the Republic. Plato understood the sequence of decline as follows: (1) a "timocractic state," which becomes increasingly militarized and less intellectual; (2) an "oligarchical state," in which the rich exploit the poor; and finally, (3) a "democracy," which permits "dissatisfied malcontents to create a tyranny," losing any sense of restraint (MacIntyre, 1966, p. 45). Plato contended that the correct forms of association and ideas matter—without them, the "right" order of the Republic collapses. Plato's politics and his morals are closely aligned in The Republic; he connected the notion of the good to the external and the transcendental. He did not view humans as imposing virtue, but, in contrast, as making virtue visible; this virtue is a priori and transcendentally given.

Plato's transcendental perspective yielded another insight, one more attentive to the footsteps of people actually living in the polis, framed by Plato's pupil, Aristotle. What Plato and Aristotle had in common was their aristocratic assumptions. Plato was from Athens and a member of the distinguished class; his father descended from the last king of Athens ("Plato," 2011). Aristotle (384–322 BCE) was born in Stagira, Chalcidice, Greece, and his father was a court physician to the grandfather of Alexander the Great, whom Aristotle later tutored ("Aristotle," 2011). The Aristotelian perspective is situational and contextual, attentive to the polis of Athens. Aristotle stressed a golden mean that requires discernment of an answer that resides between two extremes, deficiency and excess. For example, courage is the golden mean between recklessness and cowardliness; only in the actual situation within the polis is it possible to discern the correct action at a particular time. The practical wisdom of phronesis works within a "normative" set of options set within the polis (MacIntyre, 1966, p. 67).

For Plato, Greek engagement with ethics resided in the transcendental. For Aristotle, it existed in the interplay of the polis and contextual decision making, attentive to options that reside in neither excess nor deficiency. The common factor between Plato and Aristotle was that their attention was directed at the "leisured elite" (MacIntyre, 1966, p. 98). Like Plato, "Aristotle's audience was explicitly a small leisured minority. We are no longer faced with a *telos* for human life as such, but with a *telos* for one kind of life which presupposes a certain kind of hierarchical social order" (MacIntyre, 1966, p. 83). MacIntyre (1966) states that Plato's system functioned as a guardian of the ruling class, resulting in an extreme form of "fascism" (p. 98). Plato is more candid about his commitments than Aristotle, but the leisured class is the audience of concern.

MacIntyre contends that the advice of Plato and Aristotle is useless to those without power, influence, status, and property. Many are exposed to the demands of life without a safety net of privilege. MacIntyre suggests that the mystery of religion attracts such persons; the coming of Christianity opened space for those living life outside the scope of financial and social privilege. For MacIntyre, the system of ethics in the West that brings attention to those not associated with the ruling class, an ethics attentive to Otherness, does not come from the Greeks but from Christianity, which was formed within and among Hebraic, Hellenistic, and Roman traditions. Christianity is a unity of multiple traditions attentive to one God from the Hebraic tradition that continues to provide an alternative to a loyalty previously given solely to the Republic. However, the reliance upon the Greeks is not over; in the emerging world of Christian ethics, the major theologians of that time, Augustine (354–430) and Aquinas (1224–1274), engaged the Greek world of Plato and Aristotle with one added assumption—God commands loyalty not only to himself, but to others, particularly those without privilege.

The Medieval Age connected the insights of Greek philosophy with an ongoing commitment to God. The power of the state now had a rival and the multiplicity of loci of meaning continued. MacIntyre (1966) takes us to the next historical step in the West, an increasing stress upon the individual that "break[s] with the hierarchical, synthesizing society of the Middle Ages" (p. 121). MacIntyre leads with a discussion of Martin Luther (1483–1546), who counters Aristotle and stresses grace, not work, in the internal formation of the individual. Luther's rendition of the human moved from a stress on social relations and affiliations to the individual in sole judgment before God. The person who functions like Luther in the secular world is Niccolò Machiavelli (1469–1527), with the assumption that it is the responsibility of the individual to hold and retain power by attending to "political order and general prosperity" (MacIntyre, 1966, p. 127). Machiavelli recognized the transience of political power and the constancy of human nature. The task of the individual sovereign is to maintain power and political order.

In MacIntyre's story, we find increasing urgency to unleash the individual. With Luther, there is a connection to God, and with Machiavelli, there is the responsibility of the sovereign to maintain power and societal order. In the insights of Thomas Hobbes (1588–1679), we witness a further unleashing of the individual. Hobbes shifts from restraints to "desires" without an emphasis on a greatest aim or greatest good as central to the human condition (MacIntyre, 1966, p. 135). The welfare of another remains secondary to one's own well-being. Hobbes makes the case that society cannot avoid the obvious link between nature and morality—the notion of self-interest is ignored at the peril of society. Perhaps the only peer that Hobbes had was Benedict de Spinoza (1632–1677), who united philosophy and practice with the assumption that together they manifest an "impersonal love of truth" dependent upon reason (MacIntyre, 1966, p. 140). Spinoza's commitment was to reason, while Hobbes underscored the importance of desire and passion; Spinoza asserted that these emotions must be engaged with reason because they are "transformable" (MacIntyre, 1966, p. 144). Both attempted to unleash the power and autonomy of the individual.

One cannot state, however, that Spinoza's stress on reason won the day. The continuing ethics story of the West involves the desires of Hobbes and the call for reason from Spinoza. The "new values" of the emerging Enlightenment cannot escape the power of this ethical dialectic. MacIntyre (1966) emphasizes the movement to "new values" in the 17th century with an increasing urgency on individual desire and individual reason, making space for the term "atheist" (p. 146). For instance, Spinoza was expelled from the Synagogue and Hobbes was under constant attack by the Anglican Church. The emerging emphasis of the 17th century moved from God to the individual and was led by Jean-Jacques Rousseau (1712–1778) in France and Adam Smith (1723–1790) in Scotland. The era of "natural rights" had begun, stressing the mantra of proclamation for the individual (MacIntyre, 1966, p. 156). The rights of the individual trumped what had been previously situated within external authorities of the Greek polis, Roman tradition, and the

Church. Change began with the individual taking precedence over external authorities. External authority had previously shaped the West, from Greece to Rome to the medieval Catholic Church, and finally in the 18th century, we have an emerging secular bible that preaches self-reliance in the literary form of *Robinson Crusoe* (1719).

Ethics and Argument

As the world witnessed the release of the individual into a realm of increasing autonomy, we find one major theoretical experiment after another that sought to protect the rights of others. MacIntyre details two major 18th-century efforts related to rights, a British argument and a French argument. The British argument finds primary support in Hobbes and Locke and their agreement on the social nature of life, the importance of a social contract, and the evolving importance of property. Additionally, there is stress on self-interest that emerges from the perspective of sentiment. The emphasis on sentiment is central to David Hume (1711–1776) and is one of the assumptions that undergirds the work of Adam Smith and his rhetorical statement on the advancement of what we term as capitalism. They both appealed to "sympathy" for others as a guiding action (MacIntyre, 1966, p. 176). The stress on sympathy and "common sense" (MacIntyre, 1966, p. 177), which takes one into normative conventions, shapes a moment in which there is a desire to recognize individual rights while articulating ways in which restraint on the individual is still part of the conversation, from the notion of the social contract, to sympathy for others, to an emphasis on common sense.

The French argument, from this same century, consists of a conversation principally between Charles-Louis de Secondat, Baron de La Brède et de Montesquieu (1689–1755), and Jean-Jacques Rousseau, with both having differing understandings of the nature of the individual and society. Montesquieu offers restraint on the individual through his emphasis upon the division of powers among the executive, judicial, and legislative branches; he is the theoretical architect of the American Constitution (1789). Rousseau has more confidence in the individual than in the restraint of the state. The natural inclinations of the human make social life and contractual life possible. Restraints are not his focus; his stress is upon social opportunity. The problem for Rousseau was that society, not human nature, had become corrupt. The French Revolution begins with a desire to right the ship of society and ends with increasing evidence, at least as understood by Edmund Burke and Joseph Marie de Maistre, that we need to take seriously the reality of the "doctrine of original sin" (MacIntyre, 1966, pp. 188–189). The developing colonies that became the United States had followed Montesquieu, not Rousseau; they adopted a conception of life together between persons and the state that sought a balance of power among the three basic branches of government.

The boldest effort to work within a commitment to unleash the creative powers and rights of the individual, moving conversations about the loci of restraint to the individual, was undertaken by Immanuel Kant (1724–1804). Kant's moral imperative united with universal law, requiring active participation of the individual. Kant was a major representative of the Enlightenment. He contended that individual reasoning could effectively assist people and "reform institutions" (MacIntyre, 1966, p. 190). Kant assumed that reason was unconditionally good and central to the explication of "good will" toward others and toward institutions (MacIntyre, 1966, p. 192). Reason assists one in deciding between "inclination" and "duty," with the latter connected to the "moral imperative" and "universal law" (MacIntyre, 1966, p. 193). "The *ought* of the categorical imperative can only have application to an agent capable of obedience…[which] implies that one has evaded the determination of one's actions by one's inclinations…" (MacIntyre, 1966, p. 196; emphasis in original). MacIntyre concludes with the statement that Kant wanted the person to think for him or herself and to connect solely with universal moral law. However, the manner in which Kant's theory is played out in its emphasis on duty is often in stark contrast to Kant's intent. The term "duty" can easily take one off the mark, away from Kant's intent of individual and practical reasoning and onto a corporate "conformism" and allegiance to "paternalism" (MacIntyre, 1966, p. 198).

MacIntyre's story about ethics does not find a resolution to the tension between the individual and society; this tension continues. Out of the frustration, we find writers recognizing the tension between individual and society through various renditions of what MacIntyre (1966) termed "unhappy consciousness" (p. 202). The tension between individual and society emerges in the writing of Georg Wilhelm Friedrich Hegel (1770–1831) and Karl Marx (1818–1883). Hegel's conception of human life rested on change, the new subsuming the old, the thesis swallowed by the antithesis, giving rise to a novel synthesis. The stress on dialectic highlights the dilemma of being unable to extract oneself from the prevailing and changing social structures. The result of this unending loop is the social creation of individual melancholy and an "unhappy consciousness" (MacIntyre, 1966, p. 202). Hegel explicated the existence of three false solutions to a master-serf relationship, the first being that of the Stoics and their "acceptance of necessity" (MacIntyre, 1966, p. 202). The second is a frame of mind, "skepticism," within which a serf doubts beliefs enforced by a master, while existing in a world where those same beliefs are received and followed (MacIntyre, 1966, p. 202). Finally, the third is Hegel's "unhappy consciousness," what MacIntyre (1966) calls "the epoch of Catholic Christianity" (p. 202). For Hegel, the history of humankind is the movement toward freedom and the lessening of the import of the master-slave relationship. "[H]istory is an inevitable progress of freedom to higher and higher forms, the Prussian state and Hegel's own philosophy providing the culmination of this progress. But this later equation has unhappily discredited two key points that Hegel makes about freedom" (MacIntyre, 1966, p. 205). In the development of human progress, one finds the development of skepticism necessary if one is to avoid moral forms of false consciousness. The move from Hegel to Marx replaces an Absolute Idea with self-development of individualism tied to a focus on social and material conditions.

Hegel understood life within a civil society that progressively changes; Marx stressed the manipulative power of a bourgeois society composed of those who are the owners of production that set the standards for tastes and "actions" (MacIntyre, 1966, p. 213). Marx argued that the bourgeois commitment to acquiring private property puts individuality and human liberation at risk. Marx chose the working class over the bourgeoisie; he selected those who produce over those who command others to produce.

From the notion of Hegel's Absolute Idea to Marx's power of social and economic life, MacIntyre takes us to the next major step in ethical response to society, questioning narrative structures that undergird normative life. Both Kierkegaard and Nietzsche deconstructed metanarrative assumptions of society. Kierkegaard and Nietzsche provided contrasting critiques that deconstruct confidence in normative assumptions. They rejected Hegel's notion of progress and his view of social movements through the dialectic. Kierkegaard stressed the importance of choice, connected to God, without any assurance from an absolute truth. Kierkegaard recognized the increasing importance of choice in the midst of ambiguity in the atheistic, ethical, and religious domains of life, with each domain situated within an increasingly criterionless environment. Kierkegaard rejected the idealism of Hegel, which was destroyed by the events of the French Revolution (1789), with Kierkegaard and Nietzsche offering a counter to this systematic view of progress in action in human history. Kierkegaard demanded choice and Nietzsche demanded that one reject the entire moral system of Christianity, which he contended devalues the world.

Metanarrative Decline

Nietzsche's famous assertion that God is dead reflected the death of the Christian narrative and rejection of anything that evokes the master-slave relationship. MacIntyre states that 19th-century philosophers felt tremors of massive change and catastrophes that were to come in the emerging historical moment as confidence in the metanarrative of modern existence lessened. Metanarrative decline gave rise to Nietzsche's "Superman" or Overman and Kierkegaard's stress on individual choice, as each responded to this moment of historical change (MacIntyre, 1966, p. 225).

This era of emerging metanarrative decline gives rise to the importance of the heroic individual effort of choice, such as "innovators, radicals, and revolutionaries who revive old doctrines" (MacIntyre, 1966, p. 227). Thomas Paine (1737–1809) brought back into vogue the insights of Kant and natural rights. Edmund Burke (1729–1797) reintroduced the importance of tradition and prejudice. "Prejudice renders a man's virtue his habit, and not a series of unconnected acts" (MacIntyre, 1966, p. 229). William Godwin (1756–1836) then countered Burke's stress on the importance of unmasking all prejudice or tradition (MacIntyre, 1966, p. 231). Godwin was a utopianist armed with the optimism of reason. Both Godwin and Jeremy Bentham (1748–1832) are connected by their adherence to the utilitarian notion of the greatest good for the greatest number. John Stuart Mill (1806–1873) followed this same utilitarian route, adding that one must discriminate between lower- and higher-order pleasures. However, as one moves to higher pleasures, the link between self-satisfaction and the greatest good for "the greatest number could be used to defend any paternalistic or totalitarian society in which the price paid for happiness is the freedom of the individuals in that society to make their own choices" (MacIntyre, 1966, pp. 237–238). This concern for happiness and greatest good continues as later utilitarians state that "utility" is better understood as the criterion for judging "principles," not "particular actions" (MacIntyre, 1966, p. 241).

MacIntyre (1966) claims that adhesion to moral first principles is what propels Kant's stress upon "good will" (p. 248). However, the modern view of ethics moves from good will to the notion of "my" will, giving rise to what MacIntyre (1981) termed "emotivism." Emotivism, decision making by personal preference, is the ethical manifestation of individualism, which results in one walking above restraints that give one a social context and sense of tradition that carries standards of authority for evaluation and judgment.

For MacIntyre, the acid-like nature of individualism[2] eats away at the moral foundations of four centuries of what could be termed traditional society, making way for decision making that relies solely upon personal preference.

In such an era of emotivism, what increasingly operates under the guise of a philosophy of ethics is a crude moral psychology that puts the individual at the pinnacle of decision making. The goal is to enhance private satisfaction. Choices are then made without reference to a standard outside the self. No longer do we have the polis, the Republic, the Church, or multifaceted ways of offering restraint upon the individual; we find the individual at the center of choice without guidance from some form of restraint other than his or her psychological comfort (MacIntyre, 1966, p. 269). In modernity, this psychological view of ethics attempts to stand above the prejudice of tradition and any form of restraint. We unleash the individual without attentiveness to history, existence, change, and concern for Otherness; we do so under the battle cry of modernity, freedom, and liberation. We seek to liberate the "me," forgetting the social dimension of the human condition.

MacIntyre leaves his story connected to emotivism, decision making by personal preference. We now turn to the debate between utilitarianism and intuitionalism, which gives us insight into a form of pragmatism guided by moral first principles. This approach functions as an alternative to individualism and as an early historical response to what is eventually known as emotivism. Henry Sidgwick (1874/1981), an English philosopher known for his ethical theory based on utilitarianism in *The Methods of Ethics*, offers us insight into ethical dilemmas of the 19th century that continue to haunt us today.

Sidgwick: A Utilitarian Alternative

Henry Sidgwick (1838–1900) is considered by many to be the most significant 19th-century English writer of ethics. A fellow at Trinity College in Cambridge (1859), he later became a lecturer in classics, then moved to moral philosophy in 1869, becoming Knightbridge professor of moral philosophy in 1883 ("Henry Sidgwick," 2011). Sidgwick wrote what some consider one of the most important works on ethics centered in the utilitarian tradition of "happiness of all sentient beings" (Rawls, 1981, p. v). Sidgwick's utilitarian position worked to align hedonism, the idea that pleasure or happiness is the

---

2 In *Democracy in America*, Tocqueville (1835 & 1840/2000) stated that individualism is considerably more problematic than selfishness. Individualism attempts to stand above the human condition, and selfishness can be attentive to those around us, for no other reason than to protect ourselves (pp. 482–488).

sole good in life, with reasoned justification. His manner of explicating this position involved discussion of three different ethical theories that attempted to unite hedonism and reason: (1) egoistic hedonism, (2) intuitionalism, and (3) universalistic hedonism, with each tied to the classical doctrine of utilitarianism. In order to frame these approaches, Sidgwick stressed knowledge over practice—he wanted the person to know why a given action was attempted. Sidgwick explicated the utilitarian connection between ethics and philosophy of communication. One can refer to Sidgwick's (1874/1981) understanding of this approach as a philosophical explication of a "morality of common sense" that keeps before us utilitarian perspectives on ethics (p. xii).

The Interplay of Self-Interest and Duty

Sidgwick's work provides an excellent picture of issues that continue to divide us in everyday views of ethics: the argument between self-interest and duty or, put differently, the continuing debate between John Stuart Mill (1806–1873) and Immanuel Kant (1724–1804). This brief summary cannot do justice to the more than 500 pages of thoughtful discussion rendered by Sidgwick. Rather, our task is to emphasize Sidgwick's philosophical story that gives insight into a common set of ethical questions on self-interest and duty, both trying to work with Enlightenment assumptions about the importance of rationality and individual free will. Sidgwick (1874/1981) considered ethics the study of right and wrong that involves the voluntary actions of an individual, philosophically constituted by differing "practical" "methods of ethics" (p. 14). The practical focus on ethics with a solid theoretical base permits Sidgwick to conceptualize ethics in action in political life. The basic question he asked was whether a given set of political actions would generate human happiness, the highest good.

The engagement of happiness in the public domain requires attentiveness to practical reason that takes into account the "end" or the objective (Sidgwick, 1874/1981, p. 26). The connection to "end" gives insight into the political nature of this view of ethics. Sidgwick differentiated two concentrations upon the "end," one propelled by desire and the other by reason. He connected judgment to examining ethical ends and stressed reliance upon reason that invites consistency in ethical ends. Sidgwick understood the role of reasoning in conjunction with what he termed an "egoistic hedonism," a view of ethics that requires constant rational deliberation on the questions of pleasure and pain. This approach assumes that ethics connects to happiness, which then generates more pleasure than pain. "Empirical hedonism" is the method that Sidgwick associates with egoistic hedonistic ethics, requiring empirical reflection on whether or not a given action gives pleasure or pain in the actual carrying out of a given action or series of actions. The assumption of this approach is that human beings are connected to a "sympathy," a pre-mind/body reaction to the Other, which is detailed in Chapter 7 of this work, that makes them rationally attentive to sensations of pleasure and pain that requires reflection upon consequences (Sidgwick, 1874/1981, p. 170). Sidgwick (1874/1981) states that this approach ("egoistic hedonism") is a general rule that is tied to "common sense" that permits reflection upon consequences of actions related to pleasure or pain and, as a by-product, permits an ethic of egoistic hedonism to develop (p. 160). Sidgwick (1874/1981) is not satisfied with this approach and turns to "duty" as a way of pursuing happiness, leaving the realm of pleasure and principle as too general and incapable of providing enough moral height (p. 160). Sidgwick's (1874/1981) contention is that reliance on pleasure and pain is insufficient for the development of civilization; what is needed is the framing of "duty" tied to particular roles that keep the social life of a people ethical, with happiness attentive to something of greater moral height than one's own pleasure or pain (p. 174).

To pursue duty that yields happiness, one must accept the reality of uncertainty. Sidgwick (1874/1981) rejected the assumption that there is a universal that gives us complete insight; he stressed the necessity of attending to life before us, suggesting the need for "deductive hedonism" (p. 176). Deductive hedonism assists one in discerning what might be the "high priori road" to happiness (Sidgwick, 1874/1981, p. 195). The key to deductive hedonism is to work from an a priori standard that one deduces and then must be empirically ascertained; one determines a standard or conclusion and deductively works to determine the correct steps for getting there.

Intuitionism and Common Sense

The alternative that Sidgwick (1874/1981) offered as a rival to hedonistic egotism was "intuitionism" (p. 199), reliance on enlightened self-interest that uses sentiment and/or the notion of duty as a guide that must be rationally and empirically discerned. Intuitionalists work with a "first principle" that they assume guides their decision making (Sidgwick, 1874/1981, p. 201); this approach to ethics begins with what can be termed an ethical axiom that has universal appeal.

Ethical axioms take on the form of virtues, with Sidgwick (1874/1981) turning to "wisdom" as an explication of the intuitive connection of virtue and duty to forms of universal appeal (p. 231). These axioms result in habits or practices that make them actionable in everyday ethical life, inviting restraint or "self-control" in the engagement of decision making (Sidgwick, 1874/1981, p. 231). Another one of the practical virtues is "benevolence," which Sidgwick (1874/1981) calls an "architectonic virtue" that shapes practices of doing good, along with a disposition of good will toward others (p. 238). There is a duty of "good-will" with and toward others that requires additional shaping with the virtue of justice. "Impartiality" permits the discernment of judgment that does not rest on relational terms; this view of justice is akin to equality of opportunity (Sidgwick, 1874/1981, p. 267).

To ensure justice that gives opportunity and fairness, "promises" and "laws" must guide justice, with the former delivered by those who make promises that they fulfill while enacting laws that keep the public space shaped by known expectations of behavior and action (Sidgwick, 1874/1981, p. 311). In order for these social expectations to work, one must assume an intuitive given that the duty of "veracity" will guide the public forum (Sidgwick, 1874/1981, p. 315). The intuitive orientation assumes that "generosity" and "chivalry," or what is called "liberality," makes "benevolence" a natural act toward another (Sidgwick, 1874/1981, p. 326).

Sidgwick (1874/1981) envisioned a morality of "common sense" that found a harmony between "self-interest" and the virtue of "duty" (p. 327). Common sense united these two dialectical tensions with the result of a human being finding a self-identity of "dignity," "self-respect," and "pride" (Sidgwick, 1874/1981, pp. 335–336). Common sense and self-identity come alive in the interplay of duty and virtue, tying ethics to enlightened self-interest. This intuitional approach to common sense ethics involves a number of virtues about self and other that begins with human sympathy.

Intuitionalism moves from sentiment and sympathy to increasingly philosophical categories, giving rise to "utilitarianism" and the greatest good for the greatest number (Sidgwick, 1874/1981, p. 388). This approach makes a "desirable consciousness" the "ultimate good" for private and social life (Sidgwick, 1874/1981, p. 397). Sidgwick questioned whether this universal view of a desirable consciousness that has the right virtues in the correct proportions is ultimately the ethical good.

> For, whether it be true or not that the whole of morality has sprung from the root of sympathy, it is certain [Common Sense] that self-love and sympathy combined are sufficiently strong in average men to dispose them to grateful admiration of any exceptional efforts to promote the common good, even though these efforts may take a somewhat novel form. (Sidgwick, 1874/1981, p. 495)

Utilitarianism gives credence and reason to common sense assumptions about intuition and the virtues. Utilitarianism works to ensure a "general happiness" in a society, providing a moral background that undergirds law as the skeletal backbone of a society (Sidgwick, 1874/1981, p. 493). Sidgwick's assumption that ethics rests between utilitarianism and intuitionalism relies upon moral first principles that are known before the fact and fit the everyday vernacular of common sense, an alternative to the extremes of self-interest and duty.

Philosophy of Communication: *Zorba the Greek* and Ethics

This chapter underscores a historical fact—there is no longer agreed-upon certainty about what is ethical; there are multiple perspectives. The work of MacIntyre and Sidgwick outline the diversity in method, process, and style of implementing ethical matters. It is not just what we argue as ethical that matters; the manner of carrying out a given ethic shapes a philosophy of communication. In the novel *Zorba the Greek*, we discover one situation after another in which Zorba and Boss are in ethical disagreement. These two main characters also meet secondary characters in the novel whose ethical perspectives dramatically contrast with theirs.

Zorba reveals ethics at work that counter decision making by personal preference. He takes care of others and his tools. We find in the character of Zorba a kind of craftsman-like ethic, played out in his work and with his men in the mine. Zorba both protects his men and chastises them for what they forgot to protect—their tools.

> Zorba had just made firm the great prop and was running, slithering in the mire, towards the exit. Rushing headlong in the darkness, he ran into me and we accidentally fell into each other's arms. "We must get out!" he yelled. "Get out!" We ran and reached the light. The terror-stricken workmen had gathered at the entrance and were peering inside.... "You left your picks down there!" Zorba shouted angrily. The men said nothing. "Why didn't you take them with you?" he shouted again, furious. (Kazantzakis, 1946/1952, pp. 127–128)

The philosophy of communication that Zorba embraces includes the vitality of doing and caring for the tools needed for building. For Zorba, labor is not just for producing; the labor gives meaning for a life. In the eyes of Sidgwick, Zorba's actions during this incident in the mine lie in the space between self-interest and duty, a utilitarian commitment to the workers, the work, and the tools, that was not blind loyalty or individualist disregard.

The drama within the novel offers a constant reminder that we cannot take ethical agreement for granted. Ethical positions emerge from contrasting views of the good that yield different philosophies of communication, which seek to protect and promote differing conceptions of what is meaningful.

1. There is a danger of following contemporary normative conventions of decision making that are defined solely by personal preference, emotivism. One might expect Zorba to embrace emotivism, decision making by personal choice, alone. However, in Zorba we find a person attentive to others and existence. He does not impose an ethic, but responds creatively to that which he meets.

2. The hope for the capacity of reason rests with the need to have a trusted navigation system for meeting increased diversity without losing one's way. Historically in the West, hope rested with rationality, connecting ethics to rational decision making. We find this commitment in Boss. In Zorba, we witness a different set of commitments. The rational moves one to walk above the earth, beyond the messiness of everyday life—the very ground that Zorba occupied.

3. The ongoing interplay and tension between self-interest and duty continues to shape our ethical landscape today. Zorba has natural inclination toward self-interest. He takes care of the environment before him, persons, and work with full knowledge that assisting them will assist him. Zorba is an exemplar of the difference between individualism and self-interest, with the former attempting to walk above the stresses of everyday life and the latter wading into the demands of ordinary life.

4. The underlying ability to think philosophically is essential as one seeks to understand the ethical implications. The ability to think philosophically and to recognize difference is a trait that Zorba engaged in everyday life, without philosophical language. He understands that different assumptions lend to contrasting views of the world. Boss works at thinking philosophically. He must learn, however, to think beyond his own preferred system of thought. For this, Zorba is the teacher.

Zorba would, in general, approve of Sidgwick's (1874/1981) contribution, which reminds us of ongoing questions about the interplay between human self-interest and duty. We may argue with Sidgwick's terms, but we need to admire his effort to rescue society from an emerging attachment to emotivism, decision making as perceived self-interest without limits. Both Sidgwick and MacIntyre offer insight into the problematic ethical offspring of blatant individualism, which the main character of *Zorba the Greek* refutes in action.

PART III: MEANING IN ACTION

CHAPTER 12
PUBLIC DOMAIN AS THE HOME OF DIFFERENCE AND OPINION

A central issue in this historical moment is the meeting of, contributing to, and understanding of the public domain. In this chapter, we turn to two articulate spokespersons about the public domain, Hannah Arendt (1906–1975) and Jürgen Habermas (b. 1929). Their work is central to the insights of contemporary scholars seeking to understand the construction of the public domain in an era defined by difference. One of the scholars indebted to their work is Seyla Benhabib, whose insights into the public domain attend to ethics and change, relying on both Arendt and Habermas.[1]

Introduction

The erroneous commonplace assumption about the public domain is that agreement defines its reality. This assumption contrasts with the scope of this chapter. We understand the public domain as a place of difference, contrasting opinions, and differing perspectives. The public domain is a sphere for conversation and argument, not a site of presupposed agreement.

This chapter examines the public domain through the lens of two scholars central to its study, Hannah Arendt and Jürgen Habermas, in three major sections: (1) a reading of Arendt's *The Human Condition*; (2) an examination of Habermas using David Rasmussen's *Reading Habermas*; and (3) the implications of the public domain for philosophy of communication as the carrier of meaning exemplified through the story of *Zorba the Greek*.

This chapter connects philosophy of communication to the public domain with one basic assumption—the diversity of the public domain matters. Our ability to enter and influence the public domain is central to our discovery of meaning in the human condition. The public domain is the place of argument about the practices that should guide us in a given historical moment. The public domain does not offer answers; rather, it is a conversational dwelling place for differences of opinion.

---

1 Seyla Benhabib's works include: *Critique, Norm and Utopia: A Study of the Normative Foundations of Critical Theory* (1986); *Situating the Self: Gender, Community, and Postmodernism in Contemporary Ethics* (1992); *Feminism as Critique* (1986; with Drucilla Cornell); *Feminist Contentions: A Philosophical Exchange* (1994; with Judith Butler, Drucilla Cornell, & Nancy Fraser); *The Reluctant Modernism of Hannah Arendt* (2003); *The Claims of Culture: Equality and Diversity in the Global Era*, (2002); *The Rights of Others: Aliens, Citizens and Residents* (2004); and *Another Cosmopolitanism: Hospitality, Sovereignty and Democratic Iterations* (2006).

Arendt and *The Human Condition*

Hannah Arendt was born in 1906 in Hanover, Germany; she died in New York in 1975 at the age of 69. She was born of a Jewish family, witnessed two world wars, and watched the systematic destruction of those deemed "unworthy" by the Nazi machine. Arendt began her university studies in theology with Rudolf Bultmann (1884–1976) and later studied with Martin Heidegger (1889–1976) at the University of Marburg. She left Marburg to study with Edmund Husserl (1859–1938) in the fall of 1925, and then moved to Heidelberg where she studied with Karl Jaspers (1883–1969), who later became her dissertation director (Benhabib, 2003, p. 51). Arendt defended her dissertation on Augustine in 1929, which was later published as *Love and Saint Augustine* in 1996. During her lifetime, Arendt completed 22 books and 149 articles (Young-Bruehl, 2004). Her final work, *The Life of the Mind*, was edited by Mary McCarthy and published posthumously in 1978.

A Call to Reclaim the Public Domain

This chapter examines Arendt's (1958) *The Human Condition*, a central work in her conception of the public domain (Benhabib, 2003, pp. 199–200). Arendt begins the prologue of this work with her now famous conception of the danger of standing outside existence; she responds to a news headline that used the launching of Sputnik as an excuse to express a desire to escape "imprisonment to the earth" (Arendt, 1958, p. 1). The public domain is not something to escape; it is not some ethereal entity. The public domain is composed of the opinions of human beings who engage the mud of everyday life. We both live in and make up the public domain. Arendt's assertion was that we must fight the temptation to free ourselves from the earthly responsibilities of labor and thinking before, during, and after the doing of a given activity. Rather, she suggested that we embrace responsibilities necessary for the protection and the preservation of the public domain.

Arendt describes three activities as central to vita activa in the human condition: labor, work, and action. She connected labor with the "necessities" that must be fed to maintain the life processes. Labor involves the survival of the individual and the species. Work involves "unnaturalness" (Arendt, 1958, p. 7); it builds a world that can transcend and outlast the architect. Action is the point of "between" or interplay, involving the "plurality" of human participants (Arendt, 1958, p. 7).

Additionally, Arendt discussed the importance of *vita contemplativa* as an essential complement to *vita activa*. She contended that significant "works and deeds and words" produce greatness in mortals (Arendt, 1958, p. 19). The fall of the Roman Empire revealed that the great works of mortals are, indeed, not immortal. The rise of Christianity moved the striving for immortality from the grasp of *vita activa* alone, stressing the importance of a life tempered with contemplation. Just as *vita activa* and *vita contemplativa* are both needed in the human condition, so is the distinction between the public and private realms of life.

Only action requires the presence of other human beings, a society. *Societas* is a Latin term suggesting "an alliance between people for a specific purpose" (Arendt, 1958, p. 23). The development of the city-state, the polis, permitted action to be accompanied by the power of human "speech" and the shaping of the "social animal" (Arendt, 1958, p. 27). Public speech is central to the "political" domain in the polis, and private speech is central to the maintenance of the family and the "household" (Arendt, 1958, p. 29). In classical life, freedom and honor were pursued in the public domain, not in the household, where the roles were clearly established and slaves were part of everyday life. The public domain of the polis was the dwelling of "equals," a place where one could argue with another, making free use of human speech (Arendt, 1958, p. 32). However, for Arendt (1958), there was a large "gulf" between the private and the public domains with only the latter permitting the possibility of human freedom and advancement (p. 33). The polis was the locus of freedom and individuation of honor; the public arena was the place where one could differentiate oneself from others. The household was a private place in which one had a particular role that allowed for no alteration or change unless death or some other outside intervention necessitated a change. The classical understanding of the "common good" rested with the political and the public; within the medieval world, the "common good" shifted to the household (Arendt, 1958, p. 35). As the private household challenged the power of the public realm, there was a shift from the common good of the public to the private domain, which lent itself to the later Romantic stress on "individualism" and "intimacy," which levels associations in the public domain, leading to a third entry—the "social" (Arendt, 1958, pp. 38–39).

The social domain is neither public nor private; it is a dwelling between the two spheres. The social is the home of modern sitcoms where strangers gather without the intimacy of the household and with little regard for their public responsibility in and for the public domain. The social opens the door to a modern view of equality that is akin to Aristotle's (trans. 1998) view of "sameness" (1131a–1131b23). The swing from competency tested in the public domain to individual worth begins to level those participating in the public domain. Meaningfulness is found in "everyday relationships" and is no longer registered by acts of great deeds in the public domain in an era that privileges the social (Arendt, 1958, p. 42). Arendt (1958) stated that "mass society" puts at risk both the public and the private realms of the human condition (pp. 45–47). Public deeds of excellence must be vetted by "storytelling" and "publicity" (Arendt, 1958, p. 50). Public deeds of excellence lose their power in a world increasingly composed of the "social" arena, which no longer differentiates between public and private space (Arendt, 1958, p. 50). Significance then relocates, moving from the public domain to concerns about individual "private property" and individual acts of "goodness," which are increasingly separated from actualization in the public domain (Arendt, 1958, pp. 72–73).

Labor, Work, and Action

Recognizing the demise of the public domain and its function for individuation as people engaged in deeds of excellence, Arendt outlined the necessary coordinates for reinvigorating the human condition: labor, work, and action. Arendt did not frame labor in the same manner as Karl Marx (1818–1883); her emphasis was on necessities for human biological survival. Laboring does not leave anything behind; it is the doing of necessity and the engagement of temporal acts in order to assist the survival of persons. There is contempt in ancient and modern cultures for the doing of labor that results in a turn toward slave labor, giving to others the tasks of doing acts of necessity that keep people alive. The delegation of labor to others aligns the act of laboring as necessity with "contempt" for labor (Arendt, 1958, p. 93).

The classical contempt for labor was challenged by John Locke (1632–1704), who connected labor to the acquisition of private property. However, Locke's connection of labor with private property moved the societal focus from the public sense of the common. Adam Smith (1723–1790) then connected labor to accumulation of capital, and finally, "where labor became the source of all productivity and the expression of the very humanity of man" (Arendt, 1958, p. 101). Contrary to Smith, Marx wanted to eliminate labor as a necessity and moved it into the realm of freedom of choice, with labor being the manner in which one reproduces one's own life. Marx understood imposed labor as surplus for others that built a culture of consumption on the backs of a few. Marx wanted to emancipate the laborer from imposed necessity and, unfortunately, from all necessity. "The easier that life has become in a consumers' or laborers' society, the more difficult it will be to remain aware of the urges of necessity by which it is driven, even when pain and effort, the outward manifestations of necessity, are hardly noticeable at all" (Arendt, 1958, p. 135). Arendt ended her discussion of labor with the reminder that a consumption-based culture forgets the importance and power of labor, understood as a biological necessity. The twin goals of trying to eliminate labor and worshiping the act of labor failed the human condition, ignoring the fact that some things must simply be done to survive, defined by Arendt as the labor of necessity.

Work, for Arendt, moves from the act of necessity (labor) to the realm of building things that have a chance of outliving us, shifting from *animal laborans* to *homo faber*. The work of fabrication builds something. Our task is no longer to simply survive, but to leave something enduring behind. Arendt stated that *homo faber* is lord and master over productivity, which makes possible the act of destruction. Work requires intentional "tool-making," an act that prepares one for production. There is a contrast between tool and machine, however. The act of production moves one from the tool-in-hand to the machine afar, which includes making parts that another assembles, opening the door to a "meaninglessness" that a tool-in-hand does not promote (Arendt, 1958, p. 154).

Story-Laden Action

The public arena of *homo faber* is the "exchange market," which offers esteem when the products are tied to the hand, but when the products are mass produced, only commercial results drive the person in the market (Arendt, 1958, p. 159). Commodities result in a "materializing reification" (Arendt, 1958, p. 170). We cease to find meaning in what we make; instead, meaning comes, no matter how transient, from what we own. In addition to work, the other manner of discovering human meaning emerges in the public arena of freedom of voice in the diversity of opinion (action in the public arena) that constitutes the "human plurality," where there is both "equality" and "distinction" (Arendt, 1958, p. 175). The public domain is sustained by action, deeds of excellence confirmed by stories about exemplary behavior, ideas, and achievement.

The equality of the public square offers a freedom of opportunity in which one risks the possibility of distinctiveness; one must claim one's own place in the public square with ideas and actions of excellence. "In acting and speaking, men show who they are, reveal actively their unique personal identities and thus make their appearance in the human world, while their physical identities appear without any activity of their own in the unique shape of the body and sound of the voice" (Arendt, 1958, p. 179). Persons in the public domain are held together by action and speech. The actors and the speakers reveal the power of story that moves behavior into understandable action. The importance of the storyteller is akin to an Athenian historian who brings forth a story about deeds worthy of being remembered. It is through a story expressed in the public domain that behavior moves to action and deeds are remembered that give individuals distinction. Story involves deeds and other characters; indeed, "the reality of the world is guaranteed by the presence of others" (Arendt, 1958, p. 199). A person who brings together action and speech and the presence of others "preserves the public realm" (Arendt, 1958, p. 204). In contrast, a tyrant tries to function without the presence of others, imposing an individual will onto others.

Those who worship at the contemporary table of *animal laborans* often consider contemplative understanding of action and speech "idleness" (Arendt, 1958, p. 208); however, contemplation is a fundamental part of Arendt's understanding of action in the public square. Arendt (1958) contended that what withered the public arena was the move toward consumption and away from productivity, which required contemplative action (p. 220). Following an old adage, one must consider and look before one leaps; contemplation must guide action. The public arena is a place of diversity of opinion and risk. Without risk, individuation is not possible. Without contemplation, consideration of what is excellent and who is doing excellence is not possible. Contemplation gives rise to public opinion based on evidence that requires promises, necessitates forgiveness, and forgets the non-excellent that must be left behind.

Arendt concluded *The Human Condition* with a return to issues related to the major theme of her work, *vita activa*, connecting her insights to the modern age. Arendt (1958) stated that modernity is defined as a moment of "world alienation" with the collapse of public and private spheres and the loss of our sense of place (p. 254). We invite misery with a "laboring poor" and err in our demand for an "Archimedean point" from which we can make objective judgments (Arendt, 1958, p. 262). The consequence of misery in the human condition spawned "schools of suspicion"; this systematic engagement of doubt moved us from the practical reality of "appearance" to confidence in abstract reasoning, void of clear origins. We lost the "sensual world." The loss of our connection to a sensual world of existence, in which one feels sympathy for another, is fertile ground for the loss of human dignity in the public square and the rejection of traditions composed of practices of excellence. Instead, we fueled the growth of a myth, the autonomous self (Arendt, 1958, pp. 248–291).

In modernity, the person doing contemplation prior, during, and after action was replaced by the maker/imitator, leaving out the importance of creativity. "*Theoria*, in fact, is only another word for *thaumazein*; the contemplation of truth at which the philosopher ultimately arrives is the philosophically purified speechless wonder with which he began" (Arendt, 1958, p. 302). With the loss of contemplation and creative engagement in the public square, the notion of wonder no longer propels the human condition. Imposition upon existence trumped the meeting of existence, from which creativity could arise. Contrary to imposition, Arendt's notion of contemplation yields craftsmanship and participation in the public arena. Depravity enters when labor and action become unreflective practices driven solely by process, procedure, and an assumption that we can control the world. "It is quite conceivable that the modern age—which began with such an unprecedented and promising outburst of human activity—may end in the deadliest, most sterile passivity history has ever known" (Arendt, 1958, p. 322). Arendt ends, not with a call for just contemplation or action, but with the realization that both are needed—theory with practice, ideas with actions, thinking with doing, words with deeds, and behavior with story that vets the significance of human deeds. Such ingredients make the dwelling of public space possible, framed even more forcefully by Jürgen Habermas.

Rasmussen and *Reading Habermas*

A thoughtful examination of Jürgen Habermas's scholarship is offered by David Rasmussen, a leading Habermasian scholar. Rasmussen is a professor in the Department of Philosophy at Boston College. He joined the faculty in 1967, becoming full professor in 1976. He is editor-in-chief of the journal *Philosophy and Social Criticism*, which began publication in 1978, and is one of the foremost experts on critical theory in the United States. Rasmussen has authored nine books and edited works on Habermas, including a four-volume series entitled *Habermas II*, which he edited with James Swindal and published in 2009.

Modernity and the Public Domain

Rasmussen states that Habermas stresses the public domain and its place in modernity, functioning as a critic of numerous aspects of modernity. Habermas's emphasis on the public domain results in his privileging communication; he shifts from a linguistic to a communicative emphasis. Numerous scholars within the "postmodern" critical genre contend that modernity is finished (Lyotard, 1984; Vattimo, 1988). Habermas, on the other hand, suggests "[a]t its base level, the assumption is that the project of modernity can be redeemed" (Rasmussen, 1990, p. 5). Habermas's task is "a reconstructed project of modernity" (Rasmussen, 1990, p. 6). Habermas's reconstruction project is contrary to Georg Wilhelm Friedrich Hegel's (1770–1831) resistance to a "communicative solution"; Habermas pursues a communicative solution that rejects the Hegelian view of the "dialectic of enlightenment" (Rasmussen, 1990, pp. 10–11). Habermas is both part of and critical of the story of the Enlightenment. For Habermas, dialectic understanding about the Enlightenment begins with Friedrich Nietzsche (1844–1900).

Nietzsche rejected modernity's love of progress; he undermined "the theoretical history of reason, rationality, rationalization, development, progress, and evolution" (Rasmussen, 1990, p. 12). However, Nietzsche made a turn back to modernity with his use of Kant's "aesthetic" (Rasmussen, 1990, p. 12). For Nietzsche, the aesthetic becomes, ironically, another form of reasoning. Nietzsche offers a seductive alternative, pointing to the real battleground of modernity as involving the question of reason and the nature of the form that reason takes in a given historical moment. However, Habermas rejects any effort to deny reason or dethrone the position of the "philosophy of the subject" (Rasmussen, 1990, p. 16). Nietzsche accepts the critique of much of modern life; he refused to give up on the Enlightenment project of human emancipation. Habermas turns to a communicative strategy, which is played out in the two volumes of *The Theory of Communicative Action*; he offers a theory of emancipation of the individual through communication.

Habermas's effort to rehabilitate modernity begins with his use of a diachronic model for understanding language, "[u]sing Ferdinand de Saussure's [1857–1913] distinction between diachronic and synchronic as fundamental, diachronic historical-evolutionary schemes for understanding language" (Rasmussen, 1990, pp. 18–19). Habermas uses this diachronic orientation to take on two of the principal problems of modernity: (1) the modern expectation for "foundations," and (2) the modern desire to "limit" diversity and difference (Rasmussen, 1990, p. 20). Habermas places the origin of these two problems with Immanuel Kant's (1724–1804) insistence upon a "foundationalism of epistemology" (Rasmussen, 1990, p. 20). Habermas offers a "reconstructive science" that uses philosophy as a constructive empirical science (Rasmussen,

1990, p. 20). Habermas states that one must choose between capitalism and the "rationalization" outlined by Max Weber (1864–1920) (Rasmussen, 1990, p. 23). The perspectives offered by Habermas and Weber move in contrasting directions, as Habermas understands rationalization in a more textured manner than Weber, situating rationality within community. Habermas rejects an instrumental rationalization that Weber contended was a fundamental cause for increasing secularization (Rasmussen, 1990, p. 24).

Community

Attentiveness to community is important for Habermas; danger rests in stressing the "isolated subject" who is not "intersubjectively" understood (Rasmussen, 1990, p. 26). Thus, Habermas's "speech-act theory" connects "language" and the "life-world" (Rasmussen, 1990, p. 26). Habermas emphasized community and life-world, resulting in his upholding the importance of communication. He wants to regenerate reason as communicative reason that is tied to language and community in the life-world.

Habermas works with the assumption that language in the life-world is lived out in communication, which provides a location for the "justification" of communication's influence on and directing of reason (Rasmussen, 1990, p. 29). He chooses a form of language articulate with "communication," not "strategic" discourse (Rasmussen, 1990, p. 30). Rasmussen (1990) states that the communicative project of Habermas attends to a communicative community that unites "empirical theories with strong universalistic claims" (p. 36). The rejection of strategic discourse invites an emancipation of communicative reason, leaving us with the question of whether or not this work is "science" or actually "politics" (Rasmussen, 1990, p. 36).

Habermas chooses the notion of communicative action over the strategic, not because of "ought," but due to empirical reflection on how life actually proceeds (Rasmussen, 1990, p. 37). It is the "illocutionary" that Habermas offers as an alternative to what Max Weber situated as the heart of modernity, "purposive-rational activity" (Rasmussen, 1990, p. 40). Habermas offers a combination of the above, seeking "consensus" through "communicative rationality" that requires communicative agency and speaker knowledge and involvement (Rasmussen, 1990, p. 43). "As the foundation of the theory of language is the primacy of the communicative over the strategic, so the end of social theory is liberation from the consequences of strategic action in the form of the colonization of the life-world" (Rasmussen, 1990, p. 45). Communicative rationality enriches the life-world of the people, offering communicative interaction that gives people a sense of common life. The life-world is colonized when abstract principles and processes determine outcomes. The life-world is essential for the health of the "social system"; otherwise, the social system becomes isolated from criticism.

To renew the life-world, Habermas moves to "discourse ethics" to guide communicative action (Rasmussen, 1990, p. 57). Additionally, Habermas attempts to weave a theory between abstract universalism and communitarianism. In an effort to find an alternative between these two extremes, Habermas turns to the work of Lawrence Kohlberg, who moves conversation about the "moral" to the "universal," bypassing "ethics," which must languish in "cultural analysis" (Rasmussen, 1990, p. 58). Habermas's "discourse ethics" orientation uses insights from the pragmatic semiologist Charles Sanders Peirce (1839–1914), which have been reinterpreted by Karl-Otto Apel in *Charles S. Peirce: From Pragmatism to Pragmaticism* (1981). The basic supposition is that science presupposes a scientific community that assists in acts of validation. "Unlike Kant, Peirce located those conditions not in the intuitions of an investigating subject, but in the postulation of an ideal community of investigators whose mutual understanding would regulate the nature of scientific truth" (Rasmussen, 1990, p. 59). Peirce shifted the conversation from the nature of things to the nature of communities, a radical semiotic move. Habermas pursues Peirce's approach and frees discourse ethics from "institutional representation" (Rasmussen, 1990, p. 59).

Habermas includes Kant as he stresses the universal nature of discourse ethics and reconstructs the grounds for a "categorical imperative" (Rasmussen, 1990, p. 60). The categorical imperative responds to an absolute command that calls forth duty in the accomplishment of the absolute. The most famous of the categorical imperatives from Kant (1785/1981) is "Act only according to that maxim whereby you can at the same time will that it should become a universal law" (p. 30). Habermas differentiates between "norms" and "values," with the former connected to practices and habits (Rasmussen, 1990, p. 60). His work centers on norms explicated by "procedures" that invite an ideal speech situation (Rasmussen, 1990, p. 60). Habermas's objective is to search for "rational consensus" (Rasmussen, 1990, p. 61). In order to invite rational discourse that is not tainted by unreflective ground (tradition), there is a controlled enactment of an "ethics of suspicion" (Rasmussen, 1990, p. 62). Habermas's theory of communicative action works as a foundation for discourse ethics. He rejects tradition, cultural precepts, and the communitarian implications that emerge from the later John Rawls

(1921–2002). However, Habermas continues to have confidence in the universal characteristics of rationality. "Discourse ethics may be said to provide a procedural justification for truth and validity claims" (Rasmussen, 1990, p. 63). Habermas's goal is "rationally motivated consensus" with this "ideal-speech situation" becoming a "meta-norm" (Rasmussen, 1990, p. 64). The connection of universality to reason finds support within Kant's project and is rejected by the communitarians and ethics authors, such as Alasdair MacIntyre, whom we discussed in the previous chapter.

Habermas, like Seyla Benhabib, offers a dialectical meeting of the universal and community, which makes discourse ethics the intermediary between the universal and community. Like Benhabib, Habermas's understanding of ethics is linked closely to the life-world, which he does not confuse with the communitarian assumptions of Aristotle, whom he terms a dead metaphysic. Habermas argues that we must take into account this historical moment and embrace a scientific commitment that does not situate ethics in tradition, but rather in the procedures of discourse. Habermas states that the communitarian perspective has inherent "repressive characteristics" that limit discourse, and the communitarians suggest that any move that does not take into account the real life of a people shifts the discourse to a modern "abstraction," which they contend was at the center of Kant's project (Rasmussen, 1990, p. 73). As stated above, Habermas leans heavily upon Peirce's empirical view of community tied to science, rejecting community tied to tradition.[2] Habermas links discourse ethics to a radical democratic agenda.

This Kantian perspective continues to influence Habermas's differentiation of morality and ethics, with the former tied to the universal and the latter to the contextual. Habermas moves this analysis into the difference between morality, which is the foundation for procedural issues in law and the actual content of law, which is more value-based. Legitimization does not come from ethics or law, but from morality that finds life in the life-world. When there is "colonization of the life-world," one finds the invasion of abstract systems of capital and content within ethics and law that act as repressive agents (Rasmussen, 1990, p. 81). This position

---

2 Habermas and Hans-Georg Gadamer, whom we discussed in Chapter 6, engaged in a series of written exchanges revolving largely around Gadamer's work with and construct of the term "tradition." The debate began after the publication of the second edition of Gadamer's *Truth and Method* in 1965, as Gadamer responded to his critics in the preface of this volume. Habermas then countered in two major essays appearing in 1967 and 1970 (MacKendrick, 2008, p. 77).

leads Habermas to reject both "objectivism" and "formalism" as artificial substitutes for the life-world in its healthy form (Rasmussen, 1990, p. 83). Questions of morality rest within the context of a life-world, and questions of law live within rules that assume abstract and abiding importance, making it impossible for Habermas to abide by "legal positivism" (Rasmussen, 1990, p. 93). The connection between law and morality rests in procedures that demand questions that return the conversation and the judgment to the life-world, leaving a narrow and abstract understanding of justice.

Rejecting Relativism

Rasmussen concludes with a discussion of Habermas and postmodernity. In the early work of Habermas, we find two polar issues anchoring his work: the transcendental and the empirical. In later Habermas, philosophy takes on an interpretive role, assisting a new reconstitutive science that operates within the parameters or coordinates of the transcendental and the empirical. Habermas engages the "unfinished project of modernity" in a continuing effort to engage reason for "emancipatory" purposes (Rasmussen, 1990, p. 95). Habermas moves from "epistemology" to "language" to "communication" as the emancipatory key in his *The Theory of Communicative Action*, which undergirds the remainder of his work (Rasmussen, 1990, p. 95). He considers the project of modernity "noble" (Rasmussen, 1990, p. 96). Habermas's modern project embraces a "reconstructive science" that permits him to bypass two arguments about meaning and communicative action "on a purely transcendental basis as Apel does, or he would have to accede to the contextualists. In other words, without reconstructive science, discourse ethics has to be argued on a contextualist basis" (Rasmussen, 1990, p. 97). Additionally, Habermas rejects the hermeneutics of Gadamer as too relativistic. His project is a response to a tradition generated by Nazism. He has not given up on modernity and has not fallen into the extreme camps of tradition or postmodernity; rather, he contended with authors associated with both perspectives.

According to Rasmussen (1990), Habermas's initial fascination with Heidegger, and then his deep disappointment with Heidegger as he discovered his connection with the Nazi party, moved Habermas increasingly to the universal position and to a commitment to a "reconstructive science" (p. 97). Habermas refuses to give in to the critics who question the reality of moral universalism and considers the alternative dangerous, announced by the Nazi fascination with contextualism.

Habermas has been battling for the soul of continental philosophy, carrying forth a modernist unfinished project in opposition to those who turned against the assumption that links rationality and modernity, framing them as genuine emancipators. He views Heidegger as a thinker within the "shadow" of Friedrich Nietzsche. Habermas rejects the "abolition" of the subject and offers a devastating critique of Heidegger and his view of the subject (Rasmussen, 1990, p. 101). Habermas claims that Heidegger demonstrates a "history of Being" that inverts the nature of the subject, making the "they" normative—in ironical contrast to his Nietzschian task (Rasmussen, 1990, p. 108).

Habermas reads Jacques Derrida (1930–2004) as working within the shadow of Heidegger's history of Being. The deconstructive path of Derrida follows the lead of Heidegger. Derrida continued with the critique of metaphysics, failing to go beyond Heidegger, but falling behind him in an embrace of "the historical locale where mysticism once turned into enlightenment" (Rasmussen, 1990, p. 107). Unlike Derrida, Habermas continues his work centered in language and in the unfinished project of modernity. Interestingly, Habermas reads Michel Foucault (1926–1984) in a more sympathetic manner than either Heidegger or Derrida. "What seems to interest Habermas most in his reading of Foucault is the transition from archaeology to genealogy, and the subsequent preoccupation with the theory of power" (Rasmussen, 1990, p. 107). Foucault does not adhere to epistemology, structuralism, and semiotic representation; his stress on "practices" gives him a chance to reject the conventional views of the Western subject (Rasmussen, 1990, p. 108). Yet, ironically, it is the derivation of the "will to power" from Nietzsche that brings Foucault back into the problem of the "philosophy of the subject" (Rasmussen, 1990, p. 109). Habermas rejects postmodernity for its turn toward "moral vacuity" (Rasmussen, 1990, p. 109). He refuses to give up on the subject; his work is "subject-centered" (Rasmussen, 1990, p. 111). His theory fits into a larger project, "democratic" participation (Rasmussen, 1990, p. 112). He weds democratic theory, Marxism, and rationality in an ideal communicative situation, arguing for a life-world that continues to emancipate human subjects.

Philosophy of Communication: *Zorba the Greek* and the Public Domain

This chapter utilized Arendt and Habermas to frame the importance of understanding and engagement that seeks to ensure a vibrant public domain, a sphere where there is a diversity of ideas and opinions grounded in evidence rather than personal preference. Arendt offered a warning of what happens when we ignore the public domain. Her position stresses the interplay of opinion with evidence, multiplicity, and understanding of the public domain as a dwelling that offers respite for contrasting ideas. Habermas frames a communicative commitment that he contends ensures the reality of such a public domain. He frames necessary procedures for communicative engagement that seek a universal morality in communicative action. Habermas maintains an Enlightenment hope that we can discern truth in communicative action together.

Zorba meets the power of the public domain, a place of diversity that requires risk as one fights for a given position or person. We now turn to the most horrific moment in *Zorba the Greek*, when Zorba must fight for the life of another and almost loses his own in the process. He struggles for the different and the marginalized. The moment of dramatic height within *Zorba the Greek* comes with the attack upon the widow. Zorba fights to protect her life but he fails; as a consequence, the widow loses her life. In this moment of standing up for her, Zorba puts his own life at risk. Later, Boss, who saves Zorba, reminds Manolakas why Zorba has a right to have a place in the public domain of the village.

> "And don't forget, Zorba is a foreigner, a Macedonian, and it's the greatest disgrace we Cretans can bring on ourselves to raise a hand against a guest in our country.... Come now, give him your hand, that's real gallantry—and come to the hut, Manolakas. We'll drink together and roast a yard of sausage to seal our friendship!" I took Manolakas by the waist and led him a little apart. "The poor fellow's old, remember," I whispered. "A strong, young fellow like you shouldn't attack a man of his age." (Kazantzakis, 1946/1952, p. 282)

This moment in the novel is a raw announcement about the flawed nature of a public domain, when there is limited space for difference. Following a Habermasian-like lead, Boss must discover a form of rationality that makes sense to the community that has shaped Manolakas. Boss sought to enlarge this public domain as he tried to make a place for Zorba in the community. Boss's perspective is heard and the village does not experience another death; he is able to stop Manolakas from killing Zorba. Boss's struggle for Zorba reminds us that the public domain is not just full of ideas, but is composed of people who sometimes must risk much in an effort to keep the public domain more open and healthy. At times, we must find a way to engage in a rational meeting with one another, engaging that which we do not like or condone, working to enlarge the public domain for a moment to make space for another. The public domain is not just a sphere or dwelling of joy; the public domain is more accurately understood as frustrating and, at times, a place in which people must risk much in order to keep the public domain healthy and alive with diversity that makes space for difference.

The demanding sequences in *Zorba the Greek* announce two basic facts. First, the public domain consists of multiple opinions. This assertion is not demanding; however, the second truism of the public domain is difficult. There are positions in the public domain that are despicable and, at times, we must fight and contend against them. Philosophy of communication as the carrier of meaning requires multiple opinions and, at times, courage to fight for and against particular perspectives.

1. Arendt argued for three coordinates of the human condition (labor, work, and action) that shape the importance of the public and privates domains of existence. The novel reveals the necessity of labor in order to survive, the importance of work in constructing something worthwhile, and the presence of action in the public domain that calls for argument and struggle. The public domain is the dwelling place of difference, simultaneously generating new ideas and conflict.

2. The danger of the social, a blurred place of public and private, loses differentiation, eroding the public domain. A background story of the novel is the danger of blurring public and private life. Anyone who has experienced a place where another knows all about his or her life can relate to the danger of such a dwelling. If one is on the inside of such intimacy, one may feel protected; however, that protection comes at a cost—one must agree with those in power of the common assumptions. The blurring of public and private lessens diversity of ideas in the public domain; Zorba understands the need for such separation as he offers warnings to Boss.

3. The public domain is a place of diversity of opinion, not one uniform set of ideas. Uniformity is a temptation until one is on the outside of what is accepted and approved. The widow loses her life; she is an outsider. Zorba almost loses his life in an attempt to protect her. The public domain ceases to function in a healthy manner when only one set of ideas and assumptions dominate.

4. The diversity of the engagement in the public domain requires a taming of "interests" and a reliance on procedures that give life to rationality connected to the enhancement of the life-world. The example of Boss protecting Zorba displays the importance of interests guiding communicative action. Boss determines the interests of

Manolakas and argues to save Zorba's life. We may not approve of the interests of another; however, if we cannot discern those interests and work with them, our interests are likely to go unheeded.

The village that shapes the lives of Zorba and Boss and all the characters that compose the novel reveal a limited public domain, a dwelling in the hands of a small perceptual world. This place is far from cosmopolitan; one must fight for contrasting positions. The public domain is a sacred space when it is healthy and full of diverse ideas and opinions that some have fought and died to protect. The public domain is not an intellectual haven, but more like Zorba's village—a place that necessitates fighting for what one deems are good opinions. When diversity exists and the sacred space of the public domain is acknowledged, one finds increased power given to the private domain. We dialectically discover our character and identity in the exchange of public and private life.

Chapter 13

Individualism as Misstep

This chapter contends that individualism is a misstep, a caricature of the excesses of the Enlightenment carried into modernity. The rationale for this chapter rests with our understanding of a philosophy of communication that is attentive to others, the historical moment, and a given social context—a position in contrast to individualism, which attempts to walk above all constraints. This chapter distinguishes the notion of individualism from selfishness and from the individual; both of these terms are understood in a more constructive light than the mythology of standing above the human community. The philosophical acknowledgment of difference begins with an inescapable relationship between the individual and the community, with each lending insight from the other. The interplay of individual, community, and difference invites a space for philosophy of communication as the carrier of meaning.

Introduction

This chapter relies upon a philosophical picture—a critique of individualism—that recognizes the importance of the individual painted by two very different philosophers: Alexis de Tocqueville and Judith Butler. We rely on Alexis de Tocqueville's (1835, Vol. 1; 1840, Vol. 2) *Democracy in America* and Judith Butler's (2005) *Giving an Account of Oneself*. Tocqueville's (1835 & 1840) two-volume text provides historical consideration of community and democracy; he also coined the term "individualism" (p. 98). Tocqueville (1840) provides a critical look at the importance of individual and community as opposed to individualism that "appeals only to the individual effort of his own understanding" (p. 3). Butler's work is a feminist critique of individualism and, specifically, a feminist critique of how the category of "woman" is produced. Butler's work has also been described as a "radical critique" of the normative conventions associated with women's identities (Brady & Schirato, 2010, p. 30). Butler's work centers on a philosophical discovery of identification framed around an embedded individual within relationships and contexts.

This chapter examines the concept of individualism in three major sections: (1) a discussion of Tocqueville's conception of individualism as a philosophical and pragmatic misstep; (2) an examination of Butler's conception of the emergence of the individual; and (3) implications of individualism for the study of philosophy of communication understood as a philosophical painting incorporating community and difference illustrated through the characters in *Zorba the Greek*, the central story used throughout this project.

The passions of the individual temper community, and community tempers the passions of the individual; this dialectic of difference contrasts with an individualistic mythology of standing above the human condition. This chapter acknowledges the fundamental importance of a dialectic of difference between individual and community as a necessary background for a philosophy of communication capable of functioning as a temporal dwelling for human meaning. The notions of individual, community, and difference are structural elements in the human condition that counter individualism. The differences and connections between individual and community shape our understanding of philosophy of communication as the carrier of meaning. Tocqueville and Butler offer critiques of individualism that emanate from contrasting political perspectives while articulating the importance of a socially embedded understanding of the individual.

The Emergence of Individualism

Alexis de Tocqueville (1805–1859) was a French political philosopher and historian. His main concern was social equity for the individual living within a community. Tocqueville wrote *Democracy in America* during a historical moment marked by transition in the early American colonies. Like many other countries in Europe, France had internal strife for years as civil unrest flourished, precipitated by the French Revolution (1789–1799). The transitional and contentious environments that Tocqueville experienced in his youth formulated his perspective, which he displayed in writing and in public political life.

Tocqueville (1835 & 1840/1963) believed that reflection on American democracy might assist as France reconstructed its own government based upon the "sovereignty of the people" (p. cvi). While Tocqueville began from a position of hope, Volume 2 of *Democracy in America* (1840/1963) engages in harsh criticism of American individualism, warning of impending doom for the democratic experiment in America. Tocqueville described an environment that was beginning to elevate individualism over community. Tocqueville (1840/1963) depicted individualism as a novel expression that refers to "a mature and calm feeling, which disposes each member of the community to sever himself from the mass of his fellows and to draw apart with his family and his friends...he willingly leaves society at large to itself" (p. 98). Tocqueville's (1840/1963) individualism is an attempt to stand above all social constraints, a consequence of "erroneous judgment" caused by "deficiency of the mind" and "perversity of heart" (p. 98). Individualism attempts to extract one from responsibilities at the expense of the larger community. Originally, Tocqueville's (1835/1963) purpose for his visit to America was "to gain a clearer view of the polity that will be the best for us" (p. cvii). He did not come to America to critique, but to learn something about the prison system in America that might help France with its correctional system. While Tocqueville did visit several prisons, he also made numerous observations about the American democratic political structure, hoping to assist France. He later found that critique was demanded and warranted from his observations of what he believed was an American misstep toward what he defined as "individualism" (Tocqueville, 1840/1963, p. 98).

Alexis de Tocqueville was born in Paris on July 29, 1805, into an aristocratic family that had fallen out of grace and power during the French Revolution. His family lived in exile in England before returning to France during the reign of Napoleon (1769–1821). At an early age, Tocqueville was tutored at home; he later entered the Lycee Faber in Metz and began a political career as deputy of the Manche Department in 1830, which he concluded in 1851. Tocqueville held on to aristocratic values and libertarian views simultaneously. During his tenure as deputy, Tocqueville upheld abolitionist views and free trade, while also supporting the colonization of Algeria by the French. In 1831, Tocqueville received instructions to investigate prisons and penitentiaries in America (Bradley, 1963). Over the course of two years, Tocqueville traveled extensively in America and visited prisons in general. During his investigation, he maintained copious notes of his observations and reflections. He observed the American democratic system in action and wrote his now famous work on the developing young nation, *Democracy in America.*

Tocqueville held several different positions in French government, including the Chamber of Deputies from 1839 to 1848 when the Second Republic in France fell. Tocqueville assisted with the Constitutional Commission that wrote the new French Constitution of 1848, after which a new political leader was elected, Louis Napoleon Bonaparte, nephew of Napoleon I. In 1851, Louis Napoleon Bonaparte III dissolved the National Assembly because the constitution forbade his re-election. This act of dissolution turned Tocqueville away from public political engagement. Tocqueville then went into seclusion in his castle, where he died on April 16, 1859, from tuberculosis (Brogan, 2008). Tocqueville's concerns regarding community and the workings of the public political system "frame the heart of his inquiry relat[ed] to the problems posed by and resulting from social inequality and its effects on the practice of political democracy" (Bradley, 1963, p. xcvi). Tocqueville recognized the danger of gross inequality in a community; equality removes the cause for future revolution, offering reasonable security to all.

Tocqueville believed democracy must balance equality, community, and liberty in order to have lasting power. However, during his visit to America, Tocqueville discovered the dark side of equality and liberty that forgets obligation to the community, emerging in the guise of individualism. Tocqueville (1840/1963) made numerous observations that critiqued American individualism, including the connection of sovereignty with the self, disproportional power in the legislature, abuse for the love/desire for freedom, excessive equality, and a lack of respect for difference. According to Tocqueville, individualism separates individuals from others, giving rise to conflict and making one inattentive to the needs of individuals other than oneself (Brogan, 2008). Tocqueville (1840/1963) made a distinction between individualism and selfishness. He stated selfishness is "passionate and exaggerated love of self, which leads man to connect everything with himself and to prefer himself to everything in the world" (p. 98). Selfishness takes account of others in order for one to assist oneself—selfishness requires one to navigate others. On the other hand, individualism separates one from all social roots of restraint and consideration; there is a dismissive impulse behind individualism that ignores all social constraints. Selfishness emerges out of "blind instinct" and "depraved feelings" (Tocqueville, 1840/1963, p. 98). Individualism emerges from a desire to stand above human history and not to be socially connected to another.

Sovereignty of the People

In Volume 1, Tocqueville (1835/1963) identified the main principle of American democracy as the sovereignty of the people. He suggested that sovereignty of the people is "recognized by the customs and proclaimed by the laws; it spreads freely, and arrives without impediment at its most remote consequences" (Tocqueville, 1835/1963, p. 55). Tocqueville initially understood America as an ideal example of democracy centered on the principle of sovereignty for the people. America was governed by the people, who made the laws and enforced them. The sovereignty of the people emerged through the individual action of voting for representatives that had limited terms in public office. Tocqueville (1835/1963) compared American democracy to a God in which one could attribute the "cause and aim of all things" (p. 58). To Tocqueville, the American people appeared to understand themselves as omnificent.

Tocqueville (1835/1963) identified the American Constitution as the document that outlines the sovereignty of the people. However, he suggested that no document can provide the best representation because laws are "frequently defective or incomplete; they sometimes attack vested rights, or sanction others which are dangerous to the community" (Tocqueville, 1835/1963, p. 237). Tocqueville described democratic laws as promoting the welfare of the majority, even though the majority can err as they rarely assist an interest opposed to their own advantage. Tocqueville (1835/1963) compared the process of law-making between aristocratic and democratic environments; he found aristocracies better equipped to make good laws because they have self-control and do not make "errors of temporary excitement" (p. 238). Tocqueville (1835/1963) suggested that aristocracies can be more objective and patient than democracies, which almost always have "ineffective or inopportune" laws (p. 238). Tocqueville (1835/1963) also suggested that American democracy "may be best fitted to produce the prosperity of [...] community" because this form of democracy is reparable by those who make mistakes or misjudgments or commit intentional offenses—a democracy "promotes the welfare of the greatest number of people" (p. 238). A democracy can be designed with discrete terms of service, bringing diversity to the pool of those in charge of the direction of many.

Tocqueville's (1840/1963) Volume 2 critiqued the minds and intellect of those in America; he attacked the ability of the individual in America to think for her or himself. He attributed this non-thinking posture to a consequence of excessive equality, the guiding principle of American democracy. Tocqueville identified the misstep of individualism as occurring when people, in this case Americans, attempt to stand above any concern for others. Tocqueville (1840/1963) pointed to the problem of expediency, when people "are constantly brought back to their own reason," their own private view of ideas or truth (p. 4). Tocqueville contended that Americans were closed-minded and were drawn to short-term benefits; such a perspective undermines a community of diverse orientations and does not embrace the importance of taking the longer road to achievement. Additionally, Tocqueville (1840/1963) warned of the potential for great disaster when one places trust in the authority of one person, remaining closed off to other ideas and standpoints. Such action is a form of collective individualism propelled by a refusal to attend to multiple social constraints.

Tocqueville wanted Americans to place authority in themselves; such authority is illegitimate if one is incapable of learning from others. Tocqueville critiqued how individualism leads to the closure of the American mind. He wanted philosophical reflection that considers long-term consequences. Tocqueville (1840/1963) contended that Americans paid less attention to philosophy than any other country in the civilized world. He stated Americans had no philosophical school of their own and ignored philosophical schools in other countries. Tocqueville wanted to shame Americans for their lack of philosophical sophistication and their apathy for historical knowledge.

Danger of Excess

The excessive emphasis on individual sovereignty of the people, as advocated by American democracy, had an ironic twist, convincing Americans to be confident in their own experience alone. This problem sprung from an exaggerated sense of their own ability to think critically and make decisions. Tocqueville suggested that the principle of individual sovereignty created three problems: (1) disproportional power in the legislature, (2) an abuse of the love/desire for freedom, and (3) excessive focus on equality that promoted individualism—the core issue in Tocqueville's critique of America.

Disproportional power in the legislature. When anyone or anything gains too much power and privilege, there can be trouble; Tocqueville (1835/1963) observed there is disproportional power in the American legislature. He stated that the "very essence of democratic government consists in the absolute sovereignty of the majority" (Tocqueville, 1835/1963, p. 254). Even though American democracy ensures a legislature that is directly elected by the majority of the people, these measures do not protect communities from disproportional use of power that leads to misuse. When the omnipotence of the majority increases, the direct result is instability in the legislature and a disproportional balance of power. Tocqueville (1835/1963) described this imbalance as creating supremacy in the legislature where "nothing prevents them [the legislature] from accomplishing their wishes with celerity and with irresistible power" (p. 257). Such an environment creates and sustains a despotic condition; the majority then functions as an oligarchy, propelling their own agenda and self-interest.

Tocqueville's (1840/1963) ironical conclusion about American democracy was that as Americans took increasing steps toward equality, they invited "despotism" (p. 303). As power became disproportional, Tocqueville (1840/1963) stated, it would "render every day private independence more weak, more subordinate, and more precarious" (p. 303). This means that the power of the majority, without a constant check and reflection upon its own interests, endangers communities, the individual, and democratic support for difference. Tocqueville's warning about American democracy centered on actions of expediency. He critiqued intellectual apathy in America, which encouraged an average American to seek a superficial intellect and embrace short-term aims. Tocqueville contended that individualism propels a self-interest that has no long-term enlightened view of self-interest and does not foster care for community. This self-focus without concern for ties to the community results in an inability to self-reflect upon the consequences of disproportional power. Tocqueville's argument was that individualism engendered unreflective promotion of majority self-interest and a limited horizon of concern that is unresponsive to the ties of sociality.

Abuse of the love/desire for freedom. One of the more dangerous combinations in American democracy, according to Tocqueville, is the excessive desire for freedom and physical pleasure. Tocqueville (1840/1963) stated that when one is driven by passion, one is likely to "surrender to the first master who appears" (p. 140). This means that one does not think or reflect on actions and implications; instead, one succumbs to this desire in an unprincipled manner that privileges the unreflective individual self-interest over the community. Tocqueville (1835/1963) stated that the desire for freedom is closely related to materialism. When the hope for increasing self-gratification grows more aggressively than the perceived importance of education and the cultivation of free institutions, human beings lose social restraint; they relentlessly strive for more possessions and individual growth with little regard for the community. Tocqueville argued that freedom that liberates one from tyranny has a dark side if the person then feels liberated from all societal burden and concern for others.

Excessive focus on equality. Tocqueville's critique on equality emerged from an American hyper-focus on sameness of me and the other without regard for another's achievements. This hyper-focus nourishes individualism and materialism and contributes to a despotic society. Individualism changes the composition of a community, severing a human being from community and family. Materialism claims possessions, privileging things over relationships and community. Materialism teases the passions of individuals who, at all cost, strive for the acquisition of things that enslave the individual at the expense of concern for others and community. Tocqueville (1840/1963) also identified the dangers of individuals in a hurry, dissatisfied with their lot and willing to undercut those who work harder and more diligently. When a large number of people become infected by such self-serving obsessive thinking, the conditions for social unrest are sowed. Tocqueville's compelling presage about materialism is its obsessive quality, which becomes a social disease that is destructive to self and other. Individualism's effort to stand above the social fray of human constraints and community obligations moves our focus away from the reality of excessive materialism as a social danger. Tocqueville contended, however, that the mythic assumption that one can stand above history is doomed to eventually collapse under the weight of demands of others that intrude with an undeniable power and urgency.

Tocqueville described America as a place that creates individuals who are too often offensive and arrogant, demonstrating an unquenchable desire for acquisition. Tocqueville rejected the desire for the acquisition of material goods, which results in ignoring the Other and the community. The only pragmatic way to temper the social diseases of individualism and materialism is concern for community. Tocqueville considered the American dream as the dual concern for individual achievement and concern for the community. He called for a pragmatic hope in the dialectic of individual and community that lessens the missteps of deficient attentiveness to our social roots.

Difference. Tocqueville argued that excessive equality eliminates difference. This happens because "[e]veryone shuts himself up tightly within himself and insists upon judging the world from there" (Tocqueville, 1840/1963, p. 4). If one judges the world solely from one's own position, insight from another is not present. One fails to learn from difference, which tempers individualism and lack of concern for the community. Difference reminds us that the interplay of individual and community yields a multiplicity of perspectives that can inform a responsive and democratic worldview. Attentiveness to difference abolishes Tocqueville's fear of the tyranny of the majority. Difference permits the "I" to hear the call of the Other and recognize that this hailing by the community offers another account of emerging events in the human condition. Difference reminds us that the world is not about "me" alone; the heartbeat of the "American dream" is the dialectic of individual and community (Adams, 1931). When this dialectic is ruptured, society loses its ability to offer a home to a diversity of persons and perspectives. Tocqueville's project contended that individualism unreflectively dismisses the Other, encouraging a refusal to learn from, appreciate, and understand insights from those different from us. Judith Butler provides yet another critique of individualism, moving us from the 19th to the 21st century.

The Individual, Not Individualism

Judith Butler was born February 24, 1956, in Cleveland, Ohio. As a philosopher, she has influenced feminist studies, queer studies, political philosophy, and ethics. She grew up in a home with a strong guiding influence of Judaism. She attended Hebrew school with classes on Jewish ethics. Butler attended Bennington College, earning her B.A. in Philosophy in 1978, and Yale University, where she earned her Ph.D. in Philosophy in 1984. Her dissertation, entitled "Recovery and Invention: The Projects of Desire in Hegel, Kojève, Hyppolite, and Sartre," was revised and later published as *Subjects of Desire: Hegelian Reflections in Twentieth-Century France* (1987). Hegel continues to be a significant influence in her philosophy and scholarship. Butler taught at several prestigious universities before going to the University of California, Berkeley, in 1993 (Davies, 2008) and Columbia University in New York, where she is currently a visiting professor.

Butler's work centers on the idea of "woman" being a "term-in-process" (Salih, 2002, p. 7). According to Sara Salih (2002), Butler's consideration of the subject and the processes involved in subject formation provide critical and theoretical interventions across academic disciplinary boundaries. Butler has been influenced by Hegel, as well as Michel Foucault (1926–1984) and Jacques Derrida (1930–2004), who were also concerned with the ensemble of language, power, and formulations of self. Salih (2002) states that both Butler and Foucault detail the process of subject formation within historical and discursive contexts, and Butler and Derrida describe meaning between subjects as an "event" that transpires within a particular chain, having no real beginning or end (p. 5). These philosophical and theoretical influences upon Butler have contributed to her "extensive formulations of identity" (Salih, 2002, p. 1). Butler's theoretical underpinnings overlap the above philosophical perspectives while maintaining her unique scholarly framework; her work emerges from the spirit of dialectical inquiry. Butler's attention to the relationship between the individual, community, and the interplay of difference within a given context is at the core of her philosophical ruminations on the communicative self.

Judith Butler's philosophy focuses on the individual while embracing a critical discourse on identification, facilitating a broader discourse on morality and responsibility. When Butler (2005) refers to the individual, she connects us to the importance of "subject formation" and to questions about identity and subjectivity (p. 21). She argues, "I cannot explain exactly why I have emerged in this way, and my efforts at narrative reconstruction are always undergoing revision" (Butler, 2005, p. 40). Butler's guiding question regarding the general nature of her interrogation asks, "through what processes [do] subjects come into existence"? (Salih, 2002, p. 2). Butler questions the means by which structures actually shape subjects; she examines the successes and failures of formational structures. Butler (2005) announces that one's account of oneself is always partial; there is no definitive story of individual formation.

In Butler's (2005) *Giving an Account of Oneself*, she discusses ethical violence that lays the groundwork for understanding a moral position of the self as an individual. Butler (2005) states that there are sometimes "conditions under which [abstract universality] can exercise violence" (p. 7). The concept of abstract universality as a form of violence provides entrance into Butler's (2005) theoretical construct of accounting for oneself, aiding our understanding of violence that emerges from social conditions of indifference. Without situating ourselves in living with others, we remain lodged in an abstract universality of individualism where there is no provision for individual freedom or individual particularities. Our uniqueness is socially constructed, acquired, and augmented; without social conditions, without connection with others, individual differentiation is not possible. The operation of abstract universality fails to respond to social and cultural conditions as we remain disconnected from others (Butler, 2005). In contrast, Butler's (2005) understanding of the individual consists of a subject who is always embedded in something, in a context—"this self is already implicated in a social temporality that exceeds its own capacities for narration" (p. 8). The individual is the result of ongoing creative caring tension between self and a community of others.

According to Butler (2005), subject formation commences when the individual recognizes the conditions under which the self emerges as an individual. Butler (2005) explains subject formation as concerned with the individual and the embeddedness of the "I" within community (p. 8). Butler (2005) states that the "I" has no story of its own; the "I" is embedded in a web of existence, a "story of a relation" within a community (p. 8). Dialectically, Butler does not ignore the fact that undue strict conventions within a community can impede the growth of the individual and the community alike. The dialectic alternative requires finding freedom in the embeddedness of community, while rejecting a static web of social conventions. Butler connects subject formation with dynamic moral discourse—subject formation is a condition for moral inquiry.

Subject formation, whether constructive or unduly limiting, involves performativity and interpellation, which are responsible for our self-accounts. Performativity refers to the enactment of the self; prior to enactment there is no individual subject—the subject emerges as a result of the performativity

(Butler, 2005). Interpellation is the linguistic interaction between a subject and other, in which one subject is "hailed" by another (Butler, 2005, p. 78). Together, the notion of accounting for one's self through integration of performativity and interpellation gives rise to morally constituted action that acknowledges a subject's existence. Butler's project assists the moral subject in not succumbing to the missteps of individualism.

Performativity

Sara Salih's (2002) work on Butler's understanding of subject formation outlines the relationship between "interpellation" and "performativity." Salih (2002) reminds us that according to Butler, subjects are a "subject-in-process that is constructed in discourse by the acts it performs" (p. 44). Salih (2002) states that "identity is a sequence of acts" that are entangled within existential connections with others and society (p. 45).

Butler (2005) discusses the sequence of acts in performativity that presuppose existence of a subject and refer to a "scene of address" that acknowledges embeddedness between self and other (p. 50). Butler argues that one gives an account of oneself *to* another; this accounting occurs within "rhetorical conditions" that promote a responsibility that calls one to attend to self and the Other through language (p. 50). For Butler (2005), accounting for oneself is not restricted to whether or not I give an adequate account of myself, but more importantly concerns the *relationship* of "I" and the other/sociality, which demands my own account.

Butler's notion of performativity communicates an enactment of the self; it is how the "I" is reconstituted. Performativity is a non-narrative act even though it is the "fulcrum for the narrative itself" (Butler, 2005, p. 66). There is no narrative already present before the act of performativity; it is through performativity that a narrative emerges. Butler's performativity is not narrative based; it gives life to a narrative. Butler's stress on performativity is consistent with Friedrich Nietzsche's (1887) idea in Genealogy of Morals—there is no *being* behind an act; identity emerges in performativity.

Salih (2002) explains Butler's position as demonstrating a distinction between performance and performativity; performance presupposes a subject, but performativity does not carry that same presupposition. Instead, performativity contests the idea of the existence of a reified subject because the subject is performatively constituted. Performativity manifests itself in the self meeting social conditions such as language. Salih (2002) argues that there is no "I" outside of language, "since language is a signifying practice" (p. 64).

Additionally, Salih (2002) states that "culturally intelligible subjects" are the results of performativity and not the cause of it (p. 64). Butler (2006) contends that gender identities are constituted by language, which means that gender identity cannot precede language; there is no presupposed subject before language. Interpellation follows performativity; performativity gives birth to the individual and interpellation describes the actions between individuals.

Interpellation

Butler's "interpellation" is an action metaphor suggesting linguistic interaction that is multi-sided. Linguistic interaction refers to action that calls out another subject, requiring a response (Salih, 2002). Butler employs the term interpellation to "describe how subject positions are conferred and assumed through the action of 'hailing' [others]" (Salih, 2002, p. 78). Interpellation, for Butler, demonstrates a violence of the hailing of one person by another person. Butler (2005) states that we give accounts of ourselves because we are interpellated as "beings who are rendered accountable" by a system imbued with justice that must be continually constructed and continues to evolve (p. 10). For Butler, we are called to give an account of ourselves by the existence of the other and through the embeddedness of the relational context in a scene of address. Butler (2005) states it is our responsibility to give an account of ourselves. Butler's understanding of this accounting calls into question individualism, connecting the self to community responsibility. Too much stress on either the self or the community fails to acknowledge the dialectical construction of individual identity. Both dimensions of human experience, individual and community, are necessary for generating meaning that reflects our embeddedness and sense of moral calling.

Tocqueville and Butler warn us, reminding us to beware of the dark side of freedom—individualism. Alexis de Tocqueville explores individualism in America through an examination of societal structures that govern daily life. Butler's account of the individual in healthy critical tension with community emerges from a reflective critical stance situated in an examination of societal structures. Tocqueville and Butler give us insights into practices that counter the missteps of individualism.

Philosophy of Communication: *Zorba the Greek* and the Individual, Community, and Difference

The creative interplay of individual, community, and difference lessens our long-term chances of falling into the clutches of individualism. Excessive focus on the self alone or social conventions alone invites dangerous consequences in everyday existence. Butler details how we must learn to give an account of ourselves that does not excessively focus on the "I" or the other, but seeks to discover a way to mediate the desires of the individual and the community. Butler extends Tocqueville's warning about American reliance on individualism that foolishly seeks to stand above all social ties, risking the development and growth of both the individual and the community. Tocqueville considered selfishness less dangerous than individualism, which is socially sanctioned.

In *Zorba the Greek*, Zorba and Boss travel to the monastery to negotiate the purchase of land from the monks. On their way to the monastery, they run into a monk who is fleeing from the monastery. They try to converse with the monk, but he encourages them to leave as well. The monk tells Zorba and Boss that the monks at the monastery are engaging in sinful actions driven by their fleshly desires for "[m]oney, pride, and young boys" (Kazantzakis, 1946/1952, p. 213). Zorba and Boss experience dialectical tension between the individual and the community, since the monastery represents a commitment to the community, but the members of the community are acting out of their individual desires that hold power over the people they serve. There is no balance between their individual carnal desires and their commitment to serve the people in the community. Not all monks adhere to the commitment to carnal desires; a fleeing monk seeks release from the community. The community of people whom the monastery serves is forgotten in the story. The formation of the "I" is in creative response to attentiveness to others.

A community can become corrupt without the rhetorical courage of individuals. Individualism moves us away from all concern for others. *Zorba the Greek* does not give us an answer—one becomes an individual only in acknowledgment of and, at times, resistance to a given community. This dialectical struggle is in contrast to individualism that seeks to ignore all social constraints. Only a dialectical tension between self and community permits insight from difference that creates a space that calls one to responsibility.

Philosophy of communication as the carrier of meaning, understood from the interplay of individual, community, and difference, adapts the emphasis on perspectives and counters the manic stress on "my" demands. Zorba is a man propelled by desire for life, and he lives as a unique individual without falling into the trap of individualism.

1. Absolute or excessive focus on a given idea or action is generally detrimental to the human condition. Zorba lives life with passion. What keeps him from becoming a fanatic is that his passion extends to many different elements of life. Work, friendship, music, and love offer a unique form of balance; he is passionate without being obsessed. Boss, on the other hand, is a closer picture of obsession. He lacks passion and yet, he is obsessive, reminding us not to confuse the two.

2. Attentiveness to others necessitates acknowledgment of, and respect for, difference. This learning is difficult for Boss and does not characterize many of the members of the community. One wonders why Zorba is able to manifest such ability. The answer rests in one simple fact—Zorba knows this place, but has seen a wider spectrum of the world. He has experience negotiating difference.

3. Both the individual and the community depend upon one another for their own existence—difference gives each one life and meaning. The conversations in the novel announce the importance of individual and community. The setting of the inn for meals invites another glimpse of the importance of fellowship that offers a sense of meaning for the participants. Zorba functions as a catalyst for community.

4. Meaning ultimately comes from the creative dialectical tension of individual and community. The struggle between individuals and the community was often creative. The thrust of the novel takes us to the darker side of the tension between individual and community. We observe, not a fine set of relationships, but the opposing demand for domination as one finds power in the herd.

5. The pursuit of difference alone offers no answer, but attention to the call from alterity, the stranger, the other is the home of human responsibility and hope. The novel displays the importance of difference and a basic existential fact—difference does not ensure a good life. However, the danger of undue uniformity puts lives at risk; the authors lament over the evil inflicted on the widow and Zorba's inability to turn the tide and correct the actions of the crowd.

Individualism embodies a "fiendish disregard for community" (Arnett, Fritz, & Holba, 2007, p. 120). Individualism grows from an "erroneous judgment" emerging from "defects of the mind" and "vices of the heart" (Arnett, Fritz, & Holba, 2007, p. 117). One subsumed in individualism attempts "to live in a world where one can stand above the fray…to critique and judge from the outside" (Arnett, Fritz, & Holba, 2007, p. 117). Individualism denies difference and creates a problematic community. Individualism can be characterized as "a phenomenological lie with devastating empirical consequences for human communication" (Arnett, Fritz, & Holba, 2007, p. 117). We gain meaning through difference. Through individualism, we see the world from a privileged height that ignores our obligations to others.

Dialectically, we must attend to two extremes that can damage individual formation: individualism and excessive attendance to social constraint. When individualism is the guide, we ignore community. When community constraints are the sole standard, we risk mob rule or "group think" (Janis, 1982, p. 174), the demand of the "they" or the herd (Heidegger, 1962, p. 217). Difference is key in shaping how individuals live in a community, avoiding the missteps of individualism or reified social constraints. Zorba offers us a raw example of a life lived between these two extremes.

CHAPTER 14

SENSUS COMMUNIS: THE COMMUNITY MATTERS

Common sense is not innate; it is a practice learned within communities that shapes our personal and/or professional lives. Common sense is practiced communicative action and decision making, performed in multiple facets of our existence. Common sense is a natural outcome, not of instinct, but of a meaningful set of communicative practices understood within a larger community. These practices require action, mistake, success, and communal reaction, which textures the meaningfulness of given practices, moving beyond individual assessment and into the sociality of being human. Common sense is a learned communicative practice engaged in our daily interactions, both personally and professionally.

Introduction

This chapter relies on a philosophical picture of "common sense" offered by Giovanni Battista (Giambattista) Vico's (1725/2000) *New Science*; this work introduces Vico's conception of the philosophy of common sense and its pragmatic importance to human communities. Additionally, this chapter uses Thomas Paine's (1737–1809) pamphlet, *Common Sense* (1776/1953), as an exemplar of a persuasive appeal to common sense, which assisted in the uniting of people in the American colonies. Paine's work offered a shared sense of outrage against Great Britain that found currency in the Enlightenment demand for individual autonomy. Both Vico and Paine point to a philosophical picture that highlights the pragmatic importance of common sense. This perspective assists one in navigating both explicit and implicit communicative practices that give character and meaning to a given community. Common sense, as understood by Vico and Paine, is a philosophical picture of a philosophy of human communication that guides meaningful interpretation of communicative practices within a community.

This chapter consists of three major sections: (1) a discussion of Vico's understanding of common sense and its influence upon philosophy of communication; (2) an examination of Thomas Paine's perspective on common sense through his pamphlet *Common Sense*; and (3) implications of common sense for the study of philosophy of communication understood as one philosophical painting illustrated by *Zorba the Greek*, the central story used throughout this project. Common sense, understood as a philosophical painting, permits errors in judgment and encourages experience as a learning tool—experience by ourselves and experience with others.

This chapter contends that common sense is no longer a universally accessible sense of the common; this perspective was tied to the Enlightenment commitment to universal reason and rationality. Today, one would align common sense with the communicative practices of a people within a given a community, assuming that such insights are learned, not inherent. This chapter outlines a philosophical picture of common sense tied to common communicative practices and Enlightenment assumptions. One may not be born with common sense, but it is possible to convince an audience that the opposition is void of common sense. Additionally, if one is to learn about another community, then attentiveness to their communicative practices is essential as one restrains the impulse to condemn what is alien to one's own customs.

Common Sense and Unity

Giovanni Battista (Giambattista) Vico (1668–1744) was born in Naples, Italy, to a working-class family. He attended various local schools and had private Jesuit tutors due to chronic poor health. Vico attended the University of Naples from 1690 to 1694 and graduated with a degree in civil and canon law. Vico worked as a private tutor from 1686 to 1695, which provided him with living expenses during the years of his informal studies with tutors and his formal studies at the University of Naples. Vico accepted a position as professor of rhetoric at the University of Naples, which he held from 1699 to 1741. Vico sought to hold the chair of jurisprudence, but he never received that honor; his work consistently meshed with the jurisprudence theme. In 1734, Vico was appointed royal historiographer for King Charles III of Naples and offered a substantial salary that was significantly more than his professorship position; he maintained his professorship until illness forced him to step down in 1741 (Fisch & Bergin, 1963).

During his career, Vico wrote about philosophy, rhetoric, ethics, history, and science. His major work, *New Science*, was published in 1725 and later revised in 1730. Many of his ideas were not well received during his lifetime; only after his death did his writings receive attention, especially those related to common sense and civic life (Fisch & Bergin, 1963). Vico was a rhetorician and humanist who privileged civic discourse. He appealed to *phronesis* or practical wisdom, which led to his interest in *sensus communis*. Vico's ideas influenced several prominent philosophers, including Max Horkheimer (1895–1973), Isaiah Berlin (1909–1997), and Hans-Georg Gadamer (1900–2002), as well as anthropologist Edmund Leach (1910–1989) (Audi, 1995/2001).

Vico has been identified as the most important Italian humanist in the rhetorical tradition and central to the Scottish Enlightenment (Herrick,

2001). Vico valued imagination and suggested that language permits people to improve society by provoking thought and new ideas. Vico believed that decisions in public life were based upon certain conditions, which limited reason and made prudence or "practical judgment" essential in informing opinions and decisions (Herrick, 2001, p. 172). Imagination fueled Vico's perspective on rhetoric. For Vico, the language of metaphor and poetry facilitated imagination and creative decision making (Herrick, 2001). Vico was interested in the origin of human thought related to natural law and common sense played out in practical judgments in everyday experience. His early publications mainly included poetry on topics such as death and despair. His magnum opus, *New Science*, acknowledged modernity and explored its methods, making a comparison between ancient and modern methods of inquiry. Vico (1725/2000) defended the humanistic tradition in education and argued that the new science of his time was actually a compilation of the history of ideas—the sciences included logic, morality, economics, politics, astronomy, cosmology, and geography. Vico (1725/2000) stated that each science "established divine principles in all things" (p. 139), which he contended unified science within the humanistic tradition. He rejected the assumption that science and the humanistic tradition should be separate and discrete from each other.

A New Science

Vico's (1725/2000) *New Science* is a philosophical treatise connecting humankind to natural law. Vico (1725/2000) defined natural law as the Romans defined it, as "something which divine providence had ordained together with human customs of civilization" (p. 7). Natural law originates from God's law and unifies with human customs.

Vico (1725/2000) integrated poetic sensibility into his manuscript on *New Science*, which centered on poetic wisdom, poetic metaphysics, poetic logic, and poetic morality, to name but a few of the chapter subjects. Vico illuminated the poetic in philosophy; he emphasized the importance of rhetoric and eloquence. The poetic emanates from imagination; this stress on the origin of creativity and innovation is a central theme in Vico's rhetoric and philosophy. Vico's commitment to natural law made the connection to common sense a short leap. Vico accepted the common-sense fact that natural law is a collaboration of divine ordination and customs of the community. Creativity comes in response to what is naturally before us; the poetic permits adaptation and imagination to respond to natural law, forging new insights through communicative engagement of common sense and imagination.

Vico explored numerous philosophical concepts in this great treatise with, of course, common sense or *sensus communis* as one of his most lasting scholarly contributions. Generally translated as common sense, Vico (1725/2000) defined common sense as "a[n] unreflecting judgment shared by an entire social order, people, nation, or even all humankind" (p. 80). Vico's definition suggested that shared ideas and practices are situated within a community that abides by a perspectival common ground; in this case, an endorsement of natural law. The idea of common sense establishes a criterion for decision making that Vico connected to divine providence and natural law. For Vico, common sense recognizes an underlying agreement that respects natural law played out within a human community; this perspective is consistent with Vico's strong religious values and his devout support of the Catholic Church.

Vico (1725/2000) referred to common sense as a "consciousness of the certain" (p. 63), making the possibility of common knowledge dependent upon a common set of practices. Vico believed *sensus communis* is the dwelling that houses the common lived experiences of a community. For Vico, *sensus communis* is a particular and, simultaneously, a universal concept that is dialectically understood (Gadamer, 1960/1986). Common sense is particular in that *sensus communis* speaks to individual actions; common sense is universal in that shared understanding of the good is what forms particular practices that shape the common sense of a group of people. Additionally, common sense is particular and universal in that there is a mental language (universal) that is common to all nations, and common sense is expressed through numerous (particular) imaginative modifications appropriate to diverse cultures, experiences, and peoples.

Gadamer (1960/1986) stated that Vico's common sense is both particular and universal, summarizing common sense as a dialectical unity of the individual and the community. Gadamer, whose work is described in Chapter 6 on philosophical hermeneutics, reminded the interpretive community of the importance of common sense for making sense of a given event or text. Common sense is the home of everyday engagement and, specifically, the dwelling place of experts who have agreement in judgment and taste. Sense-making occurs in the imagination and creates the conditions from which human beings "create civilization out of disordered nature" (Herrick, 2001, p. 174). Vico emphasized imagination as fundamental to rhetoric, fueling innovation that influences how people color the manner and fashion in which they make sense out of the world before them.

Common sense is cultivated through experiential practices within our social and personal lives. *Sensus communis* becomes an underlying basis for judgment; it is central to the art of living and reveals a common sense reality that science alone is insufficient for making judgments in the practical sphere of everyday life (Hance, 1997). Vico's *New Science* (1725/2000) identified three kinds of jurisprudence that governed decision making: mystical theology, heroic jurisprudence, and natural equity.

Mystical theology involved "vernacular wisdom" from ancient myths that incorporated hidden mysteries in traditional stories that guide actions (Vico, 1725/2000, p. 25). Mystical theology represents archetypal knowledge crafted from ancient myths that guides actions; this knowledge is co-created by the known stories of a people, constituting a shared knowledge and understanding. Heroic jurisprudence is based upon the necessity of civic life made possible by people seeking the "common good," warding off the dangers of individual abuse of judgment and individual greed in government (Vico, 1725/2000, p. 25). Heroic jurisprudence is based upon civil equity composed of public investment in ideas, interests, and values that undergird decisions and choices. Civil equity cultivates common sense as truth based upon shared practices and experiences. Natural equity invites individuals to seek their own particular good, which aligns with the good of others. Together, a community of individuals can pursue "equal benefits" in society; these benefits are then available to all (Vico, 1725/2000, pp. 27, 405–406). Natural equity reinforces the idea of natural law as a common set of shared connections between persons. Natural equity privileges each individual and balances the individual and community through joint experiences and a commitment to natural law. Natural equity is consistent with Vico's devotion to the Catholic Church. These three forms of jurisprudence informed Vico's subsequent development of common sense. Vico (1725/2000) stated that common sense is "necessary and useful to humankind" (p. 79), constituted by people committed to practices that keep a community vibrant and creatively engaged.

We now move from Italy to Thomas Paine's influence on the American Revolution. In his case, common sense does not simply bring unity, but announces difference and the need for separation. Paine stressed a common sense that gave testimony to a natural call for separation.

Common Sense and Separation

Thomas Paine was born in Thetford, England, in 1737. Paine has been referred to as a "child of violence," reflecting his experiences as a young child growing up next to an execution site that had been in existence for six centuries (Keane, 2003). Down the street from Paine's home, the local jail had a long public presence since it was build in 1271 during the reign of Edward I (1239–1307) (Keane, 2003). Every spring during Paine's youth, he witnessed convicted men herded up the hill from the local jail. This final place of lodging was a three-story structure that included a dungeon basement. This particular jail has been described as a "hellish maze of bars and doors," the "black hole of Calcutta," and "a sewer of vice" (Keane, 2003, p. 4). The young Thomas Paine experienced a parade of death that generated a public spectacle, as the condemned walked through the village and up to Gallows Hill, which was adjacent to Paine's home.

Villagers followed behind the criminals, which provided a better view of those on their way to a public death. Voyeurism at the last gasps of human life was the beginning drama of Paine's life. His biographers suggest that he witnessed many of these public executions and related horrific events. Paine's early encounter with the governing law of England brought him face to face with a horrific drama played out by those involved in "executing" the law of the land (Keane, 2003). Paine grew up in the presence of a constant public reminder of the extent of governmental influence on the lives of people to the point of being able to terminate life when deemed appropriate by the authorities. He witnessed the dark side of politics in his backyard. Paine's youth was shaped by the activities at the jail and on Gallows Hill, which would be his initial introduction to the rule of England.

Continuing Personal Struggle

Paine attended grammar school in Thetford from 1744 to 1749. In 1750, at the age of 13, Paine apprenticed with his father who was a tailor, a corset maker. By 1759, Paine opened his own tailor shop after having a brief experience working for the navy as a privateer, a private individual commissioned by the navy to attack enemy ships and confiscate the bounty. Privateers were commonly used between the 16th and 17th centuries to save the navy money, as private investors funded their exploits (Keane, 2003). Paine's sense of adventure took him into marriage and into business with similar results. Paine married Mary Lambert in 1759; his business failed that same year. Paine and his wife moved to Margate where Mary became pregnant, but sadly, both she and her child died. Paine found himself a poor widower. In 1761, Paine returned to Thetford to work as a supernumerary, a temporary employee for an organization. In 1762, Paine took a position as an excise officer in Grantham, Lincolnshire, where he conducted inspections for the government. In 1765, he was fired from this position for failing to conduct an inspection even though he had stated that he had done it. In 1766, Paine filed a petition to be reinstated in his position; although his request was granted, he did not wait for an opening. While waiting for reinstatement, Paine worked as a tailor and servant. He even applied to be a church minister, but was then hired as a schoolteacher in London in 1767. Because of his short-lived professional projects and his early background where he was confronted with the dark side of civic life, Paine decided to make a difference by entering public civic life (Keane, 2003).

Paine became active in church and in city governance. In 1771, Paine married his landlord's daughter, Elizabeth Ollive; in 1773, Paine was reappointed as excise officer in East Sussex. It was here where he wrote his first political publication on the office of excise and requested better pay and working conditions. In 1774, Paine was fired from his new position for allegedly not being at his post when he should have been. He and Elizabeth separated shortly after, and in April 1774, Paine sold his home and possessions to avoid being cast into a debtor's prison (Keane, 2003).

A New Start and More Disappointment

Paine then returned to London where he met Benjamin Franklin (1706–1790), who recommended that Paine move to America. Franklin wrote him a letter of recommendation, and Paine arrived in Philadelphia in November 1774 (Keane, 2003). Paine was ill when he arrived in Philadelphia; his recovery took six weeks, but afterward, he officially became a citizen of Philadelphia, and by January 1775, Paine was editor of *Philadelphia Magazine*. This man, who had met difficulty at each step in his life, understood that common sense does not always unify; common sense can and does separate us from others who support practices other than our own. Paine wrote *Common Sense* within a year after arriving in America (Keane, 2003). He believed that the American colonists were being subjected to unfair governance by Britain. He became an "apostle of freedom" (Keane, 2003, p. xix). Paine championed the cause of the colonists as a personal civic duty. The results of his writing *Common Sense* have been described as "world-shattering" (Keane, 2003, p. xix), perhaps due to the fact that Paine intended to frame common sense as an examination of practices that can unify the colonies and also divide them from Great Britain.

After the American Revolution, Paine was no longer politically involved. Instead, he worked as an inventor. Paine designed bridges and invented the smokeless candle as well as collaborated on the invention of the steam engine (Keane, 2003). In 1778, Paine left America and returned to England, where he resumed his political interests and wrote his most famous treatise, *On the Rights of Man*; the two-part volume was published in 1791 and 1792, respectively. This publication revived his popularity with the common people but not with Britain's government. Paine was forced to flee England in 1792 and was declared an outlaw by the British government. Paine went to France where he again became involved with politics during the political turmoil of the French Revolution (1789–1799). Paine wrote the French Declaration of the Rights of Man and a new Constitution for France. He argued that the new government in France should adopt these organizing documents; however, the French were convinced that they must execute King Louis XVI. Paine, while supportive of the revolution and the new form of government that was emerging, pleaded with the French people to end the monarchy, but to do so without bloodshed. This position of not seeing the guillotine as the answer branded him a traitor, despite his support of the French Revolution. Paine was then imprisoned in Luxembourg from December 1793 until the American ambassador to France, James Monroe, negotiated his release in November 1794.

During Paine's imprisonment, he began writing *The Age of Reason*, which was published in 1795. Paine's rationale for writing *The Age of Reason* originated from his desire to write about his perspective on religion—a topic he admittedly knew would spark controversial discussion. Paine stayed in France for a few years and then moved back to America in 1802. While Paine was initially well received in America, he began to fall out of public favor for a letter he wrote to George Washington in 1796, in which he criticized some of Washington's policies as the first president of the United States. Consequently, Paine became an outcast and unwelcomed. Paine became an alcoholic and lived in poverty. Afflicted by poor health, poor nutrition, and excessive abuse of alcohol, Paine died in 1809 while living in New York as a pauper and an outcast (Keane, 2003).

A Lasting Contribution

Even though the end of Paine's life was dominated by poverty and despair, one cannot forget the importance of his intellectual contribution to the Western world. The most significant contribution that Paine made to the American colonies was, of course, *Common Sense* (1776/1953). Paine's early life had exposed him to government policies that resorted to taking the life of another. He had worked for low wages. His private life had been defined by sadness and disappointment. He had suffered for his outspoken comments about working conditions. All these events gave Paine a sense of sympathy necessary to understand the American experience contra Britain. His dissenting voice and his ability to use words with eloquence moved human beings to act with common sense against the British. Paine's communicative sophistication helped precipitate a revolution. He provided a voice for a new nation rallying together, which helped America create a unified voice that stood up for individual rights, a just community, and the necessity of separation from Great Britain. Paine's life experiences had prepared him to understand the power of common sense, which not only unifies, but separates. The practices we hold in common constitute a unique community, which is often in contrast with the practices and assumptions of another community.

Paine published *Common Sense* anonymously in 1776; it was immediately an influential pamphlet. He argued for the separation of the 13 American colonies from Great Britain and thus, British rule and subjugation. The American Revolution had officially begun when the United States Declaration of Independence was signed in July 1776. Up until the signing of this document, there were constant disagreements and tensions between residents of the colonies and Great Britain. The American Revolution ended in 1781 with the defeat of Great Britain and the end of its hold on the colonies, thus liberating the American colonies and giving them a chance to develop a representative democracy.

Paine's pamphlet, *Common Sense*, contributed to success in inspiration, ideas, and financial developments; the pamphlet was printed and sold in the streets for public consumption. According to the Thomas Paine Society, the publisher set the price of the pamphlet at two shillings; at that time, the cost of the pamphlet was more than one day's wage. Paine thought this price was too high; however, the pamphlet sold well despite his discontent, selling more than 150,000 copies in its first printing. This number of sales would have made Paine a rich man; however, he took no proceeds from the publication—the money was used to fund the revolution.

The power of this document ignited the common sense of the people, appealing to their minds, hearts, and subsequent actions (Adkins, 1953). Rather than using the sophisticated language of Enlightenment philosophers at the time, Paine spoke to the people through everyday language and examples. Paine used common sense, or *sensus communis*, to make visible an argument that demanded separation from Great Britain. His common-sense argument was an appeal to metaphors that functioned as a philosophical picture capable of driving persons to action.

Before Paine introduced a metaphor or argument in general, he appealed to the sense of the common by explicitly referencing undeniable arguments about why it was necessary to separate from Great Britain.

> The cause of America is in a great measure the cause of all mankind. Many circumstances have and will arise which are not local but universal, and through which the principles of all lovers of mankind are affected and in the event of which their affections are interested. (Paine, 1776/1953, p. 3)

Paine argued that there are universal issues common to all people. He contended that the issues of the American Revolution announced that there is no one in the world unaffected by the struggle for universal rights—they are common sense.

Paine acknowledged the importance of shared experience as he argued that governments are unavoidable and follow the natural development and growth of a society. He concurred that all human beings experience, in some form or another, a system of governing. A society requires some form of governing order. After establishing the necessity of government, which avoided the delusion of innocence, Paine then offered an argument against England. Indeed, "the palaces of kings are built on the ruins of lost innocence" (Paine, 1776/1953, p. 4). Paine stated that the monarchy was at odds with the growing demand and recognition of the importance of individual autonomy. He termed this moment an "Age of Reason" (Keane, 2003). Paine focused persons on an emerging common-sense assumption that was central to the 18th century and to the Enlightenment—autonomy matters.

Common sense aligned with individual autonomy permitted Paine to question the paternalism of Britain. In *Common Sense*, Paine wrote that paternalism is a fallacious argument that supports the spirit of the monarchy. He used this metaphor to assist people in understanding the difference between the appropriate actions used toward a child versus an adult. Paine (1776/1953) stated that Britain used parenting metaphors that generated the image of "[t]he infant state of the Colonies" and the assumption that "[y]outh is the seedtime of good habits, as well in nations as in individuals" (p. 40). Paine appealed to the common sense of families in the colonies that wished greater success for their offspring than for themselves. Paine reminded his audience that brutes do not devour their children, unlike the king who wanted to devour the colonies like a savage.

An Enlightenment commitment to common sense stresses autonomy that gives increasing power to the cry for "freedom of religion" and "diversity of religious opinions" (Paine, 1776/1953, p. 41). For a society like the colonies, in which many lived in accordance with faiths and practices that were different from that of the monarch, the call for increased religious freedom was common sense. The demand for religious freedom made a common-sense plea for autonomy and separation from Great Britain.

Finally, autonomy requires that one understand the common-sense importance of being entrusted with control over one's own finances and one's own defense. For example, Paine provided detailed cost-benefit analyses to the colonists, making it clear that they must develop their own navy, earn their own money through trade, and protect the colonies from bandits on the seas. Paine reminded the colonists that many natural resources and materials were present on American soil and were being exploited by England. He argued that Americans should make many goods themselves without parental interference. Paine argued that a change in their financial independence would require a minimal investment from the colonies, which would pay great dividends in the end. Thomas Paine's *Common Sense* exemplifies a philosophical picture of *sensus communis*, which enabled people to understand the issues relevant to everyday life. He argued for employing the common sense of particulars, understood against the backdrop of a privileged Enlightenment universal—individual autonomy. Thomas Paine's essay exemplifies common sense in action; the interplay of the particular and the universal is capable of moving individuals to shared action. For Paine, common sense demanded that one understand that the practices we embrace will not only unite us, but will separate us from those pursuing different perspectives than what we term as common sense. Common sense not only unites; it separates, divides, and makes differentiated identity of a community possible.

Philosophy of Communication: *Zorba the Greek* and Common Sense

Common sense requires cultivating ideas through education, practices, and the co-sharing of experiences that shape common perspectives. Engagement in common practices demands thoughtful reflection upon common practices in a given community. Through reflection we can identify actions and practices that make sense in a particular place at a particular time; after a period of time reflections fade into agreed-upon practices, moving us to what is termed common sense. We are not born with common sense; we are born with the capacity to develop common sense through experience and practice. Common sense informs a philosophy of communication in the ongoing interplay of action/practices, reflection, and the discovery of meaning.

Common sense requires an understanding of the practices that shape one's environment, permitting effective and appropriate judgments and decisions to guide. Common-sense wisdom emerges through experience, learned in daily routine with a group of people. Common sense is given birth as we pay attention to our environments in which we are embedded. The cost of not learning common sense within a given community elicits a high toll. In the story of *Zorba the Greek*, Boss reflects upon the danger of impatience and forcing one's own abstract demands upon a situation without first learning about the place, the people, and the creatures that give shape to a given community. During a nature walk, Boss comes upon a cocoon and tries to force out a butterfly before its natural time, going against the common-sense practices of the natural world.

> My breath had forced the butterfly to appear, all crumpled, before its time. It struggled desperately and, a few seconds later, died in the palm of my hand. That little body is, I do believe, the greatest weight I have on my conscience. For I realize today that it is a mortal sin to violate the great laws of nature. We should not hurry, we should not be impatient, but we should confidently obey the eternal rhythm. (Kazantzakis, 1946/1952, p. 139)

Boss fails the first test of common sense—good decisions are optimized if we know the environment in which we are embedded. Common sense comes from knowing one's environment and understanding its natural rhythms. For Boss, this experience stays with him, weighing heavily upon his mind. Common sense requires us to attend to the practices, persons, creatures, and events before us, not our demands about an abstract truth. Common sense is contrary to one's demand that the world should and must function as one thinks it ought.

Zorba is a master of common sense in this terrain. He reveals that philosophy of communication as the carrier of meaning, understood from the point of common sense, is tied to the place and the persons with whom one interacts. Common sense shapes philosophy of communication through agreed-upon practices that give identity to a given community.

1. One must be open to learning through education and literacy about the practices of a community. Boss learns common sense about books through practice, just as Zorba does through practices in his local environment. Both sought to teach the other new practices, augmenting what we term common sense. When a group of persons

collectively work with a given set of practices, common sense is the natural outcome of their life together. Common sense is derivative of the practices we learn and repeatedly enact.

2. Human beings are not born with common sense; common sense develops from experience and reflection upon practices held in common. The fact that common sense is not innate not only means that the practices must be learned, but that whatever common sense one has does not often translate from one community or environment to another. Zorba has common sense about mining. He does not have common sense about books or philosophy. The reverse is true of Boss—common sense rests with our practices.

3. Common-sense practices offer meaning that can unite us. Boss identifies with the books he reads and finds meaning in their practices, just as Zorba does with a much different sort of practices. Meaning emerges from practices, which are not to be confused with repetition. The difference between repetition and practice exemplifies why some do not get better at what they do and others become experts. Common sense augmentation requires attention to practice, not repetition.

4. Common sense practices offer meaning that can separate us. Ultimately, Zorba and Boss part. We are saddened at the end of the novel to witness these two friends going their separate ways. Finally, their common sense understanding of meaning takes them down different roads. Most of us have had a "best friend" whom we lost touch with as our practices made us value different forms of common sense.

5. Common-sense shapes a particular rationality tied to the practices of a given community. For us to consider the thought of another as rational, we need to understand their practices to have appreciation for their common sense. Rationality requires common-sense approval of the connections between ideas. For example, the most dramatic differences in common sense emerge with words such as "terrorist" and "freedom fighter." Common sense connected to given perceptual practices determine what one observes in the other. Both Boss and Zorba are appalled with the manner of the widow's death; however, only Zorba can understand the "common sense" of those taking a life. Indeed, not all common sense is common and not all common sense is something that we would want to practice. Differing views of what constitutes common sense can invite intense conflict.

Both Zorba and Boss display a common sense that unites education/learning, experience, and practices. The presence of common sense can both unite and divide persons; common sense is not a communicative phenomenon that automatically brings us together. Common sense is only common through the doing of common practices; thus, the semblance of a common world is given birth by education, experience, practices, and our willingness to learn about alterity, the differences that confront us.

This final chapter serves as a quasi-conclusion, relying upon two scholars, Seyla Benhabib and Calvin O. Schrag, whose works point to a thoughtful and textured conception of philosophy of communication. If you know someone who attends to the dimension of communication that is the unsaid, and the inarticulate that is ever present without being obvious, then you can conceptualize the texture that gives tone to human meaning. Philosophy of communication attentive to human meaning is a form of music that offers insight even when the pitch varies. It is possible to have perfect pitch and make a choir less attentive to its own unique tone. Relative pitch is attentive to others and the environment; relative pitch, not perfect pitch, can move a good choir to an outstanding performance. A textured understanding of meaning in philosophy of communication is akin to relative pitch, connected to a dimension of meaning that lives in a realm that is beyond accumulation of information alone.

Introduction

Philosophy of communication is not deemed correct or valid by abstract proof or some form of perfect pitch; philosophy of communication is tested in human living. Philosophy of communication invites meaning to manifest itself within a special context of others, in a particular time and a given place, guided by an ear to the unsaid and the inarticulate. Benhabib and Schrag point us in this direction. Additionally, in *Zorba the Greek*, Boss yearns for an ability to hear the unsaid. It is Zorba, however, who offers us a life attentive to relative pitch.

This chapter examines philosophy of communication as story-centered meaning through the work of Seyla Benhabib and Calvin O. Schrag in three sections: (1) a reading of Benhabib's *Situating the Self: Gender, Community and Postmodernism in Contemporary Ethics*; (2) an examination of Schrag's *Communicative Praxis and the Space of Subjectivity*; and (3) the implications of discernment of meaning for philosophy of communication, exemplified through the characters of *Zorba the Greek*.

We end this work as we began it, attending to meaning that emerges between and among persons in a historical moment in a particular existence; philosophy of communication is a textured fabric that weaves in and through human life. We thankfully understand that the conversation about textured meaning has no end, no final answer. In this project, we attended to multiple theories that offer a particular form of meaning, and to the two major characters in *Zorba the Greek* who seek meaning in contrasting fashions. Boss and Zorba meet life differently, both attending to the reality of a place in a given time that embeds and textures meaning, offering insights, limits, and blind spots about the human condition. Zorba is known for his famous dance tied to relative pitch that kept him attentive to existence. He offers us a philosophical picture of a person whose life is a philosophy of communication grounded in an existential dance.

Benhabib's *Situating the Self*

Seyla Benhabib is a central voice in our understanding of the praxis of meaning as story centered. She is the Eugene Meyer Professor of Political Science and Philosophy at Yale University and former director of the university's Ethics, Politics, and Economics Program (2002–2008). Benhabib (1992) understands the story of our epoch as shaped by "profound transformations," "fractured spirit," and a rejection of the Enlightenment assumption of metanarratives (p. 1). This perspective is in stark contrast to the end of history predicted by Georg Wilhelm Friedrich Hegel (1770–1831) and by Francis Fukuyama (b. 1952) in his essay, "The End of History?" (1989) (Benhabib, 1992, p. 1). Benhabib (1992) offers a counter story of "reconstruction" of Enlightenment thinking and the notion of "universalism" (p. 2). She frames "a post-Enlightenment defense of universalism" without ignoring gender and difference in context (Benhabib, 1992, p. 3). She provides an "interactive," not "legislative," story of this historical moment (Benhabib, 1992, p. 3). Benhabib's project reformulates the universal story without adhering to metaphysical assumptions that undergird the Enlightenment. "The first step then in the formulation of a post-metaphysical universalist position is to shift from a substantialistic to a discursive, communicative concept of rationality" (Benhabib, 1992, p. 5). Her story connects communication, community, and difference to rationality, rejecting the assumption that we are capable of grounding rationality in an abstraction that stands above everyday life.

Narrative and Discourse Ethics

Benhabib (1992) understands the identity of the "I" as a result of a narrative framing of the self, which is responsive to human stories (p. 5). Her position is in contrast to the Enlightenment assumption that one can understand identity in the abstract as a "disembedded cogito" (Benhabib, 1992, p. 5). Alternatively, she turns to "practical reason" that is "interactionist," not "legislative" (Benhabib, 1992, p. 6). Benhabib (1992) narrates a story about practical reason that is opposed to the abstract consideration of "legalistic universalism" that was central to the work of Immanuel Kant (1724–1804) and John Rawls (1921–2002) (p. 9). Benhabib (1992) offers a "proceduralist" universal that is "participatory" and "interactionist," functioning in the "public domain" without losing sight of the feminist reservation about artificial lines drawn between the public and the private (pp. 10–12). Benhabib (1992) embraces the necessity of dialectical inquiry, engaging the opposing interplay of "generalized" and "concrete" others in human communities (p. 10).

Benhabib's project is a dialectical effort to reformulate the universal within communities, historicality, and temporality. Her work is an ongoing oxymoron, a "unity of contraries" (Buber, 1965/1966, p. 111). She turns to Hegel's critique of Kant's assertion that one should not act unless one can legitimize the action as a "universal law" (Benhabib, 1992, p. 26). Hegel's response to Kant was simple—universal law does not necessarily equate with what is morally right; there is a difference between perfect and relative pitch. The demand for the morally right comes closer to the needs of a community and real people than to adherence to an abstract universal law. "With this reformulation, universalizability is defined as an intersubjective procedure of argumentation, geared to attain communicative agreement" (Benhabib, 1992, p. 28). Benhabib's interactional view of conversation assumes: (1) "universal moral respect," (2) "egalitarian reciprocity," and (3) attentiveness to a "significant other" defined by someone who has been given the rights of "reciprocity"—a "universal pragmatic" that attends to conversational partners (Benhabib, 1992, pp. 30–32). This framework also defines Habermas's framing of discourse ethics.

Habermas's position, however, is called into question by Agnes Heller (b. 1929), the Hannah Arendt Visiting Professor of Philosophy and Political Science at the New School for Social Research, and by Charles Taylor (b. 1931), with each scholar warning about the danger of assuming legitimization without validation and confusing the notion of "right" with that of the "good" (Benhabib, 1992, pp. 36–38). They contend against a view of discourse ethics as morally "neutral," a position refuted by Benhabib (1992) on behalf of Habermas (p. 39). Benhabib's (1992) response differentiates "moral reflexivity" from "moral conventionalism," countering the notion of moral neutrality (p. 43). Benhabib's understanding of discourse ethics begins with admission of two metanorms: universal respect and universal egalitarian reciprocity. She contends that these two assumptions place discourse ethics neither at the door of an "anti-institutionalist" assertion nor at the behest of the "anarchistic" (Benhabib, 1992, p. 47). Additionally, Benhabib attends to the importance and power of community, taking into account emotive life, unlike previous cognitive and procedural processes that have been utilized since Kant. The upholding of the importance of community counters the mythology of the autonomous moral agent who assumes the ability to stand above human existence and render pristine objective judgments.

Benhabib stresses that discourse ethics requires reversibility of understanding, taking the standpoint of another, facilitating dialogic understanding that invites intersubjective reason, and being attentive to context, which gives rise to judgment that requires both narrative and interpretive skills. We cannot stand above the fray of persons, communities, and cultures in the engagement of decision making; this perspective is divergent from pure liberalism and Marxism, which are tied to modernity and the autonomous agent. Both communitarians and postmodernists distrust the notions of progress and metanarrative. For Benhabib, discourse ethics does not accept the above criticisms at face value; their resolution emerges through dialectical understanding of "differentiation," "individuation," and "democratization," consistent with Habermas's effort to revitalize modernity (Benhabib, 1992, pp. 80–81). The key is participation; otherwise, we limit democracy to mere administration.

Benhabib and Arendt

Benhabib (1992) then turns to Hannah Arendt (1906–1975) to discuss the importance of participation and the advancement of a vibrant public domain, moving from a Kantian "legalistic" public domain to a "discursive public space" (p. 89). Arendt stressed the public domain as the place of human "freedom"; the public domain permits examination of the question of "justice" (Benhabib, 1992, p. 94). Such judgments do not rest in "neutrality" (Benhabib, 1992, p. 102). "It is neutrality that destroys dialogue…[its] dialectical character" (Benhabib, 1992, p. 102). The lack of neutrality does not rest, however, in an unexamined "tradition," but in "discursive will formation" that works within radical proceduralism and constraints respectful of discursive equality, which lessens the hegemony of "majoritarian politics" (Benhabib, 1992, pp. 104–105).

Benhabib cites Arendt, who stressed a public domain that distinguishes between public and private realms; Benhabib (1992) states, "feminist theory itself sorely needs a model of public space and public speech" (p. 112). The re-engagement of public space brings dialectical understanding to everyday engagement of terms such as public, private, justice, good life, right actions, needs, interests, and feminist commitments to context and person. Dialectic in action assists "judgment," which is not possible in acts of "thoughtlessness"; instead, there is a commitment to attentive thinking about the particulars that assist in the construction of public narrativity and storytelling about the why and how of human action (Benhabib, 1992, p. 122).

Arendt understood Kant's universal of the morally good and the particularity of the morally right as the heart of thinking that invites an "enlarged mentality"; such thinking requires "reflective judgment" and is textured by thinking that is an inner dialogue (Benhabib, 1992, pp. 132–133). Benhabib (1992) accepts this perspective, rejecting answers that come from ideologies propelled by "purity of heart," which lessen the demand to think, consider, and then judge (p. 132). An enlarged mentality requires "a civic culture of public participation" (Benhabib, 1992, p. 140), an understanding of "autonomy" that requires "reversibility of positions," and the ability to take the "standpoint of others," both "generalized" and "concrete" (Benhabib, 1992, pp. 145–146). The objective is to make a space for the "excluded other" (Benhabib, 1992, pp. 190–191).

> As Hannah Arendt has emphasized, from the time of our birth we are immersed in "a web of narratives," of which we are both the author and the object. The self is both the teller of tales and that about whom tales are told. The individual with a coherent sense of self-identity is the one who succeeds in integrating these tales and perspectives into a meaningful life history. (Benhabib, 1992, p. 198)

Benhabib envisions a world full of dialectical tension, not reified in tradition while attentive to community, and ever cognizant of the importance of differentiation between public and private realms within a life-world composed of a web of narratives.

Responding to Postmodernity

Benhabib (1992) responds to the "constitutive" and "evaluative" nature of both postmodernity and feminism (p. 203). Postmodernity works with the assumption of the "temporary" and the "performativity" in that "knowledge is power" with a focus on "critical," not "functional," knowledge; this contrasts with the "modern epistemological subject" who lives without transcendental guarantees (Benhabib, 1992, pp. 204–206). Postmodernity announced the "death of man," the "death of history," and the "death of metaphysics" (Benhabib, 1992, p. 211). Feminism deals with this same trinity, but with texture attentive to inclusion—opening the world to gender, engendering narration, and recognizing "interests" in metaphysics (Benhabib, 1992, p. 212). Some are wary of an alliance between feminism and postmodernity (Marshall, 2005, p. 84; Mann, 2006, p. 75). Benhabib (1992), on the other hand, conceptualizes an alliance between feminism and postmodernity in that both critique "progress" (p. 218). Feminism requires "situated criticism" attentive to the practices within given "local narratives" from the standpoint of a social critic in exile (Benhabib, 1992, p. 225). Postmodernity reminds us that utopian thinking and foundational thinking take us in problematic directions, with feminism reminding us that the communicative agent should be understood as the keeper of change and hope.

Language can be viewed as the "symbolic universe" of the "father," requiring a focus on "consciousness" that lends itself to the discovery of a "discourse of empowerment" (Benhabib, 1992, pp. 243–244); such a view of discourse begins with the restoration of the importance of the dialectic that opens up closed structures and conversations, making human liberation possible. Benhabib announces a story of discourse ethics that dialectically engages the stories of our time, postmodernity, feminism, and the insights of the communitarians. She utilizes an ironical understanding of dialectic that does not fall prey to the "locomotive of history," the problematic mythology of the Enlightenment—progress (Benhabib, 1992, p. 256). Benhabib's story of situated discourse and situated communicative agents finds a companion in the hermeneutic insights of Calvin O. Schrag.

Schrag and Communicative Praxis

Calvin O. Schrag (b. 1928), the George Ade Distinguished Professor of Philosophy Emeritus at Purdue University, takes us into a world of "communicative praxis," which is defined throughout his work *Communicative Praxis and the Space of Subjectivity* (1986). His initial discussion centers on the importance of "prepositions" that emphasize connection and texture between and among ideas and events. Schrag (1986) highlights a communicative space that is given shape and dimension by prepositions: "for" someone, "by" someone, and "about" something (pp. 1–2). Schrag's (1986) project centers on a philosophical picture of "decentered subjectivity" that stresses the pragmatic importance of context, within which events and communicative agents are embedded and situated (p. 11). Additionally, Schrag (1986) emphasizes "metaphors" as philosophical pictures that illuminate, point, and guide (p. 3). A metaphor functions as a potential headline for a given narrative, lending insight into the importance and significance of communicative praxis implications. For Schrag (1986), as for Benhabib, "[d]iscourse becomes the Rosetta Stone" of understanding between and among persons (p. 12). He does hermeneutics, interpretation within a space that is moving, temporal, and contextual, within what he terms as the "space of subjectivity in communicative praxis" (Schrag, 1986, p. 12).

The notion of "praxis" trumps the convention of "practice" for Schrag (1986, p. 18). He considers practice unreflective, more akin to routine, a seemingly changeless set of actions. The word "practice" fits a traditional society, exemplified by the blacksmith. Praxis combines both action and reflection prior to, during, and after action, necessitating a theory or a story as a guide. The rationale for the importance of such reflection is that our historical moment requires public blueprints of communicative reasons for action, which assist necessary changes and yield opportunity for investigating issues that have gone otherwise than expected.

Communicative Texture

Schrag (1986) stresses the importance of "texture," which is not present in the term "practice" (p. 23). Texture implies the sense and depth of events, taking us beyond the limits of optics without falling into pure subjectivism. Texture implies a sense of weightiness, importance, and spatial significance. Schrag moves beyond practice, calling us to learning that is attentive to multiple dimensions of the context and events before us.

Schrag's (1986) story frames "communicative praxis as expression," implying that communicative meaning unfolds in this textured sense of space called communicative praxis, offering a "figuration of texture" or a "displayed reference" often understood through "gesture," which unites discourse and action (pp. 32–34). Schrag's perspective leans on Maurice Merleau-Ponty (1908–1961) and his stress upon embodiment. Texture is an embodied metaphor that engages communicative space, not as linear information, but as a collection or possession.

Schrag continues with metaphors that texture communicative space within communicative praxis: distanciation, idealization, and recollection. Schrag (1986) acknowledges that Jacques Derrida's (1930–2004) project of deconstructing meaning assists in his project in that Derrida reinstitutes "meaning within the hermeneutical and holistic space of communicative praxis" (p. 53). "Distanciation" requires space for reflection that is better understood as initiated from the side, not from above (Schrag, 1986, p.

49). "Idealization" brings forth ideas that require critique; otherwise, we are vulnerable to "self-deception and on the sedimentation of ideology" (Schrag, 1986, p. 63). Schrag (1986) cites Kierkegaard, stating that "recollection" occurs as we meet that which is before us—it is "recollected forwards" (p. 65). Existence calls for an awakening, a connection to the not present that is simultaneously present.

Through acts of distanciation, reflection, critique, and emergent and responsive recollection, Schrag frames the interplay of understanding and explanation in the interpretive meeting of the space of communicative praxis. This space is a dwelling for a "surplus of meaning" that emerges in the historical moment of engagement of interpreter and text in which neither can overwhelm the other (Schrag, 1986, p. 77). Interpretive meaning emerges in the between of "whole" and "part" (Schrag, 1986, p. 80). Interpretation happens in a space composed of the particular, the moment of engagement, in interaction with a longer view. As one gathers more detail, the longer view makes more sense, and as one understands in an increasingly textured fashion, the longer-view detail becomes clearer. Interpretation, for Schrag, happens in textured spatial dimensions.

Schrag's (1986) textured conception of interpretation comprehensively unites understanding and explanation within "the density of the facticity of our discourse and action" (p. 85). Understanding and explanation illuminate one another. Such is the reason that a person who acts as a mentee must also mentor; understanding and explanation are companions in interpretive comprehension. Schrag recognizes the importance of reciprocity and interplay between understanding and explanation, working within a context of whole and part textured by metaphor and action. Schrag rejects conventional hermeneutic mythology that lends undue confidence in the use of metaphor, which dismisses the vitality and necessity of action. Texture in human meaning comes from a variety of sources, including metaphor and action, understanding and explanation, interpersonal relations, and "the fibers of institutional life" (Schrag, 1986, p. 92).

Learning in Action

One learns in the midst of action in the interspaces between and among; this learning in action is then story-vetted and shaped, moving us away from what Schrag (1986) understands as the "illusion of foundationalism" (p. 94). René Descartes (1596–1650) used "systematic doubt" with the hope of rebuilding foundations (Schrag, 1986, p. 94). John Locke (1632–1704) looked for the building of foundations with his focus on "exterior" (sensations from the outside) and "inner" (reflection upon those sensations); together, Descartes and Locke lend mistaken credence to the reality of foundations springing from "fountains of knowledge" (Schrag, 1986, p. 94). Immanuel Kant moved the issue of foundational knowledge to a deeper level; he added the transcendental with a transcendental ego that stands above the material conditions and builds a purer foundation of knowledge.

Schrag then turns to those that offer an alternative to the modern obsession with foundation; he attends to the pivotal questions offered by postmodern writers and central to the deconstruction project of Friedrich Nietzsche (1844–1900). Nietzsche undercut the foundationalist assumption, a root "prejudice" of modernity (Schrag, 1986, p. 101). In a traditional culture, the foundation rests with blood relations and with practices that bind a group of people together. In modernity, foundation is not the connection with people and their practices, but adherence/connection to a metanarrative that functions as a universal tied to reason. Reason then locates its power in abstract universal assumptions, ignoring the ground under us; such a view of reason calls for the adoption of the magic of standing above all constraint and sociality, losing the ground from under our feet. Modernity offers a false substitute for the ground of tradition, providing mythology for an abstract universal reason that permits "objective" understanding. Modernity, from the eyes of postmodern scholarship, looks like an abstract set of assumptions; it is a form of mythology in the contemporary world.

Schrag underscores the danger of foundationalism while reminding us that communicative praxis is "about" something; the referent in a given communication matters. We have all been in conversation with someone who spoke for an extended period, only to discover that we erroneously thought we were discussing a different topic. The confusion emerged because there was no clear referent for the conversation. For Schrag, the referent rests in the interplay of metaphor and action—the referent establishes part of the background dwelling for sense making. The referent gives one retrieval power, something concrete to which one can respond to and from which one can push off. Recognition of the referent in action permits a "dialectic of conservation and innovation, repetition and novelty" (Schrag, 1986, p. 109). Schrag moves us from an epistemological foundation to conversation responsive to the interplay of metaphor and action that is directly attentive to a given referent; this understanding of communicative praxis keeps interpretation from falling prey to the myth of an abstract universal assumption on the one hand, and into the grasp of one's own fantasy about what the conversation "should" be about on the other hand. The referent grounds communicative praxis.

Following the insights of phenomenology, Schrag (1986) underscores "intentionality," in its connection to the referent, as the inevitable interplay of subject and object, seer and seen, hearer and heard; intentionality implicates meaning as mutually constituted and influential (p. 115). Schrag stresses "self-implication" as one attends to a given referent; it is impossible for the interpreter to avoid influencing a given reading or observation. One is constantly involved in some degree of "self-implicature" and attentiveness to a given referent (Schrag, 1986, p. 115). Again, the interplay of action with metaphor dialectically moves us out of extreme positions. Schrag does not place subjectivity inherently within the communicator, but within a limited space in which the discourse takes place. In that space, there is subjective action toward Otherness and to the Same (oneself). This subjectivity is influenced by the referent and a communicative agent with limited ability to recognize "self-implicature" in a given historical moment. For Schrag (1986), the communicator is simultaneously "actor," "narrator," and "respondent" embedded in "social practices" that are understood only in the textured interplay of metaphor and action, part and whole (p. 138).

Decentered Subject

Schrag (1986) understands the power of the phrase "Death of Man" as an argument that the human being is no longer the king or queen of a subjectivity that can be imposed upon a given object (p. 117). On the other hand, Schrag assumes that the human being does, indeed, make a difference; in one's gaze, one conceptualizes not only part of a given object, but glimpses part of oneself. Schrag does not want to bury subjectivity; he tempers its impact by acknowledging our participation. His statement that there is always "saying of something by someone" gives space for subjectivity without contending that the "I" can be an island unto itself (Schrag, 1986, p. 123).

Recognition of the embeddedness of the human communicator leads to Schrag's (1986) description of the "decentered subject" without denying the subject or replacing the subject; he "resituates" the subject within a "hermeneutical space of communicative praxis" (p. 139). Schrag wants to revisit and recapture subjectivity that emerges from a space of conversation and social practices within a given historical moment. The decentered subject is understood through a number of dimensions within a space of "embodied" subjectivity that is "temporal" and tied to "multiplicity" in a textured fashion, yielding a unique voice that is not solely owned by the communicator (Schrag, 1986, pp. 146–152). This perspective is contrary to a hyper-focus on the self, which emphasizes a reified unity of identity; instead, Schrag points to a layered complexity of difference that shapes and drives communicative praxis. "The decentered subject as embodied is already *at* the world and already *in* the social practices" (Schrag, 1986, p. 152). The decentered subject ceases to be understood within theatrical terms of "roles, drama, and enactment"; Schrag (1986) moves closer to the public domain of embodied action of the decentered subject with metaphors that are political and ethical in nature (pp. 150–155). We no longer assume that a "literary" and an "artistic" vocabulary can address the embodied life of a decentered subject that enters the arenas of conversation, action, and decision making.

Perhaps the more accurate way to detail this world of a decentered subject is with the metaphor of "dialogical consciousness" (Schrag, 1986, p. 158). Dialogic praxis is not chosen; it emerges as a natural reflection of reality as one participates in the world. This view of consciousness assumes that intentionality is given in human communication, connecting subject and object in a space of subjectivity with or without our approval. Schrag (1986) critiques the story of modern philosophy as a tale about "monological consciousness" (p. 160). The key for Schrag's (1986) story is the turn toward dialogic consciousness that is not driven solely by choice and away from the power and the habit of ego "possession" of an object (p. 162). Schrag is not suggesting a new metaphysic; he is detailing a phenomenological rendering or description of how we learn and meet information in the human condition. The impulse of possession is part of the mythology of modernity that Schrag seeks to deconstruct. The act of possession rests within a rigid tradition and in a modern transcendental understanding of the ego that finds support from an "abstract" and "purified" subjectivity, permitting one to "know" without reservation; such confidence is the stuff of imperialism and colonialism that abides by the assumption that truth has been found and one must find another way to see the truth (Schrag, 1986, p. 164). One can sense, in Schrag's (1986) understanding of dialogic consciousness and his critique of the transcendental, a movement to what he termed the "transversal" (p. 164). Again, Schrag does not totally forgo conventions; he engages them in a different key of yes and no simultaneously, a "unity of contraries" (Buber, 1965/1966, p. 111). Schrag offers a decentered understanding of consciousness that rejects transcendental rationality; instead, he embraces a transversal rationality that moves learning and human engagement within the sphere of dialogic consciousness and a space of subjectivity. He walks from the delusion that one can discern pristine truth to an understanding of learning connected and situated within a complexity of phenomena. Schrag's story offers a reason for his critique of abstract modernist assumptions about the infallibility of an individual's ability to know.

The Rhetorical Turn

Schrag assumes that a dialogic consciousness situated within a space of subjectivity no longer adheres to universals connected to truth that give one the right to impose a position upon another. His situated view of truth takes him to rhetoric and the need to persuade another about the correctness of one's position. Schrag's (1986) position takes a "rhetorical turn" in which one must argue why a given position makes sense in a particular setting in a unique historical moment (p. 179). Schrag understands rhetoric as integral, a natural outgrowth of the deconstruction of a pristine universal understanding of truth. Without the universal connection to truth, Schrag understands the connection between rhetoric (persuasion) and hermeneutics (interpretation) as naturally mandated. The task of rhetoric is to explicate a position that requires interpretation and simultaneously involves self and other. In the process of doing rhetoric tied to hermeneutics, one moves from sheer tenacity to the communicative act of convincing another about the importance of a particular learning. Schrag's understanding of rhetoric is from the dangers of sophistry, which can be colloquially defined as persuasion without a soul, without a sense of conviction, and without consideration for a world wider and deeper than oneself. Schrag's rhetoric takes us from an epistemology composed of the accumulation of information to hermeneutics with a stress on interpretative perspectives that shift and alter the meaning of information. Rhetoric takes us to the engagement of information on the move, interpreted and understood in the communicative action of human engagement.

Schrag (1986) argues for a "new humanism," one that is more humbly responsive to the world around us (p. 197). He reminds us that we are situated beings and that others, both known and unknown, and existence, both near and far, make the human condition and human identity possible. Schrag (1986) does not abide by humanism that is colonially defined as the "custodian of values" (p. 197). Instead of assuming there are values that must be preserved, Schrag's new humanism leans toward alterity, otherness, shaping our ability to learn from all that is different than us. Schrag's shift is from preservation to learning. Human identity continues to evolve in meetings and in responses to that which is different than our limited perspectives. This form of humanism rests, not in what we know, but in meeting the new and unknown, uniting alterity and difference with learning. A life of "discourse and action" makes possible Schrag's (1986) new humanism, demanding only one ingredient from a communicative agent—constant learning (p. 200). Schrag gives us a philosophical picture of communication in which the communicative agent is a participant who must meet and respond to existence on its terms, no longer part of a legend that one can become the sole master of one's own fate or the providence of another.

Philosophy of Communication: *Zorba the Greek* and Story-Centered Meaning

Both Benhabib and Schrag offer philosophical pictures about the discernment of meaning through a texture that does not ignore communal conventions and, at the same time, is not captive to them. Additionally, Benhabib refuses to give up on the public domain and the importance of rationality, as she textures her position with dialectical conversation from Enlightenment, feminist, and postmodern scholarship. She takes a middle road, not a path of compromise, but a direction that emerges from a dialectical and story-driven understanding of philosophy of communication. Her project moves the focus from the individual and the desire to cling to a rigid ideology that is erroneously supported by the assumption that there is one metanarrative, one truth, to a dialectical story of action. Benhabib textures conversation with relationships and reminders of before, now, and what is not yet. She seeks to liberate the human being within contexts responsive to people, environments, multiple generations, institutions, and ideas that situate us within embedded contexts, within an unending conversation alert to shifting historical demands.

Schrag reminds us of space in which subjectivity finds form and reality—in communicative praxis discourse that is about something, by someone, and for someone, temporally understood and explained within an interpretive context of part and whole. Schrag's communicative praxis moves communication from the abstract to concrete engagement attentive to genuine consequences. Schrag connects texture to a three-dimensional understanding of communication in action. We learn on the run, attending to ideas as they come to life before our eyes. A metaphysical statement about the world that never phenomenologically manifested itself in human existence is not a story, but rather a fantasy, a wish or demand for life to conform to the ambitions of a sole communicative agent. Together, Schrag and Benhabib frame philosophy of communication as story-centered. A philosophy of communication is a guiding story that is tested in our ongoing engagement with existence.

Our story-centered view of philosophy of communication made the selection of a novel a natural gesture. *Zorba the Greek* ends in the textured interplay of a common critique of modernity—community matters, and it is not a facile experience. Both Boss and Zorba walk away from a culture absorbed in individualism. The limits of this story (individualism) are central, unmasked in multiple projects by Robert Bellah (Bellah, Madsen, Sullivan, Swidler, & Tipton, 1985; Bellah, 1992) and Robert D. Putnam (2000). Recognition of this misstep gives us a chance to witness a practical counter, the practices and the story of human friendship.[1] Zorba and Boss, with all their flaws, give us a philosophical picture of friendship, and Zorba reminds us of the possibility of loving life right up to one's last breath. We now turn to Zorba's final moments, which were communicated to Boss in a letter written by a schoolmaster in the town where Zorba now lived with his wife.

> He [Zorba] then sat up in his bed, threw back the sheets and tried to get up. We ran to prevent him—Lyuba, his wife, and I, along with several sturdy neighbors. But he brushed us all roughly aside, jumped out of bed and went to the window. There, he gripped the frame, looked out far into the mountains, opened wide his eyes and began to laugh, then to whinny like a horse. It was thus, standing, with his nails dug into the window frame, that death came to him.
>
> His wife Lyuba asked me to write to you and send her respects. The deceased often talked about you, she says, and left instructions that a santuri of his should be given to you after his death to help you to remember him. (Kazantzakis, 1946/1952, p. 346)

Zorba is a walking embodiment of philosophy of communication, manifesting passion for life, love for music, care of friendship, and the importance and dignity of work. As he made his final stand "with his nails dug into the window frame" (Kazantzakis, 1946/1952, p. 246), Zorba looked out into the distance, whinnied like a horse, and died—Zorba the Greek's last moments on Earth were an existential dance. Zorba announced the importance of joy that comes from meeting existence on its own terms and then offering a response with one's whole being.

---

1 See for example the work of William K. Rawlins, *Friendship Matters: Communication, Dialectics, and the Life Course* (1992) and *The Compass of Friendship: Narratives, Identities, and Dialogues* (2009).

Zorba and Boss offer us a powerful story about human friendship. The following are our final coordinates, which tender a philosophy of communication that is story laden.

1. Philosophy of communication attentive to story-centered meaning is textured with multiple influences, from persons to context, to interpretive perspectives, to the historical moment, and to the dialectical interplay of part and whole. Zorba has a large presence in the novel, but he is still only a part. One observes that place, other persons, the historical moment, and all the events are co-actors in the story.

2. Philosophy of communication attentive to story-centered meaning does not disregard the moments of relational connection between ideas, generations, persons, and institutions. Throughout the novel, we encounter the importance of ideas, persons, and institutions from the past. A story-centered view of philosophy of communication brings the past into the present, keeping practices alive with meaning, not mindless repetition. One watches Zorba do the same practices time and time again, with each effort being novel and unique.

3. Philosophy of communication attentive to story-centered meaning responds to real meeting and real life, offering deconstruction of abstract mythology of the individual alone. Zorba is a unique and powerful figure in the novel. We chose him as an exemplar of ruggedness and passion that does not fall prey to individualism. Others matter to him. He walks in the mud of everyday life; he is not tempted to stand above the pain of existence. Zorba both loves and suffers; his life is not lived in abstraction.

4. Philosophy of communication attentive to story-centered meaning takes discourse seriously, remembering that communication is about something, by someone, and for someone. Boss has to learn the hard way that there are consequences to the stories that are told and connect us to persons and topics, shaping our own identities. Zorba understands this philosophical position in practical terms. The stories that are told and lived matter.

5. Philosophy of communication attentive to people, context (immediate and extended), ideas, relationships, and the historical moment understood in its uniqueness give rise to a sense of story-centered meaning. Zorba is alert; he lives in a world of attentiveness. Boss is

often lost in abstraction until existence demands acknowledgment. Zorba offers us a portrait of attentiveness in action, reminding us to attend to the sign of existence.

The novel *Zorba the Greek* gives us a story about philosophy of communication that is attentive to story-centered meaning that is embodied in human existence. Zorba takes life seriously on its own terms, not as a fantasy, a wish, or a demand for life to emerge on particular terms that concur with the ambition of the communicative agent alone. Zorba demonstrates the importance of finding meaning as it emerges from our meeting and responsiveness to existence. Philosophy of communication attentive to story-centered meaning demands agility, an ability to dance with existence and encounter others with a voice attentive to relative pitch. One brings relative pitch to sociality within the human condition. Zorba gives us insight into his unique version of relative pitch. If you have ever known someone with the characteristic of relative pitch, you understand that it is possible to engage life with an existential dance, willing to love life when the world refuses to abide by one's own personal demands.

Throughout this work, *An Overture to Philosophy of Communication: The Carrier of Meaning*, we have painted Zorba the Greek as a standard bearer of a life of meaning. As stated in Chapter 1, we intentionally did not choose Boss. Rather, we chose the character in the story that reminds us that an existential dance is possible. Perhaps, at best, philosophy of communication attentive to meaning is judged by its ability to help us dance, to love life, to assist us in attending to relationships, to call us to notice that which is before us—right up to the last moment of digging our nails into something in order to stand upright while screaming with our last breath a thanks for existence itself.

Zorba is a character who repeatedly says "yes" to life; however, more importantly in everyday existence, we encounter people who display such a commitment to nonstop learning from difference—people who, regardless of the circumstances, never cease loving the world around them. Such persons are standard bearers of a philosophy of communication as a carrier of meaning, reminding us of the importance of learning from "difference" (Allen, 2010), the importance of an "enlarged mentality" (Kant, 1790/1951, pp. 136–137; Arendt 1992) that keeps us attentive to and appreciative of the human condition, and the genuine possibility of engaging joy as the heart of life. As the ethicist of our time, Emmanuel Levinas, repeatedly reminded us, joy is not a cosmetic liking, but rather a tenacious passion for meeting and responding to existence on its own terms. In Levinasian terms, a philosophy of communication as a carrier of meaning helps us meet existence on its own terms, finding joy as we understand and practice the profound difference between love and liking. Zorba does not cease loving his existence, even when great dislike functioned as a shadow over all.

The following material offers a bibliography of scholarship from communication journals and books. This scholarship aligns with the conceptual engagements reflected in each chapter. This appendix is offered for assistance and further research, and more importantly, for acknowledgment and thanks for the thoughtful work done by so many on the philosophy of communication themes discussed throughout this work.

Chapter 1
Philosophy of Communication: "Habits of the Heart"

Arneson, P. (2007). *Perspectives on philosophy of communication*. West Lafayette, IN: Purdue University Press.

Arnett, R. C. (1990). The practical philosophy of communication ethics and free speech as the foundation for speech communication. *Communication Quarterly*, 38(3), 208–217.

Arnett, R. C. (2010). Defining philosophy of communication: Difference and identity. *Qualitative Research Reports in Communication*, 11(1), 1–6.

Barnlud, D. C. (1962). Toward a meaning-centered philosophy of communication. *Journal of Communication*, 12(4), 197–211.

Bergman, M. (2009). Experience, purpose, and the value of vagueness: On C. S. Peirce's contribution to the philosophy of communication. *Communication Theory*, 19(3), 248–277.

Bergman, M. (2009). *Peirce's philosophy of communication: The rhetorical underpinnings of the theory of signs*. New York: Continuum.

Cook, M., & Holba, A. (Eds.). (2008). *Philosophies of communication: Implications for everyday experience*. New York: Peter Lang.

Dresner, E. (2006). Davidson's philosophy of communication. *Communication Theory*, 16(2), 155-172.

Grant, C. B. (2010). *Beyond universal pragmatics: Studies in the philosophy of communication*. New York: Peter Lang.

Kelley, V. (2002). "Good speech": An interpretive essay investigating an African philosophy of communication. *Western Journal of Black Studies*, 26(1), 44–54.

Kelly, J. C. (1981). *A philosophy of communication: Explorations for a systematic model*. London, U.K.: Centre for the Study of Communications and Culture.

Langsdorf, L., & Smith, A. R. (1995). *Recovering pragmatism's voice: The classical tradition, Rorty, and the philosophy of communication*. Albany, NY: State University of New York Press.

Lillywhite, H. (1952). *Toward a philosophy of communication. Journal of Communication*, 2(1), 29–32.

Martinez-Ramos, D. (2009). On rational madness: Love and reason in Socrates and Lacan. *Communication Review*, 12(2), 162–173.

Phillips, D. E. (1981). *Karl Barth's philosophy of communication*. New York: Georg Olms Verlag.

Radford, G. P. (2005). *On the philosophy of communication*. Belmont, CA: Thomson Wadsworth.

Ramsey, E. R. (1998). *The long path to nearness: A contribution to a corporeal philosophy of communication and the groundwork for an ethics of relief*. Amherst, NY: Humanity Books.

Stern, B. B. (1984). A philosophy of communications for the marketing manager: Three "T's" in an MBA course. *Business Communication Quarterly*, 47(1), 28–30.

Stewart, J. R. (1995). *Language as articulate contact: Toward a post-semiotic philosophy of communication*. Albany, NY: State University of New York Press.

Voudoures, K. I., & Poulakos, J. (2002). *Greek philosophy of communication*. Athens, Greece: Ionia Publications.

Chapter 2
Zorba's Dance
Novel
(These essays point to the importance of the novel as a form of an elongated literary case study.)

Alberts, J. K. (1986). The role of couples' conversations in relational development: A content analysis of courtship talk in Harlequin Romance novels. *Communication Quarterly*, 34(2), 127–142.

Bowman, M. S. (1995). "Novelizing" the stage: Chamber theatre after Breen and Bakhtin. *Text & Performance*, 15(1), 1–23.

Hart, J. L., Walker, K. L., & Gregg, J. L. (2007). Communication ethics and *My Sister's Keeper*. *Communication Teacher*, 21(4), 123–127.

Heston, L. A. (1973). A note on prose fiction: The performance of dialogue tags. *The Speech Teacher*, 22(1), 69–72.

Heston, L. A. (1975). The solo performance of prose fiction. *The Speech Teacher*, 24(3), 269–277.

Hubbard, R. C. (1985). Relationship styles in popular romance novels, 1950 to 1983. *Communication Quarterly*, 33(2), 113–125.

Kougl, K. M. (1983). Novels as a source for heuristics about interpersonal communication. *Communication Quarterly*, 31(4), 282–289.

Maddux, K. (2008). *The Da Vinci Code* and the regressive gender politics of celebrating women. *Critical Studies in Media Communication*, 25(3), 225–248.

Ott, B. L., & Bonnstetter, B. (2007). "We're at now, now": *Spaceballs* as parodic tourism. *Southern Communication Journal*, 72(4), 309–327.

Picart, C. J. S. (1998). Rebirthing the monstrous: James Whale's (mis)reading of Mary Shelley's *Frankenstein*. *Critical Studies in Mass Communication*, 15(4), 382–404.

Pollock, D. (1988). The play as novel: Reappropriating Brecht's drums in the night. *Quarterly Journal of Speech*, 74(3), 296–309.

Ramsey, B. A. (1972). An interdisciplinary course in the rhetoric of literature. *The Speech Teacher*, 21(4), 319–321.

Striphas, T. (2003). A dialectic with the everyday: Communication and cultural politics on Oprah Winfrey's Book Club. *Critical Studies in Media Communication*, 20(3), 195–316.

Striphas, T. (2010). The abuses of literacy: Amazon Kindle and the right to read. *Communication & Critical/Cultural Studies*, 7(3), 297–317.

Yarbrough, S. R. (1994). Misdirected sentiment: Conflicting rhetorical strategies in *Uncle Tom's Cabin*. *Rhetorica: A Journal of the History of Rhetoric*, 12(2), 191–210.

Chapter 3
Communicative Dwellings
Antiquity

Cox, V. (1999). Ciceronian rhetoric in Italy, 1260–1350. *Rhetorica: A Journal of the History of Rhetoric*, 17(3), 239–288.

Leff, M. C. (1973). The Latin stylistic rhetorics of antiquity. *Speech Monographs*, 40(4), 273–279.

Weaver, B. J. (1979). Cultural determination of rhetorical styles: A study in Greek oratory. *Communication Quarterly*, 27(2), 12–18.

Middle Ages

Briggs, C. F. (2007). Aristotle's rhetoric in the later medieval universities: A reassessment. *Rhetorica: A Journal of the History of Rhetoric, 25*(3), 243–268.

Dieter, O. A. (1965). Arbor picta: The medieval tree of preaching. *Quarterly Journal of Speech, 51*(2), 123–144.

Kernodle, G. R., & Kernodle, P. (1942). Dramatic aspects of the medieval tournament. *Speech Monographs, 9*(1), 161–172.

Lemen Clark, D. (1959). Rhetoric and the literature of the English Middle Ages. *Quarterly Journal of Speech, 45*(1), 19–28.

Murphy, J. J. (1966). Aristotle's rhetoric in the Middle Ages. *Quarterly Journal of Speech, 52*(2), 109–115.

Murphy, J. J. (1967). Cicero's rhetoric in the Middle Ages. *Quarterly Journal of Speech, 53*(4), 334–341.

Pellegrini, A. M. (1942). Renaissance and medieval antecedents of debate. *Quarterly Journal of Speech, 28*(1), 14–19.

Prill, P. E. (1987). Rhetoric and poetics in the early Middle Ages. *Rhetorica: A Journal of the History of Rhetoric, 5*(2), 129–147.

Purcell, W. (1987). Transsumptio: A rhetorical doctrine of the thirteenth century. *Rhetorica: A Journal of the History of Rhetoric, 5*(4), 369–410.

Soffer, O. (2005). The textual pendulum. *Communication Theory, 15*(3), 266–291.

Tade, G. T. (1965). Rhetorical aspects of the spiritual exercises in the medieval tradition of preaching. *Quarterly Journal of Speech, 51*(4), 409–418.

Wallace, W. A. (1989). Aristotelian science and rhetoric in transition: The Middle Ages and the Renaissance. *Rhetorica: A Journal of the History of Rhetoric, 7*(1), 7-21.

Ward, J. O. (1995). Quintilian and the rhetorical revolution of the Middle Ages. *Rhetorica: A Journal of the History of Rhetoric, 13*(3), 231–284.

Ward, J. O. (2001). Rhetorical theory and the rise and decline of Dictamen in the Middle Ages and early Renaissance. *Rhetorica: A Journal of the History of Rhetoric, 19*(2), 175–223.

Renaissance

Achter, P. J. (2004). TV, technology, and McCarthyism: Crafting the democratic renaissance in an age of fear. *Quarterly Journal of Speech, 90*(3), 307–326.

Bowen, B. C. (1998). Ciceronian wit and renaissance rhetoric. *Rhetorica: A Journal of the History of Rhetoric, 16*(4), 409–429.

Brennan, J. X. (1960). The epitome Troporum ac Schematum: The genesis of a Renaissance rhetorical text. *Quarterly Journal of Speech, 46*(1), 59–71.

Cleary, J. W. (1959). John Bulwer: Renaissance communications. *Quarterly Journal of Speech, 45*(4), 391–398.

Lucas, S. E. (1988). The renaissance of American public address: Text and context in rhetorical criticism. *Quarterly Journal of Speech, 74*(2), 241–260.

Mohrmann, G. P. (1972). The civile conversation: Communication in the Renaissance. *Speech Monographs, 39*(3), 193–204.

Murphy, J. J. (1969). Mis-titling and other problems in the field of Renaissance rhetorical scholarship. *Quarterly Journal of Speech, 55*(1), 78–82.

Murphy, J. J. (1989). Implications of the "renaissance of rhetoric" in English departments. *Quarterly Journal of Speech, 75*(3), 335–343.

Nadeau, R. (1950). A Renaissance schoolmaster on practice. *Speech Monographs*, 17(2), 171–179.

Nadeau, R. (1950). Thomas Farnaby: Schoolmaster and rhetorician of the English Renaissance. *Quarterly Journal of Speech*, 36(3), 340–344.

Pellegrini, A. M. (1942). Renaissance and medieval antecedents of debates. *Quarterly Journal of Speech*, 28(1), 14–19.

Rebhorn, W. A. (1993). Baldesar Castiglione, Thomas Wilson, and the courtly body of Renaissance rhetoric. *Rhetorica: A Journal of the History of Rhetoric*, 11(3), 241–274.

Sloan, T. O. (1969). A Renaissance controversialist on rhetoric: Thomas Wright's passions of the minde in generall. *Speech Monographs*, 36(1), 38–54.

Ward, J. O. (1988). Magic and rhetoric from antiquity to the Renaissance: Some ruminations. *Rhetorica: A Journal of the History of Rhetoric*, 6(1), 57–118.

Ward, J. O. (2001). Rhetorical theory and the rise and decline of Dictamen in the Middle Ages and early Renaissance. Rhetorica: *A Journal of the History of Rhetoric*, 19(2), 175–223.

Modernity

Greifinger, J. (1995). Therapeutic discourse as moral conversation: Psychoanalysis, modernity, and the ideal of authenticity. *The Communication Review*, 1(1), 53–81.

Hasian M. Jr., (2003). Franklin D. Roosevelt, the Holocaust, and modernity's rescue rhetorics. *Communication Quarterly*, 51(2), 154–173.

Hier, S. P. (2008). Transformative democracy in the age of second modernity: Cosmopolitanization, communicative agency and the reflexive subject. *New Media & Society*, 10(1), 27–44.

Rajagopal, A. (1996). Mediating modernity: Theorizing reception in a non-Western society. *Communication Review*, 1(4), 441–469.

Tell, D. (2012). Rhetoric, modality, modernity. *Quarterly Journal of Speech*, 98(1), 124–127.

Postmodernity

Andrucki, M. (1990). "Ah the old questions, the old answers. . .": Postmodernism and poetic justice in the plays of Charles Ludlam. *Text & Performance Quarterly*, 10(4), 294–305.

Ashton, W. (2003). Critical theory versus postmodernism. *Review of Communication*, 3(2), 145–149.

Blair, C., Jeppeson, M. S., & Pucci E. Jr., (1991). Public memorializing in postmodernity: The Vietnam Veteran Memorial as prototype. *Quarterly Journal of Speech*, 77(3), 263–288.

Bowman, M., & Pollock, D. (1989). "This spectacular visible body": Politics and postmodernism in Pina Bausch's *Tanztheater*. *Text & Performance Quarterly*, 9(2), 113–118.

Browning, L. D., & Hawes, L. C. (1991). Style, process, surface, context: Consulting as postmodern art. *Journal of Applied Communication Research*, 19(1/2), 32–54.

Carmichael, T. (1991). Postmodernism, symbolicity, and the rhetoric of the hyperreal: Kenneth Burke, Fredric Jameson, and Jean Baudrillard. *Text & Performance Quarterly*, 11(4), 319–324.

Ferris, D. S. (2003). Post-modern interdisciplinarity: Kant, Diderot and the encyclopedia project. *MLN*, 118(5), 1251–1277.

Gray, P. H. (1989). Performance, postmodernism, and politics. *Text & Performance Quarterly*, 9(4), 342–347.

Grayson Seymour, C. (2011). A place for the premodern: A review of modern and postmodern intimate interpersonal communication frames. *Review of Communication*, 11(4), 286–309.

Hamera, J. (1986). Postmodern performance, postmodern criticism. *Literature & Performance*, 7(1), 13–20.

Harms, J. B., & Dickens, D. R. (1996). Postmodern media studies: Analysis or symptom? *Critical Studies in Mass Communication*, 13(3), 210–227.

Hasian, M. J. (2008). Iconic materials, hermeneutics of faith, and the postmodern reproduction of public democracies. *The Review of Communication*, 8(1), 1–15.

Herman, A., & Sloop, J. M. (1998). The politics of authenticity in postmodern rock culture: The case of Negativland and the letter "U" and the numeral "2." *Critical Studies in Mass Communication*, 15(1), 1–20.

Kacandes, I. (1993). Are you in the text?: The "literary performative" in postmodernist fiction. *Text & Performance Quarterly*, 13(2), 139–153.

Lippucci, A. (1992). Social theorizing on the operatic stage: Jean-Pierre Ponnelle's postmodern humanist production of Verdi's *La Traviata*. *Text & Performance Quarterly*, 12(3), 245–273.

McPhee, R. D. (2004). Clegg and Giddens on power and (post)modernity. *Management Communication Quarterly*, 18(1), 129–145.

Moore, R. (2004). Postmodernism and punk subculture: Cultures of authenticity and deconstruction. *The Communication Review*, 7(3), 305–327.

Nudd, D. M. (1995). The postmodern heroine(s) of *Lardo Weeping*. *Text & Performance Quarterly*, 15(1), 24-43.

Peterson, E. E. (1989). On the boundaries of postmodern aesthetics. *Text & Performance Quarterly*, 9(2), 165–169.

Pollock, D., & Cox, J. R. (1991). Historicizing "reason": Critical theory, practice, and postmodernity. *Communication Monographs*, 58(2), 170–178.

Rice, J. (2004). A critical review of visual rhetoric in a postmodern age: Complementing, extending, and presenting new ideas. *Review of Communication*, 4(1/2), 63–74.

Stengrim, L. A. (2005). Negotiating postmodern democracy, political activism, and knowledge production: Indymedia's grassroots and e-savvy answer to media oligopoly. *Communication & Critical/Cultural Studies*, 2(4), 281–304.

Wilferth, J. (2003). Generative essays from Wilchelns to postmodernity. *Review of Communication*, 3(1), 99–101.

Chapter 4
Knowledge and Meaning through Epistemology

Epistemology

Aguado, J. M. (2009). Self-observation, self-reference and operational coupling in social systems: Steps toward a coherent epistemology of mass media. *Empedocles: European Journal for the Philosophy of Communication*, 1(1), 59–74.

Berger, C. R., & Douglas, W. (1981). Studies in interpersonal epistemology: III. Anticipated interaction, self-monitoring, and observational context selection. *Communication Monographs*, 48(3), 183–196.

Bertelsen, D. A. (1993). Sophistry, epistemology, and the media context. *Philosophy & Rhetoric*, 26(4), 296–301.

Brock, B. L. (1985). Epistemology and ontology in Kenneth Burke's Dramatism. *Communication Quarterly*, 33(2), 94–104.

Brock, B. L., Burke, K., Burgess, P. G., & Simons, H. W. (1985). Dramatism as ontology or epistemology: A symposium. *Communication Quarterly*, 33(1) 17–33.

Brummett, B. (1990). A eulogy for epistemic rhetoric. *Quarterly Journal of Speech*, 76(1), 69–72.

Caraher, B. G. (1981). Metaphor as contradiction: A grammar and epistemology of poetic metaphor. *Philosophy & Rhetoric*, 14(2), 69–88.

Cherwitz, R. A., & Darwin, T. J. (1995). Why the "epistemic" in epistemic rhetoric? The paradox of rhetoric as performance. *Text & Performance Quarterly*, 15(3), 189–205.

Cherwitz, R. A., & Hikins, J. W. (1979). John Stuart Mill's *On Liberty*: Implications for the epistemology of the new rhetoric. *Quarterly Journal of Speech*, 65(1), 12–24.

Cherwitz, R. A., & Hikins, J. W. (1990). Burying the undertaker: A eulogy for the eulogists of rhetorical epistemology. *Quarterly Journal of Speech*, 76(1), 73–77.

Chesebro, J. W. (1988). Epistemology and ontology as dialectical modes in the writings of Kenneth Burke. *Communication Quarterly*, 36(3), 175–191.

Crable, R. E. (1982). Knowledge-as-status: On argument and epistemology. *Communication Monographs*, 49(4), 249–262.

Davis, S. (2002). Conversation, epistemology and norms. *Mind & Language*, 17(5), 513–537.

Engnell, R. A. (1973). Implication for communication of the rhetorical epistemology of Gorgias of Leontini. *Western Speech*, 37(3), 175–184.

Enos, R. L. (1976). The epistemology of Gorgias' rhetoric: A re-examination. *Southern Speech Communication Journal*, 42, 35–51.

Farrell, T. B. (1990). From the Parthenon to the bassinet: Death and rebirth along the epistemic trail. *Quarterly Journal of Speech*, 76(1), 78–84.

Goodman, M., & Gring, M. (2000). The radio act of 1927: Progressive ideology, epistemology, and praxis. *Rhetoric & Public Affairs*, 3(3), 397–418.

Gozzi, R. J. (1992). Electric media and electric epistemology: Empathy at a distance. *Critical Studies in Mass Communication*, 9(3), 217–228.

Greenwood, J. D. (2007). Unnatural epistemology. *Mind & Language*, 22(2), 132–149.

Gregg, R. B. (1987). Communication epistemology: A study in the "language" of cognition. *Quarterly Journal of Speech*, 73(2), 232–242.

Gresson, A. D. (1977). Minority epistemology and the rhetoric of creation. *Philosophy & Rhetoric*, 10(4), 244–262.

Harris, R. (2011). Tropical truth(s): The epistemology of metaphor and other tropes. *Quarterly Journal of Speech*, 97(4), 473–477.

Haskell, R. E., & Hauser, G. A. (1978). Rhetorical structure: Truth and method in Weaver's epistemology. *Quarterly Journal of Speech*, 64(3), 233–245.

Hsiang-Ann, L. (2006). Toward an epistemology of participatory communication: A feminist perspective. *Howard Journal of Communications*, 17(2), 101–118.

Katz, S. B. (1995). The epistemology of the Kabbalah: Toward a Jewish philosophy of rhetoric. *Rhetoric Society Quarterly*, 25, 107–122.

Kitcher, P. (1995). Revisiting Kant's epistemology: Skepticism, apriority, and psychologism. *Noûs*, 29(3), 285–315.

Lankshear, C. (2003). The challenge of digital epistemologies. *Education, Communication, & Information*, 3(2), 167–186.

Lillis, T., & Scott, M. (2007). Defining academic literacies research: Issues of epistemology, ideology and strategy. *Journal of Applied Linguistics*, 4(1), 5–32.

Liska, J., & Cronkhite, G. (1977). Epilogue for apologia: On the convergent validation of epistemologies. *Western Journal of Speech Communication*, 41(1), 57–65.

McDermid, D. J. (2000). Does epistemology rest on a mistake? Understanding Rorty on skepticism. *Critica: Revista Hispanoamericana de Filosofia*, 32(96), 3–42.

McNamee, S. (1988). Accepting research as social intervention: Implications of a systemic epistemology. *Communication Quarterly*, 36(1), 50–68.

Miller, K. D. (1988). Epistemology of a drum major: Martin Luther King, Jr. and the black folk pulpit. *Rhetoric Society Quarterly*, 18(3/4), 225–236.

Miller, K. D. (1989). Voice merging and self-making: The epistemology of "I Have a Dream." *Rhetoric Society Quarterly*, 19(1), 23–31.

Morgenstern, S. (1992). The epistemic autonomy of mass media audiences. *Critical Studies in Mass Communication*, 9(3), 293–310.

Moore, R. C. (1999). Where epistemology meets ecology: Can environmental news reporting survive postmodernism? *Mass Communication & Society*, 2(1/2), 3–25.

Ortega, L. (2005). Methodology, epistemology, and ethics in instructed SLA research: An introduction. *Modern Language Journal*, 89(3), 317–327.

Pinchevski, A. (2005). Displacing incommunicability: Autism as an epistemological boundary. *Communication & Critical/Cultural Studies*, 2(2), 163–184.

Pullman, G. L. (1994). Reconsidering sophistic rhetoric in light of skeptical epistemology. *Rhetoric Review*, 13(1), 50–68.

Rodríguez, J. I., & Cai, D. A. (1994). When your epistemology gets in the way: A response to Sprague. *Communication Education*, 43(4), 263–272.

Schowalter, D. F. (2004). Hallucination as epistemology: Critiquing the visual in Ken Burns' *The West*. *Communication & Critical/Cultural Studies*, 1(3), 250–270.

Sinntt-Armstrong, W. (2000). From "is" to "ought" in moral epistemology. *Argumentation*, 14(2), 159–174.

Smudde, P. (2004). Concerning the epistemology and ontology of public relations literature. *Review of Communication*, 4(3/4), 163–175.

Supa, D. W. (2009). The origins of empirical versus critical epistemology in American communication. *American Communication Journal*, 11(3), 1–11.

Swanson, D. L. (1977). A reflective view of the epistemology of critical inquiry. *Communication Monographs*, 44(3), 207–219.

Taylor, S. S. (2003). Knowing in your gut and in your head: Doing theater and my underlying epistemology of communication. *Management Communication Quarterly*, 17(2), 272–279.

Tell, D. (2004). Burke's encounter with ransom: Rhetoric and epistemology in "four master tropes." *Rhetoric Society Quarterly*, 34(4), 33–54.

Thomas, D. (1994). Reflections on a Nietzschean turn in rhetorical theory: Rhetoric without epistemology? *Quarterly Journal of Speech*, 80(1), 71–76.

Thorne, S. L. (2005). Epistemology, politics, and ethics in sociocultural theory. *Modern Language Journal*, 89(3), 393–409.

Veit, W. (1984). The potency of imagery: The impotence of rational language: Ernesto Grassi's contribution to modern epistemology. *Philosophy & Rhetoric*, 17(4), 221–239.

Verdicchio, M. (1986). The rhetoric of epistemology in Vico's *New Science*. *Philosophy & Rhetoric*, 19(3), 178–193.

Watson-Gegeo, K. (2004). Mind, language, and epistemology: Toward a language socialization paradigm for SLA. *Modern Language Journal*, 88(3), 331–350.

Kant

Abbott, D. (2007). Kant, Theremin, and the morality of rhetoric. *Philosophy & Rhetoric*, 40(3), 274–292.

Aune, J. A. (2008). Modernity as a rhetorical problem: Phronesis, forms, and forums in *Norms of Rhetorical Culture*. *Philosophy & Rhetoric*, 41(4), 402–420.

Bahti, T. (1987). Histories of the university: Kant and Humboldt. *MLN*, 102(3), 437–460.

Baker, E. (1998). Fables of the sublime: Kant, Schiller, Kleist. *MLN*, 113(3), 524–536.

Corngold, S. (1987). Wit and judgment in the eighteenth century: Lessing and Kant. *MLN*, 102(3), 461–482.

Crisman, W. (1991). "Thus far had the work been transcribed": Coleridge's use of Kant's precritical writings and the rhetoric of *On the Imagination*. *Modern Language Quarterly*, 52(4), 404–422.

Dostal, R. J. (1980). Kant and rhetoric. *Philosophy & Rhetoric*, 13(4), 223–244.

Feldman, K. (2009). De Man's Kant and Goebbels' Schiller: The ideology of reception. *MLN*, 124(5), 1170–1187.

Ferris, D. S. (2003). Post-modern interdisciplinarity: Kant, Diderot and the encyclopedia project. *MLN*, 118(5), 1251–1277.

Flannery, A. (2007). The passion of the sign: Revolution and language in Kant, Goethe, and Kleist. *MLN*, 122(3), 672–674.

Gehrke, P. J. (2002). Turning Kant against the priority of autonomy: Communication ethics and the duty to community. *Philosophy & Rhetoric*, 35(1), 1–21.

Hove, T. (2009). Communicative implications of Kant's aesthetic theory. *Philosophy & Rhetoric*, 42(2), 103–114.

McCormick, S. (2005). The artistry of obedience: From Kant to kingship. *Philosophy & Rhetoric*, 38(4), 302–327.

Nikolopoulou, K. (2006). As if: Kant, Adorno, and the politics of poetry. *MLN*, 121(3), 757–773.

Peck, L. (2007). Sapere aude! The importance of a moral education in Kant's doctrine of virtue. *Journal of Mass Media Ethics*, 22(2/3), 208–214.

Pfau, T. (1999). The voice of critique: Aesthetic cognition after Kant. *Modern Language Quarterly*, 60(3), 321–352.

Posy, C. J. (1997). Between Leibniz and Mill: Kant's critique of music. *Philosophy & Rhetoric*, 30(3), 243–270.

Reed, A. (1980). The debt of disinterest: Kant's critique of music. *MLN*, 95(3), 563–584.

Reinhard, K. (1995). Kant with Sade, Lacan with Levinas. *MLN*, 110(4), 785–808.

Smith, J. H. (1985). Dialogic midwifery in Kleist's *Marquise von O* and the hermeneutics of telling the untold in Kant and Plato. *PMLA*, 100(2), 203–219.

Stroud, S. R. (2005). Rhetoric and moral progress in Kant's ethical community. *Philosophy & Rhetoric*, 38(4), 328–354.

Stroud, S. R. (2006). Kant on community: A reply to Gehrke. *Philosophy & Rhetoric*, 39(2), 157–165.

Stroud, S. R. (2011). Kant on education and the rhetorical force of the example. *Rhetoric Society Quarterly*, 41(5), 416–438.

Taylor, M. (2009). Critical absorption: Kant's theory of taste. *MLN*, 124(3), 572–591.

Van de Vijver, G. (1990). Schematism and schematat: Kant and the P. D. P. *Communication & Cognition*, 23(2/3), 223–233.

Vuksanovic, D. (1996). Immanuel Kant's philosophy of consciousness in light of the Jungian typology of personalities. *Communication & Cognition*, 29(1), 121–130.

Warminski, A. (2001). Returns of the sublime: Positing and performative in Kant, Fichte, and Schiller. *MLN*, 116(5), 964–978.

Chapter 5
Existential Engagement

Existentialism

Smith, C. R., & Arntson, P. H. (1991). Identification in interpersonal relationships: One foundation of creativity. *The Southern Communication Journal*, 57(1), 61–118.

Dostoevsky

Patterson, D. (1994). The dialogic of the elsewhere in Danow's analysis of Dostoevsky. *The Dialogic Sign: Essays on the Major Novels of Dostoevsky*, 98(3/4), 397–409.

Jaspers

Gordon, R. D. (2000). Karl Jaspers: Existential philosopher of dialogical communication. *The Southern Communication Journal*, 65(2/3), 105–118.

Hyde, M. J., & Sargent, D. K. (1993). The performance of play, the Great Poem, and ethics. *Text & Performance Quarterly*, 13(2), 122–138.

Kierkegaard

Althouse, M. T. (2004). Moving Kierkegaard toward critical rhetoric. *The Review of Communication*, 4(3/4), 321–323.

Althouse, M. T. (2010). Reading the Baptist schism of 2000: Kierkegaardian hermeneutics and religious freedom. *Atlantic Journal of Communication*, 18(4), 177–193.

Anderson, R. E. (1963). Kierkegaard's theory of communication. *Speech Monographs*, 30(1), 1–14.

Ercolini, G. L. (2003). Burke contra Kierkegaard: Kenneth Burke's dialectic via reading Søren Kierkegaard. *Philosophy & Rhetoric*, 36(3), 207–222.

Hawes, L. C. (1999). The dialogics of conversation: Power, control, vulnerability. *Communication Theory*, 9(3), 229–264.

Herrmann, A. F. (2008). Kierkegaard and dialogue: The communication of capability. *Communication Theory*, 18(1), 71–98.

Galati, M. (1969). A rhetoric for the subjectivist in a world of untruth: The tasks and strategy of Søren Kierkegaard. *Quarterly Journal of Speech*, 55(4), 372–380.

Jansen, N. (1987). Kierkegaard news from abroad. *Communicatio South African Journal for Communication Theory and Research*, 13(2), 45–46.

Turnbull, J. (2009). Kierkegaard, indirect communication, and ambiguity. *The Heythrop Journal*, 50(1), 13–22.

Heidegger

Anton, C. (1999). Beyond the constitutive-representational dichotomy: The phenomenological notion of intentionality. *Communication Theory*, 9(1), 26–57.

Arnett, R. C., & Nakagawa, G. (1983). The assumptive roots of empathic listening: A critique. *Communication Education*, 32(4), 368–378.

Arthos, J. (2002). Chapman's *Coatesville Address*: A hermeneutic reading. *Quarterly Journal of Speech*, 88(2), 193–208.

Chaudhary, Z. R. (2010). The labor of mimesis. *Social Semiotics*, 20(4), 357–365.

Couldry, N., & Markham, T. (2008). Troubled closeness or satisfied distance? Researching media consumption and public orientation. *Media, Culture, & Society*, 30(1), 5–21.

Desilet, G. (1991). Heidegger and Derrida: The conflict between hermeneutics and deconstruction in the context of rhetorical and communication theory. *Quarterly Journal of Speech*, 77(2), 152–175.

Elden, S. (2005). Reading Logos as speech: Heidegger, Aristotle and rhetorical politics. *Philosophy & Rhetoric*, 38(4), 281–301.

Heidlebaugh, N. J. (2008). Invention and public dialogue: Lessons from rhetorical theories. *Communication Theory, 18*(1), 27–50.

Heitsch, D. B. (1999). Nietzsche and Montaigne: Concepts of style. *Rhetorica, 18*(4), 411–431.

Johnson, R. R. (2010). The ubiquity paradox: Further thinking on the concept of user centeredness. *Technical Communication Quarterly, 19*(4), 335–351.

Lipari, L. (2010). Listening, thinking, being. *Communication Theory, 20*(3), 348–362.

MacDonald, M. (2006). Empire and communication: The media wars of Marshall McLuhan. *Media, Culture, & Society, 28*(4), 505–520.

McBeath, G., & Webb, S. A. (2000). On the nature of future worlds? Considerations of virtuality and utopias. *Information, Communication, & Society, 3*(1), 1–16.

McOmber, J. B. (1999). Technological autonomy and three definitions of technology. *Journal of Communication, 49*(3), 137–153.

Oakley, S. S. (2008). Commonplace: Rhetorical figures of difference in Heidegger and Glissant. *Philosophy & Rhetoric, 41*(1), 1–21.

Pender, K. (2008). Negation and the contradictory technics of rhetoric. *Rhetoric Society Quarterly, 38*(1), 2–24.

Ramsey, R. E. (1997). Communication and eschatology: The work of waiting, an ethics of relief, and areligious religiosity. *Communication Theory, 7*(4), 343–361.

Scult, A. (1992). The limits of narrative: Truth aspiring discourse in the Bible. *Rhetorica, 10*(4), 345–365.

Scult, A. (1999). Aristotle's Rhetoric as ontology: A Heideggerian reading. *Philosophy & Rhetoric, 32*(2), 146–159.

Sikka, T. (2011). Technology, communication, and society: From Heidegger and Habermas to Feenberg. *Review of Communication, 11*(2), 93–106.

Smith, D. L. (2003). Intensifying phronesis: Heidegger, Aristotle, and rhetorical culture. *Philosophy & Rhetoric, 36*(1), 77–102.

Stewart, J. (1983). Interpretive listening: An alternative to empathy. *Communication Education, 32*(4), 379–391.

Stewart, J. (1986). Speech and human being: A complement to semiotics. *Quarterly Journal of Speech, 72*(1), 55–73.

Struever, N. S. (2009). Rhetorical definition: A French initiative. *Philosophy & Rhetoric, 42*(4), 401–423.

Sutton, J. (1986). The death of rhetoric and its rebirth in philosophy. *Rhetorica, 4*(3), 203–226.

Taylor, P. A. (2008). From Mit-Sein to Bit-Sein: Informational pattern recognition and the chronicle of a life foretold. *Information, Communication & Society, 11*(6), 781–798.

Zeytinoglu, C. (2011). Appositional (communication) ethics: Listening to Heidegger and Levinas in chorus. *Review of Communication, 11*(4), 272–285.

Zickmund, S. (2007). Deliberation, phronesis, and authenticity: Heidegger's early conception of rhetoric. *Philosophy & Rhetoric, 40*(4), 406–415.

Chapter 6
Philosophical Hermeneutics as Interpretation and Meaning

Arnett, R. C., Arneson, P., & Holba, A. (2008). Bridges not walls: The communicative enactment of dialogic storytelling. *Review of Communication, 8*(3), 217–234.

Bineham, J. L. (1994). Displacing Descartes: Philosophical hermeneutics and rhetorical studies. *Philosophy & Rhetoric, 27*(4), 300–312.

Hatch, J. B. (2006). The hope of reconciliation: Continuing the conversation. *Rhetoric & Public Affairs, 9*(2), 259–277.

Gadamer

Arnett, R. C. (2001). Dialogic civility as pragmatic ethical praxis: An interpersonal metaphor for the public domain. *Communication Theory, 11*(3), 315–338.

Arnett, R. C., Arneson, P., & Holba, A. (2008). Bridges not walls: The communicative enactment of dialogic storytelling. *Review of Communication, 8*(3), 217–234.

Arnett, R. C., Bell, L. M., & Fritz, J. M. H. (2010). Dialogic learning as first principle in communication ethics. *Atlantic Journal of Communication, 18*(3), 111–126.

Arthos, J. (2000). Who are we and who am I? Gadamer's communal ontology as palimpsest. *Communication Studies, 51*(1), 15–34.

Arthos, J. (2007). A hermeneutic interpretation of civic humanism and liberal education. *Philosophy & Rhetoric, 40*(2), 189–200.

Arthos, J. (2008). Gadamer's rhetorical imaginary. *Rhetoric Society Quarterly, 38*(2), 171–197.

Aune, J. A. (2007). Only connect: Between morality and ethics in Habermas. *Communication Theory, 17*(4), 340–347.

Brook, J. (2010). An elaboration of the transformative approach to practical theory: Its connections with Gadamer's philosophical hermeneutics. *Communication Theory, 20*(4), 405–426.

Campbell, J. A. (1978). Hans-Georg Gadamer's truth and method. *Quarterly Journal of Speech, 64*(1), 101–110.

Chen, K. H. (1987). Beyond truth and method: On misreading Gadamer's praxical hermeneutics. *Quarterly Journal of Speech, 73*(2), 183–199.

Deetz, S. (1978). Conceptualizing human understanding: Gadamer's hermeneutics and American communication studies. *Communication Quarterly, 26*(2), 12–23.

Gadamer, H. G. (1990). Hearing—seeing—reading. (R.C. Norton, Trans.). *Language & Communication, 10*(1), 87–92.

Mailloux, S. (2000). Disciplinary identities: On the rhetorical paths between English and communication studies. *Rhetoric Society Quarterly, 30*(2), 5–29.

Mootz, F. J., III, (2010). Perelman's theory of argumentation and natural law. *Philosophy & Rhetoric, 43*(4), 383–402.

Mumby, D. K. (1997). Modernism, postmodernism, and communication studies: A rereading of an ongoing debate. *Communication Theory, 7*(1), 1–28.

Porter, W. M. (1990). Cicero's pro archia and the responsibilities of reading. *Rhetorica: A Journal of the History of Rhetoric, 8*(2), 137–152.

Rubini, R. (2009). Humanism as philosophia (perennis): Grassi's Platonic rhetoric between Gadamer and Kristeller. *Philosophy & Rhetoric, 42*(3), 242–278.

Roy, A., & Starosta, W. J. (2001). Hans-Georg Gadamer, language, and intercultural communication. *Language & Intercultural Communication, 1*(1), 6–20.

Ryan, K. J., & Natalle, E. J. (2001). Fusing horizons: Standpoint hermeneutics and invitational rhetoric. *Rhetoric Society Quarterly, 31*(2), 69–90.

Sandvig, C. (2006). The Internet at play: Child users of public Internet connections. *Journal of Computer-Mediated Communication, 11*(4), 932–956.

Tillery, D. (2001). Power, language, and professional choices: A hermeneutic approach to teaching technical communication. *Technical Communication Quarterly, 10*(1), 97–116.

Ricoeur

Abbott, D. P. (2006). Splendor and misery: Semiotics and the end of rhetoric. *Rhetorica: A Journal of the History of Rhetoric, 24*(3), 303–323.

Arnett, R. C., Arneson, P., & Holba, A. (2008). Bridges not walls: The communicative enactment of dialogic storytelling. *Review of Communication*, 8(3), 217–234.

Brauer, D. (2010). Alternate readings: Student hermeneutics and academic discourse. *Rhetoric Review*, 29(1), 69–87.

Descombes, V. (2007). A philosophy of the first-person singular. *Communication Theory*, 17(1), 4–15.

Doxtader, E. (2007). The faith and struggle of beginning (with) words: On the turn between reconciliation and recognition. *Philosophy & Rhetoric*, 40(1), 119–146.

Franke, W. (2000). Metaphor and the making of sense: The contemporary metaphor renaissance. *Philosophy & Rhetoric*, 33(2), 137–153.

Gross, A. (2010). Rhetoric, narrative, and the lifeworld: The construction of collective identity. *Philosophy & Rhetoric*, 43(2), 118–138.

Hasian, M. J. (2008). Iconic materials, hermeneutics of faith, and the postmodern reproduction of public democracies. *The Review of Communication*, 8(1), 1–15.

Hatch, J. B. (2009). Dialogic rhetoric in letters across the divide: A dance of (good) faith toward racial reconciliation. *Rhetoric & Public Affairs*, 12(4), 485–532.

Kaneva, N. (2007). Remembering communist violence: The Bulgarian Gulag and the conscience of the west. *Journal of Communication Inquiry*, 31(1), 44–61.

McCarron, G. (2002). Moralizing uncertainty: Suspicion and faith in Hitchcock's *Suspicion*. *Canadian Journal of Communication*, 27(1), 47–62.

Watts, R. B. (2008). Paul Ricoeur's innovative perspective on the rhetorical tradition. *Review of Communication*, 8(1), 44–46.

Chapter 7
Empathy and the Other: A Phenomenological Perspective

Allison, J. M. Jr., (1994). Narrative and time: A phenomenological reconsideration. *Text & Performance Quarterly*, 14(2), 108–125.

Anderson, R. (1982). Phenomenological dialogue, humanistic psychology, and pseudo-walls: A response and extension. *The Western Journal of Speech Communication*, 46(4), 344–357.

Anton, C. (1999). Beyond the constitutive-representational dichotomy: The phenomenological notion of intentionality. *Communication Theory*, 9(1), 26–57.

Arnett, R. C. (1981). Toward a phenomenological dialogue. *The Western Journal of Speech Communication*, 45(3), 201–212.

Bayer, T. I. (2009). Hegelian rhetoric. *Philosophy & Rhetoric*, 42(3), 203–219.

Bemis, J. L., & Phillips, G. M. (1964). A phenomenological approach to communication theory. *Communication Theory*, 13(4), 262–269.

Bergo, B. (2005). What is Levinas doing? Phenomenology and the rhetoric of an ethical unconscious. *Philosophy & Rhetoric*, 38(2), 122–144.

Bialostosky, D. (2006). Architectonics, rhetoric, and poetics in the Bakhtin school's early phenomenological and sociological texts. *Rhetoric Society Quarterly*, 36(4), 355–377.

Bradac, J. J., Sandell, K. L., & Wenner, L. A. (1979). The phenomenology of evidence: Information-source utility in decision making. *Communication Quarterly*, 27(4), 35–46.

Cahn, D. D., & Hanford, J. T. (1984). Perspectives on human communication research: Behaviorism, phenomenology, and an integrated view. *The Western Journal of Speech Communication*, 48(3), 277–292.

Cornett-DeVito, M. M., & Worley, D. W. (2005). A front row seat: A phenomenological investigation of learning disabilities. *Communication Education*, 54(4), 312–333.

Couldry, N., & Markham, T. (2008). Troubled closeness or satisfied distance? Researching media consumption and public orientation. *Media, Culture, & Society, 30*(1), 5–21.

Davis, D. K. (1987). Phenomenology of media audiences. *Critical Studies in Mass Communication, 4*(3), 301–324.

Deetz, S. (1973). Words without things: Toward a social phenomenology of language. *Quarterly Journal of Speech, 59*(1), 40–51.

Fausti, R. P., & Luker, A. H. (1965). A phenomenological approach to discussion. *The Speech Teacher, 14*(1), 19–23.

Felts, A. A. (1978). Hermeneutic phenomenology: A critique of Leonard Hawes' conception. *Communication Quarterly, 26*(4), 58-64.

Fish, S. L. (1976). A phenomenological examination of femininity. *Journal of Applied Communication Research, 4*(2), 43–53.

Fish, S. L., & Dorris, J. M. (1975). Phenomenology and communication research. *Journal of Applied Communication Research, 3*(1), 9–26.

Friesen, N., Feenberg, A., & Smith, G. (2009). Phenomenology and surveillance studies: Returning to the things themselves. *The Information Society, 25*(2), 84–90.

Garrett, E. A. (2011). The rhetoric of antiblack racism: Lewis R. Gordon's radical phenomenology of embodiment. *Atlantic Journal of Communication, 19*(1), 6–16.

Gresson, A. D., III. (1978). Phenomenology and the rhetoric of identification: A neglected dimension of coalition communication inquiry. *Communication Quarterly, 26*(4), 14–23.

Gronbeck, B. E. (1972). Gorgias on rhetoric and poetic: A rehabilitation. *The Southern Speech Communication Journal, 38*(1), 27–38.

Hariman, R. (1996). Political styles and political feelings: Introduction prophecy, phenomenology, and democratic politics: A review of Hart's *Seducing America. Critical Studies in Mass Communication, 13*(2), 180–186.

Hawes, L. C. (1977). Toward a hermeneutic phenomenology of communication. *Communication Quarterly, 25*(3), 30–41.

Haynes, W. L. (1988). Of that which we cannot write: Some notes on the phenomenology of media. *Quarterly Journal of Speech, 74*(1), 71–101.

Hyde, M. J. (1980). The experience of anxiety: A phenomenological investigation. *Quarterly Journal of Speech, 66*(2), 140–154.

Ihde, D. (1982). Phenomenology and deconstructive strategy. *Semiotica, 41*(1/4), 5–24.

Kenny, R. W. (2003). Husserl at the limits of phenomenology: Including texts by Edmund Husserl. *Philosophy & Rhetoric, 36*(4), 379–383.

Kristjánsdóttir, E. S. (2009). Invisibility dreaded and desired: Phenomenological inquiry of Sojourners' cross-cultural adaptation. *The Howard Journal of Communication, 20*(2), 129–146.

Langellier, K. M. (1983). A phenomenological approach to audience. *Literature & Performance, 3* (2), 34–39.

Lanigan, R. L. (1982). Semiotic phenomenology: A theory of human communication praxis. *Journal of Applied Communication Research, 10*(1), 62–73.

Lanigan, R. L. (1988). Is Erving Goffman a phenomenologist? *Critical Studies in Mass Communication, 5*(4), 335–345.

Logan, C. (2005). The space between: Phenomenologies of audience, performer, and place for three performances of menopause and desire. *Text & Performance Quarterly, 25*(3), 282–289.

Lundy, J. C. (1996). General semantics and phenomenology on conducting classroom discussion: The E*D*I*T* System. *The New Jersey Journal of Communication, 4*(1), 91–98.

Macsoud, S. J. (1971). Phenomenology, experience, and interpretation. *Philosophy & Rhetoric, 4* (3), 139–149.

Martinez, J. M. (2008). Semiotic phenomenology and the "dialectical approach" to intercultural communication: Paradigm crisis and the actualities of research practice. *Semiotica*, 169(1/4), 135–153.

Maxcy, D. J. (1994). Meaning in nature: Rhetoric, phenomenology, and the question of environmental value. *Philosophy & Rhetoric*, 27(4), 330–346.

Orbe, M. P. (1998). From the standpoint(s) of traditionally muted groups: Explicating a co-cultural communication theoretical model. *Communication Theory*, 8(1), 1–26.

Orbe, M. P. (2005). "The more things change . . .": Civil rights health assessment in a "majority-minority" U.S. community. *The Howard Journal of Communication*, 16(3), 177–199.

Peterson, E. E. (1987). Media consumption and girls who want to have fun. *Critical Studies in Mass Communication*, 4(1), 37–50.

Picart, C. J. (2004). A metaphysics of the transcendent through a phenomenology of film: Choosing metaphysics over politics. *Review of Communication*, 4(3/4), 316–320.

Pilotta, J. (2005). A critical background of philcom: Phenomenology and Marxism. *The Communication Review*, 8(4), 405–414.

Scannell, P. (1995). For a phenomenology of radio and television. *Journal of Communication*, 45(3), 4–19.

Simpson Stern, C. (1983). Deconstruction and the phenomenological alternative. *Literature & Performance*, 4(1), 41–44.

Smith, C. A., & Smith, K. B. (1980). Trees or forest? A response to Gresson's *Phenomenology and the Rhetoric of Identification. Communication Theory*, 28(2), 57–62.

Stewart, J. (1981). Philosophy of qualitative inquiry: Hermeneutic phenomenology and communication research. *Quarterly Journal of Speech*, 67(1), 109–121.

Tomlinson, J. (1994). A phenomenology of globalization? Giddens on global modernity. *European Journal of Communication*, 9(2), 149–172.

Traudt, P. J., Anderson, J. A., & Meyer, T. P. (1987). Phenomenology, empiricism, and media experience. *Critical Studies in Media Communication*, 4(3), 302–310.

Tucker, R. E. (2001). Figure, ground and presence: A phenomenology of meaning in rhetoric. *Quarterly Journal of Speech*, 87(4), 396–414.

Warnick, B. (1979). Structuralism vs. phenomenology: Implications for rhetorical criticism. *Quarterly Journal of Speech*, 65(3), 250–261.

Young, K. (1982). Edgework: Frame and boundary in the phenomenology of narrative communication. *Semiotica*, 41(1/4), 277–315.

Young, K. (1989). Disembodiment: The phenomenology of the body in medical examinations. *Semiotica*, 73(1/2), 43–66.

Young, K. (2000). Gestures and the phenomenology of emotion in narrative. *Semiotica*, 131 (1/2), 79–112.

Chapter 8
Analytic Discernment
Analytic Discernment

Dresner, E. (2006). Davidson's philosophy of communication. *Communication Theory*, 16(2), 155–172.

Ludwig Wittgenstein

Altieri, C. (1976). Wittgenstein on consciousness and language: A challenge to Derridean literary theory. *MLN*, 91(6), 1397–1423.

Baker, G. P. (1999). Italics in Wittgenstein. *Language & Communication, 19*(3), 181–211.

Baker, G. P. (2001). Wittgenstein's "depth grammar." *Language & Communication, 21*(4), 303–319.

Berenbeim, R. (2002). Wittgenstein's bedrock. *Vital Speeches of the Day, 69*(3), 90–92.

Berenbeim, R. (2002/2003). Wittgenstein's bedrock: What business ethicists do. *Executive Speeches, 17*(3), 22–24.

Bertman, M. (1975). Wittgenstein's doctrine of the tyranny of language: An historical and critical examination of the *Blue Book*. *Philosophy & Rhetoric, 8*(2), 131–133.

Buttny, R. (1986). The ascription of meaning: A Wittgensteinian perspective. *Quarterly Journal of Speech, 72*(3), 261–273.

Canfield, J. (1995). The living language: Wittgenstein and the empirical study of communication. *Language Sciences, 15*(3), 165–193.

Copeland, B. J., & Proudfoot, D. (2000). What Turing did after he invented the universal Turing machine. *Journal of Logic, Language, & Information, 9*(4), 491–509.

Creadon, M. (1984). Wittgenstein's forms of life: Language and literature as a heuristic tool. *Studies in Language & Communication, 19*(1), 69–95.

Elkins, J. (1996). Between picture and proposition: Torturing paintings in Wittgenstein's *Tractatus*. *Visible Language, 30*(1), 72–95.

Engle, L. (1989). Afloat in thick deeps: Shakespeare's sonnets on certainty. *PMLA, 104*(5), 832–843.

Falzer, P. R. (1992). Wittgenstein's path to rapprochement. *Philosophy & Rhetoric, 25*(1), 45–58.

Gotman, A. (1994). Disinheritance, squandering and filiation: Is Wittgenstein a modern? *Communications, 59*, 149–175.

Greenfield, M. (1995). Coetzee's *Foe* and Wittgenstein's *Philosophical Investigations*: Confession, authority, and private languages. *The Journal of Narrative Technique, 25*(3), 223–237.

Holiday, A. (1985). Wittgenstein's silence: Philosophy, ritual and the limits of language. *Language & Communication, 5*(2), 133–142.

Kaha, C. (1988). Wittgenstein, Merleau-Ponty, and the poetic gestalt. *Studies in Symbolic Interaction, 9*, 33–50.

Livingston, P. (2010). Wittgenstein, Turing and the "finitude" of language. *Linguistic & Philosophical Investigation 9*, 215–247.

Olteteanu, I. (2011). Wittgenstein's attitude toward language as music. *Linguistic & Philosophical Investigations, 10*, 156–161.

Proudfoot, D. (2002). Wittgenstein's deflationary account of reference. *Language & Communication, 22*(3), 331–351.

Sheehan, T. (2002). Wittgenstein and Vertov: Aspectuality and anarchy. *Discourse, 24*(3), 95–113, 115.

Shotter, J. (1996). Talking of saying, showing, gesturing, and feeling in Wittgenstein and Vygotsky. *Communication Review, 1*(4), 471–495.

Skupien, J. (1997). From the *Begriffsschrift* to the *Philosophical Investigations*: Frege and Wittgenstein on the semantics of natural language. *Language & Communication, 17*(1), 1–17.

Smit, D. W. (1991). The rhetorical method of Ludwig Wittgenstein. *Rhetoric Review, 10*(1), 31–51.

Tamen, M. (1995). "Beautiful communication": Schiller, Wittgenstein, and the rhetoric of the aesthetic. *Argumentation, 9*(3), 481–488.

Todd, D. (1975). Wittgenstein's language. *Philosophy & Rhetoric, 8*(3), 187–189.

Verheggen, C. (2005). Stroud on Wittgenstein, meaning and community. *Dialogue, 44*(1), 67–85.

Chapter 9
Pragmatism: An American Practice
Pragmatism

Andrews, J. R. (1967). Piety and pragmatism: Rhetorical aspects of the early British peace movement. *Speech Monographs, 34*(4), 423–436.

Baldwin, J. (2005). Shibutani and pragmatism. *Symbolic Interaction, 28*(4), 487–504.

Bennett, W. L. (1977). The ritualistic and pragmatic bases of political campaign discourse. *Quarterly Journal of Speech, 63*(3), 219–238.

Campbell, J. (1983). Mead and pragmatism. *Symbolic Interaction, 6*(1), 155–164.

Conner, J. D. (1995). Rhetoric, sophistry, pragmatism. *MLN, 110*(4), 979–983.

Cornell, S. (2001). Iran and the Caucasus: The triumph of pragmatism over ideology. *Global Dialogue, 3*(2/3), 80–92.

Crable, R. E. (1990). "Organizational rhetoric" as the fourth great system: Theoretical, critical, and pragmatic implications. *Journal of Applied Communication Research, 18*(2), 115–128.

Denzin, N. (1996). Post-pragmatism. *Symbolic Interaction, 19*(1), 61–75.

Denzin, N. (1996). Prophetic pragmatism and the postmodern: A comment on Maines. *Symbolic Interaction, 19*(4), 341–355.

Fisher, B. A. (1982). Communication pragmatism: Another legacy of Gregory Bateson. *Journal of Applied Communication Research, 10*(1), 38–49.

Ganesh, S., & Holmes, P. (2011). Positioning intercultural dialogue: Theories, pragmatics, and an agenda. *Journal of International & Intercultural Communication, 4*(2), 81–86.

Glogowska, M. (2011). Paradigms, pragmatism and possibilities: Mixed-methods research in speech and language therapy. *International Journal of Language & Communication Disorders, 46*(3), 251–260.

Goodnight, G. T. (1981). Conspiracy rhetoric: From pragmatism to fantasy in public discourse. *Western Journal of Speech Communication, 45*(4), 299–316.

Hannan, J. (2011). Pragmatism, democracy, and communication: Three rival perspectives. *Review of Communication, 11*(2), 107–121.

Hardt, H. (1989). Cultural studies between pragmatism and Marxism. *Critical Studies in Mass Communication, 6*(4), 421–426.

Holba, A. M. (2010). Neo-pragmatism, communication, and the culture of creative democracy, by Omar Swartz, Katia Campbell, and Christina Pestana. *Quarterly Journal of Speech, 96*(3), 349–352.

Jackson, B. (2008). Pragmatism, democracy, and the necessity of rhetoric. *Rhetoric Society Quarterly, 38*(2), 219–223.

Jackson, S., & Jacobs, S. (1980). Structure of conversational argument: Pragmatic bases for the enthymeme. *Quarterly Journal of Speech, 66*(3), 251–265.

Jay, P. (2002). Reception histories: Rhetoric, pragmatism, and American cultural politics. *Modern Philology, 99*(4), 677–680.

Laufer, R. (2009). New rhetoric's empire: Pragmatism, dogmatism, and sophism. *Philosophy & Rhetoric, 42*(4), 326–348.

Lee, M. (2009). Pragmatism, democracy, and the necessity of rhetoric. *Argumentation & Advocacy, 45*(3), 174–176.

Maines, D. R. (1996). On postmodernism, pragmatism, and plasterers: Some interactionist thoughts and queries. *Symbolic Interaction, 19*(4), 323–340.

Payne, M. (2006). On being vatic: Pindar, pragmatism, and historicism. *American Journal of*

Philology, 127(2), 159–184.

Rochberg-Halton, E. (1983). The real nature of pragmatism and Chicago sociology. *Symbolic Interaction, 6*(1), 139–153.

Rowland, R. C. (2006). Reagan at the Brandenburg gate: Moral clarity tempered by pragmatism. *Rhetoric & Public Affairs, 9*(1), 21–50.

Russill, C. (2007). Communication problems in a pragmatist perspective. *Communication Monographs, 74*(1), 125–130.

Schalin, D. N. (1992). Introduction: Habermas, pragmatism, interactionism. *Symbolic Interaction, 15*(3), 251–259.

Smeltzer, M. (1996). Gorgias on arrangement: A search for pragmatism amidst the art and epistemology of Gorgias of Leontini. *The Southern Communication Journal, 61*(2), 156–165.

Stob, P. (2011). Pragmatism, experience, and William James' politics of blindness. *Philosophy & Rhetoric, 44*(3), 227–249.

Stroud, S. (2009). Pragmatism and the methodology of comparative rhetoric. *Rhetoric Society Quarterly, 39*(4), 353–379.

Suttie, P. (1998). Edmund Spenser's political pragmatism. *Studies in Philology, 95*(1), 56–76.

Thayer, H. S. (1952). *The logic of pragmatism: An examination of John Dewey's logic.* New York: Greenwood Press.

Thayer, H. S. (1953). *Newton's philosophy of nature: Selections from his writings.* New York: Macmillan.

Thayer, H. S. (1968). *Meaning and action: A critical history of pragmatism.* New York: Bobbs-Merrill.

Thayer, H. S. (1982). *Pragmatism: The classical writings.* Cambridge, MA: Hackett Publishing.

Thompson, J. (2011). Magic for a people trained in pragmatism: Kenneth Burke, *Mein Kampf,* and the early 9/11 oratory of George W. Bush. *Rhetoric Review, 30*(4), 350–371.

Volz, Y. Z. (2009). American pragmatism and Chinese modernization: Importing the Missouri model of journalism education to modern China. *Media, Culture, & Society, 31*(5), 711–730.

Wilde, N. (1914). The pragmatism of Pascal. *The Philosophical Review, 23*(5), 540–549.

Rorty

Ankersmit, F. (2010). Truth in history and literature. *Narrative, 18*(1), 29–50.

Bruffee, K. A., & Bialostosky, D. H. (1987). Rorty and dialogic discourse. *PMLA, 102*(2), 216–218.

Crick, N. (2003). Composition as experience: John Dewey on creative expression and the origins of "mind." *College Composition & Communication, 55*(2), 254–275.

Dobrowski, P. M. (2002). Language and empiricism. *Journal of Technical Writing & Communication, 32*(1), 3–21.

Halton, E. (1992). Habermas and Rorty: Between Scylla and Charybdis. *Symbolic Interaction, 15*(3), 333–358.

Horne, J. (1989). Rhetoric after Rorty. *Western Journal of Speech Communication, 53*(3), 247–259.

Horne, J. (1993). Rorty's circumvention of argument: Redescribing rhetoric. *The Southern Communication Journal, 58*(3), 169–181.

Moore, R. C. (1999). Where epistemology meets ecology: Can environmental news reporting survive postmodernism? *Mass Communication and Society, 2*(1/2), 3–25.

Smith, R. E., III, (1989). Reconsidering Richard Rorty. *Rhetoric Society Quarterly, 19*(4), 349–364.

Rondel, D. (2011). On Rorty's evangelical metaphilosophy. *Philosophy & Rhetoric, 44*(2), 150–170.

Chapter 10
Dialectical Differentiation
Dialectic

Allen, J. (2007). Aristotle on the disciplines of argument: Rhetoric, dialectic, analytic. *Rhetorica: A Journal of the History of Rhetoric, 25*(1), 87–108.

Altman, I. (1993). Dialectics, physical environments, and personal relationships. *Communication Monographs, 60*(1), 26–34.

Apker, J., Propp, K. M., & Zabava Ford, W. S. (2005). Negotiating status and identity tensions in healthcare team interactions: An exploration of nurse role dialectics. *Journal of Applied Communication Research, 33*(2), 93–115.

Arden Ford, L., Berlin Ray, E., & Hartman Ellis, B. (1999). Translating scholarship on intrafamilial sexual abuse: The utility of a dialectical perspective for adult survivors. *Journal of Applied Communication Research, 27*(2), 139–157.

Ashworth, E. J. (1991). Logic in late sixteenth-century England: Humanist dialectic and the new Aristotelianism. *Studies in Philology, 88*(2), 224–236.

Bator, P. G. (1988). The "good reasons movement": A "confounding" of dialectic and rhetoric? *Philosophy & Rhetoric, 21*(1), 38–47.

Baus, R. D. (1995). Using performance to increase retention of dialectic tension management strategies. *Journal of Applied Communication Research, 23*(3), 230–238.

Baynes, K. (1994). Communicative ethics, the public sphere and communication media. *Critical Studies in Mass Communication, 11*(4), 315–326.

Benjamin, J. (1983). Eristic, dialectic, and rhetoric. *Communication Quarterly, 31*(1), 21–26.

Braithwaite, D. O., & Baxter, L. A. (2006). "You're my parent but you're not": Dialectical tensions in stepchildren's perceptions about communicating with the nonresidential parent. *Journal of Applied Communication Research, 34*(1), 30–48.

Braithwaite, D. O., Toller, P. W., Daas, K. L., Surham, W. T., & Jones, A. C. (2008). Centered but not caught in the middle: Stepchildren's perceptions of dialectical contradictions in the communication of co-parents. *Journal of Applied Communication Research, 36*(1), 33–55.

Brownstein, O. L. (1965). Plato's *Phaedrus*: Dialectic as the genuine art of speaking. *Quarterly Journal of Speech, 51*(4), 392–398.

Burgess, P. G. (1985). The dialectic of substance: Rhetoric vs poetry. *Communication Quarterly, 33*(2), 105–112.

Burke, R. (1974). Rhetoric, dialectic, and force. *Philosophy & Rhetoric, 7*(3), 154–165.

Capo, K. E. (1983). Performance of literature as social dialectic. *Literature & Performance, 4*(1), 31–36.

Carroll, J. (2004). Essence, stasis, and dialectic: Ways that key terms can mean. *Rhetoric Review, 23*(2), 156–170.

Cheong, P. H., & Gray, K. (2011). Mediated intercultural dialectics: Identity perceptions and performances in virtual worlds. *Journal of International & Intercultural Communication, 4*(4), 265–271.

Chesebro, J. W. (1988). Epistemology and ontology as dialectical modes in the writings of Kenneth Burke. *Communication Quarterly, 36*(3), 175–191.

Cissna, K. N., Bochner, A. P., & Cox, D. E. (1990). The dialectic of marital and parental relationships within the stepfamily. *Communication Monographs, 57*(1), 44–61.

Cloud, D. L. (2008). On dialectics and "duelism": A reply to Jennifer Daryl Slack. *Communication & Critical/Cultural Studies, 5*(1), 102–107.

Cook, A. (1985). Dialectic, irony, and myth in Plato's *Phaedrus*. *The American Journal of Philology, 106*(4), 427-441.

Crable, B. (2003). Symbolizing motion: Burke's dialectic and rhetoric of the body. *Rhetoric Review, 22*(2), 121–137.

Crusius, T. W. (1986). A case for Kenneth Burke's dialectic and rhetoric. *Philosophy & Rhetoric, 19*(1), 23–37.

Crusius, T. W. (1988). Kenneth Burke's auscultation: A "de-struction" of Marxist dialectic and rhetoric. *Rhetorica: A Journal of the History of Rhetoric, 6*(4), 355–379.

Crusius, T. W. (1988). Orality in Kenneth Burke's dialectic. *Philosophy & Rhetoric, 21*(2), 116–130.

Desmond, W. (1985). Hegel, dialectic, and deconstruction. *Philosophy & Rhetoric, 18*(4), 244–263.

Dimmick, J., & Rothenbuhler, E. W. (1986). Critical response and reply: Comments on Kaul and McKerns' *Dialectic ecology*. *Critical Studies in Mass Communication, 3*(3), 380–383.

Dorter, K. (1992). A dual dialectic in the "symposium." *Philosophy & Rhetoric, 25*(3), 253–270.

Duran, R. L., Kelly, L., & Rotaru, T. (2011). Mobile phones in romantic relationships and the dialectic of autonomy versus connection. *Communication Quarterly, 59*(1), 19–36.

Erickson, K. V. (1982). Aristotle's rhetoric 1354a 1–11: Art, dialectic, and philosophical rhetoric. *Rhetoric Society Quarterly, 12*(1), 9–12.

Ercolini, G. L. (2003). Burke contra Kierkegaard: Kenneth Burke's dialectic via reading Søren Kierkegaard. *Philosophy & Rhetoric, 36*(3), 207–222.

Gage, J. T. (1982). Rhetoric and dialectic in Robert Frost's A Masque of Reason. *Pacific Coast Philology, 17*(1/2), 82–91.

Gill, J. M. (1959). Newman's dialectic in the idea of a university. *Quarterly Journal of Speech, 45*(4), 415–418.

Gordon, J. (1996). Dialectic, dialogue, and transformation of the self. *Philosophy & Rhetoric, 29*(3), 259–278.

Grossberg, L. (1979). Marxist dialectics and rhetorical criticism. *Quarterly Journal of Speech, 65*(3), 235-249.

Gutenberg, N., & Johnstone, H. W. J. (1994). On the category of the controversial: An approach through Schleiermacher's dialectic. *Philosophy & Rhetoric, 27*(4), 347–358.

Haahr, J. G. (1992). Criseyde's inner debate: The dialectic of enamorment in the "filostrato" and the "troilus." *Studies in Philology, 89*(3), 257–271.

Hance, K. G. (1939). The dialectic method in debate. *Quarterly Journal of Speech, 25*(2), 243–248.

Harpine, W. D. (1985). Can rhetoric and dialectic serve the purposes of logic? *Philosophy & Rhetoric, 18*(2), 96–112.

Howard, L. A., & Geist, P. (1995). Ideological positioning in organizational change: The dialectic of control in a merging organization. *Communication Monographs, 62*(2), 110–131.

Howell, W. S. (1934). Nathaniel Carpenter's place in the controversy between dialectic and rhetoric. *Speech Monographs, 1*(1), 20–41.

Hunt, E. L. (1921). Dialectic: A neglected method of argument. *Quarterly Journal of Speech, 7*(3), 221–232.

Janssens, E., & Johnstone, H.W.J. (1968). The concept of dialectic in the ancient world. *Philosophy & Rhetoric, 1*(3), 174–181.

Jiménez, A. M. (1995). Rhetoric, dialectic, and literature in the work of Francisco Sánchez, El Brocense. *Rhetorica: A Journal of the History of Rhetoric, 13*(1), 43–59.

Johnson, A. J., Wittenberg, E., Villagran, M. M., Mazur, M., & Villagran, P. (2003). Relational progression as a dialectic: Examining turning points in communication among friends. *Communication Monographs, 70*(3), 230–249.

Jones, T. S., & Bodtker, A. (1998). A dialectical analysis of a social justice process: International collaboration in South Africa. *Journal of Applied Communication Research, 26*(4), 357–373.

Kaul, A. J., & McKerns, J. P. (1985). The dialectic ecology of the newspaper. *Critical Studies in Mass Communication, 2*(3), 217–233.

Keith, P. M. (1979). Burkeian invention, from pentad to dialectic. *Rhetoric Society Quarterly, 9* (3), 137–141.

Kenny, R. W. (2000). The constitutional dialectic. *Quarterly Journal of Speech, 86*(4), 454–464.

Kramer, M. W. (2004). Toward a communication theory of group dialectics: An ethnographic study of a community theater group. *Communication Monographs, 71*(3), 311–332.

Lake, R. A. (1986). The rhetor as dialectician in "last chance for survival." *Communication Monographs, 53*(3), 201–220.

Low, A. (1997). The return of dialectic to its place in intellectual life. *Rhetoric Review, 15*(2), 365–381.

McAdon, B. (2001). Rhetoric is a counterpart of dialectic. *Philosophy & Rhetoric, 34*(2), 113–150.

McBurney, J. H. (1937). Some contributions of classical dialectic and rhetoric to a philosophy of discussion. *Quarterly Journal of Speech, 23*(1), 1–13.

McNally, J. R. (1966). Dux illa directrixque atrium: Rudolph Agricola's dialectical system. *Quarterly Journal of Speech, 52*(4), 337–347.

Meyer, M. D. E. (2003). "It's me. I'm it.": Defining adolescent sexual identity through relational dialectics in *Dawson's Creek. Communication Quarterly, 51*(3), 262–276.

Mezo, R. E. (1974). Rhetoric, dialectic, and protest. *Newsletter: Rhetoric Society of America, 4* (3), 3–4.

Monfasani, J. (1995). Renaissance argument: Valla and Agricola in the tradition of rhetoric and dialectic. *Rhetorica: A Journal of the History of Rhetoric, 13*(1), 91–97.

Murray, J. S. (1988). Disputation, deception, and dialectic: Plato on the true rhetoric. *Philosophy & Rhetoric, 21*(4), 279–289.

Murray, J. W. (1998). Constructing the ordinary: The dialectical development of Nazi ideology. *Communication Quarterly, 46.*

Norander, S. (2009). Charting the dialectics of social change: A journey through four tensions in four contexts. *Review of Communication, 9*(1), 42–46.

Pawlowski, D. R. (1998). Dialectical tensions in marital partners' accounts of their relationships. *Communication Quarterly, 40*(4), 396–416.

Pitts, M. J., Fowler, C., Kaplan, M. S., Nussbaum, J., & Becker, J. C. (2009). Dialectical tensions underpinning family farm succession planning. *Journal of Applied Communication Research, 37*(1), 59–79.

Raign, K. A. (1994). Teaching stones to talk: Using stasis theory to teach students the art of dialectic. *Rhetoric Society Quarterly, 24*(3/4), 88–95.

Sabourin, T. C., & Stamp, G. H. (1995). Communication and the experience of dialectical tensions in family life: An examination of abusive and nonabusive families. *Communication Monographs, 62*(3), 213–242.

Sahlstein, E., Maguire, K. C., & Timmerman, L. (2009). Contradictions and praxis contextualized by wartime deployment: Wives' perspectives revealed through relational dialectics. *Communication Monographs, 76*(4), 421–442.

Sattler, W. M. (1943). Socratic dialectic and modern group discussion. *Quarterly Journal of Speech, 29*(2), 152–157.

Scott, R. L. (1993). Dialectical tensions of speaking and silence. *Quarterly Journal of Speech, 79*(1), 1–18.

Scott, R. L. (2000). The forum between silence and certainty: A codicil to "dialectical tensions of speaking and silence." *Quarterly Journal of Speech, 86*(1), 108–110.

Striphas, T. (2003). A dialectic with the everyday: Communication and cultural politics on Oprah Winfrey's Book Club. *Critical Studies in Media Communication, 20*(3), 295–316.

Toller, P. W. (2005). Negotiation of dialectical contradictions by parents who have experienced the death of a child. *Journal of Applied Communication Research, 33*(1), 46–66.

Toyosaki, S. (2011). Critical complete-member ethnography: Theorizing dialectics of consensus and conflict in intracultural communication. *Journal of International & Intercultural Communication, 4*(1), 62–80.

Tracy, S. J. (2004). Dialectic, contradiction, or double bind? Analyzing and theorizing employee reactions to organizational tension. *Journal of Applied Communication Research, 32*(2), 119–146.

Trahair, L. (2002). Short-circuiting the dialectic: Narrative and slapstick in the cinema of Buster Keaton. *Narrative, 10*(3), 307–325.

Watt, A. (1998). Burke on narrative: The dialectic of temporal embodiment and eternal essence. *Narrative, 6*(1), 49–71.

Plato

Abrams, J. A. (1981). Plato's rhetoric as rendered by the pentad. *Rhetoric Society Quarterly, 11*(1), 24–28.

Adams, J. C. (1996). The rhetorical significance of the conversion of the lover's soul in Plato's *Phaedrus*. *Rhetoric Society Quarterly, 26*(3), 7–16.

Balla, C. (2007). Plato and Aristotle on rhetorical empiricism. *Rhetorica: A Journal of the History of Rhetoric, 25*(1), 73–85.

Baracchi, C. (2001). Beyond the comedy and tragedy of authority: The invisible father in Plato's *Republic*. *Philosophy & Rhetoric, 34*(2), 151–176.

Belfiore, E. (2006). Dancing with the gods: The myth of the chariot in Plato's *Phaedrus*. *The American Journal of Philology, 127*(2), 185–217.

Benitez, E. (1992). Argument, rhetoric, and philosophic method: Plato's *Protagoras*. *Philosophy & Rhetoric, 25*(3), 222–252.

Benoit, W. L. (1991). Isocrates and Plato on rhetoric and rhetorical education. *Rhetoric Society Quarterly, 21*(1), 60–71.

Biesecker-Mast, G. J. (1994). Forensic rhetoric and the constitution of the subject: Innocence, truth, and wisdom in Gorgias' *Palamedes* and Plato's *Apology*. *Rhetoric Society Quarterly, 24*(3/4), 148–166.

Black, E. (1958). Plato's view of rhetoric. *Quarterly Journal of Speech, 44*(4), 361–374.

Blyth, D. (1997). The ever-moving soul in Plato's *Phaedrus*. *The American Journal of Philology, 118*(2), 185–217.

Blyth, D. (2000). Socrates' trial and conviction of the jurors in Plato's Apology. *Philosophy & Rhetoric, 33*(1), 1–22.

Bowie, E. L. (1993). Greek table-talk before Plato. *Rhetorica: A Journal of the History of Rhetoric, 11*(4), 355–371.

Brandt, T. C. (1971). Wolfram von Eschenbach's references to Plato and the Sibyl: A report on their sources. *MLN, 86*(3), 381–384.

Brinton, A. (1983). Quintillian, Plato, and the "vir bonus." *Philosophy & Rhetoric, 16*(3), 167–184.

Brownson, C. L. (1897). Reasons for Plato's hostility to the poets. *Transaction & Proceedings of the American Philological Association, 28*, 5–41.

Brownstein, O. L. (1965). Plato's *Phaedrus*: Dialectic as the genuine art of speaking. *Quarterly Journal of Speech, 51*(4), 392–398.

Bryant, D. C. (1981). The most significant passage (for the moment) in Plato's *Phaedrus*. *Rhetoric Society Quarterly, 11*(1), 9–11.

Buonanno, M. (2009). My media studies: Shadows in Plato's cave. *Television & New Media, 10*(1), 31–33.

Cherniss, H. (1932). On Plato's *Republic* X597B. *The American Journal of Philology*, 53(3),233–242.

Cherniss, H. (1947). Some war-time publications concerning Plato. I. *The American Journal of Philology*, 68(2), 113–146.

Cherniss, H. (1957). The relation of the *Timaeus* to Plato's later dialogues. *The American Journal of Philology*, 78(3), 225–266.

Cook, A. (1985). Dialectic, irony, and myth in Plato's *Phaedrus*. *The American Journal of Philology*, 106(4), 427–441.

Cossutta, F. (2003). Dialogic characteristics of philosophical discourse: The case of Plato's dialogues. *Philosophy & Rhetoric*, 36(1), 48–76.

Coulter, J. A. (1964). The relation of the *Apology of Socrates* to Gorgias' *Defense of Palamedes* and Plato's critique of Gorgianic rhetoric. *Harvard Studies in Classical Philology*, 68, 269–303.

Crick, N., & Poulakos, J. (2008). Go tell Alcibiades: Tragedy, comedy, and rhetoric in Plato's *Symposium*. *Quarterly Journal of Speech*, 94(1), 1–22.

Curran, J. V. (1986). The rhetorical technique of Plato's *Phaedrus*. *Philosophy & Rhetoric*, 19(1), 66–72.

Dainotto, R. M. (2011). With Plato in Italy: The value of literary fiction in Napoleonic Italy. *Modern Language Quarterly*, 72(3), 399–418.

Danzig, G. (2003). Apologizing for Socrates: Plato and Xenophon on Socrates' behavior in court. *Transactions of the American Philological Association*, 133(2), 281–321.

Delacy, P. H. (1939). The problem of causation in Plato's philosophy. *Classical Philology*, 34(2), 97–115.

Derrida, J. (1984). An idea of Flaubert: "Plato's letter." *MLN*, 99(4), 748–768.

Dickie, M. W. (1993). "Hermeias on Plato *Phaedrus* 238d and *Synesius Dion* 14.2." *The American Journal of Philology*, 114(3), 421–440.

Dimock, G. E., Jr. (1952). Alla in Lysias and Plato's *Phaedrus*. *The American Journal of Philology*, 73(4), 381–396.

Donovan, B. R. (2003). The do-it-yourselfer in Plato's *Republic*. *The American Journal of Philology*, 124(1), 1–18.

Dorter, K. (1996). Incantation and aporia in Plato's rhetoric. *Philosophy & Rhetoric*, 29(3), v–vi.

Eades, T. (1996). Plato, rhetoric, and silence. *Philosophy & Rhetoric*, 29(3), 244–258.

Edelstein, L. (1945). The role of Eryximachus in Plato's *Symposium*. *Transaction & Proceedings of the American Philological Association*, 76, 85–103.

Edmonds, R. G., III. (2000). Socrates the beautiful: Role reversal and midwifery in Plato's *Symposium*. *Transactions of the American Philological Association*, 130, 261–285.

Enos, R. L. (1981). The most significant passage in Plato's *Phaedrus*: A personal nomination. *Rhetoric Society Quarterly*, 11(1), 15–18.

Erickson, K. V. (1977). Plato's philosophy of rhetoric: A research guide. *Rhetoric Society Quarterly*, 7(3), 78–90.

Ervin, E. (1993). Plato the pederast: Rhetoric and cultural procreation in the dialogues. *Pre Text: A Journal of Rhetorical Theory*, 14(1/2), 73–98.

Fixler, M. (1977). Plato's four furors and the real structure of *Paradise Lost*. *PMLA*, 92(5), 952–962.

France, P. (1998). The reader's figure: Epidictic rhetoric in Plato, Aristotle, Bossuet, Racine, and Pascal. *Rhetorica: A Journal of the History of Rhetoric*, 16(3), 312–314.

Frentz, T. (2006). Memory, myth, and rhetoric in Plato's *Phaedrus*. *Rhetoric Society Quarterly*, 36(3), 243–262.

Gagarin, M. (1969). The purpose of Plato's *Protagoras*. *Transactions and Proceedings of the American Philological Association*, 100, 133–164.

Gaines, R. N. (1981). A note on the significance of Plato's *Phaedrus* 271AB. *Rhetoric Society Quarterly, 11*(1), 19–21.

Garver, E. (2006). The rhetoric of friendship in Plato's *Lysis*. *Rhetorica: A Journal of the History of Rhetoric, 24*(2), 127–146.

Giannopoulou, Z. (2010). Enacting the other, being oneself: The drama of rhetoric and philosophy in Plato's *Phaedrus*. *Classical Philology, 105*(2), 146–161.

Giguette, R. (2006). Building objects out of Plato: Applying philosophy, symbolism, and analogy to software design. *Communications of the ACM, 49*(10), 66–71.

Goggin, M. D., & Long, E. (1993). A tincture of philosophy, a tincture of hope: The portrayal of Isocrates in Plato's *Phaedrus*. *Rhetoric Review, 11*(2), 301–324.

Goodell, T. D. (1921). Plato's hedonism. *The American Journal of Philology, 42*(1), 25–39.

Gold, B. K. (1980). A question of genre: Plato's *Symposium* as novel. *MLN, 95*(5), 1353–1359.

Greene, W. C. (1918). Plato's view of poetry. *Harvard Studies in Classical Philology, 29*, 1–75.

Greene, W. C. (1920). The spirit of comedy in Plato. *Harvard Studies in Classical Philology, 31*, 63–123.

Hamilton, M. (2000). Plato on rhetoric and language. *Journal of Technical Writing & Communication, 30*(4), 416–418.

Hammond, M. (1958). Plato and Ovid's exile. *Harvard Studies in Classical Philology, 63*, 347–361.

Hammond, W. A. (1892). On the notion of virtue in the dialogues of Plato, with particular reference to those of the first period and to the third and fourth books of the *Republic*. *Harvard Studies in Classical Philology, 3*, 131–180.

Haskins, E. V. (2000). "Mimesis" between poetics and rhetoric: Performance culture and civic education in Plato, Isocrates, and Aristotle. *Rhetoric Society Quarterly, 30*(3), 7–33.

Havelock, E. (1990). Plato's politics and the American Constitution. *Harvard Studies in Classical Philology, 93*, 1–24.

Howes, G. E. (1895). Homeric quotations in Plato and Aristotle. *Harvard Studies in Classical Philology, 6*, 153–237.

Howland, J. (2004). Plato's reply to Lysias: *Republic* 1 and 2 and *Against Eratosthenes*. *The American Journal of Philology, 125*(2), 179–208.

Hunt, E. L. (1920). Plato on rhetoric and rhetoricians. *Quarterly Journal of Speech, 6*(3), 33–53.

Jenks, R. (2007). The sounds of silence: Rhetoric and dialectic in the refutation of Callicles in Plato's *Gorgias*. *Philosophy & Rhetoric, 40*(2), 201–215.

Johnson, R. R. (1999). Does Plato's myth of Er contribute to the argument of the *Republic? Philosophy & Rhetoric, 32*(1), 1–13.

Johnson, W. A. (1998). Dramatic frame and philosophic idea in Plato. *The American Journal of Philology, 119*(4), 577–598.

Kahn, C. H. (1963). Plato's funeral oration: The motive of the menexenus. *Classical Philology, 58*(4), 220–234.

Kastely, J. L. (1991). In defense of Plato's *Gorgias*. *PMLA, 106*(1), 96–109.

Kastely, J. L. (1996). Plato's *Protagoras*: Revisionary history as sophistical comedy. *Rhetoric Review, 15*(1), 26–43.

Kastely, J. L. (2002). Respecting the rupture: Not solving the problem of unity in Plato's *Phaedrus*. *Philosophy & Rhetoric, 35*(2), 138–152.

Kaufer, D. (1978). The influence of Plato's developing psychology on his views of rhetoric. *Quarterly Journal of Speech, 64*(1), 63–78.

Kirby, J. T. (1997). A classicist's approach to rhetoric in Plato. *Philosophy & Rhetoric, 30*(2), 190–202.

Klosko, G. (1987). Plato and the morality of fallacy. *The American Journal of Philology, 108*(4), 612–626.

Kroeker, K. L. (2010). Celebrating the legacy of Plato. *Communications of the ACM*, *53*(8), 19–20.

Kuhn, H. (1941). The true tragedy: On the relationship between Greek tragedy and Plato, I. *Harvard Studies in Classical Philology*, *52*, 1–40.

Kutash, E. (1993). Anaxagoras and the rhetoric of Plato's middle dialogue theory of forms. *Philosophy & Rhetoric*, *26*(2), 134–152.

LaRusso, D. A. (1965). A neo-platonic dialogue: Is rhetoric an art? An introduction and a translation. *Speech Monographs*, *32*(4), 393–410.

Leff, M. C. (1981). The forms of reality in Plato's *Phaedrus*. *Rhetoric Society Quarterly*, *11*(1), 21–23.

Lenz, F. W. (1946). The quotations from Aelius Aristeides in Olympiodorus' commentary on Plato's *Gorgias*. *The American Journal of Philology*, *67*(2), 103–128.

Lenz, T. M. (1983). The third place from truth: Plato's paradoxical attack on writing. *Communication Quarterly*, *31*(4), 290–301.

Lewis, V. B. (2000). The rhetoric of philosophical politics in Plato's *Seventh Letter*. *Philosophy & Rhetoric*, *33*(1), 23–38.

Liebersohn, Y. (2011). The problem of rhetoric's material in Plato's *Gorgias* (449c9–d9). *Rhetorica*, *29*(1), 1–22.

Linck, M. S. (2003). Unmastering speech: Irony in Plato's *Phaedrus*. *Philosophy & Rhetoric*, *36* (3), 264–276.

Logie, J. (2004). Lost in translation: The influence of 20th-century literary theory on Plato's texts. *Rhetoric Society Quarterly*, *34*(1), 47–71.

Maguire, J. P. (1964). The differentiation of art in Plato's aesthetics. *Harvard Studies in Classical Philology*, *68*, 389–410.

Maguire, J. P. (1965). Beauty and the fine arts in Plato: Some aporiai. *Harvard Studies in Classical Philology*, *70*, 171–193.

Marback, R. C. (1994). Rethinking Plato's legacy: Neoplatonic readings of Plato's sophist. *Rhetoric Review*, *13*(1), 30–49.

Marback, R. C. (1995). The phoenix of Hermes, or the rebirth of Plato in the eighteenth century. *Rhetorica: A Journal of the History of Rhetoric*, *13*(1), 61–86.

Marsh, C. W. Jr. (2001). Public relations ethics: Contrasting models from the rhetorics of Plato, Aristotle, and Isocrates. *Journal of Mass Media Ethics*, *16*(2/3), 79–98.

McAdon, B. (2004). Plato's denunciation of rhetoric in the *Phaedrus*. *Rhetoric Review*, *23*(1), 21–39.

McComiskey, B. (1992). Disassembling Plato's critique of rhetoric in the *Gorgias* (447a–466a). *Rhetoric Review*, *11*(1), 79–90.

McDonough, R. (1991). Plato's anti-mechanistic account of communication. *Language & Communication*, *11*(3), 165–179.

Michels, A. K. (1945). The golden bough of Plato. *The American Journal of Philology*, *66*(1), 59–63.

Moline, J. (1988). Plato on persuasion and credibility. *Philosophy & Rhetoric*, *21*(4), 260–278.

Moore, J. D. (1973). Limitation and design in Plato's *Ion*. *Pacific Coast Philology*, *8*, 45–51.

Mortensen, C. (2000). Plato's pharmacy and Derrida's drugstore. *Language & Communication*, *20* (4), 329–346.

Muckelbauer, J. (2001). Sophistic travel: Inheriting the simulacrum through Plato's *The Sophist*. *Philosophy & Rhetoric*, *34*(3), 225–244.

Murley, C. (1940). Plato's *Phaedrus* and theocritean pastoral. *Transactions & Proceedings of the American Philological Association*, *71*, 281-295.

Murphy, J. J. (1971). The metarhetorics of Plato, Augustine, and McLuhan: A pointing essay. *Philosophy & Rhetoric, 4*(4), 201–214.

Murray, J. S. (1988). Disputation, deception, and dialectic: Plato on the true rhetoric (*Phaedrus* 261–266). *Philosophy & Rhetoric, 21*(4), 279–289.

Murray, J. S. (2001). "Plato on power, moral responsibility and the alleged neutrality of *Gorgias* art of rhetoric (*Gorgias* 456c–457b)." *Philosophy & Rhetoric, 34*(4), 355–363.

Neumann, H. (1969). Socrates in Plato and Aristophanes: In memory of Ludwig Edelstein (1902–1965). *The American Journal of Philology, 90*(2), 201–214.

Nightingale, A. (1993). Writing/reading a sacred text: A literary interpretation of Plato's laws. *Classical Philology, 88*(4), 279–300.

Notopoulos, J. A. (1942). Plato's epitaph. *The American Journal of Philology, 63*(3), 272–293.

Notopoulos, J. A. (1944). The symbolism of the sun and light in the republic of Plato. II. *Classical Philology, 39*(4), 223–240.

Packard, L. R. (1877). Notes on certain passages in the *Phaedo* and the *Gorgias* of Plato. *Transaction of the American Philological Association, 8*, 5–17.

Partee, M. H. (1972). Plato's theory of language. *Foundations of Language, 8*(1), 113–132.

Petruzzi, A. (1996). Rereading Plato's rhetoric. *Rhetoric Review,15*(1), 5–25.

Petruzzi, A. (1999). The effects of the hegemony of the idea upon the understanding of Plato's rhetoric. *Philosophy & Rhetoric, 32*(4), 368–380.

Phillips, K. R. (2010). The failure of memory: Reflections on rhetoric and public remembrance. *Western Journal of Communication, 74*(2), 208–223.

Poster, C. (2005). Framing *Theaetetus*: Plato and rhetorical (mis)representation. *Rhetoric Society Quarterly, 35*(3), 31–73.

Quandahl, E. (1989). What is Plato? Inference and allusion in Plato's *Sophist. Rhetoric Review, 7* (2), 338–348.

Quandt, K. (1982). Socratic consolation: Rhetoric and philosophy in Plato's *Crito. Philosophy & Rhetoric, 15*(4), 238–256.

Quimby, R. W. (1974). The growth of Plato's perception of rhetoric. *Philosophy & Rhetoric, 7* (2), 71–79.

Rafferty, S. F. (2009). The politics of sincerity: Plato, frank speech, and democratic judgment, by Elizabeth Markovits. *Quarterly Journal of Speech, 95*(1), 117–121.

Rappe, S. (2000). Father of dogs? Tracking the cynics in Plato's *Euthydemus. Classical Philology, 95*(3), 282–303.

Reid, R. S. (1997). "Neither oratory nor dialogue": Dionysius of Halicarnassus and the genre of Plato's *Apology. Rhetoric Society Quarterly, 27*(4), 63–90.

Rendall, S. (1977). Dialogue, philosophy, and rhetoric: The example of Plato's *Gorgias. Philosophy & Rhetoric, 10*(3), 165–179.

Roochnik, D. (1991). In defense of Plato: A short polemic. *Philosophy & Rhetoric, 24*(2), 153–158.

Roochnik, D. (1994). Counting on number: Plato on the goodness of *Arithmos. The American Journal of Philology, (4)*, 543–563.

Runciman, W. G. (1959). Plato's *Parmenides. Harvard Studies in Classical Philology, 64*, 89–120.

Samuel, I. (1976). Swift's reading of Plato. *Studies in Philology, 73*(4), 440–462.

Sanders, H. N. (1916). An with the future: I. On the occurrences in Plato. *The American Journal of Philology.37*(1), 42–61.

Sansone, D. (1993). Towards a new doctrine of the article in Greek: Some observations on the definite article in Plato. *Classical Philology, 88*(3), 191–205.

Sattler, W. M. (1949). Some platonic influences in the rhetorical works of Cicero. *Quarterly Journal of Speech, 35*(2), 164–169.

Schiappa, E. (1990). Did Plato coin Rhetorike. *The American Journal of Philology*, 111(4), 457–470.

Schildknecht, C. (1996). Knowledge that the mind seeks: The epistemic impact of Plato's form of discourse. *Philosophy & Rhetoric*, 29(3), 225–243.

Shorey, P. (1901). Plato, Lucretius, and Epicurus. *Harvard Studies in Classical Philology*, 12, 201–210.

Shorey, P. (1914). Plato's laws and the unity of Plato's thought. I. *Classical Philology*, 9(4), 345–369.

Segvic, H. (2006). Homer in Plato's *Protagoras*. *Classical Philology*, 101(3), 247–262.

Slaveva-Griffin, S. (2003). Of gods, philosophers, and charioteers: Content and form in Parmenides' Proem and Plato's *Phaedrus*. *Transactions of the American Philological Association*, 133(2), 227–253.

Smith, J. H. (1985). Dialogic midwifery in Kleist's *Marquise von O* and the hermeneutics of telling the untold in Kant and Plato. *PMLA*, 100(2), 203–219.

Steckerl, F. (1945). Plato, Hippocrates, and the Menon papyrus. *Classical Philology*, 40(3), 166–180.

Svoboda, M. (2006). The unity of Plato's *Gorgias*: Rhetoric, justice, and the philosophic life. *Rhetoric Society Quarterly*, 36(4), 473–477.

Svoboda, M. (2007). Athens, the unjust student of rhetoric: A dramatic historical interpretation of Plato's *Gorgias*. *Rhetoric Society Quarterly*, 37(3), 275–305.

Swearingen, C. J. (1992). Plato's feminine: Appropriation, impersonation, and metaphorical polemic. *Rhetoric Society Quarterly*, 22(1), 109–123.

Tejera, V. (1978). History and rhetoric in Plato's *Meno*, or on the difficulties of communicating human excellence. *Philosophy & Rhetoric*, 11(1), 19–42.

Thomas, M. (2003). Plato's problems and Plato's problem. *Language & Communication*, 23(1), 81–92.

Tigner, S. S. (1970). Plato's philosophical uses of the dream metaphor. *The American Journal of Philology*, 91(2), 204–212.

Timmerman, D. (1993). Ancient Greek origins of argumentation theory: Plato's transformation of "Dialegesthai" to dialectic. *Argumentation & Advocacy*, 29(3), 116–123.

Vlastos, G. (1988). Elenchus and mathematics: A turning-point in Plato's philosophical development. *The American Journal of Philology*, 109(3), 362–396.

Walter, O. M. (1984). Plato's idea of rhetoric for contemporary students: Theory and composition assignments. *College Composition & Communication*, 35(1), 20–30.

Weiss, R. (2003). Oh, brother! The fraternity of rhetoric and philosophy in Plato's *Gorgias*. *Interpretation*, 30(2), 195–206.

Welch, K. E. (1988). The Platonic paradox: Plato's rhetoric in contemporary rhetoric and composition studies. *Written Communication*, 5(1), 3–21.

Werner, D. (2010). Rhetoric and philosophy in Plato's *Phaedrus*. *Greece and Rome*, 57(1), 21–46.

Whedbee, K. (2007). An English Plato: J.S. Mill's *Gorgias*. *Rhetoric Society Quarterly*, 37(1), 19–41.

Wickkiser, B. L. (1999). Speech in context: Plato's *Menexenus* and the ritual of Athenian public burial. *Rhetoric Society Quarterly*, 29(2), 65–74.

Wiegmann, H., & Johnston, H. W. Jr. (1990). Plato's critique of the poets and the misunderstanding of his epistemological argumentation. *Philosophy & Rhetoric*, 23(2), 109–124.

Yunis, H. (1993). The rhetoric of morality and philosophy: Plato's *Gorgias* and *Phaedrus*. *Rhetorica: A Journal of the History of Rhetoric*, 11(3), 343–344.

Zyskind, H. (1992). Plato's *Republic* book I: An equitable rhetoric. *Philosophy & Rhetoric*, 25(3), 205–221.

Hegel

Burke, V. I. (1999). From desire to fascination: Hegel and Blanchot on negativity. *MLN*, *114*(4), 848–856.

De Boer, K. (2001). The infinite movement of self-conception and its inconceivable finitude: Hegel on logos and language. *Dialogue*, *40*(1), 75–97.

Desmond, W. (1985). Hegel, dialectic, and deconstruction. *Philosophy & Rhetoric*, *18*(4), 244–263.

Fay, E. (2003). Archaic contamination: Hegel and the history of dead matter. *PMLA*, *118*(3), 581–590.

Gearhart, S. (1986). The dialectic and its aesthetic other: Hegel and Diderot. *MLN*, *101*(5), 1042–1066.

Geller, J. (1992). Hegel's self-conscious woman. *Modern Language Quarterly*, *53*(2), 173–199.

Geroulanos, S. (2003). French Hegel: From surrealism to postmodernism. *MLN*, *118*(5), 1332–1336.

Heckner, E. (1996). Feminist interpretations of G. W. F. Hegel. *MLN*, *111*(5), 1026–1034.

Holmstron, L. L., Karp, D. A., & Gray, P. S. (2002). Why laundry, not Hegel? Social class, transition to college, and pathways to adulthood. *Symbolic Interaction*, *25*(4), 437–462.

Johnstone, H. W. Jr. (1985). Aristotle, Hegel, and argumentum ad hominem. *Rhetoric Society Quarterly*, *15*(3/4), 131–144.

Joseph, G. (1981). The Antigone as cultural touchstone: Matthew Arnold, Hegel, George Eliot, Virginia Woolf, and Margaret Drabble. *PMLA*, *96*(1), 22–35.

Kainz, H. (1995). Hegel on the Bacchanalian revel of truth. *Philosophy & Rhetoric*, *28*(2), 146–152.

Koschorke, A. (2001). Mastery and slavery: A masochist falls asleep reading Hegel. *MLN*, *116*(3), 551–563.

Labarriere, P. (1977). Hegel: A "philosophy of right." *Communications*, *26*, 159–167.

MacDonald, M. J. (2005). Losing spirit: Hegel, Levinas, and the limits of narrative. *Narrative*, *13*(2), 182–194.

MacDonald, M. J. (2006). Encomium of Hegel. *Philosophy & Rhetoric*, *39*(1), 22–44.

MacKay, L. A. (1962). Antigone, Coriolanus, and Hegel. *Transactions & Proceedings of the American Philological Association*, *93*, 166–174.

Morresi, R. (2005). Rhetoric in Hegel and Hegel's rhetoric. *Rhetorica: A Journal of the History of Rhetoric*, *23*(4), 347–362.

Poulakos, J. (1990). Hegel's reception of the Sophists. *Western Journal of Speech Communication*, *54*(2), 160–171.

Presner, T. S. (2003). Jews on ships: Or, how Heine's reisebilder deconstruct Hegel's *Philosophy of World History*. *PMLA*, *118*(3), 521–538.

Reid, J. (2006). Hegel's ontological grasp of judgment and the original dividing of identity into difference. *Dialogue*, *45*(1), 29–43.

Rowe, J. C. (1980). The internal conflict on romantic narrative: Hegel's phenomenology and Hawthorne's *The Scarlet Letter*. *MLN*, *95*(5), 1203–1231.

Roy, A. (2009). Hegel contra Schlegel; Kierkegaard contra de Man. *PMLA*, *124*(1), 107–126.

Self, C. (2010). Hegel, Habermas, and community: The public in the new media era. *International Journal of Strategic Communication*, *4*(2), 78–92.

Shapiro, G. (1975). Hegel on the meaning of poetry. *Philosophy & Rhetoric*, *8*(2), 88–107.

Shuter, W. (1971). History as palingenesis in Pater and Hegel. *PMLA*, *86*(3), 411–421.

Smith, J. H. (1985). Rhetorical polemics and the dialectics of "Kritik" in Hegel's Jena essays. *Philosophy & Rhetoric*, *18*(1), 31–57.

Stansfield, A. (1934). Das dritte reich: A contribution to the study of the idea of the "Third Kingdom" in German literature from Herder to Hegel. *The Modern Language Review*, *29*(2), 156–172.

Van Dooren, W. (1975). Language in the philosophy of Hegel. *Lingua, 37*(1), 86–88.

Whyte, P. (2001). Subjects of terror: Nerval, Hegel and the modern self. *Modern Language Review, 96,* 512–513.

Chapter 11
Ethics and Diversity
Ethics

Aune, J. A. (2007). "Only connect": Between morality and ethics in Habermas' communication theory. *Communication Theory, 17*(4), 340–347.

Amare, N., & Manning, A. (2009). Writing for the robot: How employer search tools have influenced résumé rhetoric and ethics. *Business Communication Quarterly, 72*(1), 35–60.

Arnett, R. C. (1990). The practical philosophy of communication ethics and free speech as the foundation for speech communication. *Communication Quarterly, 38*(3), 208–217.

Arnett, R. C. (2001). Dialogic civility as pragmatic ethical praxis: An interpersonal metaphor for the public domain. *Communication Theory, 11*(3), 315–338.

Arnett, R. C. (2008). Pointing the way to communication ethics theory: The life-giving gift of acknowledgement. *Review of Communication, 8*(1), 21–28.

Arnett, R. C., Arneson, P., & Bell, L. M. (2006). Communication ethics: The dialogic turn. *Review of Communication, 6*(1/2), 62–92.

Arnett, R. C., Bell, L. M., & Fritz, J. M. H. (2010). Dialogic learning as first principle in communication ethics. *Atlantic Journal of Communication, 18*(3), 111–126.

Baker, S., & Martinson, D. L. (2001). The TARES test: Five principles for ethical persuasion. *Journal of Mass Media Ethics, 16*(2–3), 148–175.

Banaji, S., & Buckingham, D. (2009). The civic sell: Young people, the Internet, and ethical consumption. *Information, Communication, & Society, 12*(8), 1197–1223.

Barnes, M. C. (2006). Ethics in conflict: Making the case for a critical pedagogy. *Business Communication Quarterly, 69*(2), 144–157.

Barney, R. D. (1997). "Journals" as dialogue assignments in ethics courses. *Journal of Mass Media Ethics, 12*(4), 243–245.

Barton, E., & Eggly, S. (2009). Ethical or unethical persuasion?: The rhetoric of offers to participate in clinical trials. *Written Communication, 26*(3), 295–319.

Beard, D. (2009). A broader understanding of the ethics of listening: Philosophy, cultural studies, media studies and the ethical listening subject. *The International Journal of Listening, 23*(1), 7–20.

Behme, T. (2004). Isocrates on the ethics of authorship. *Rhetoric Review, 23*(3), 197–215.

Benton, C. L. (1993). Performance: Ethical concerns and moral dilemmas. *Text & Performance Quarterly, 13*(1), 97–103.

Berkowitz, D., & Limor, Y. (2003). Professional confidence and situational ethics: Assessing the social-professional dialectic in journalistic ethics decisions. *Journalism & Mass Communication Quarterly, 80*(4), 783–801.

Bettina, B. (2005). What is Levinas doing? Phenomenology and the rhetoric of an ethical unconscious. *Philosophy & Rhetoric, 38*(2), 122–144.

Bivins, T. H., & Newton, J. H. (2003). The real, the virtual, and the moral: Ethics at the intersection of consciousness. *Journal of Mass Media Ethics, 18*(3–4), 213–229.

Black, J. (2008). An informal agenda for media ethicists. *Journal of Mass Media Ethics, 23*(1), 28–35.

Bloom, M. M. (1990). Sex differences in ethical systems: A useful framework for interpreting communication research. *Communication Quarterly, 38*(3), 244–254.

Boileau, D. M. (1985). Eric report: Ethics and speech: An inherent or irrelevant relationship? *Communication Education*, 34(3), 259–265.

Booth-Butterfield, S., & Cottone, R. R. (1991). Ethical issues in the treatment of communication apprehension and avoidance. *Communication Education*, 40(2), 172–179.

Borden, S. L. (1997). Choice processes in a newspaper ethics case. *Communication Monographs*, 64 (1), 65–81.

Borden, S. L. (2003). Deviance mitigation in the ethical discourse of journalists. *The Southern Communication Journal*, 68(3), 231–249.

Bormann, E. G. (1961). Ethics of ghostwritten speeches. *Quarterly Journal of Speech*, 47(3), 262–267.

Borton, I. M. (2008). Getting beyond easy dichotomies: Thinking otherwise about ICT and ethics. *Review of Communication*, 8(4), 405–408.

Bowen, S. A. (2004). Expansion of ethics as the tenth generic principle of public relations excellence: A Kantian theory and model for managing ethical issues. *Journal of Public Relations Research*, 16(1), 65–92.

Bowen, S. A. (2008). A state of neglect: Public relations as "corporate conscience" or ethics counsel. *Journal of Public Relations Research*, 20(3), 271–296.

Bracci, S. (2001). Managing health care in Oregon: The search for a civic bioethics. *Journal of Applied Communication Research*, 29(2), 171–194.

Brown, W. J., & Singhal, A. (1990). Ethical dilemmas of prosocial television. *Communication Quarterly*, 38(3), 268–280.

Browning, L. D. (1982). The ethics of intervention: A communication consultant's apology. *Journal of Applied Communication Research*, 10(2), 101–116.

Bugeja, M. (2007). Making whole: The ethics of correction. *Journal of Mass Media Ethics*, 22 (1), 49–65.

Burks, D. M. (1966). On the ethics of speaking. *The Speech Teacher*, 15(4), 336–339.

Butchart, G. C. (2006). On ethics and documentary: A real and actual truth. *Communication Theory*, 16(4), 427–452.

Cabot, M. (2005). Moral development and PR ethics. *Journal of Mass Media Ethics*, 20(4), 321–332.

Canary, H. E. (2007). Teaching ethics in communication courses: An investigation of instructional methods, course foci, and student outcomes. *Communication Education*, 56 (2), 193–208.

Carmack, H. J. (2010). Bearing witness to the ethics of practice: Storying physicians' medical mistake narratives. *Health Communication*, 25(5), 449–458.

Carpenter, R. H. (1975). Alfred Thayer Mahan's style on sea power: A paramessage conducing to ethos. *Speech Monographs*, 42(3), 190–202.

Cenite, M., Detenber, B. H., Koh, A. W. K., Lim, A. L. H., & Soon, N. E. (2009). Doing the right thing online: A survey of bloggers' ethical beliefs and practices. *New Media & Society*, 11(4), 575–597.

Chase, K. R. (2009). Constructing ethics through rhetoric: Isocrates and piety. *Quarterly Journal of Speech*, 95(3), 239–262.

Cheney, G. (2004). Bringing ethics in from the margins. *Australian Journal of Communication*, 31 (3), 35–40.

Cheney, G. (2008). Encountering the ethics of engaged scholarship. *Journal of Applied Communication Research*, 36(3), 281–288.

Christians, C. G. (2004). Ubuntu and communitarianism in media ethics. *Ecquid novi*, 25(2), 235–256.

Christians, C. G., & Lambeth, E. B. (1996). The status of ethics instruction in communication departments. *Communication Education, 45*(3), 236–243.

Cline, A. R. (2008). Ethics and ethos: Writing an effective newspaper ombudsman position. *Journal of Mass Media Ethics, 23*(2), 79–89.

Conn, C. E. (2009). Talking about problematic issues in employment backgrounds: Lessons in ethical and effective interviewing strategies. *Communication Teacher, 23*(1), 52–57.

Conway, M., & Groshek, J. (2009). Forgive me now, fire me later: Mass communication students' ethics gap concerning school and journalism. *Communication Education, 58*(4), 461–482.

Correa, T. (2009). Does class matter? The effect of social class on journalists' ethical decision making. *Journalism & Mass Communication Quarterly, 86*(3), 654–672.

Crable, R. E. (1978). Ethical codes, accountability, and argumentation. *Quarterly Journal of Speech, 64*(1), 23–32.

Craig, D. A., & Ferré, J. P. (2006). Agape as an ethic of care for journalism. *Journal of Mass Media Ethics, 21*(2–3), 123–140.

Crick, N., & Gabriel, J. (2010). The conduit between lifeworld and system: Habermas and the rhetoric of public scientific controversies. *Rhetoric Society Quarterly, 40*(3), 201–223.

Cripe, N. M. (1957). Debating both sides in tournaments is ethical. *The Speech Teacher, 6*(3), 209–212.

Deetz, S. (1990). Reclaiming the subject matter as a guide to mutual understanding: Effectiveness and ethics in interpersonal interaction. *Communication Quarterly, 38*(3), 226–243.

Diggs, B. J. (1964). Persuasion and ethics. *Quarterly Journal of Speech, 50*(4), 359–373.

Dougherty, D. S., Mobley, S. K., & Smith, S. E. (2010). Language convergence and meaning divergence: A theory of intercultural communication. *Journal of International & Intercultural Communication, 3*(2), 164–186.

Erzikova, E. (2010). University teachers' perceptions and evaluations of ethics instruction in the public relations curriculum. *Public Relations Review, 36*(3), 316–318.

Fawkes, J. (2010). The shadow of excellence: A Jungian approach to public-relations ethics. *Review of Communication, 10*(3), 211–227.

Fekete, L. (2006). The ethics of economic interactions in the network economy. *Information, Communication, & Society, 9*(6), 737–760.

Fenske, M. (2004). The aesthetic of the unfinished: Ethics and performance. *Text & Performance Quarterly, 24*(1), 1–19.

Ferré, J. P. (1980). Contemporary approaches to journalistic ethics. *Communication Quarterly, 28*(2), 44–48.

Ferré, J. P. (1990). Communication ethics and the political realism of Reinhold Niebuhr. *Communication Quarterly, 38*(3), 218–225.

Fitzpatrick, K. (2002). Evolving standards in public relations: A historical examination of PRSA's code of ethics. *Journal of Mass Media Ethics, 17*(2), 89–110.

Fitzpatrick, K., & Gauthier, C. (2001). Toward a professional responsibility theory of public relations ethics. *Journal of Mass Media Ethics, 16*(2/3), 193–212.

Flynn, L. J. (1957). The Aristotelian basis for the ethics of speaking. *The Speech Teacher, 6*(3), 179–187.

Fuse, K., Land, M., & Lambiase, J. J. (2010). Expanding the philosophical base for ethical public relations practice: Cross-cultural case application of non-western ethical philosophies. *Western Journal of Communication, 74*(4), 436–455.

Galewski, E. (2008). Foundering to me is sweet in this sea: Agamben's theory of ethical life. *Review of Communication, 8*(4), 395–404.

Garvey, T. G. (2000). The value of opacity: A Bakhtinian analysis of Habermas's discourse ethics. *Philosophy & Rhetoric, 33*(4), 370–390.

Gehrke, P. J. (2007). Historical study as ethical and political action. *Quarterly Journal of Speech, 93*(3), 355–357.

Gehrke, P. J. (2010). Being for the Other-to-the-Other: Justice and communication in Levinasian ethics. *Review of Communication, 10*(1), 5–19.

Glasser, T. L. & Ettema, J. S. (2008). Ethics and eloquence in journalism: An approach to press accountability. *Journalism Studies, 9*(4), pp. 512–534.

Goodnight, G. T. (2009). The bourgeois virtues: Ethics for an age of commerce. *Quarterly Journal of Speech, 95*(3), 346–351.

Gunkel, D., & Hawhee, D. (2003). Virtual alterity and the reformatting of ethics. *Journal of Mass Media Ethics, 18*(3/4), 173–193.

Gunson, D., & Collins, C. (1997). From the I to the we: Discourse ethics, identity, and the pragmatics of partnership in the west of Scotland. *Communication Theory, 7*(4), 278–300.

Haiman, F. S. (1958). Democratic ethics and the hidden persuaders. *Quarterly Journal of Speech, 44*(4), 385–392.

Haiman, F. S. (1967). The rhetoric of the streets: Some legal and ethical considerations. *Quarterly Journal of Speech, 53*(2), 99–114.

Halese, C., & Honey, A. (2007). Rethinking ethics review as institutional discourse. *Qualitative Inquiry, 13*(3), 336–352.

Hallstein, D. L. O. (1999). A postmodern caring: Feminist standpoint theories, revisioned caring, and communication ethics. *Western Journal of Communication, 63*(1), 32–56.

Hamilton, J., & Mueller, A. (2010). Ethics simulations as preparation for public discourse. *Communication Teacher, 24*(1), 1–8.

Harpole, C. H. (1975). Eric report: Rape, seduction, and love. Ethics in public and private communication. *The Speech Teacher, 24*(4), 303–308.

Hart, J. L., Walker, K. L., & Gregg, J. L. (2007). Communication ethics and My Sister's Keeper. *Communication Teacher, 21*(4), 123–127.

Herrick, J. A. (1992). Rhetoric, ethics, and virtue. *Communication Studies, 43*(3), 133–149.

Herrscher, R. (2002). A universal code of journalism ethics: Problems, limitations, and proposals. *Journal of Mass Media Ethics, 17*(4), 277–289.

Hill, R. T. (1995). The Nakwa Powamu ceremony as rehearsal: Authority, ethics and ritual appropriation. *Text and Performance Quarterly, 15*(4), 301–320.

Himelboim, I., & Limor, Y. (2008). Media perception of freedom of the press: A comparative international analysis of 242 codes of ethics. *Journalism, 9*(3), 235–265.

Hope, D. S. (2009). Reporting the future: A visual parable of environmental ethics in Robert and Shana Parke Harrison's *The Architect's Brother*. *Visual Communication Quarterly, 16*(1), 32–49.

Hopkins, R. (1977). Refocusing on ethics. *Communication Education, 26*(4), 359–360.

Howell, W. S. (1934). Nathaniel Carpenter's place in the controversy between dialectic and rhetoric. *Speech Monographs, 1*(1), 20–41.

Hyde, M. J., & King, N. M. P. (2010). Communication ethics and bioethics: An interface. *Review of Communication, 10*(2), 156–171.

Hyde, M. J., & Sargent, D. K. (1993). The performance of play, the "great poem," and ethics. *Text & Performance Quarterly, 13*(2), 122–138.

Jacobson, T. L. (1998). Discourse ethics and the right to communicate. *Gazette, 60*(5), 395–413.

Jensen, J. V. (1985). Teaching ethics in speech communication. *Communication Education, 34*(4), 324–330.

Johnson, R. C. (1970). Teaching speech ethics in the beginning speech course. *The Speech Teacher, 19*(10), 58–61.

Jovanovic, S., & Wood, R.V. (2004). Speaking from the Bedrock of ethics. *Philosophy & Rhetoric, 37*(4), 317–334.

Jovanovic, S., & Wood, R.V. (2006). Communication ethics and ethical culture: A study of the ethics initiative in Denver city government. *Journal of Applied Communication Research, 34* (4), 386–405.

Kang, J. A. (2010). Ethical conflict and job satisfaction of public relations practitioners. *Public Relations Review, 36* (2), 152–156.

Keeble, R., & Cohen-Almagor, R. (2010). Ethical space: Journal with a difference. *Review of Communication, 10*(3), 228–235.

Keith, S., Schwalbe, C. B., & Silcock, B. W. (2006). Images in ethics codes in an era of violence and tragedy. *Journal of Mass Media Ethics, 21*(4), 245–264.

Keith, W. (2012). The ethics and politics of speech. *Quarterly Journal of Speech, 98*(1), 118–121.

Kennamer, D. (2005). What journalists and researchers have in common about ethics. *Journal of Mass Media Ethics, 20*(1), 77–89.

Kennedy, K. (1999). Cynic rhetoric: The ethics and tactics of resistance. *Rhetoric Review, 18* (1), 26–45.

Kienzler, D. (2001). Ethics, critical thinking, and professional communication pedagogy. *Technical Communication Quarterly, 10*(3), 319–339.

Kienzler, D. (2004). Teaching ethics isn't enough: The challenge of being ethical teachers. *Journal of Business Communication, 41*(3), 292–301.

Kienzler, D., & David, C. (2003). After Enron: Integrating ethics into the professional communication curriculum. *Journal of Business and Technical Communication, 17*(4), 474–489.

Kirkwood, W. G., & Ralston, S. M. (1996). Ethics and teaching employment interviewing. *Communication Education, 45*(2), 167–179.

Kittross, J. M., & Gordon, A. D. (2003). The academy and cyberspace ethics. *Journal of Mass Media Ethics, 18*(3–4), 286–307.

Kroll, B. (1997). Arguing about public issues: What can we learn from practical ethics? *Rhetoric Review, 16*(1), 105–119.

Kruger, A. N. (1967). The ethics of persuasion: A re-examination. *The Speech Teacher, 16*(4), 295–305.

Kuhn, M. (2007). Interactivity and prioritizing the human: A code of blogging ethics. *Journal of Mass Media Ethics, 22*(1), 18–36.

Lair, D. J., Sullivan, K., & Cheney, G. (2005). Marketization and the recasting of the professional self: The rhetoric and ethics of personal branding. *Management Communication Quarterly, 18* (3), 307–343.

LaRusso, D. A. (1965). A neo-platonic dialogue: Is rhetoric an art? An introduction and a translation. *Speech Monographs, 32*(4), 393–410.

Lewis, P. V., & Speck, H. E., III (1990). Ethical orientations for understanding business ethics. *The Journal of Business Communication, 27*(3), 213–232.

Lipari, L. (2004). Listening for the other: Ethical implications of the Buber-Levinas encounter. *Communication Theory, 14*(2), 122–141.

Lipari, L. (2009). Listening otherwise: The voice of ethics. *The International Journal of Listening, 23* (1), 44–59.

Lo, V. H., & Wei, R. (2008). Ethical risk perception of freebies and effects on journalists' ethical reasoning. *Chinese Journal of Communication, 1*(1), 25–37.

Longaker, M. G. (2005). Beyond ethics: Notes toward a historical materialist paideia in the professional writing classroom. *Journal of Business & Technical Communication, 19*(1), 78–97.

Lyon, A., & Mirivel, J. C. (2011). Reconstructing Merck's practical theory of communication: The ethics of pharmaceutical sales representative-physician encounters. *Communication Monographs, 78*(1), 53–72.

Macaulay, R. (1952). Scholars' ethics. *Quarterly Journal of Speech, 38*(1), 56.

Marsh, C. W. J. (2001). Public relations ethics: Contrasting models from the rhetorics of Plato, Aristotle, and Isocrates. *Journal of Mass Media Ethics, 16*(2/3), 78–98.

Maxwell, R., & Miller, T. (2008). Ecological ethics and media technology. *International Journal of Communication, 2*, 331–353.

McCaleb, J. L., & Dean, K. W. (1987). Ethics and communication education: Empowering teachers. *Communication Education, 36*(4), 410–416.

McEuen, V. S., Gordon, R. D., & Todd-Mancillas, W. R. (1990). A survey of doctoral education in communication research ethics. *Communication Quarterly, 38*(3), 281–290.

McLeod, A. L. (1957). The ethics of radio announcing: A dilemma. *Today's Speech, 5*(2), 30–31.

McQueeney, E. (2006). Making ethics come alive. *Business Communication Quarterly, 69*(2), 158–171.

Medhurst, M. J. (1987). Ghostwritten speeches: Ethics isn't the only lesson. *Communication Education, 36*(3), 241–249.

Meisenbach, R. J. (2006). Habermas's discourse ethics and principle of universalization as a moral framework for organizational communication. *Management Communication Quarterly, 20*(1), 39–62.

Mirando, J. A. (1998). Lessons on ethics in news reporting textbooks, 1897–1997. *Journal of Mass Media Ethics, 13*(1), 26–39.

Murphy, R. (1957). The ethics of debating both sides. *The Speech Teacher, 6*(1), 1–9.

Murphy, J. B., Ward, S. J. A., & Donovan, A. (2006). Ethical ideals in journalism: Civic uplift or telling the truth. *Journal of Mass Media Ethics, 21*(4), 322–337.

Murray, J. W. (1998). An other ethics for Kenneth Burke. *Communication Studies, 49*(1), 29–48.

Nicotera, A. M., & Cushman, D. P. (1992). Organizational ethics: A within organization view. *Journal of Applied Communication Research, 20*(4), 437–462.

O'Gorman, N. (2005). "Telling the Truth": Dietrich Bonhoeffer's rhetorical discourse ethic. *Journal of Communication & Religion, 28*(2), 224–248.

Oates, T. P., & Pauly, J. (2007). Sports journalism as moral and ethical discourse. *Journal of Mass Media Ethics, 22*(4), 332–347.

Palmer-Mehta, V. (2009). Motivational appeals and ethics. *Communication Teacher, 23*(1), 41–47.

Pearson, J. C., Child, J. T., Mattern, J. L., & Kahl, D. H. Jr. (2006). What are students being taught about ethics in public speaking textbooks? *Communication Quarterly, 54*(4), 507–521.

Peek, L., Peek, G., Roxas, M., Robichaud, Y., & Blanco, H. (2007). Team learning and communication: The effectiveness of email-based ethics discussions. *Business Communication Quarterly, 70*(2), 166–185.

Petrilli, S. (2009). Semiotics as semioethics in the era of global communication. *Semiotica, 173*(1/4), 343–397.

Phillips, A. (2010). Transparency and the new ethics of journalism. *Journalism Practice, 4* (3), 373–382.

Phillips, G. M. (1958). Use of authorities as ethical proof in the Talmudic discourse. *Speech Monographs, 25*(1), 67–75.

Pöttker, H. (2005). What is journalism for? Professional ethics between philosophy and practice. *Communications, 30*(1), 109–116.

Powell, A. C., III. (1998). Satellite imagery: The ethics of a new technology. *Journal of Mass Media Ethics, 13*(2), 93–98.

Prellwitz, J. H. (2011). Nietzschean genealogy and communication ethics. *Review of Communication, 11*(1), 1–19.

Pritchard, D. (2010). Media convergence and changes in Québec journalists' professional values. *Canadian Journal of Communication, 35*(4), 595–607.

Rao, S., & Ting Lee, S. (2005). Globalizing media ethics? An assessment of universal ethics among international political journalists. *Journal of Mass Media Ethics, 20*(2/3), 99–120.

Reich, W. T. (1988). Experiential ethics as a foundation for dialogue between health communication and health-care ethics. *Journal of Applied Communication Research, 16*(1), 16–28.

Rogge, E. (1959). Evaluating the ethics of a speaker in a democracy. *Quarterly Journal of Speech, 45*(4), 419–425.

Rubin, R. B., & Yoder, J. (1985). Ethical issues in the evaluation of communication behavior. *Communication Education, 34*(1), 13–17.

Salvo, M. J. (2001). Ethics of engagement: User-centered design and rhetorical methodology. *Technical Communication Quarterly, 10*(3), 273–290.

Sanders, W. (2010). Documentary filmmaking and ethics: Concepts, responsibilities, and the need for empirical research. *Mass Communication and Society, 13*(5), 528–553.

Sattler, W. M. (1947). Conceptions of ethos in ancient rhetoric. *Speech Monographs, 14*(1/2), 55–65.

Schrier, W. (1930). The ethics of persuasion (A defense of rhetoric). *Quarterly Journal of Speech, 16*(4), 476–486.

Sinnreich, A., Latonero, M., & Gluck, M. (2009). Ethics reconfigured: How today's media consumers evaluate the role of creative reappropriation. *Information, Communication, and Society, 12*(8), 1242–1260.

Smudde, P. M. (2011). Focus on ethics and public relations practice in a university classroom. *Communication Teacher, 25*(3), 154–158.

Spigelman, C., & Grobman, L. (2006). Why we chose rhetoric: Necessity, ethics, and the (re)making of a professional writing program. *Journal of Business and Technical Communication, 20*(1), 48–64.

Sproule, J. M. (1987). Whose ethics in the classroom? An historical survey. *Communication Education, 36*(4), 317–326.

Strentz, H. (2002). Universal ethical standards? *Journal of Mass Media Ethics, 17*(4), 263–276.

Stroud, S. R. (2005). Rhetoric and moral progress in Kant's ethical community. *Philosophy & Rhetoric, 38*(4), 328–354.

Struever, N. S. (1998). The rhetoric of familiarity: A pedagogy of ethics. *Philosophy & Rhetoric, 31*(2), 91–106.

Son, T. (2002). Leaks: How do codes of ethics address them? *Journal of Mass Media Ethics, 17*(2), 155–173.

Thompson, T. L. (2009). The applicability of narrative ethics. *Journal of Applied Communication Research, 37*(2), 188–195.

Tomaselli, K. G. (2009). (Afri)ethics, communitarianism and Libertarianism. *International Communication Gazette, 71*(7), 577–594.

Tompkins Pribble, P. (1990). Making an ethical commitment: A rhetorical case study of organizational socialization. *Communication Quarterly, 38*(3), 255–267.

Tucker, E. M., & Stout, D. A. (1999). Teaching ethics: The moral development of educators. *Journal of Mass Media Ethics, 14*(2), 107–118.

Valentine, K. B. (2002). Yaqui Easter ceremonies and the ethics of intense spectatorship. *Text & Performance Quarterly, 22*(4), 280–296.

Vanacker, B., & Breslin, J. (2006). Ethics of care: More than just another tool to bash the media? *Journal of Mass Media Ethics, 21*(2/3), 196–214.

Wasserman, H., & Rao, S. (2008). The glocalization of journalism ethics. *Journalism, 9*(2), 163–181.

Watkins, L. I. (1959). Ethical problems in debating: A symposium. *The Speech Teacher, 8*(2), 150–156.

Wieman, H. N., & Walter, O. M. (1957). Toward an analysis of ethics for rhetoric. *Quarterly Journal of Speech, 43*(3), 266–270.

Williams, L. S. (2008) Strengthening the ethics and visual rhetoric of sales letters. *Business Communication Quarterly, 71*(1), 44–52.

Winegarden, A. D., Fuss-Reineck, M., & Charron, L. J. (1993). Using *Star Trek: The Next Generation* to teach concepts in persuasion, family communication, and communication ethics. *Communication Education, 42*(2), 179–188.

Wood, J. T. (1998). Ethics, justice, and the "private sphere." *Women's Studies in Communication, 21* (2), 127–149.

Wyatt, W. N. (2008). Being Aristotelian: Using virtue ethics in an applied media ethics course. *Journal of Mass Media Ethics, 23*(4), 296–307.

Zeytinoglu, C. (2011). Appositional (communication) ethics: Listening to Heidegger and Levinas in chorus. *Review of Communication, 11*(4), 272–285.

Zhong, B. (2008). Thinking along the cultural line: A cross-cultural inquiry of ethical decision making among U.S. and Chinese journalism students. *Journalism & Mass Communication Educator, 63*(2), 110–126.

MacIntyre

Arnett, R. C. (2001). Dialogic civility as pragmatic ethical praxis: An interpersonal metaphor for the public domain. *Communication Theory, 11*(3), 315–338.

Arnett, R. C., Arneson, P., & Bell, L. M. (2006). Communication ethics: The dialogic turn. *The Review of Communication, 6*(1/2), 62–92.

Arnett, R. C., Arneson, P., & Holba, A. (2008). Bridges Not Walls: The communicative enactment of dialogic storytelling. *The Review of Communication, 8*(3), 217–234.

Aucoin, J. (1992). The Arizona Project as a MacIntyrean moment. *Journal of Mass Media Ethics, 7*(3), 169–183.

Aune, J. A. (2008). Modernity as a rhetorical problem: Phronesis, forms, and forums in norms of rhetorical culture. *Philosophy & Rhetoric, 41*(4), 402–420.

Barr, J. (2006). Reframing the idea of an educated public. *Discourse: Studies in the Cultural Politics of Education, 27*(2), 225–239.

Breit, R. A. (2008). Journalistic self-regulation in Australia: Is it ready for the information society? *International Communication Gazette, 70*(6), 505–528.

Charland, M. (1994). Norms and laughter in rhetorical culture. *The Quarterly Journal of Speech, 80* (3), 339–342.

Frentz, T. S. (1985). Rhetorical conversation, time, and moral action. *The Quarterly Journal of Speech, 71*(1), 1–18.

Inglis, F. (2007). Richard Hoggart: The intellectual as politician. *International Journal of Cultural Studies, 10*(1), 21–28.

Lambeth, E. B. (1990). Waiting for a new St. Benedict: Alasdair MacIntyre and the theory and practice of journalism. *Journal of Mass Media Ethics, 5*(2), 75–87.

Leeper, R. V., & Leeper, K. A. (2001). Public relations as "practice": Applying the theory of Alasdair MacIntyre. *Public Relations Review, 27*(4), 461–473.

Pearce, W. B. (1984). On being sufficiently radical in gender research: Some lessons from critical theory, Kant, Milan, and MacIntrye. *Women's Studies in Communication*, 7(2), 65–68.

Plaisance, P. L. (2005). The mass media as discursive network: Building on the implications of Libertarian and communitarian claims for news media ethics theory. *Communication Theory*, 15(3), 292–313.

Shotter, J. (1997). On a different ground: From contests between monologues to dialogical contest. *Argumentation*, 11(1), 95–112.

Sparks, R. L., & Granschow, L. (1995). A strong influence approach to causal factors in foreign language learning: A response to MacIntyre. *The Modern Language Journal*, 79(2), 235–244.

Sullivan, D. L., & Martin, M. S. (2001). Habit formation and storytelling: A theory for guiding ethical action. *Technical Communication Quarterly*, 10(3), 251–272.

Sidgwick

Jarratt, S. C. (1987). The first Sophists and the uses of history. *Rhetoric Review*, 6(1), 67–78.

Chapter 12:
Public Domain as the Home of Difference and Opinion

Public Domain

Ananny, M., & Kriess, D. (2011). A new contract for the press: Copyright, public domain journalism, and self-governance in a digital age. *Critical Studies in Media Communication*, 28(4), 314–333.

Arnett, R. (2001). Dialogic civility as pragmatic ethical praxis: An interpersonal metaphor for the public domain. *Communication Theory*, 11(3), 315–338.

Buchholz, W. (1988). Computers and communication: Computer software in the public domain: An academic bazaar. *Business Communication Quarterly*, 51(4), 1–4.

Eltit, D. (2009). Public domain. *PMLA*, 124(5), 1800–1805.

Frost, R. (2005). Call for a public-domain speechweb. *Communications of the ACM*, 48(11), 45–49.

Narula, M. (2002). Sarai: One year in the public domain. *Television and New Media*, 3(4), 387–395.

Nduku Kioko, A., & Jepkirui Muthwii, M. (2003). English variety for the public domain in Kenya: Speakers' attitudes and views. *Language, Culture, & Curriculum*, 16(2), 130–145.

Rawlins, W. (1998). Theorizing public and private domains and practices of communication: Introductory concerns. *Communication Theory*, 8(4), 369–380.

Smiers, J. (2000). The abolition of copyright: Better for artists, third-world countries and the public domain. *International Communication Gazette*, 62(5), 379–406.

Zhao, S., & Elesh, D. (2008). Copresence as "being with": Social contact in online public domains. *Information, Communication & Society*, 11(4), 565–583.

Arendt

Bernstein, S. (2003). Regions of sorrow-anxiety and messianism in Hannah Arendt and W. H. Auden. *MLN*, 118(5), 1317–1323.

Boltanski, L., & Sawchuk, K. (2002). Distant suffering: Morality, media and politics. *Canadian Journal of Communication*, 27(1), 93–96.

Chapman, O. (2011). The elusive allure of "aura": Sample-based music and Benjamin's practice of quotation. *Canadian Journal of Communication*, 36(2), 243–261.

Curthoys, N. (2002). Hannah Arendt and the politics of narrative. *Journal of Narrative Theory, 32* (3), 348–370.

Jiwani, Y., & Young, M. L. (2006). Missing and murdered women: Reproducing marginality in news discourse. *Canadian Journal of Communication, 31*(4), 895–917.

Jung, V. (2004). Writing Germany in exile—The bilingual author as cultural mediator: Klaus Mann, Stefan Heym, Rudolf Arnheim, and Hannah Arendt. *Journal of Multicultural Development, 25*(5/6), 529–546.

Kaposi, D. (2010). Between orient and occident: Tradition, politics and the limits of criticism in the Scholem-Arendt exchange. *Journal of Language and Politics, 9*(3), 409–432.

Lee, H. (2010). Enemy under my skin: Eileen Chang's lust, caution and the politics of transcendence. *PMLA, 125*(3), 640–656.

Logan, M. (2001). Hannah Arendt: Nature-human, sacred, and stateless. *AUMLA: Journal of the Australasian University Modern Language, 96,* 49–71.

Long, C. (2007). Hannah Arendt—Leidenschaften, Menschen und Bücher. *MLN, 122*(3), 674–677, 679.

Martín-Barbero, J. (2011). In memoriam: Technical reason and political reason. Spaces/times not considered. *Canadian Journal of Communication, 36*(2), 325–339.

Murphy, B. (2002). Arendt, Kristeva, and Arthur Miller: Forgiveness and promise in *After the Fall. PMLA, 117*(2), 314–316.

O'Connell, D. C., & Kowal, S. (1998). Orality and literacy in public discourse: An interview of Hannah Arendt. *Journal of Pragmatics, 30*(5), 543–564.

Roberts-Miller, P. (2006). Agonism, wrangling, and John Quincy Adams. *Rhetoric Review, 25* (2), 141–161.

Rosenfield, L. W. (1984). Hanna Arendt's legacy. *Quarterly Journal of Speech, 70*(1), 90–96.

Weigel, S., & Kyburz, M. (2002). Secularization and sacralization, normalization and rupture: Kristeva and Arendt on forgiveness. *PMLA, 117*(2), 320–323.

Weiland, S. (1999). Biography, rhetoric, and intellectual careers: Writing the life of Hannah Arendt. *Biography, 22*(3), 370–398.

Habermas

Antonio, R. J. (1992). Communication, modernity, and democracy in Habermas and Dewey. *Symbolic Interaction, 15*(3), 277–297.

Ashley, D. (1982). Jürgen Habermas and the rationalization of communicative interaction. *Symbolic Interaction, 5*(1), 79–96.

Bohman, J. F. (1988). Emancipation and rhetoric: The perlocutions and illocutions of the social critic. *Philosophy & Rhetoric, 21*(3), 185–204.

Burkart, R. (2007). On Jürgen Habermas and public relations. *Public Relations Review, 33*(3), 249–254.

Burleson, B. R., & Kline, S. L. (1979). Habermas' theory of communication: A critical explication. *Quarterly Journal of Speech, 65*(4), 412–428.

Chang, L., & Jacobson, T. (2010). Measuring participation as communicative action: A case study of citizen involvement in and assessment of a city's smoking cessation policy-making process. *Journal of Communication, 60*(4), 660–679.

Cooren, F. (2000). Toward another ideal speech situation: A critique of Habermas' reinterpretation of speech act theory. *Quarterly Journal of Speech, 86*(3), 295–317.

David, C., & Kienzler, D. (1999). Towards an emancipatory pedagogy in service courses and user departments. *Technical Communication Quarterly, 8*(3), 269–283.

Dorland, M., Charland, M., & Angus, I. (2004). Law, rhetoric and irony in the formation of Canadian civil culture. *Canadian Journal of Communication, 29*(1), 86–89.

Finnegan, C. A., & Jiyeon, K. (2004). "Sighting" the public: Iconoclasm and public sphere theory. *Quarterly Journal of Speech, 90*(4), 377–402.

Francesconi, R. (1986). The implications of Habermas's theory of legitimation for rhetorical criticism. *Communication Monographs, 53*(1), 16–35.

Gareis, E. (2010). Habermas to the rescue. *Business Communication Quarterly, 73*(2), 166–173.

Garvey, T. G. (2000). The value of opacity: A Bakhtinian analysis of Habermas's discourse ethics. *Philosophy & Rhetoric, 33*(4), 370–390.

Gunaratne, S. A. (2006). Public sphere and communicative rationality: Interrogating Habermas's eurocentrism. *Journalism & Communication Monographs, 8*(2), 93–156.

Guss, D. L. (1991). Enlightenment as process: Milton and Habermas. *PMLA, 106*(5), 1156–1169.

Haas, T. (2004). The public sphere as a sphere of publics: Rethinking Habermas's theory of the public sphere. *Journal of Communication, 54*(1), 178–184.

Habermas, J., & Hill, J. (2002). The postnational constellation: Political essays. *Canadian Journal of Communication, 27*(4), 558–561.

Habermas, J., & Russill, C. (2003). On the pragmatics of social interaction: Preliminary studies in the theory of communicative action. *Canadian Journal of Communication, 28*(1), 128–130.

Huspek, M. (1991). Taking aim on Habermas's critical theory: On the road toward a critical hermeneutics. *Communication Monographs, 58*(2), 225–233.

Halton, E. (1992). Habermas and Rorty: Between Scylla and Charybdis. *Symbolic Interaction, 15*(3), 333–358.

Hinkle, G. J. (1992). Habermas, Mead, and rationality. *Symbolic Interaction, 15*(3), 315–331.

Jacobson, T. L. (1998). Discourse ethics and the right to communicate. *International Journal for Communication Studies, 60*(5), 395–413.

Kahn, V. (1990). Habermas, Machiavelli, and the humanist critique of ideology. *PMLA, 105*(3), 464–476.

Kernstock, J., & Brexendorf, T. O. (2009). Implications of Habermas's "theory of communicative action" for corporate brand management. *Corporate Communications, 14*(4), 389–403.

Koerber, A., Arnett, E. J., & Cumbie, T. (2008). Distortion and the politics of pain relief: A Habermasian analysis of medicine in the media. *Journal of Business & Technical Communication, 22*(3), 364–391.

Leeper, R. (1996). Moral objectivity, Jürgen Habermas's discourse ethics, and public relations. *Public Relations Review, 22*(2), 133–150.

McBurney, P., & Parsons, S. (2001). Intelligent systems to support deliberative democracy in environmental regulation. *Information & Communications Technology Law, 10*(1) 79–89.

McLuskie, E. (1993). Against transformations of communication into control: The philosophical discourse of modernity by Jürgen Habermas. *Journal of Communication, 43*(1), 154–165.

Meisenbach, R. (2006). Habermas's discourse ethics and principle of universalization as a moral framework for organizational communication. *Management Communication Quarterly, 20*(1), 39–62.

Mitchell, G. R. (2003). Did Habermas cede nature to the positivists? *Philosophy & Rhetoric, 36*(1), 1–21.

Omachonu, J. O., & Healey, K. (2009). Media concentration and minority ownership: The intersection of Ellul and Habermas. *Journal of Mass Media Ethics, 24*(2/3), 90–109.

Ongstad, S. (2002). Positioning early research on writing in Norway. *Written Communication, 19*(3), 345–381.

Ornebring, H. (2003). Televising the public sphere: Forty years of current affairs debate programmes on Swedish television. *European Journal of Communication, 18*(4), 501–527.

Petric, G., Petrovcic, A., & Vehovar, V. (2011). Social uses of interpersonal communication technologies in a complex media environment. *European Journal of Communication, 26*(2), 116–132.

Pinter, A. (2004). Public sphere and history: Historians' response to Habermas on the "worth" of the past. *Journal of Communication Inquiry, 28*(3), 217–232.

Remer, G. (2008). Genres of political speech: Oratory and conversation, today and in antiquity. *Language and Communication, 28*(2), 182–196.

Roberts, P. (1996). Habermas, "philosophes", and Puritans: Rationality and exclusion in the dialectical public sphere. *Rhetoric Society Quarterly, 26*(1), 47–68.

Saccamano, N. (1991). The consolations of ambivalence: Habermas and the public sphere. *MLN, 106*(3), 685–698.

Sciulli, D. (1992). Habermas, critical theory, and the relativistic predicament. *Symbolic Interaction, 15*(3), 299–313.

Seccombe Eastland, L. (1994). Habermas, emancipation, and relationship change: An exploration of recovery processes as a model for social transformation. *Journal of Applied Communication Research, 22*(2), 162–176.

Self, C. (2010). Hegel, Habermas, and community: The public in the new media era. *International Journal of Strategic Communication, 4*(2), 78–92.

Shalin, D.N. (1992). Introduction: Habermas, pragmatism, interactionism. *Symbolic Interaction, 15* (3), 251–259.

Sikka, T. (2011). Technology, communication, and society: From Heidegger and Habermas to Feenburg. *Review of Communication, 11*(2), 93–106.

Socolow, M. (2010). A profitable public sphere: The creation of the *New York Times* op-ed page. *Journalism and Mass Communication Quarterly, 87*(2), 281–296.

Terjera, V. (1986). Community, communication, and meaning: Theories of Buchler and Habermas. *Symbolic Interaction, 9*(1), 83–104.

Thorne, C. (2001). Thumbing our nose at the public sphere: Satire, the market, and the invention of literature. *PMLA, 116*(3), 531–544.

Wahl-Jorgensen, K., & Galperin, H. (2000). Discourse ethics and the regulation of media: The case of the U.S. newspaper. *Journal of Communication Inquiry, 24*(1), 19–40.

Weigand, H., Schoop, M., de Moor, A., & Dignum, F. (2003). B2B negotiation support: The need for a communication perspective. *Group Decision & Negotiation, 12*(1), 3–56.

Williams, S. D. (2010). Interpretive discourse and other models from communication studies: Expanding the values of technical communication. *Journal of Technical Writing & Communication, 40*(4), 429–446.

Chapter 13:
Individualism as Misstep

Individualism

Allison, M., & Emmers-Sommer, T. M. (2011). Beyond individualism-collectivism and conflict style: Considering acculturation and media use. *Journal of Intercultural Communication Research, 40*(2), 135–152.

Cai, D., & Fink, E. (2002). Conflict style differences between individualists and collectivists. *Communication Monographs, 69*(1), 67–87.

Campbell, S. (2008). Perceptions of mobile phone use in public: The roles of individualism, collectivism, and focus of the setting. *Communication Reports, 21*(2), 70–81.

Cheng, M. (2000). Elia Arce's performance art: Transculturation, feminism, politicized individualism. *Text and Performance Quarterly, 20*(2), 150–181.

Crowell, T. L. (1948). Opinions on onomastic individualism. *American Speech, 23(3/4),* 265–272.

Dragan, N., & Sherblom, J. C. (2008). The influence of cultural individualism and collectivism on U.S. and post-Soviet listening styles. *Human Communication, 11*(2), 177–192.

Foth, M., & Hearn, G. (2007). Networked individualism of urban residents: Discovering the communicative ecology in inner-city apartment buildings. *Communication & Society, 10*(5), 749–772.

Fuyuan, S., & Edwards, H. H. (2005). Economic individualism, humanitarianism, and welfare reform: A value-based account of framing effects. *Journal of Communication, 55*(4), 795–809.

Gardner, W. L., Reithel, B. J., Foley, R. T., Cogliser, C. C., & Walumbwa, F. O. (2009). Attraction to organizational culture profiles: Effects of realistic recruitment and vertical and horizontal individualism-collectivism. *Management Communication Quarterly, 22*(3), 437–472.

Gudykunst, W. B., Yoon, Y. C., & Nishida, T. (1987). The influence of individualism collectivism on perceptions of communication in ingroup and outgroup relationships. *Communication Monographs, 54*(3), 295–306.

Hammerback, J. C. (1972). Barry Goldwater's rhetoric of rugged individualism. *Quarterly Journal of Speech, 58*(2), 175–183.

Heuterman, T. H. (1976). Assessing the "press on wheels" individualism in frontier journalism. *Journalism Quarterly, 53*(3), 423–428.

Hindman, E. B. (2004). The chickens have come home to roost: Individualism, collectivism, and conflict in commercial speech doctrine. *Communication Law & Policy, 9*(2), 237–271.

Horowitz, A. (2009). Individualism and narrow content. *Linguistic & Philosophical Investigations, 8,* 139–153.

Kim, M. S., Hunter, J. E., Miyahara, A., Horvath, A. M., Bresnahan, M., & Yoon, H. J. (1996). Individual- vs. culture-level dimensions of individualism and collectivism: Effects on preferred conversational styles. *Communication Monographs, 63*(1), 29–49.

Lee, W., & Chio, S. M. (2005). The role of horizontal and vertical individualism and collectivism in online consumers' responses toward persuasive communication on the web. *Journal of Computer-Mediated Communication, 11*(1), 317–336.

Lucaites, J. L. (1997). Visualizing "the people": Individualism vs. collectivism in *Let Us Now Praise Famous Men. Quarterly Journal of Speech, 83*(3), 269–288.

Mortenson, S. T. (2002). Sex, communication values, and cultural values: Individualism-collectivism as a mediator of sex differences in communication values in two cultures. *Communication Reports, 15*(1), 57–70.

Nelson, N. (1933). Individualism as a criterion of the Renaissance. *The Journal of English & Germanic Philology, 32*(3), 316–334.

Peters, J. D. (1989). John Locke, the individual, and the origin of communication. *Quarterly Journal of Speech, 75*(4), 387–399.

Pyles, T. (1947). Onomastic individualism in Oklahoma. *American Speech, 22*(4), 257–264.

Sefcovic, E. M. I. (2002). Cultural memory and the cultural legacy of individualism and community in two classic films about labor unions. *Critical Studies in Media Communication, 19* (3), 329–351.

Soutar, L. (2010). British female converts to Islam: Choosing Islam as a rejection of individualism. *Language & Intercultural Communication, 10*(1), 3–16.

Thatcher, M. S. (2006). Bakhtin applied: Employing dialogism to analyze the interplay of the ideologies of individualism and community within the discourse of Alcoholics Anonymous. *Journal of Applied Communication Research, 34*(4), 349–367.

Thayer, F. (1979). Methodological individualism, values, ethics. *Dialogue, 2*(2), 12–13.

Thompson, J. M. (1995). Incarcerated souls: Women as individuals in Margaret Fuller's *Woman in the Nineteenth Century. Communication Quarterly, 43*(1), 53–63.

Zhang, Y. (2009). Individualism or collectivism? Cultural orientations in Chinese TV commercials and analysis of some moderating factors. *Journalism & Mass Communication Quarterly, 86*(3), 630–653.

Tocqueville

Fried, A. (2006). The personalization of collective memory: The Smithsonian's September 11 exhibit. *Political Communication, 23*(4), 387–405.

Gastil, J., Black, L. W., Deess, E. P., & Leighter, J. (2008). From group member to democratic citizen: How deliberating with fellow jurors reshapes civic attitudes. *Human Communication Research, 34*(1), 137–169.

Lupton, J. R. (2011). Re-vamp: A response. PMLA: *Publications of the Modern Language Association of America, 126*(2), 467–471.

Whedbee, K. (1998). Authority, freedom and liberal judgment: The presumptions and presumptuousness of Whately, Mill, and Tocqueville. *The Quarterly Journal of Speech, 84* (2), 171–189.

Winick, C., & Winich, M. P. (1974). Courtroom drama on television. *Journal of Communication, 24*(4), 67–73.

Chapter 14
Sensus Communis: The Community Matters

Common Sense

Agnew, L. (2000). The "perplexity" of George Campbell's rhetoric: The epistemic function of common sense. *Rhetorica: A Journal of the History of Rhetoric, 18*(1), 79–101.

Bineha,, J. L. (1991). Against common sense: Avoiding Cartesian anxiety. *Philosophy & Rhetoric, 24*(2), 159–163.

Bormann, D. R. (1985). Some "common sense" about Campbell, Hume, and Reid: The extrinsic evidence. *Quarterly Journal of Speech, 71*(4), 395–421.

Brock, I. W. (1936). The magic of common sense. *Modern Language Journal, 20*(4), 209–211.

Campbell, J. A. (1985). Insight and understanding: The "common sense" rhetoric of Bernard Lonergan. *Quarterly Journal of Speech, 71*(4), 476–488.

Chappell, V. A. (1995). Expert testimony, "regular people," and public values: Arguing common sense at a death penalty trial. *Rhetoric Review, 13*(2), 391–408.

Claussen, D. (2008). The age of American unreason/common sense: Intelligence as presented on popular television. *Journalism and Mass Communication Educator, 63*(1), 71–74.

Daniel, S. H. (1985). The philosophy of ingenuity: Vico on proto-philosophy. *Philosophy & Rhetoric, 18*(4), 236–243.

Douglas, S. (1998). Sir James Wilson and his common-sense approach to the Scots language. *Scottish Language, 17*, 16–29.

Glasser, T. L., & Etterna, J. S. (1989). Common sense and education of young journalists. *Journalism Educator, 44*(2), 18–75.

Grishakova, M. (2009). Beyond the frame: Cognitive science, common sense and fiction. *Narrative, 17*(2), 188–199.

Heorl, K. (2008). Cinematic jujitsu: Resisting white hegemony through the American dream in Spike Lee's *Malcolm X*. *Communication Studies, 59*(4), 355–370.

Hoffman, D. C. (2006). Paine and prejudice: Rhetorical leadership through perceptual framing in *Common Sense*. *Rhetoric & Public Affairs, 9*(3), 373–410.

Hogan, J. M., & Williams, G. (2000). Republican charisma and the American Revolution: The textual persona of Thomas Paine's *Common Sense*. *The Quarterly Journal of Speech, 86*(1), 1–18.

Ivie, R. L. (1984). Speaking "common sense" about the Soviet threat: Reagan's rhetorical stance. *Journal of Speech Communication, 48*(1), 39–50.

Lewis, C. (1992). Making sense of common sense: A framework for tracking hegemony. *Critical Studies in Mass Communication, 9*(3), 277–292.

Lyne, J. (2005). Science controversy, common sense, and the third culture. *Argumentation & Advocacy, 42*(1), 38–42.

Macdonald, C. (2002). Theories of mind and "The Commonsense View." *Mind & Language, 17*(5), 467–488.

Mahaffey, J. D. (2010). Converting Tories to Whigs: Religion and imagined authorship in Thomas Paine's *Common Sense*. *Southern Communication Journal, 75*(5), 488–504.

Malone, J. (1997). Technology vs. bureaucracy: Common-sense government in the post-industrial age. *Vital Speeches of the Day, 63*(16), 492–494.

McGrane, L. (2005). Fielding's fallen oracles: Print culture and the elusiveness of common sense. *Modern Language Quarterly, 66*(2), 173–196.

Miller, S., & Jenson, A. (2009). Language choice and management in Danish multinational companies: The role of common sense. *Sociolinguistica, 23*, 86–103.

Morrow, T. (1999). Common-sense deliberative practice: John Witherspoon, James Madison, and the U.S. Constitution. *Rhetoric Society Quarterly, 29*(1), 25–47.

Praetorius, P. (2002). Technical communicators as purveyors of common sense. *Journal of Technical Writing & Communication, 32*(4), 337–351.

Rees, R. (1994). Common sense in Catullus 64. *The American Journal of Philology, 115*(1), 75–88.

Riecken, D. (2001). A commonsense opportunity for computing. *Communications of the ACM, 44*(3), 132–133.

Severtson, D., Baumann, L., & Brown, R. (2008). Applying the common-sense model to measure representations of arsenic-contaminated well water. *Journal of Health Communication, 13*(6), 538–554.

Siciliano, E. A. (1960). Common sense in the oral approach. *Modern Language Journal, 44*(1), 3–4.

Sullivan, P. A. (1993). Signification and African-American rhetoric: A case study of Jesse Jackson's *Common Ground and Common Sense* speech. *Communication Quarterly, 41*(1), 1–15.

Thompson, W. N. (1975). Aristotle as a predecessor to Reid's "common sense." *Speech Monographs, 42*(3), 209–220.

Van den Braden, R. (2009). From common sense to common knowledge. And vice versa. *Literary & Linguistic Computing, 24*(2), 235–241.

Wallace, M., & Wray A. (2002). The fall and rise of linguists in education policy making: From *Common Sense* to common ground. *Language Policy, 1*(1), 75–98.

Wikelund, P. R. (1962). A "common sense" for English. *College Composition & Communication, 13*(1), 47–51.

Williams, R. B. (1933). Observations on the use of "horse sense" in language teaching. *Modern Language Journal, 17*(7), 506–511.

Wilson, W. (1942). Breath control: A common-sense summary. *Quarterly Journal of Speech, 28*(3), 338–343.

Yarmey, A. D. (2004). Common-sense beliefs, recognition and the identification of familiar and unfamiliar speakers from verbal and non-linguistic vocalizations. *Speech, Language, & the Law, 11*(2), 267–277.

Vico

Abbott, D. P. (1985). Vico in the tradition of rhetoric. *Rhetorica: A Journal of the History of Rhetoric, 3*(4), 297–299.

Abbott, D. P. (1988). The doctrine of double form: Benedetto Croce on rhetoric and poetics. *Philosophy & Rhetoric, 21*(1), 1–18.

Beasley Von Burg, A. (2010). Caught between history and imagination: Vico's ingenium for a rhetorical renovation of citizenship. *Philosophy & Rhetoric, 43*(1), 26–53.

Bevilacqua, V. M. (1972). Vico, rhetorical humanism, and the study methods of our time. *Quarterly Journal of Speech, 58*(1), 70–83.

Bevilacqua, V. M. (1974). Vico, "process," and the nature of rhetorical investigation: An epistemological perspective. *Philosophy & Rhetoric, 7*(3), 166–174.

Bevilacqua, V. M. (1983). Campbell, Vico, and the rhetorical science of human nature. *Rhetoric Society Quarterly, 13*(1), 5–11.

Black, D. (1994). Rhetoric and the narration of conscience. *Philosophy & Rhetoric, 27*(4), 359–373.

Bryan, F. J. (1986). Vico on metaphor: Implications for rhetorical criticism. *Philosophy & Rhetoric, 19*(4), 255–265.

Clark, R. T. Jr. (1947). Herder, Cesarotti, and Vico. *Studies in Philology, 44*(4), 645–671.

Danesi, M., & Hatch, G. (1995). Vico, metaphor, and the origin of language. *Discourse & Society, 6*(4), 538–539.

Daniel, S. H. (1985). The philosophy of ingenuity: Vico on proto-philosophy. *Philosophy & Rhetoric, 18*(4), 236–243.

Daniel, S. H. (1988). The narrative character of myth and philosophy in Vico. *International Studies in Philosophy, 20*, 1–9.

Fisch, M. H. (1943). The Coleridges, Dr. Prati, and Vico. *Modern Philology, 41*(2), 111–122.

Gensini, S. (2004). Metaphor according to Giambattista Vico: An exemplary case of iconic theory. *Logos and Language: Journal of General Linguistics and Language Theory, 5*(1), 35–38.

Golden, J. L. (1970). The influence of rhetoric on the social science theories of Giambattista Vico and David Hume. *Western Speech, 34*(3), 170–180.

Grant, A. J. (2000). Vico and Bultmann on myth: The problem with demythologizing. *RSQ: Rhetoric Society Quarterly, 30*(4), 49–82.

Gross, D. M. (1996). Metaphor and definition in Vico's *New Science. Rhetorica: A Journal of the History of Rhetoric, 14*(4), 359–381.

Jung, H. Y. (1982). Vico's rhetoric: A note on Verene's Vico's *Science of Imagination. Philosophy & Rhetoric, 15*(3), 187–202.

Land, S. (1976). The account of language in Vico's *Scienze Nuova*: A critical analysis. *Philological Quarterly, 55*(3), 354–372.

Levin, S. R. (1987). Catachresis: Vico and Joyce. *Philosophy & Rhetoric, 20*(2), 94–105.

Lucente, G. L. (1982). Vico's notion of "divine providence" and the limits of human knowledge, freedom, and will. *MLN, 97*(1), 183–191.

Moevs, C. (2003). The new map of the world: The poetic philosophy of Giambattista Vico. *MLN, 118*(1), 264–267.

Morrison, J. C. (1979). How to interpret the idea of divine providence in Vico's *New Science. Philosophy & Rhetoric, 12*(4), 256–261.

Roush, S. (2003). The Donna me prega of the Seicento? Reassessing Vico's unautobiographical Affetti di un disperato. *MLN, 118*(1), 147–167.

Said, E. W. (1976). Vico on the discipline of bodies and texts. *MLN, 91*(5), 817–826.

Samuels, M. (1987). Is technical communication "literature"? Current writing scholarship and Vico's cycles of knowledge. *Iowa State Journal of Business and Technical Communication, 1*(1), 48–67.

Schaeffer, J. D. (1981). Vico's rhetorical model of the mind: Sensus communis in the de nostril temporis studiorum ratione. *Philosophy & Rhetoric, 14*(3), 152–167.

Schaeffer, J. D. (1996). Vico and Kenneth Burke. *RSQ: Rhetoric Society Quarterly, 26*(2), 7–17.

Schaeffer, J. D. (1997). From natural religion to natural law in Vico: Rhetoric, poetic, and Vico's imaginative universals. *Rhetorica: A Journal of the History of Rhetoric, 15*(1), 41–51.

Schefer, J. (1977). Historical matter and legal matter: Vico. *Communications, 26*, 168–184.

Struever, N. (1976). Vico and Herder: Two studies in the history of ideas. *MLN, 91*(6), 1625–1627.

Struever, N. (1999). Vico's axioms: The geometry of the human world. *Rhetorica: A Journal of the History of Rhetoric, 17*(2), 222–227.

Veit, W. (1984). The potency of imagery—the impotence of rational language: Ernesto Grassi's contribution to modern epistemology. *Philosophy & Rhetoric, 17*(4), 221–239.

Verdicchio, M. (1986). The rhetoric of epistemology in Vico's *New Science. Philosophy & Rhetoric, 15*(3), 203–206.

Vickers, B. (1988). The atrophy of modern rhetoric, Vico to De Man. *Rhetorica: A Journal of the History of Rhetoric, 6*(1), 21–56.

Von Burg, A. B. (2010). Caught between history and imagination: Vico's Ingenium for a rhetorical renovation of citizenship. *Philosophy & Rhetoric, 43*(1), 26–53.

Thomas Paine

Clark, T. (1978). A note on Tom Paine's "vulgar style." *Communication Quarterly, 26*(2), 31–34.

Hoffman, D. C. (2006). Paine and prejudice: Rhetorical leadership through perceptual framing in *Common Sense. Rhetoric & Public Affairs, 9*(3), 373–410.

Hogan, J. M., & Williams, G. (2000). Republican charisma and the American Revolution: The textual persona of Thomas Paine's *Common Sense. The Quarterly Journal of Speech, 86*(1), 1–18.

Kelsall, M. (1999). Crisis in representation: Thomas Paine, Mary Wollestonecraft, Helen Maria Williams, and the rewriting of the French Revolution. *Modern Language Review, 94*, 794–795.

Kennerly, M. (2010). Getting carried away: How rhetorical transport gets judgment going. *Rhetoric Society Quarterly, 40*(3), 269–291.

Lamar, A. (1998). Should Tom Paine have filed with the FEC?: The loss of common sense in campaign finance reform. *Vital Speeches of the Day, 64*(12), 381–384.

Mahaffey, J. D. (2010). Converting Tories to Whigs: Religion and imagined authorship in Thomas Paine's *Common Sense. Southern Communication Journal, 75*(5), 488–504.

Samet, E. D. (2003). Spectacular history and the politics of theater: Sympathetic arts in the shadow of the Bastille. *PMLA, 118*(5), 1305–1319.

Touba, M. (1994). Tom Paine's plan for revolutionizing America: Diplomacy, politics, and the evolution of a newspaper rumor. *Journal History, 20*(3/4), 116–124.

Chapter 15
Story-Centered Meaning: Beyond Information

Schrag

Arnett, R. C. (2011). Civic rhetoric—Meeting the communal interplay of the provincial and the cosmopolitan: Barack Obama's Notre Dame speech, May 17, 2009. *Rhetoric & Public Affairs, 14*(4), 631–671.

Schrag, C. O. (1985). Rhetoric resituated at the end of philosophy. *Quarterly Journal of Speech, 71*(2), 164–174.

Sweet, D. R. (2005). More than goth: The rhetorical reclamation of the subcultural self. *Popular Communication, 3*(4), 239–264.

Vicaro, M. P. (2011). A liberal use of "torture": Pain, personhood, and precedent in the U.S. federal definition of torture. *Rhetoric & Public Affairs, 14*(3), 401–426.

Benhabib

Asen, R. (2002). Imagining in the public sphere. *Philosophy & Rhetoric, 34*(4), 345–367.

Welsh, S. (2002). Deliberative democracy and the rhetorical production of political culture. *Rhetoric & Public Affairs, 5*(4), 679–707.

REFERENCES

Adams, J. T. (1931). *The epic of America*. Boston, MA: Little, Brown & Company.

Adkins, N. F. (Ed.). (1953). Introduction. In *"Common Sense" and other political writings* (pp. xi–xlix). New York: Bobbs-Merrill.

"Albert Camus." (2010). In *Encyclopaedia Britannica Online*. Retrieved from http://www.britannica.com/EBchecked/topic/91464/Albert-Camus

Allen, B. (2010). *Difference matters: Communicating social identity*. Long Grove, IL: Waveland Press.

Anderson, R., & Cissna, K. N. (1997). *The Martin Buber–Carl Rogers dialogue: A new transcript with commentary*. Albany, NY: State University of New York Press.

Anton, C. (2010). *Sources of significance: Worldly rejuvenation and neo-stoic heroism*. West Lafayette, IN: Purdue University Press.

Apel, K.-O. (1981). *Charles S. Peirce: From pragmatism to pragmaticism* (R. Bernstein, Trans.). Amherst, MA: University of Massachusetts Press.

Arendt, H. (1958). *The human condition*. Chicago, IL: University of Chicago Press.

Arendt, H. (1992). *Lectures on Kant's political philosophy* (R. Beiner, Ed.). Chicago, IL: University of Chicago Press.

Arendt, H. (1978). *The life of the mind* (M. McCarthy, Ed.). San Diego, CA: Harcourt, Brace & Company.

Aristotle. (1998). *The Nicomachean ethics* (W. D. Ross, Trans., J. L. Ackrill, & J. O. Urmson, Eds.). Oxford, U.K.: Oxford University Press.

Aristotle. (2007). *On rhetoric: A theory of civic discourse* (2nd ed., G. Kennedy, Trans.). New York: Oxford University Press.

"Aristotle." (2011). In *Encyclopaedia Britannica Online*. Retrieved from http://www.britannica.com/EBchecked/topic/34560/Aristotle

Arneson, P. (Ed.). (2007). *Perspectives on philosophy of communication*. West Lafayette, IN: Purdue University Press.

Arnett, R. C. (1994). Existential homelessness: A contemporary case for dialogue. In R. Anderson, K. Cissna, & R. C. Arnett (Eds.), *The reach of dialogue: Confirmation, voice, and community* (pp. 229–245). Cresskill, NJ: Hampton Press.

Arnett, R. C. (2007). Hannah Arendt: Dialectical communicative labor. In P. Arneson, (Ed.), *Perspectives on philosophy of communication* (pp. 67–88). West Lafayette, IN: Purdue University Press.

Arnett, R. C. (2008). Rhetoric and ethics. In W. Donsbach (Ed.), *International encyclopedia of communication* (pp. 4242–4246). Hoboken, NJ: Wiley-Blackwell/International Communication Association.

Arnett, R. C. (2009). Emmanuel Levinas: Priority of the other. In C. G. Christians & J. C. Merrill (Eds.), *Ethical communication: Moral stances in human dialogue* (pp. 200–206). Columbia, MO: University of Missouri Press.

Arnett, R. C. (2010). Defining philosophy of communication: Difference and identity. *Qualitative Research Reports in Communication*, 11(1), 57–62.

Arnett, R. C., Fritz, J. M. H, & Bell, L. M. (2009). *Communication ethics literacy: Dialogue and difference*. Thousand Oaks, CA: Sage.

Arnett, R. C., Fritz, J. M. H., & Holba, A. M. (2007). The rhetorical turn to otherness: Otherwise than humanism. *Cosmos and History: The Journal of Natural and Social Philosophy*, 3(1), 115–133.

Audi, R. (Ed.). (1995/2001). *Cambridge dictionary of philosophy*. New York: Cambridge University Press.

Barrett, W. (1958). *Irrational man: A study in existential philosophy.* Garden City, NY: Doubleday Anchor.

Baseheart, M. C. (1997). *Person in the world: Introduction to the philosophy of Edith Stein.* Dordecht, Netherlands: Kluwer Academic Publishers.

Bellah, R. N. (1992). *The broken covenant: American civil religion in time of trial* (2nd ed.). Chicago, IL: University of Chicago Press.

Bellah, R. N., Madsen, R., Sullivan, W. M., Swidler, A., & Tipton, S. M. (1985). *Habits of the heart: Individualism and commitment in American life.* Berkeley, CA: University of California Press.

Benhabib, S. (1992). *Situating the self: Gender, community and postmodernism in contemporary ethics.* New York: Routledge.

Benhabib, S. (2003). *The reluctant modernism of Hannah Arendt* (2nd Ed.). Lanham, MD: Rowman & Littlefield.

Bergson, H. (1911). *Creative evolution* (A. Mitchell, Trans.). New York: Henry Holt & Company.

Bernstein, R. J. (1983). *Beyond objectivism and relativism: Science, hermeneutics, and praxis.* Philadelphia, PA: University of Pennsylvania Press.

Bertalanffy, L. (1968). *General systems theory: Foundations, development, applications.* New York: George Braziller.

Bien, P. (1972). *Nikos Kazantzakis.* New York: Columbia University Press.

Bradley, P. (1963). Introduction. In A. de Tocqueville, *Democracy in America* (pp. viii–c). New York: Alfred A Knopf.

Brady, A., & Schirato, T. (2010). *Understanding Judith Butler.* Thousand Oaks, CA: Sage

Brogan, H. (2008). *Alexis de Tocqueville: A life.* New Haven, CT: Yale University Press.

Brownstein, O. L. (1965). Plato's Phaedrus: Dialectic as the genuine art of speaking. *Quarterly Journal of Speech, 51*(4), 392–398.

Buber, M. (1958). *Hasidism and modern man* (M. Friedman, Ed. & Trans.). New York: Horizon Press.

Buber, M. (1965/1966). *The knowledge of man: A philosophy of the interhuman.* New York: Harper & Row.

Buber, M. (1972). *Between man and man.* New York: Macmillan.

Butler, J. (1987). *Subjects of desire: Hegelian reflections in twentieth-century France.* New York: Columbia University Press.

Butler, J. (2005). *Giving an account of oneself.* New York: Fordham University Press.

Butler, J. (2006). *Gender trouble: Feminism and the subversion of identity.* New York: Routledge.

Camus, A. (1947/1948). *The plague* (S. Gilbert, Trans.). New York: Alfred Knopf.

Carnap, R. (1934). The rejection of metaphysics. *Psyche: An Annual of General and Linguistic Philosophy. 14,* 100–111.

Cheney, G. (2008). Encountering the ethics of engaged scholarship. *Journal of Applied Communication Research, 36*(3), 281–288.

Cheney, G., Wilhelmsson, M., & Zorn, T. E. Jr. (2002). 10 strategies for engaged scholarship. *Management Communication Quarterly, 16*(1), 92–100.

Cohen, R. A. (1998). Forward. In E. Levinas, *Otherwise than being or beyond essence* (A. Lingis, Trans.) (pp. xi–xvi). Pittsburgh, PA: Duquesne University Press.

Cook, M. A., & Holba, A. M. (Eds.). (2008). *Philosophies of communication: Implications for everyday experience.* New York: Peter Lang.

Cooren, F. (2010). *Action and agency in dialogue: Passion, incarnation and ventriloquism.* Amsterdam, Netherlands: John Benjamins.

Cronen, V. E., & Pearce, W. B. (1980). *Communication, action, and meaning: The creation of social realities.* New York: Praeger.

D'Andrea, T. D. (2006). *Tradition, rationality, and virtue: The thought of Alasdair MacIntyre.* Burlington, VT: Ashgate.

Danto, A. C. (1997). *After the end of art: Contemporary art and the pale of history.* Princeton, NJ: Princeton University Press.

Darwin, C. (1859). *Origin of species.* London: John Murray.

Davies, B. (2008). *Judith Butler in conversation: Analyzing the texts and talk of everyday life.* New York: Columbia University Press.

Deontological Ethics. (2011). In *Encyclopaedia Britannica Online.* Retrieved from http://plato.stanford.edu/entries/ethics-deontological/

Descartes, R. (1637/2008). *Discourse on the method* (J. Veitch, Trans.). New York: Cosimo.

Dijksterhuis, E. J. (1983). *Archimedes* (C. Dikshoorn, Trans.). Princeton, NJ: Princeton University Press.

Dostoevsky, F. M. (1862/1965). *Memoirs from the house of the dead* (J. Coulson, Trans.). London, U.K.: Oxford University Press.

Dostoevsky, F. M. (1864/1956). Notes from underground. In W. Kaufmann (Ed.)., *Existentialism from Dostoevsky to Sartre* (pp. 52–82). Cleveland, OH: Meridian.

Downs, E. (2010). *Eighteenth-century video games: Using the Hegelian dialectic to explain how individuals identify with avatars during game play.* Conference paper presented at the International Communication Association.

Dresner, E. (2006). Davidson's philosophy of communication. *Communication Theory, 16,* 155–172.

Dworkin, R. (1986). *Law's empire.* Cambridge, MA: Harvard University Press.

Eicher-Catt, D., & Catt, I. E. (Eds.). (2010). *Communicology: The new science of embodied discourse.* Cranbury, NJ: Rosemont.

"Ferdinand Tönnies." (2011). In *Encyclopedia Britannica Online.* Retrieved from http://www.britannica.com/EBchecked/topic/599337/Ferdinand-Tonnies

Fisch, M. H., & Bergin, T. G. (1963). *The autobiography of Giambattista Vico.* Ithaca, NY: Cornell University Press.

Frankl, V. (1959/1992). *Man's search for meaning: An introduction to logotherapy* (I. Lasch, Trans.). Boston, MA: Beacon Press.

"Franz Brentano." (2011). In *Encyclopaedia Britannica Online.* Retrieved from http://www.britannica.com/EBchecked/topic/78835/Franz-Brentano

Friedman, M. (1981). *Martin Buber's life and work.* New York: E. P. Dutton.

"Fulcrum." (n.d.). In *Merriam-Webster's online dictionary.* Retrieved from http://www.merriam-webster.com/dictionary/fulcrum

Gadamer, H.-G. (1960/1980). *Dialogue and dialectic: Eight hermeneutical studies on Plato* (P. C. Smith, Trans.). New Haven, CT: Yale University Press.

Gadamer, H.-G. (1960/1986). *Truth and method.* New York: Crossroads.

Gálvez, J. P. (Ed.). (2010). *Philosophical anthropology: Wittgenstein's perspective.* Piscataway, NJ: Transaction.

Gehrke, P. J. (2009). *The ethics and politics of speech: Communication and rhetoric in the twentieth century.* Carbondale, IL: Southern Illinois University Press.

Gladwell, M. (2008). *Outliers: The story of success.* New York: Little, Brown & Company.

"Greco-Turkish Wars." (2011). In *Encyclopaedia Britannica Online.* Retrieved from http://www.britannica.com/EBchecked/topic/244151/Greco-Turkish-wars

Griffin, J. (1986). Introduction. In J. Boardman, J. Griffin, & O. Murray (Eds.), *The Oxford history of the classical world.* New York: Oxford University Press.

Gross, B. (1970). *Analytic philosophy: An historical introduction.* New York: Bobbs- Merrill.

Habermas, J. (1977). A review of Gadamer's *Truth and Method*. In F. R. Dallmayr & T. A. McCarthy (Eds.), *Understanding and social inquiry* (pp. 335–363). Notre Dame, IN: Notre Dame University Press.

Habermas, J. (1980). The hermeneutic claim to universality. In J. Bleicher (Ed.), *Contemporary hermeneutics: Method, philosophy, and critique* (pp. 181–212). London, U.K.: Routledge & Kegan Paul.

Habermas, J. (1987). *Knowledge and human interests*. Boston, MA: Polity Press.

Hance, A. (1997). The hermeneutic significance of sensus communis. *International Philosophical Quarterly*, 37(2), 133–149.

Hegel, G. W. F. (1807/1979). *The phenomenology of spirit*. (A. V. Miller, Trans.). New York: Oxford University Press.

Hegel, G. W. F.. (1811–1816/1969). *The science of logic*. London, U.K.: George Allen & Unwin.

Hegel, G. W. F. (1816/1991). *The encyclopaedia of logic: Part one of the encyclopaedia of the philosophical sciences with the Zusatze* (T. F. Geraets, W. A. Suchting, & H. S. Harris, Trans.). New York: Hackett.

Hegel, G. W. F. (1820). *Elements of the philosophy of right*. (H. B. Nisbet, Trans.) (Allen W. Wood, ed.) New York: Cambridge University Press.

Hegel, G. W. F. (1825–1826/1956). *The philosophy of history*. New York: Dover.

Heidegger, M. (1949/1956). The way back into the ground of metaphysics. In W. Kaufmann (Ed.)., *Existentialism from Dostoevsky to Sartre* (pp. 206–221). Cleveland, OH: Meridian.

Heidegger, M. (1962). *Being and time* (J. Macquarrie & E. Robinson, Trans.). San Francisco, CA: HarperCollins.

Hendricks, V. F. (2007). *Mainstream and formal epistemology*. New York: Cambridge University Press.

"Henry Sidgwick." (2011). In *Encyclopaedia Britannica Online*. Retrieved from http://www.britannica.com/EBchecked/topic/543074/Henry-Sidgwick

Herrick, J. A. (2001). *The history and theory of rhetoric: An introduction*. Needham Heights, MA: Allyn & Bacon.

Honan, W. H. (1992, September 10). William Barrett, 78, a professor and interpreter of existentialism. *New York Times*. Retrieved from http://www.nytimes.com/1992/09/10/arts/william-barrett-78-a-professor-and-interpreter-of-existentialism.html

Hornblower, S., & Spawforth, T. (2000). *Who's who in the classical world*. New York: Oxford University Press.

Husserl, E. (1931/1991). *Cartesian meditations: An introduction to phenomenology*. New York: Springer.

Husserl, E.. (1970). *The crisis of European sciences and transcendental phenomenology: An introduction to phenomenological philosophy* (D. Carr, Trans.). Evanston, IL: Northwestern University Press.

Husserl, E.. (1973). *Experience and judgment* (L. Landgrebe, Ed.; J. S. Churchill & K. Ameriks, Trans.). Evanston, IL: Northwestern University Press.

Hyde, M. J. (1982). *Communication philosophy and the technological age*. Tuscaloosa, AL: University of Alabama Press.

Hyde, M. J. (2001). *The call of conscience: Heidegger and Levinas, rhetoric and the euthanasia debate*. Columbia, SC: University of South Carolina Press

Hyde, M. J. (2004). *The ethos of rhetoric*. Columbia, SC: University of South Carolina Press.

Hyde, M. J. (2006). *The life-giving gift of acknowledgment*. West Lafayette, IN: Purdue University Press.

Hyde, M. J. (2010). *Perfection: Coming to terms with being human*. Waco, TX: Baylor University Press.

James, D. (2007). *Hegel: A guide for the perplexed*. New York: Continuum.

Janis, I. L. (1982). *Groupthink: Psychological studies of policy decisions and fiascos*. Boston, MA: Wadsworth.

Janssens, E., & Johnstone, H. W. J. (1968). The concept of dialectic in the ancient world. *Philosophy & Rhetoric* 1(3), 174–181.

Jaspers, K. (1956). Existenzphilosophie. In W. Kaufmann (Ed.), *Existentialism from Dostoevsky to Sartre* (pp. 131–205). Cleveland, OH: Meridian.

Joachim, H. H. (1997). *Descartes's rules for the direction of the mind*. Chicago, IL: St. Augustine Press.

Johnstone, C. L. (2009). *Listening to the logos: Speech and the coming of wisdom in Ancient Greece*. Columbia, SC: University of South Carolina Press.

Kant, I. (1781/1965). *Critique of pure reason* (P. Guyer & A. W. Wood, Eds.). New York: Cambridge University Press.

Kant, I. (1785/1981). *Grounding for the metaphysics of morals: On a supposed right to lie because of philanthropic concerns* (J. W. Ellington, Trans.). Indianapolis, IN: Hackett.

Kant, I. (1788/1998). *Critique of practical reason*. Milwaukee, WI: Marquette University Press.

Kant, I. (1790/1951). *Critique of judgment* (J. H. Bernard, Trans.). New York: Hafner Press.

Kant, I. (1800/2006). *Anthropology from a pragmatic point of view* (R. B. Louden, Ed.). New York: Cambridge University Press.

Kant, I. (1959). *Foundations of the metaphysics of morals, and what is enlightenment?* (L. W. Beck, Trans.). New York: Macmillan.

Kaufmann, W. (Ed.). (1956). *Existentialism from Dostoevsky to Sartre*. Cleveland, OH: Meridian.

Kazantzakis, N. (1946/1952). *Zorba the Greek* (C. Wildman, Trans.). New York: Ballantine.

Kazantzakis, N. (1960). *The saviors of God: Spiritual exercises* (K. Friar, Trans.). New York: Simon & Schuster.

Keane, J. (2003). *Tom Paine: A political life*. New York: Grove Press.

Kierkegaard, S. (1956). On himself. In W. Kaufmann (Ed.), *Existentialism from Dostoevsky to Sartre* (pp. 83–99). Cleveland, OH: Meridian.

Kristeller, P. O. (1979). *Renaissance thought and its sources*. New York: Columbia University Press.

Lorenz Krüger (1984). Why do we study the history of philosophy? In Rorty, R., Schneewind, J. B., & Skinner, Q. (eds.), *Philosophy in history: Essays in the historiography of philosophy*. New York: Cambridge University Press.

Kuehn, M. (2001). *Kant: A biography*. New York: Cambridge University Press.

Kuklick, B. (1984). Seven thinkers and how they grew: Descartes, Spinoza, Leibniz; Locke, Berkeley, Hume; Kant. In R. Rorty, L. B. Schneewind, & Q. Skinner (Eds.), *Philosophy in history* (pp. 125–139). New York: Cambridge University Press.

Langsdorf, L. (2002). In defense of poiesis: The performance of self in communicative praxis. In M. B. Matustík & W. L. McBride (Eds.), *Calvin O. Schrag and the task of philosophy after postmodernity*. Evanston, IL: Northwestern University Press.

Langsdorf, L., & Smith, A. R. (1995). *Recovering pragmatism's voice: The classical tradition, Rorty, and the philosophy of communication*. Albany, NY: State University of New York Press.

Lanigan, R. L. (1972). *Speaking and semiology: Maurice Merleau-Ponty's phenomenological theory of existential communication*. The Hague, Netherlands: Mouton.

Lanigan, R. L. (1988). *Phenomenology of communication: Merleau-Ponty's thematics in communicology and semiology*. Pittsburgh, PA: Duquesne University Press.

Lanigan, R. L. (1992). *The human science of communicology: A phenomenology of discourse in Foucault and Merleau-Ponty*. Pittsburgh, PA: Duquesne University Press.

Lea, J. F. (1979). *Kazantzakis: The politics of salvation*. Tuscaloosa, AL: University of Alabama Press.

"Léon Blum." (2011). *In Encyclopaedia Britannica Online*. Retrieved from http://www.britannica.com/EBchecked/topic/70542/Leon-Blum

Levinas, E. (1997). *Difficult freedom: Essays on Judaism* (S. Hand, Trans.). Baltimore, MD: Johns Hopkins University Press.

Levinas, E. (1998). *Otherwise than being or beyond essence* (A. Lingis, Trans.). Pittsburgh, P A : Duquesne University Press.

Lipari, L. (2004). Listening for the other: Ethical implications of the Buber-Levinas encounter. *Communication Theory, 14*(2), 122–141.

Lyotard, J. F. (1984). *The postmodern condition: A report on knowledge*. Minneapolis, MN: University of Minnesota Press.

MacIntyre, A. (1966). *A short history of ethics*. New York: Collier.

MacIntyre, A. (1981). *After virtue: A study in moral theory*. Notre Dame, IN: University of Notre Dame Press.

MacIntyre, A. (2006). *Edith Stein: A philosophical prologue 1913–1922*. Lanham, MD: Rowman & Littlefield.

MacKendrick, K. G. (2008). *Discourse, desire, and fantasy in Jürgen Habermas' critical theory*. New York: Routledge.

Malachowski, A. (2002). *Richard Rorty*. Princeton, NJ: Princeton University Press.

Malpas, J. (2009). Hans-Georg Gadamer. In E. N. Zalta (Ed.), *The Stanford encyclopedia of philosophy* (Summer 2009 ed.). Retrieved from http://plato.stanford.edu/archives/sum2009/entries/gadamer/

Mann, B. (2006). *Women's liberation and the sublime: Feminism, postmodernism, environment*. New York: Oxford University Press.

Marlowe, C. (1604/1905). *The tragical history of Doctor Faustus* (I. Gollancz, Ed.). London, U.K.: J. M. Dent & Company.

Marshall, J. (2005). *Humanity, freedom and feminism*. Burlington, VT: Ashgate.

Montague, F. C. (1885). *The limits of individual liberty*. London, U.K.: Rivingtons.

Mueller-Vollmer, K. (Ed.). (1985/2006). The historicity of understanding: Hans-Georg Gadamer. In *The hermeneutics reader* (pp. 256–292). New York: Continuum.

Murray, C. (Ed.). (2010). *Amputation, prosthesis use, and phantom limb pain: An interdisciplinary Perspective*. New York: Springer.

Nietzsche, F. W. (1887/1967). *Genealogy of morals*. (Walter A. Kaufmann, Trans.). New York: Vintage Books.

Nietzsche, F. (1956). "Live dangerously." In W. Kaufmann (Ed.), *Existentialism from Dostoevsky to Sartre* (pp. 100–112). Cleveland, OH: Meridian.

Nikulin, D. (2010). *Dialectic and dialogue*. Stanford, CA: Stanford University Press.

O'Neil, P. M. (Ed.). (2004). *Great world writers: Twentieth century*. New York: Marshall Cavendish.

Paine, T. (1776/1953). *Common sense*. In N. F. Adkins, (Ed.), "*Common Sense and other political writings* (pp. 3–54).

Paine, T. (1791 & 1792/1961). *On the rights of man*. El Reno, OK: Heritage Press.

Paine, T. (1795/2010). *The age of reason*. Washington, DC: Merchant Books.

"Parmenides." (2010). In *Encyclopaedia Britannica Online*. Retrieved from http://www.britannica.com/EBchecked/topic/444361/Parmenides

Pearce, W. B. (1989). *Communication and the human condition*. Carbondale, IL: Southern Illinois University Press.

Pieper, J. (1960/2001). *Scholasticism: Personalities and problems of medieval philosophy*. South Bend, IN: St. Augustine's Press.

Piercey, R. (2009). *The uses of the past from Heidegger to Rorty: Doing philosophy historically*. Cambridge, U.K.: Cambridge University Press.

Pinkard, T. (1988). *Hegel's dialectic: The explanation of possibility*. Philadelphia, PA: Temple University Press.

Pinkard, T. (2001). *Hegel: A biography*. New York: Cambridge University Press.

Plato. (1951). *The republic* (F. M. Cornford, Trans.). New York: Oxford University Press.

Plato. (2005). *Phaedrus* (C. Rowe, Trans.). New York: Penguin Classics.

Plato. (2010). *The apology*. New York: Create Space.

Plato. (2011). In *Encyclopaedia Britannica Online*. Retrieved from http://www.britannica.com/EBchecked/topic/464109/Plato

Popkin, R. H. (2003). *The history of skepticism from Savonarola to Bayle*. New York: Oxford University Press.

"Positivism." (2011). In *Encyclopaedia Britannica Online*. Retrieved from http://www.britannica.com/EBchecked/topic/471865/positivism

Preston, A. (2007). *Analytic philosophy: The history of an illusion*. New York: Continuum.

Putman, R. D. (2000). *Bowling alone: The collapse and revival of American community*. New York: Simon & Schuster.

Radford, G. P. (2004). *On the philosophy of communication*. Boston, MA: Wadsworth.

Ramsey, R. E. (1998). *Long path to nearness: A contribution to a corporeal philosophy of communication and the groundwork for an ethics of relief*. Amherst, NY: Humanity.

Ramsey, E. R., & Miller, D. J. (Eds.). (2003). *Experiences between philosophy and communication: Engaging the philosophical contributions of Calvin O. Schrag*. Albany, NY: State University of New York Press.

Rasmussen, D. M. (1990). *Reading Habermas*. Cambridge, MA: Basil Blackwell.

Rasmussen, D., & Swindal, J. (2009). *Habermas II*. Thousand Oaks, CA: Sage.

Rawls, J. (1971). *A theory of justice*. Cambridge, MA: Harvard University Press.

Rawls, J. (1981). Foreword. In H. Sidgwick, *The methods of ethics* (pp. v–vi). Indianapolis, IN: Hackett.

Reagan, C. E. (1996). *Paul Ricoeur: His life and his work*. Chicago, IL: University of Chicago Press.

Ricoeur, P. (1950/1966). *Freedom and nature: The voluntary and the involuntary* (E. V. Kohak, Trans.). Evanston, IL: Northwestern University Press.

Ricoeur, P. (1970). *Freud and philosophy: An essay on interpretation*. New Haven, CT: Yale University Press.

Ricoeur, P. (1984). *Time and narrative* (Vol. 1). (K. McLaughlin & D. Pellauer, Trans.). Chicago, IL: University of Chicago Press.

Rilke, R. M. (1910/1956). The notes of Malte Laurids Brigge. In W. Kaufmann (Ed.), *Existentialism from Dostoevsky to Sartre* (pp. 113–120). Cleveland, OH: Meridian.

Ritzer, G. (1996). *The McDonaldization of society: An investigation into the changing character of contemporary social life*. Thousand Oaks, CA: Pine Forge Press/Sage.

Rorty, R. (1979). *Philosophy and the mirror of nature*. Princeton, NJ: Princeton University Press.

Rorty, R. (1982). *Consequences of Pragmatism*. Minneapolis, MN: University of Minnesota Press.

Rorty, R. (1984). Introduction. In R. Rorty, L. B. Schneewind, & Q. Skinner (Eds.), *Philosophy in history* (pp. 1–14). New York: Cambridge University Press.

Rosenstock-Huessy, E. (1970/2001). *I am an impure thinker*. Essex, VT: Argo.

Rousseau, J. J. (1762/2008). *The social contract*. New York: Cosimo.

Rowling, J. K. (1998). *Harry Potter and the sorcerer's stone*. New York: A. A. Levine.

Russell, B. (1912/2011). *The problems of philosophy*. New York: Simon & Brown.

Russill, C. (2003). *Towards a pragmatist philosophy of communication: William James's radical empiricism and the problem of indeterminacy*. Paper presented at the meeting of the International Communication Association, San Diego, CA.

Russill, C. (2007). Communication problems in a pragmatist perspective. *Communication Monographs*, 74(1), 125–130.

Salih, S. (2002). *Judith Butler*. New York: Routledge.

Salih, S.. (2004). *The Judith Butler reader*. Malden, MA: Blackwell.

Schrag, C. O. (1986). *Communicative praxis and the space of subjectivity*. Bloomington, IN: Indiana University Press.

Schrag, C. O. (2010). *Doing philosophy with others: Conversations, reminiscences, and reflections*. West Lafayette, IN: Purdue University Press.

Sedgwick, M. (2009). *Against the modern world: Traditionalism and the secret intellectual history of the twentieth century*. New York: Oxford University Press.

Seneca, L. A. (1969). Letter XVI. In Robin A. Campbell (Ed.), *Seneca: Letters from a Stoic: Epistulae morales* (p. 65). New York: Penguin Classics.

Sennett, R. (2006). *The culture of the new capitalism*. New Haven, CT: Yale University Press.

Sennett, R. (2008). *The craftsman*. New Haven, CT: Yale University Press.

Sidgwick, H. (1874/1981). *The methods of ethics* (7th Ed.). Indianapolis, IN: Hackett.

Sim, S. (1999). *Critical dictionary of postmodern thought*. New York: Routledge.

Smith, J. E. (1978). *Purpose and thought: The meaning of pragmatism*. New Haven, CT: Yale University Press.

"Sophist." (2011). In *Encyclopaedia Britannica Online*. Retrieved from http://www.britannica.com/EBchecked/topic/554705/Sophist

Spencer, H. (1866). *The principles of biology* (Vol. 1). New York: D. Appleton & Company.

Stein, E. (1989). *The collected works of Edith Stein: On the problem of empathy* (Vol. 3; W. Stein, Trans.). Washington, DC: ICS Publications.

Swift, G. (1726). *Gulliver's travels*. London, U.K.: Jones & Company.

Taylor, C. (1984). Philosophy and its history. In R. Rorty, L. B. Schneewind, & Q. Skinner (Eds.), *Philosophy in history* (pp. 17–30). New York: Cambridge University Press.

Taylor, C. (1989). *Sources of the self: The making of modern identity*. Cambridge, MA: Harvard University Press.

Taylor, C. (2007). *A secular age*. Cambridge, MA: Harvard University Press.

"Teleology." (2011). In *Encyclopaedia Britannica Online*. Retrieved from http://www.britannica.com/EBchecked/topic/585947/teleology

Thayer, H. S. (1952). *The logic of pragmatism: An examination of John Dewey's logic*. New York: Greenwood Press.

Thayer, H. S. (1953). *Newton's philosophy of nature: Selections from his writings*. New York: Macmillan.

Thayer, H. S. (1968). *Meaning and action: A critical history of pragmatism*. New York: Bobbs-Merrill.

Thayer, H. S. (1982). *Pragmatism: The classical writings*. Cambridge, MA: Hackett Publishing.

Tocqueville, A. de (1835 & 1840/1963). *Democracy in America*. New York: Alfred Knopf.

Tocqueville, A. de. (1835 & 1840/2000). *Democracy in America* (H. C. Mansfield & D. Winthrop, Trans. & Ed.). Chicago, IL: University of Chicago Press.

Tolkien, J. R. R. (1954). *The two towers: Being the second part of the lord of the rings*. New York: Ballantine.

Upgren, A. (1998). *Night has a thousand eyes*. New York: Perseus.

Vattimo, G. (1988). *The end of modernity* (J. R. Snyder, Trans.). Baltimore, MD: John Hopkins University and Polity Press.

Vico, G. (1725/2000). *New science* (D. Marsh, Trans.). New York: Penguin.

Voltaire. (1759/1993). *Candide* (S. Weller, Ed. & Trans.). New York: Dover.

Voparil, C. J. (2010). Introduction. In C. J. Voparil & R. J. Berstein (Eds.), *The Rorty reader.* pp. 1–52. Malden, MA: Wiley-Blackwell.

Walker, M. U. (2007). *Moral understandings: A feminist study in ethics* (2nd Ed.). Oxford, U.K.: Oxford University Press.

"Walter A. Kaufmann." (2011). In *Princeton University, Department of Philosophy.* Retrieved from http://philosophy.princeton.edu/walter-a-kaufmann.html

Warnke, G. (1987). *Gadamer: Hermeneutics, tradition, and reason.* Stanford, CA: Stanford University Press.

Warnock, G. J. (1958). *English philosophy since 1900.* New York: Oxford University Press.

Watt, I. (1957). *The rise of the novel.* Berkeley, CA: University of California Press.

Weitz, M. (1966). *Twentieth-century philosophy: The analytic tradition.* New York: The Free Press.

Wilshire, B. (2000). *The primal roots of American philosophy: Pragmatism, phenomenology, and Native American thought.* University Park, PA: Pennsylvania State University Press.

"William James" (2010). In *Encyclopaedia Britannica Online.* Retrieved from http://www.britannica.com/EBchecked/topic/299871/William-James

Wispé, L. (1987). History of the concept of empathy. In N. Eisenberg & J. Strayer (Eds.), *Empathy and its development* (pp. 17–37). Cambridge, U.K.: Cambridge University Press.

Wittgenstein, L. (1922). *Tractatus logico-philosophicus.* London, U.K.: Kegan Paul.

Wittgenstein, L. (1953). *Philosophical investigations.* Malden MA: Blackwell.

Young-Bruehl, E. (2004). *Hannah Arendt: For love of the world* (2nd ed.). New Haven, CT: Yale University Press.

INDEX